DOSTOEVSKY

JOHN JONES

Oxford   New York

OXFORD UNIVERSITY PRESS

1985

Oxford University Press, Walton Street, Oxford OX2 6DP

London New York Toronto
Delhi Bombay Calcutta Madras Karachi
Kuala Lumpur Singapore Hong Kong Tokyo
Nairobi Dar es Salaam Cape Town
Melbourne Auckland

and associated companies in
Beirut Berlin Ibadan Mexico City Nicosia

Oxford is a trade mark of Oxford University Press

© John Jones 1983

First published 1983 by Oxford University Press
First published as an Oxford University Press paperback 1985

British Library Cataloguing in Publication Data
Jones, John, 1924 May 6–
Dostoevsky.
1. Dostoevskii, F. M. — Criticism and interpretation
I. Title
891.73'3   PG3328.Z6
ISBN 0-19-281868-6

Library of Congress Cataloging in Publication Data
Jones, John, 1924–
Dostoevsky.
(Oxford paperbacks)
Reprint. Originally published: Oxford: Clarendon Press;
New York: Oxford University Press, 1983.
Includes bibliographical references and index.
1. Dostoyevsky, Fyodor, 1821–1881 — Criticism and
interpretation.   I. Title.
PG3328.Z6J59 1985   891.73'3   84-27285
ISBN 0-19-281868-6 (pbk.)

Printed in Great Britain by
Richard Clay (The Chaucer Press) Ltd.
Bungay, Suffolk

For

JANET AND JEREMY JONES

Contents

First

Watch somebody with *Crime and Punishment* in his hands, unable to put the book down. Plainly he doesn't need to know the language of the original to get the message — anyhow to get *a* message. Or to convey it for that matter; John Middleton Murry's *Fyodor Dostoevsky* remains one of the best, and Murry had no Russian.

Also, when the children shout to Alyosha 'We love you, Karamazov!' the surname stands with the whole weight of the novel behind it for readers who have arrived at these final pages in translation. And even in *The Possessed*, where Kirillov is asked to help a woman in labour and blunders into a tangle of Russian word forms — 'I don't know how to bring birth about' — 'I don't know how to say it' — even there the linguistic comedy, the transposed obstetric charade, the fumbling, the weirdness — everything plays itself out in English well enough.

I shan't mention these instances again. They are objects hauled out and dropped back into the Dostoevsky ocean, tokens of his accessibility. They belong to my prefatory here and now because like many people I remember in adolescence reading Constance Garnett's translations and being left aghast with admiration, dazed, lost, yet sure I had the flavour and drift of what mattered most; but I do sometimes attend to the Russian in the pages ahead.

These pages must carry their own justification, and carry it in every line. I certainly do not set out to fuss over trifles, or to show off when I note mistranslations by Mrs Garnett and others and find fault with the team of Soviet editors labouring in the Leningrad Pushkin House at this moment. Details are meant to have diagnostic interest at least, and often to be intimate with big unorthodox conclusions.

They also serve a humanistic, old-fashioned if you like, approach to the critical and interpretative job: asserting which,

I will appear like a shop assistant caught with his fingers in the till and explaining he just loves the feel of money — an encouragingly Dostoevskian scene, thought there can be no denying that I handle questions of form and technique at least as much as is good for them.

You are going to read about conspiracies between novelist and reader behind the back of the narrator and his narrative. Also about things called authorlessness and authorial un-accountability, and about doubles and doubling, and about stories with frames and without frames. You are even going to meet Dostoevsky with a frame round him, in one of his notebooks, like this: $\boxed{\textit{'it's a chronicle'}}$ — himself inside the chronicle box because 'I am a character' in the chronicle. Some flaunted frames turn out to be ghost-frames, and the last novel, *The Brothers Karamazov*, concerns itself with events which happen 'now' and which the 'real' story is about; but this 'now' never comes.

The chronicle box looks like a doodle in the notebook and like typographic fooling as I reproduce it here; and the stuff about authors present and absent, accountable and unaccount-able, a dry technical dalliance; and the unarriving 'now', a hoax. Yes and no. These are of course devices, but deep-lying ones. They marry what the form will allow to what the artist has in him to say.

Therefore the reason no extended discussion of *The Idiot* occurs here is both that the novel lacks these devices and that it is, as Dostoevsky insisted it was — once he had written it — a failure. The purpureal, hymeneal splendour of Nastasya is nevertheless trashy, and the huge distinction of Myshkin not imagined through and through. The marvels of *The Idiot* survive, thrive even, in spite of its falling about in all directions, as if blown up from inside. I maintain that this novelist could only promote his dearest interests by stealth, by stalking them, by creeping up on them as they dozed or believed themselves safe with the enemy; but in *The Idiot* he approached them head on and wrecked his book. Humanly, it is forced, hysteri-cal, hyperbolic, nasty, and boring. But formally it adopts a calm and classic third-person narrative mode — which is just the trouble.

J.J.

Note

I refer to Constance Garnett's translation throughout. Single works appear under their volume title: *Poor People* under *The Gambler*, for example, and *The Double* under *The Eternal Husband*. My Russian text is the Soviet Academy's edition of the Complete Works, *Polnoe Sobranie Sochinenii* (hereafter *PSS*), which has reached the twenty-third of its projected thirty volumes. There are no more novels to come, so we now possess what we very much wanted.

PART ONE: POET

Chapter 1:   *Poor People*

(i)

When Dostoevsky finished his first book, a short novel called *Poor People*, he told his elder brother Mikhail he would never have begun the thing if he had known how much effort it would cost him.[1]

How much was 'how much'? His drafts of the novel are lost. There were certainly two of these and probably more, perhaps many more; but the work trail emerges plain for all to see in the text which the magazine *Petersburg Miscellany* printed in 1846, and from there it can be followed to *Poor People*'s appearance in volume form in 1847, and then to the first (1860) and finally to the second (1865) collected edition of his novels and short stories. At each of these stages he added, subtracted, reshaped. There's really no surprise about his letter to Mikhail, because on the evidence of the printed texts alone it is easy to believe that the earlier scene was a reeking slaughter-house of words that wouldn't do.

Now at first sight this is not our Dostoevsky. Our man goes for broad strong effects, an attacker of his subject if ever there was one, impetuous in himself and incensed by finesse in others, a sort of malign Goya, an echo of the master who grabbed the court portrait-painter's wrist because 'I cannot bear to watch your niggling brush' — spiteful Dostoevsky, eager (for example) to get a grip on Turgenev's sweet, clear, considered Russian by way of parody and lampoon.

But then *Poor People* is not our Dostoevsky either. I mean: the young Socialist, the hospital doctor's son who wrote about life in Petersburg's attics and kitchens and those partitioned-off spaces they called corners, is not the man we are interested in. We are waiting (so to speak) for him to get sent to Siberia so he can return in middle age and give the

[1]   Letter of 4 May 1845.

world *Crime and Punishment, The Idiot, The Possessed, The Brothers Karamazov.*

(ii)

Thus, with no frills, the West. Whereas in modern Russia discussion always begins, and often ends, with the twenty-four-year-old chronicler of the helpless urban poor and the people and forces exploiting them. It is agreed that his Socialism was sadly frenchified and utopian, but his heart was sound, and his heart ruled his pen. Then came Siberia. Siberia has its dialectical uses since the change from 'Property is theft' to a highly idiosyncratic Church-and-State conservatism must have a cause and some Russians say Dostoevsky was driven mad by his sufferings in prison. The more moderate view is that his vision was permanently distorted. As a result the later books all need careful doctoring, and *The Possessed* with its sustained attack on socialism and atheism is perhaps beyond cure. Indeed, after the Revolution it became difficult — and dangerous — to get your hands on *The Possessed*, while at the same time the State Publishing House set about issuing hundreds of thousands of cheap copies of *Poor People*.

So Russia and the West divide over Dostoevsky, and if you set *Poor People* against *The Possessed* as I have just done, the division seems extremely sharp. And in a way it is sharp. But not in a very interesting way. On their side there is a lot of ideology involved and official direction of taste and limitation of choice. None of this has much to do with art. And in any case how deep does it run? When, in 1971, the crowds queued through the night to get their names on the subscription list for the new Soviet Academy edition of their loved author's writings, who can say what they were really queuing for? And on our side there is widespread ignorance of the early work which in any case doesn't translate well. We can't have an informed view of what we don't know; whereas our commitment to the later novels, though based on knowledge, suffers from a slow coral-growth of dogmatic, devotional inertia, and needs prodding. I wonder — to start just one hare and let it run for the time being — how many readers of *The Idiot* have finished the book in astonishment that it can be thought capable of surviving alongside *Karamazov*, and then have supposed with a shrug that oh well, the people who established the classical canon must know best.

But while the division between Russia and the West is less radical, resonant, rewarding, than it appears, the opposite is the truth about the not so obvious agreement between them. This agreement revolves round two fixed points, both of which have been touched on already.

The first is Siberia. I find it less interesting, less of the essence, that East and West interpret Siberia differently than that they experience the same shock of crisis. We, as I said, tend to ignore the pre-Siberian Dostoevsky who has yet to walk through the initiatory fire, while the Russians want to 'save' the post-Siberian books by assimilation, however tenuous, to the social and humanitarian motifs of the early ones — and by this very effort, by this protesting too much, for example by insulating Ivan Karamazov's powerful fustian about the whole God business not being worth the pain of one ill-treated child, they show that the rest of this novel frightens them, that they too see a changed man after Siberia.

The second fixed point of agreement is best dramatized as a conspiracy. East and West have ganged up on the Dostoevsky who wrote to his brother about the fearful toil of composition and who left behind four texts of one short novel to give us a rough idea what he meant, even with all the manuscripts lost. This was his first book, and the story with the other ones was often of louder complaints and larger quantities of creative debris — long before the thirty-volume edition began to display the facts more fully.

With western readers the conspiracy is a matter of turning our backs on the word and saluting the message. We take message in Dostoevsky in a way that seems to me worth distinguishing. We don't regard him as an out-and-out hijacker of the novel form who wants to propagandize his way to a destination of his own choosing, like Rousseau; nor as an exponent of the less extreme *roman à thèse* which aims at an honourable settlement with the claims of art, like Disraeli's political novels and *Lady Chatterley*. We have only to think of a novelist with obvious resemblances to Dostoevsky, Dickens, and then of an interest which they share, money, to sense dimly that we are on to something strange. This something is not a question of how we look at foreign writers generally, for if we now proceed to throw in Balzac's novels where money also looms large, we realize, again obscurely, that the Englishman and the Frenchman are together, and Dostoevsky is alone. Nor are we pursuing a characteristic of the Russians, though their way of chewing their themes — think of Tolstoy and marriage — might lead us to suspect we were. Of course all novels are, or were until the other day, *about* something. They have a purchase on life, whether paraded or masked, which the common reader applies as he goes along and takes to himself, and which the professional literary man writes books and articles about. In this residual sense we are saluting the message all the time. But having saluted it, indeed — important correction! — in the act of saluting it, we do something with it. As we read about little Paul Dombey asking his father what money is, and Mr Dombey, 'quite disconcerted', replying 'Gold, and silver, and copper. Guineas, shillings, half-pence. You know what they are?', we refer the moment to the small boy and the businessman, and to a world of getting and spending which is very Victorian and also recognizably our own.[2] And so, *mutatis mutandis*, we refer money in Balzac and Thackeray and Fontane.

But money in Dostoevsky is not referred, it is waiting to be referred as if it were money found lying in the street. For a moment we stare at it and do nothing, and to do nothing is to do potentially anything — we might leave it where it is or pocket it or hand it in to the police. Or we might behave like one of his characters. Nastasya Filippovna in *The Idiot* throws a bundle of it on the fire. The pawnbroker in *Crime and Punishment* just stashes it away, while Luzhin in the same novel plants a hundred-rouble note on Sonya Marmeladov to incriminate her. A crumpled blue five-rouble note is the insult offered by the self-styled antihero of *Notes from Underground* to the girl he has slept with. The heroine of *The Gambler* flings twenty-five thousand German florins in the hero's face. Old Karamazov makes a fussy package of it in his

[2] Ch. VIII.

bedroom to entice a girl, while his son Dmitry sews some money in a bag around his neck and pours away other money in rainbow-coloured torrents in exchange for Strasburg pies and champagne.

Of course this Dostoevsky money has different auras of human cruelty, lust, bounty, avarice. But then money found in the street has different auras too, of lamp light or gutter smells or whatever. The aura doesn't of itself impel us beyond staring blankly at the money, whereas to read the Dickens scene and imagine Mr Dombey jingling the coins in his pocket as he answers his little boy, is to do something with them, even if we get no further than wondering whether we have ever thought what money is ourselves.

Doestoevsky money is stuff, rather as stuffs in Ben Jonson's comedies — taffeta and furs and ambergris — are stuff; it is not bourgeois money, inherited or ill-gotten or earned, it is not like money in a nineteenth-century novel at all; its colour, always prominent, is closer to the glass beads with which the trader beguiles the savage than to a world of denominations and legal tender; it solicits an eager, naive, even barbaric regard, fierce or wondering, a psychic impregnation which runs to the root both of money and the human self in Dostoevsky. Staring at the stuff, doing nothing, about to do potentially anything, we unite extreme fixity with equally extreme instability. His money is stubbornly, unbudgeably the stuff it is, and at the same time perched on the brink of non-being, at the mercy of the next human will to bump into it. Nastasya Filippovna gives the paper bundle a push towards non-being by throwing it on the fire, but her action also acknowledges its absurd yet maddening thereness like that of the pea under the mattress of the princess in the fairy story, which prevented her from sleeping.

To contemplate disposing of the thing, money or offending pea, is to embrace fixity and instability, and also to reveal what is so special about message in Dostoevsky. Money is everywhere in his novels, and it slips off the tongue to say money is a Dostoevsky theme; but theme proves to be an amalgam of brute stuff and stirring will, will poised for decision, mind not made up. This means that money has all and more than the thematic assertiveness of Mr Dombey's guineas, shillings, and halfpence, but none of the stabilizing, defining context which Dickens's memorable scene provides, a context which is linguistic as well as social and economic, for however deeply we get lost in the story we know we have a nineteenth-century classic in front of us, and novels are made of words. But in Dostoevsky the words drop out with the rest of the stabilizing context, and we are left with no middle ground, no mediation, between earthbound objects and a weightless mental orbiting. I hope the picture is becoming recognizable. Things are so *there* in Dostoevsky, yet the whole creation is unclinched and giddy. To stay with money for a moment, its dug-in fixity resembles the obtrusiveness of message in other people's old-fashioned bad novels, while the empty yet restless money mentality is incomparable and itself alone. We rush into the expectant void and in this sense make up the message for ourselves — as we couldn't invade and articulate the return-to-nature message of *La Nouvelle Héloïse*, for example, even if we wanted to, because Rousseau is securely in residence with his ideas unpacked.

And as with money, so with crime and religion and sex and the other cardinal features of the Dostoevsky landscape. This world of handkerchiefs that have gone into crusty balls with dried blood, and large-hipped girls who walk almost noiselessly and whose bodies seem as sugary as their voices, and obscene photographs slipped in among copies of the Holy Gospel — this world can be, has been invaded and taken over by religious and mystically minded people, by political theorists of every colour except liberal, by philosophers and psychologists among whom Nietzsche and Freud are the most eminent. All these have in their day moved in, not merely to find examples and ammunition as they might with any writer, but to appropriate an *oeuvre*. I cannot think of a modern parallel.

Soviet experts, as they survey this scene, have a rather piquant way of calling the western tradition of Dostoevsky studies 'arbitrary'. They sometimes go on to claim a contrasting self-consistency for Russia, which has some justice but is nothing to boast about since its rationale is censorship and repressive government. The so-called Socialist Realism of today is a business of the party line. This was not true of the

Naturalism of the 1840s or of the more confused literary milieu under the later tsars, or even of Social Realism in the first flush of the Revolution. But all these belong to a world without a free press, where journalists and academic commentators are silenced or tamed, or at best keep a wary eye about them, and sometimes invite martyrdom, and where a lot of the work of investigation and social criticism falls to the novelist. This is the bond uniting the humanitarian poet Nekrasov who woke the author of *Poor People* at four in the morning to tell him he was a new inspiration to the radical young, and the man who wrote in last week's and will write in next week's *Literaturnaya Gazeta* about Dostoevsky's understanding of the masses.

Thus the Russians also shun the word and salute the message. Unlike us, they nowadays, at least in public, salute the same message and thus obscure a marvel which our 'arbitrary' approach lays bare, namely Dostoevsky's power to generate seemingly inexhaustible psychic energy in the form of his readers' diverse intellectual passions: he could never have incited us to burst in and make up our various messages simply by leaving his house of fiction empty. But, postponing the case of Formalist criticism, we find the Russians no more prepared than ourselves — and it is after all their language — to concentrate on the man who spent his life trying to get his words right. This isn't at all the same thing as refusing to take a narrow aesthetic view of Dostoevsky. It is indeed a grand East-and-West conspiracy, and, like the Siberian crisis, it enfolds a large and sensitive area of debate which the moment has come to enter.

(iii)

In the event Dostoevsky's first step towards getting his own words right was to put another man's words right. He headed *Poor People* with an Epigraph in the form of a quotation from a contemporary writer, Prince Odoevsky. It runs:

Oh, these story tellers! If only they'd write something useful, pleasant, soothing — but they will drag all sorts of skeletons out of cupboards! I tell you I'd prohibit their writing! Why, it's too bad; you read, and willy nilly you get thinking — and then all sorts of rubbish

comes into your head: yes really I would prohibit their writing; I mean
it — I would simply prohibit their writing altogether.

Like the Epigraphs of *The Possessed* and *Karamazov*
towards the end of his career, this one at the very beginning
has been carefully picked and pitched in relation to the work
it introduces. It makes several points glancingly: the everpresent censorship ('prohibit'), Dostoevsky's own *unpleasant*
Freudian flair for 'skeletons', and — more important — his
way of provoking his readers to do the work (what I called
making up the message: 'willy nilly you get thinking'). Finally,
it alters its original. The reiterated 'I would prohibit their
writing' at the end had been in Odoevsky 'their writing ought
to be prohibited' — an apparently pointless tinkering with a
near-repetition, a doublet.[3]

But then I see doublets and doubling everywhere in *Poor
People*, this exchange of letters between a middle-aged clerk
and a girl who lives opposite him across the yard. It is an
exchange with no frame to it — no author to introduce or
close the correspondence, no commentary or linking passages.
We just have the letters. Indeed we haven't in some sense got
all of them. I say in some sense because we may proceed
naturalistically in terms of letters being dreamed up by the
lovers or lost or intercepted, or we may sweep aside the
device of authorlessness and contemplate the young novelist
brazenly, non-naturalistically teasing his readers. Thus the
girl mentions her lover being 'afraid' and writing to her
about his fears, but we haven't got his letter. Later she says
she didn't complete her last letter, and yet it shows no sign
of being unfinished. Later again, she says it is three days
since she wrote to him, but her previous letter is dated eight
days earlier.[4]

Tricks like this are very unsettling, as Dostoevsky meant
them to be. They maximize the doubling effect of letter
following letter following letter. We have nothing else to
hang on to in our struggle after what fits, matches, confirms,
returns and augments the cumulative likeness which is the
story. The reader who misses some gaps and dislocations

---

[3]   *PSS*, Vol. I, p. 480.   [4]   *The Gambler*, pp. 194, 216, 237.

will notice others. All readers will notice those which are unequivocally naturalistic, as when despair drives the clerk across the yard to his girl's room. She is out. He reports: 'On your table I found a piece of paper with the words "Dear Makar Alexevich, I hasten" — and that was all. Somebody must have interrupted you at the most interesting place.'[5] Note that surreal 'interesting'. Who but Dostoevsky? The reader has to supply the interest for himself. He has also, again in a sense, to finish the book. The last letter, undated and unsigned, is possibly a deathbed effort by the clerk; he mentions two letters earlier, as if it were a tiresome triviality, that he has caught a cold.[6] There's no telling what else if anything he wanted to say. The words stop and the reader's imagining goes on.

It goes on inside as well as at the end of the unframed story. The five-word scrap which the clerk found on the girl's table is by no means the only occasion for 'interesting' speculation. *Poor People* is a novel of echoes and reflections, of news, often unreliable or gappy, which the lovers have of each other from third parties and which they relay to each other, often sketchily; and there are snatched meetings between them in a public park, at church, once at the theatre. They refer to these, to what was said and done, in the allusive, heady way one does in love letters after meetings.

And the beginning is 'interesting' too, no more convincing as beginning than the end as end. The novel drifts in out of nowhere and we learn that the clerk has only very recently moved to his present horrible lodgings. Why? It transpires they are cheaper than his old ones, and he can see his girl's window from them. These two reasons not only don't clash but support each other reassuringly since he is spending his money on her and cannot spend enough. But then he writes *en passant* that his old landlady is dead. 'We had a happy life, Varenka; and there it was, we lived together for almost twenty years.'[7] Then she died. That's all. What happened after that? Were the lodgings closed? Was there a new, disagreeable landlady? Or is the old landlady's death irrelevant to his move, just a fact he happens to tell Varenka?

---

[5] Ibid., p. 244.   [6] Ibid., p. 243.   [7] Ibid., p. 141.

No matter — the damage has been done, and the two earlier reasons are now mocked for the very neatness with which they married up. The attentive reader feels he is being chased out of the novel by something he can't distinguish from the mess and muddle he picked up the novel to escape from in the first place. 'One of the damned thing (*sic*) is ample', as Rebecca West remarked apropos the familiar thought that novels imitate life. And here is a timid government employee, a copying clerk with weak eyes and a bald patch and slavish, alas crass, devotion, who is made to measure for a highly stylized novel in letters, but who also has his untidy memories and dreams, not concealed nor yet paraded but just his, a ragbag of personal elsewheres whose homing instinct is a bedrock affirmation of selfhood. In the words Shakespeare gave to Parolles, 'Simply the thing I am shall make me live.'

Poor People's doublings introduce the unsettled and profoundly unsettling relationship of art and life throughout Dostoevsky. His life-simulation continues as it begins, a grit-under-the-fingernails affair. His books are at once tight and slack, claustrophobically artful and spilling out lifewards in a seemingly patternless process which I shall call parajournalism. His readers have got to get used to living in closet bedrooms and also in cheap eating-houses with swinging doors and endless comings and goings — both of which he loved to write about. In terms of *Poor People* the reader is left contemplating a form, a pretty doublet, or he feels at a loose end and, as the Odoevsky Epigraph put it, he 'gets thinking'.

The doubling, the stroke of art, may take place above the heads of the two letter-writers, leaving the novel's author and its reader smiling knowingly at each other. On April 8, in his first letter, the clerk describes his new lodgings: 'It's true there are even better lodgings, perhaps there are much better ones, — but convenience is the main thing; you see I've arranged it all for convenience and don't you imagine it was for anything else . . . . No, it was convenience made me take them, just convenience prompted me.'[8] In his next letter, answering her reply to this one — the correspondence opens with a burst of three letters written on the same day and

---

[8] Ibid., p. 136.

carried across the yard by one of the servants in his lodgings
and by her woman companion — he scolds her: 'What are you
doing writing about convenience and peace and quiet and all
sorts of rigmarole?'[9] But he is really scolding himself. It was
he who latched on to this word as a *convenient* form of
lexical tiptoeing through the facts of his squalid domestic
circumstances without telling a direct lie. She had scarcely
made contact with, let alone initiated, this obsessive 'convenience' talk; there is a remote flashback when she expresses
anxiety that he will be 'cramped, uncomfortable'[10] (comfort
and convenience being one word in Russian) — but this is all
that happens on her side, whereas he promptly forgets he has
just been chiding her and climbs back on his hobby-horse:
'I have already described the lay-out of the rooms to you;
there's no denying it's convenient, it *is* convenient, but in a
way it's stuffy . . . '.[11]

With a difference, however. The hobby-horse is of course
the 'convenience' tic. This is the doublet of repetition. The
difference lies in the sudden deflecting touch of 'but' which
sets in motion 'but in a way it's stuffy, that's not to say
there's a bad smell but, if one may so express it, a slightly
decaying, a sort of sharpish-sweetish smell'. This difference
also falls within the overall doubling rhythm of *Poor People*,
since the novel's doublets cannot break out of the blank
iteration of 'convenient is convenient' without asserting
difference as well as identity, without narrative growth as
well as repetition. Any fool could think of a word and then
go on repeating it. Only a writer with his wits about him,
quick to exploit a particular surprising word-shortage in a
language with a large vocabulary, would have produced the
convenient/comfortable ghost-echo of Varenka's 'uncomfortable'. Whereas to study the ways in which convenient/com-
fortable belongs both to the clerk who uses it and the novel
which contains him, is to enter an area beyond quick wits
and what is teachable.

Convenient/comfortable (*udobni*) is a demure word, and
the clerk who uses it is a prim and modest man. His name is
Mr Devushkin, Mr Girly, and he is forty-seven. His old-

[9] Ibid., p. 140.   [10] Ibid., p. 138.   [11] Ibid, p. 143.

maidishness comes across as a cluster of mild habits deeply grooved. Over a lot of what he says there hangs a smell of genteel equivocation — indeed he has just been talking about smell, and we observe him twisting and turning with remarkable nimbleness, and comedy for ourselves, rather than call a stink a stink. Now this equivocation belongs to him as humble government employee as well as old maid; he's a civil servant, and the linguistic mores of the bureaucracy percolate down to Titular Councillor Devushkin near the bottom of the fourteen semi-military grades established by Peter the Great in the early Eighteenth Century and not abolished until 1917. His way of life makes for much tortured officialese, and for pompous locutions sprinkled with blunders of word-formation and grammar and syntax; but it also breeds a certain verbal cunning. Convenient/comfortable is after all a shrewd stroke in a tight corner. It fends off Varenka as she tries to get at the truth about his lodgings, very much as an official government communication might fend off a private suppliant. This is what petty officials are like. It shows a resourcefulness beyond Mr Devushkin's apparent personal capacity because he has the wisdom of the tribe — the terrible bureaucracy — to draw on.

Thus convenient/comfortable has rubbed off on Mr Devushkin as well as being conjured from within. Both the personal trait and the type feature appear, as do the convenient and comfortable aspects of the single word, when he tells Varenka: 'it's comfortable, and there's a window and the lot — in short, every convenience.'[12] The comfort, such as it is, belongs to his dreams and his glass of tea and 'couple of chairs' and similar indulgencies proper to the poor, while the convenience is a smart equivocation touched off by the window which has (one must concede) the supreme convenience that he can see her window, and occasionally herself, through it. There's plenty of room for argument over details, but it can't be questioned that the manipulation of *udobni* is dauntingly careful through *Poor People*'s opening pages, in this tone-setting flurry of letters.

[12]   Ibid., p. 136.

(iv)

Shunning the word, therefore, is no way to begin. The young Dostoevsky is a linguistic novelist in a way in which it would be absurd to speak of Walter Scott or Victor Hugo, to name two men he greatly admired; or Balzac, whose *Eugénie Grandet* he translated the year before he published his own first novel. His work is close and very conscious. It does not follow he is a 'fine writer', a Flaubert or Turgenev. Indeed fine writing (except in the context of parody) is the only area where his care with his words cannot be studied with much profit — even if fine writing be interpreted widely enough to include the mental after-taste of Tolstoy's prose which, unlike its bits and pieces while the eye moves past them, has the almost featureless distinction of what countrymen call good water.

Positively bad writing affords a handhold here. Recall Mr Devushkin's description of the smell in his new lodgings. If Dostoevsky took this along with him to a school of creative writing one can imagine the instructor striking out 'in a way' and 'that's not to say' and 'sort of', and telling his pupil that if the smell is bad he should say so, and nothing is gained, on the contrary something is lost, by wrapping verbal cotton wool round his description.

If Dostoevsky were to reply that the cotton wool is in character and forms part of the ageing girly syndrome, the instructor might well say 'OK, then carry on' — for this makes sense in terms of naturalism and the nineteenth-century novel, and the instructor hasn't got his pupil's complete works in front of him. But if he had he would discover that Dostoevsky was being, as so often, disingenuous. The cotton-wool phenomenon appears throughout the collected fiction, early and late, major and minor, dialogue and narrative, and has no naturalistic link with character at all beyond the fact that it becomes particularly insistent with Mr Devushkin and half-educated people like him — too like him if the individuation of, say, Dickens's little men is to be one's criterion of excellence. It is impossible to read more than a few pages, outside set pieces like the Grand Inquisitor, without being struck by 'kind of', 'sort of', 'somehow', 'in a way', 'as it

were' — all sort of kind of slovenly and loafing, all idle even
by the standards of Russian which is a lazy language. They
litter the page. English and German translators tend to drop
about one in three, and Frenchmen about half. Constance
Garnett is worse at Russian than some translators, but better
at Dostoevsky than any over the wide span. She made a lot of
mistakes. Occasionally she bowdlerized. The early work
presents special difficulties, and one meets such minor
disasters — not so much errors as tonal mishaps — as 'convenient' for Mr Devushkin's *old* lodgings, when Dostoevsky's
word is something like 'free and easy' (*privolni*).[13] But she
worked fast and caught a crucial consistency and truth, one
aspect of which is her courage over 'sort of' and 'somehow'
and the rest. She leaves us facing an uncomfortable page of
English, at once fusty and fretful, in need of cleaning up and
calming down.

There is no quicker or more complete way to get Dostoevsky wrong than to sweep the repellent features of his
genius under the carpet. His books don't make creative sense
without them, back to the beginning of the beginning when
he prefaced his first novel with an Epigraph which says the
same thing — 'I would prohibit their writing' — three times
in about fifty words. This nagging iteration, untypical only in
its irascible tone (but then it is pretending to be outside the
novel) affirms the dominant role of the classic *Poor People*
doublet which is to make a thing more possible or credible,
or to make it the case, by repeating it. In his gentle way Mr
Devushkin loves doing this, especially at the end of letters:

I'll come to you Varenka my own when it gets dark, I'll drop in for an
hour or so. It'll get dark early today, then I'll drop in. I'll certainly
come to you my darling for an hour or so today. You're expecting
Bykov now, but when he goes, then — You wait a bit darling, I'll drop
in —

Makar Devushkin[14]

It may or may not seem a modest creation, Mr Devushkin's
little hurdy-gurdy tune. Anyhow Dostoevsky took trouble
with it. He tinkered with the rhythms of 'I'll come' and 'I'll
drop in', and the gesture towards silence with the break at

[13] Ibid., p. 140.   [14] Ibid., pp. 240–1.

'when he goes, then —' is an idea which came to him when he was revising the magazine text for publication in hard covers.[15] And then there are the lost manuscripts behind these alterations.

But to what end Dostoevsky's hard work? Replying to criticisms that he was not true to life, or simply asserting himself (a thing nobody can deny he was fond of), he used to say that his goal was a deeper realism than that of the writers whom the world called Realists. Mr Devushkin says he will certainly drop in. He is using words as incantation, magically. Somehow he sort of knows — cotton wool again, an encouraging sign like the show of life in a water-diviner's twig — he knows he won't drop in by going on saying he will. But if Mr Devushkin is irrational, so are the rest of us. We know what he knows and we use language as he does.

Dostoevsky is making capital out of a fact of normal psychology. He is also working towards an end-product of extreme immediacy. Now there are different sorts of immediacy. One would know roughly what an admirer of Hopkins's *Windhover* meant if he said that reading the poem is more like watching a hawk than any hawk-watching he has gone in for himself is like watching a hawk. The affronting radiance of Blake's great lyrics is also immediate, but quite different from Hopkins and more of a prodigy. 'Full fathom five' is different again though a bit like Blake. '*Ô saisons, ô châteaux*' is yet another thing. But they all share a feature which is of the essence of Mr Devushkin's immediacy; that is (though my English examples may feign otherwise: 'I saw this morning' and so forth) they do not stand to one side of their theme as description or confession or analysis or any other second addressing itself to a first. The sense is single, as of an enactment, the difference between Mr Devushkin's letter and the others being that they are done complete so that we are happy to call them art; whereas his is in the provisional mode and carefully careless. Macbeth's 'On the torture of the mind to lie/In restless ecstasy' is not an enactment. It is a monument which stands as verbal index of mental pain, clinching and very grand. The last word on the subject! Contrast the shape which fidgets and grows at the tip of Mr Devushkin's quill pen. It *is* the subject. It is mental pain's linguistic physique. Indeed, trying to get to grips with what is involved here is very like being thrown in at the deep end of a philosphical mind-and-body debate. We find ourselves floundering next to the Hopkins enthusiast as we try to improve on the thought that reading Mr Devushkin's letter feels more like experiencing mental pain than contemplating it.

But, as I observed, Mr Devushkin is much like other petty clerks in Dostoevsky; the immediacy that is being thrust upon the reader has nothing to do with individuation. Consider the import of this. Imagine the sufferings of Anna Karenina or Isobel Archer in disconnection from their enormously circumstantial selfhood. It can't be done. Their pain, slow in both cases, is the main process, the leading voice by which that selfhood is articulated. To separate the pain would be to take a big step towards making dummy keyboards of two fictional human natures. Whereas in *Poor People* Mr Devushkin's pain is merely attributed to him in virtue of his age and poverty and shyness and love of Varenka. It has to be his, of course, in order to get and keep the story going, but no creative strength flows from this attribution. Or, putting it another way, Mr Devushkin's tune of 'I'll drop in' is interestingly painful but not interestingly his.[16]

(v)

And now to another petty clerk, Mr Marmeladov, and another tune, his tirade about his wife very early on in *Crime and Punishment*, delivered to Raskolnikov inside a filthy public house. I want to think of his words as a creation in the mouth to be placed alongside Dostoevsky's creation at the tip of Mr Devushkin's pen.

'She married her first husband, an infantry officer, for love, and ran away with him from her father's house. She loved her husband very

[16] The matter admits of degree. If little Copperfield or old Goriot are substituted for the two young women, the contrast with Dostoevsky becomes less clear-cut. And who can doubt that he is closer to Dickens and Balzac than to Tolstoy and James?

much indeed, but he took to gambling, fell foul of the law, and with
that he died. He beat her towards the end; and though she made him
pay for it — I know this for certain and have documentary proof — even
so she still remembers him with tears and casts him in my teeth, and
I'm glad, I'm glad, for though it's her imagination she does feel she was
happy once — And she was left at his death with three young children
in a remote and wild district where I happened to be at the time; and
she was left in such hopeless want that though I've seen a lot of ups
and downs in my life I don't feel equal to describing it even. Her
relatives had all abandoned her. And she was proud, inordinately proud
— And then my dear sir, I having also lost my spouse and with a daughter
of fourteen left me by my first wife — then I offered her my hand
because I could not bear to see such suffering. You can judge the extent
of her calamities by the fact that she, an educated woman and cultured
and of good family, should have agreed to marry me. But she did!
Weeping and sobbing and wringing her hands — she married me! For she
had nowhere to go. Do you understand, do you understand my dear sir
what it means when you have nowhere to go? No! You don't understand that yet — And for a whole year I carried out my duties conscien-
tiously and with devotion and did not touch this' (he poked his finger
at the jug) 'for I have my feelings. But even so there was no pleasing
her; and then I lost my job, and again it wasn't my fault but through
changes at the office, and then I did touch it!'[17]

Many people will remember reading this for the first time,
perhaps in adolescence, and wondering what was happening
to them. Marmeladov comes from nowhere. He is a sideshow
and gets no reflected interest from the main story of murder
and detection. He looks like a retired clerk. He is dirty and
has been drinking. That is about all. The book has scarcely
begun. He will be dead, though we aren't to know, long
before half-way. He buttonholes Raskolnikov. He is a tavern
bore. Then this voice, and a simultaneous onslaught on intellect and emotions that is more like being cuffed about by a
god than reading a book.

What is it, for example, that stops the reader in his tracks
and sends him reeling, while within and groping, at Marmeladov
asking his second wife to marry him 'because I could not bear
to see such suffering'? No apparent work has gone into
committing us to Marmeladov, and there is no access at all to
his wife except through the vodka haze of his story, at once
gappy and repetitious and muffled by the at-one-remove of

[17] *Crime and Punishment*, pp. 13-14.

retrospect, a story within a story. The attribution of pain and poverty to Marmeladov is even more bare than to Mr Devushkin because the absence of circumstantial selfhood is more complete, and the narrative of years gone by stands at the opposite pole from *Poor People* where the novel in letters, as used by Dostoevsky, is a here-and-now device helping him towards that immediacy which is celebrated at the tip of a hovering, plunging, flashing pen.

The twenty years between *Poor People* and *Crime and Punishment* see the development of powers which Dostoevsky had used as well as owned from the beginning. I asked why we are moved by Marmeladov's proposal of marriage to his second wife. Well, why did he approach her? His reason, his 'because', is not so much revealing as resonant — resonant with paradox, *non sequitur*, the rumbling belch of farce, and tragedy. Setting up together was crazy but noble — but crazy. It was out of the frying-pan into the fire for both of them. Dostoevsky seems to have taken in both *King Lear* and Petersburg vaudeville with his mother's milk, as he does the selfish selflessness which prompted Marmeladov to assume the burden of his shrewish wife — 'even so there was no pleasing her' — because it hurt so much to watch her suffer, and as he does those reasons that are also no reasons: Marmeladov never hints that he expected either of them to suffer less by uniting their fates.

Of course one may step forward and protest that Marmeladov surely hoped and expected all sorts of things despite his silence, and that he must have pitied her even if he doesn't say so, and that we all know shared troubles are easier to bear — while realizing the Marmeladovs aren't the sort of reflective people who talk like that.

This is what I mean by the reader entering and making up the message. He is enticed in by a 'because' which lies on the very brink of 'I married her because I married her', a blank iteration. He moves in and (to quote again the Odoevsky Epigraph to *Poor People*) he 'gets thinking'. It doesn't feel like hard work, unlike what modern highbrow novels expect of readers, because it is an act of secondary creation into which life and Dostoevsky are both pouring energy. Life heaves us forward with a shove of recognition which is our experience that lots of life's big decisions are made more or less because they *are* made, in a paradoxical quagmire of you first and me first where reasons are mental toys; and Dostoevsky has written the novel.

Everything I have said about tragedy and farce, selfish selflessness, reasons that are also no reasons, making up the message, is observable in *Poor People* in a more narrowly witty and a lighter form, like that 'interesting' letter which the reader is left to write because Varenka has been interrupted at 'I hasten'. Conversely, the traits that might be thought peculiar to *Poor People* as a young man's first book and as a novel in letters can be traced in *Crime and Punishment*, even in that small chunk of Marmeladov's tirade, but reduced and rendered down, chafed by time and work into a fine loam. These traits are the attitudes struck by the phenomenon I have called doubling: repetition, snowballing accretion, uneasy half-confirmation and half-denial, the whole structure of answer and exchange which constitutes the 'authorless' novel in letters.

In Marmeladov's monologue the doubling is of course self-doubling, a tragicomic sodden and sublime pursuit of the man he was and is. When tears leap to the eyes, I hope not just in adolescence, at 'because I could not bear to see such suffering', we are half remembering that Marmeladov could not bring himself 'even to describe' the *misère* — *misère* renders *nishcheta* better than want or destitution[18] — of the widow and three little children. There is no sense that he was tender-hearted or that he was anybody in particular, as a yeasting pressure builds up and the doors of personality burst open upon a scene of absolute extremity and despair which, however affected readers may be by the almost unqualitied speaker, the life-soiled Russian drunkard, they are not taking so to say on trust from him. They have been there themselves — in the spirit, in the universality of 'nowhere to go' and 'do you understand?', intertwined and both repeated, a double doublet. Marmeladov voices nowhere to go and nobody to be, Dostoevsky's overarching preoccupations from first to last. He is himself one exposed scrap under this open sky.

[18] 'Do you know what *misère* means?' in *The Idiot* (p. 191) translates *nishcheta* into French.

Also, his job lost, sleeping in river hay barges rather than face his wife, he is experiencing this nowhere and nobody in the flesh and proclaiming it with a slight hectoring aggressiveness which vodka lends. 'I did not touch this.' The heart attends wonderingly. '— and then I did touch it!' A doubling antiphon, and at the same time a drinker's words, and an effect beyond laconicism.

Marmeladov tells Raskolnikov that his wife's past happiness is her present fancy; he says that it is self-engendered, not that she is self-deceiving: she has her dream as surely as she is spitting blood. Similarly, he doesn't say he is the dregs of humanity, he says Raskolnikov can judge his wife's state by the fact that she married him. And the love between them — we can't believe there was no love — is wordless now. The obliquenesses, and the gaps and holes themselves, the gaps between and the holes under the words, are potent beyond anything we can apprehend in the man sitting in the public house with bits of hay still sticking to him. And we get no hint of the novelist manipulating his character. Indeed the forces at work here seem beyond Dostoevsky too, rather as death's approach in 'such a tide as moving seems asleep' appears totally uncomprehended by the Victorian voice as it affirms 'I hope to meet my Pilot face to face' — and yet Tennyson wrote the whole lyric. Hence the reader's impression of doing a lot of work. But grateful and induced work. It must *also* be true that Dostoevsky is underneath the lot, calculating gaps and holes and those oblique surprises which unsettle what would otherwise be fixed human points on his novel's map.

How much the man knows what the artist is up to, none of us can say. The deeper realism is also, in this respect, obscurer. Dostoevsky's positively bad writing — one of the damned thing is enough! — is very like life, and we may have here the area in which his condition of overdriven hack releases the most frantic and relevant energies. Certainly *A Raw Youth* is a failure, and it is the full-length novel that was written under least stress. Not that I see how to make a virtue of stress, or of 'sort of' and 'somehow' and the other habits that would earn Dostoevsky a low place in the creative writing class; or how to link 'sort of' and stress except at the obvious level of haste. Or why the way his things and people turn 'strange' and 'indescribable', just when we want to know what they are really like, exhilarates when it ought to madden. *Really* is the nub. His genius is inexhaustibly devious in its jinks and feints and its beginnings of gestures. Notice how, apropos Mrs Marmeladov, 'inordinately proud' bobs up and is gone, leaving the reader to round out the ellipse (is she *really* very proud? what would *she* have said?) while Dostoevsky, with a light guiding hand on the truant husband and what is just his story, brings his main strength to bear obliquely on a thickening of narrative texture which comes through at the receiving end as a blanket *misère*.

(vi)

Supreme among the continuities between *Poor People* and *Crime and Punishment*, and a focus of much hard work in both novels, is that effect of forwardness which I described as creation in Marmeladov's mouth and at the tip of Mr Devushkin's pen:

I live in the kitchen, or rather it would be much more accurate to say there's a particular room here alongside the kitchen (and I must tell you, over here the kitchen's clean and light and very nice), a small room, just a modest little corner — or rather, to express it even better, this kitchen's a big one with three windows, so I've got a partition running along the inside wall, so it comes to a sort of extra room, an additional lodging in the house, plenty of elbow-room, it's comfortable, and there's a window and the lot — in short, every convenience. Well, that's my little corner and don't you go thinking there's anything else about it, any hidden meaning; 'the kitchen's what it is!' you'll say — and look at it like that and all right I do live in the one room, behind the partition, but it doesn't matter, I'm tucked away on my own . . . .[19]

The shifting, crumbling surface of this prose evokes again the *Poor People* circularities, equivocations, half-contradictions, where smells aren't exactly bad but slightly decaying, and convenience/comfort is juggled from hand to hand to avoid the downright lie. Here the overall pattern runs 'I live in the kitchen, no really I sort of don't live in the kitchen, so you mustn't go thinking I live in the kitchen, but if you look at it like that I sort of do live in the kitchen'. Dostoevsky reworked its internal rhythms for the second

[19] *The Gambler*, pp. 135-6.

printed text of 1847, making the doublings more nimble, the shifts at once sharper and more tender on the mind's ear; and then, still unsatisfied, he added the 'every convenience' touch for his first collected edition of 1860.[20]

This was close work with a vengeance. 'Honour and glory to the young poet', wrote Belinsky in his famous review of *Poor People*; and 'poet' fits what we have just seen of Mr Devushkin's kitchen fuss being shaped into an obsessive little round. But Belinsky continued: '. . . whose muse loves people in attics and basements' — and so Dostoevsky's naturalism and realism were defined for posterity.

The reason for preferring Poet to Realist is that it points at the words, the doubling tunes, the distinctive flavour of the book, and not at its people and places. This room or corner of Mr Devushkin's is the first interior in all Dostoevsky, just as he is the first character. He and it both raise doubts about the attics and basements mentioned by Belinsky; not of course about Dostoevsky's care for the people who live there but about how he makes art of it. The difficulty, I believe the impossibility, is to get a purchase on *Poor People* and the books which follow by means of a head-on realism of loving attention such as Belinsky is hinting at.

For all Dostoevsky's staircases and landings and muddy yards and rotten fences and miserable town dogs and back-alleys are, as we loosely say, the same. There are dozens of interiors which can be itemized in a coarse Identikit way in terms of shabby sofa covered with oil-cloth, unlit stove, partition down one wall, the cold scraps of a meal, icon in a corner. Many readers, coming to these straight from Balzac and Dickens where every napkin-ring seems creatively breathed upon, will have felt surprise and disappointment at what seems perfunctory and lazily generalized. But soon they will have begun to realize in their bones that this fiction's genius is other. Take the unlit stoves. There is not a single stove in Dostoevsky which is alight and healthy and doing its job (except in memory or wishful dream or ironic juxtaposition with death),[21] as Russian *pechka* and Indo-European hearth, the literal *focus*. And this may seem a damaging fact from the

---

[20]   *PSS*, Vol. I, p. 441.
[21]   Thus, 'an evening samovar . . . hot comfortable stoves . . . the quintessence

standpoint of Realism since fire is prominent among the good things of the poor, and the whole point is they do sometimes have it: all writers know this, and many from Euripides to Joyce and Lawrence have made an issue of it.

But my argument is precisely that the standpoint of Realism is unavailing. Obviously we aren't to imagine a young writer resolving never to have a healthy fire in the thousands of pages of fiction he will compose during the next thirty-five years, but a man in the grip of his daemon whose fires' importance rests in their malfunctioning, from the one which poisons people with its fumes in *Karamazov* to the one which stares at Shatov cold and empty when his wife comes back to him to have Stavrogin's baby:

'Oh, I'll get some logs at once, some logs — I've got logs!' Shatov was all astir. 'Logs — I mean — but I'll get tea at once,' he said, waving a hand as though with desperate determination; and he snatched up his cap.[22]

Further creation in the mouth, but at the same time, as with Marmeladov's 'nowhere to go', the more convulsive and local the plight — 'Logs — I mean — but I'll get tea at once' — the more impassively quotidian the sorrow investing yet another undescribed, merely discovered empty grate.

And yet another cobwebby teapot abandoned somewhere, and an unlighted samovar. The samovar, that second centre of Russian family and home, bends to the same rhythm as the stove; there are no happy samovars in Dostoevsky. But there are many funny ones, including the first. In Mr Devushkin's lodgings which are a blend of boarding school, barracks, and prison, the inmates line up in front of the samovars, 'and if anyone goes up with his teapot out of turn, he catches it then and there. In fact I made that mistake first time — but anyhow, why describe it!'[23] And the fires and stoves of *Poor People* are either the lost happy ones of memory or the unseen sources of the smells of stale stewing food and dirty washing which permeate the furniture and even get into the lodgers' clothes.

---

of pancakes . . . . He knew his dream was unattainable' (*Crime and Punishment*, p. 227). Food and drink are touched with natural dying in Stepan Verkhovensky and with suicide in Kirillov, both from *The Possessed*.

[22] *The Possessed*, p. 517.

[23] *The Gambler*, pp. 143–4.

'But it doesn't matter', Mr Devushkin tells Varenka; 'in time you get used to anything.' He has this way, as with 'but why describe it!' of allowing an entire saturated hell of ill-defined smells and noises and man's petty and comic and cumulatively agonizing cruelty to man to dissolve into near-nothingness, an urban *lacrimae rerum* like the white nights of the Petersburg climate. He also niggles minutely at definition, as we have seen, with the frenetic zeal of a man who thinks he would do something about his surroundings if only he could describe them right. Often and most characteristically, he is doing both at once; the doubling dance which he executes about living and not living in the kitchen is simultaneously exhaustive and empty, a feat of style which we apprehend as a self-lacerating inertia which knows neither change nor repose.

The young poet is in a mood of art like that shown by Mr Prufrock in his deployment of interrogative forms:

> And should I then presume?
> And how should I begin?
> Shall I say . . . ?

where Modernism is doing Macbeth's restless ecstasy again, in a world without pushy wives and royal guests and murders and usurpations. The absence of these tremendous circumstances, or suburban ambitions, does not make Mr Prufrock's questions unurgent. But then neither does the absence of convincing fruit make his 'Do I dare to eat a peach?' unreal. Eliot's whole address is simply not that of Shakespeare's naturalism or of what we usually associate with the nineteenth-century novel: which is also the case with the attics and basements of *Poor People*, and why I prefer to turn my back on Belinsky and the tradition and attempt a direct traverse from the words as mental pain's linguistic physique to Dostoevsky's claim for a deeper realism.

We are all familiar with the saloon bar sentence that begins 'Let's face it'; and glancing up at the speaker we are usually left in no doubt that he hasn't the slightest intention of facing anything just now except the glass in his hand.

Almost any writer might observe this little life-pattern, and then go on to conjure the expense-account lunchtime drinking and absent wife and children and temporarily forgotten mortgage; and he might also remark how odd it is that escapist contexts seem to provoke their linguistic contraries. 'Let's face it' — the perfect saloon-bar sentiment.

This is Dostoevsky country, but with a difference. The Russian writer gives no hint of ever having *observed* his countless equivalents of 'Let's face it'. His fiction reads as if born to them. If he were to do my saloon-bar scene there would be no mention of temporarily dismissed cares, nor of the mordant clash of fact and language. The words would be said. The gin and tonic would sparkle in the hand. No reflective authorial point would be made; but the uncanny — yet normal — mental life under the words and the absolute object in the hand would reek of Dostoevsky.

Particular banalities like 'Let's face it' come and go in a few decades, whereas compulsions to say, do, be the opposite, are with us always. The opposite of what? leads most obviously to *The Double*, the second novel to be written. Nevertheless the figuring of an *alter ego*, and self-repudiation taken sometimes to the point of notional self-annihilation (the literal suicides come later), are here from the start in *Poor People*. These obscure compulsions are the heartland of Freudian commentary because they have no link in common sense with self-interest or in morality with unselfishness — for example the scene in *The Idiot* where Myshkin knows the one thing he must not do is smash a particular vase in the room, so he begins by sitting as far away from it as possible and ends by breaking it.[24] The texture here is untypically neat and thin, in contrast with the luminous cat-and-mouse density of *Crime and Punishment* where Raskolnikov's hunting himself down undercuts all attempts by the *bien pensant* reader — and the novel's own Epilogue — to make the process more correct and comfortable by lucid moralizing. A man with a bad conscience is easier to contemplate than one whose shaving-mirror reveals each morning his natural prey.

Mr Devushkin pursues himself with the agile lightness and flair of his creator's youth. Telling Varenka she must not read

[24] pp. 536–7.

any hidden meaning into his farrago about living and not living in the kitchen was the surest way to bring suspicion on his head. And his frenzied urge to sacrifice himself to Varenka makes her his victim too. Don't you go worrying about this and that is one of his most stubborn tics, meant protectively but achieving nothing except damage to her peace of mind. Once he inflicts on her the fantastic yet everyday (though not saloon-bar) formula: 'No, we had better not think of that, Varenka, and break our hearts in advance with such ideas. That's why I'm writing this — to warn you not to think about it and torment yourself with evil notions.'[25]

The authorial slyness of 'to warn you not to think about it' is typical. Let's *not* face it! Most of these jokes, if that's the right word, are reversible. Extreme instability characterizes the airy lunar wit of *Poor People* — as the lives of poor people are themselves unstable. The intellectualism and the human truth of this brilliant little book meet at the point of Mr Devushkin's pen.

His pen rather than Varenka's because her letters are without the forwardness or tip effect which is the essence of the novel's precocity. The four printed texts show some mannerisms like 'really and truly' and 'so there!' being worked up in order to fix her voice for us more firmly. She is in place all right and has her own human truth. While her lover darts about we imagine her through her letters sitting in her room, her wings furled. She plays opposite Mr Devushkin in an epistolary Double Act — contrast and not mere foil. She is the first of Dostoevsky's exploited Petersburg seamstresses, as he is the first 'office rat'. While he is forty-seven and shabby beyond seediness, she is young and ill. 'If work does come my way', she asks, 'how am I to work?'[26] He could never have said that. He would have shuffled and fumbled. He would never have met extremity head on as she does. She counsels him: 'You really mustn't give way to despair. There's trouble enough without that.' And although she is less than half his age, the admonition convinces. It reaches back to those places where all women are older than all men, to birth and death and the small and big interim crises of household and home. 'There's trouble enough without that.'[27] It echoes

---

[25] *The Gambler*, p. 206.   [26] Ibid., p. 219.   [27] Ibid., p. 207.

through the domestic imagination until we feel that not merely Mr Devushkin but no other member of his sex could have said it. This really is a prodigy, this generic feminine touch which pervades the whole book, from Varenka's twitching of her curtains in the opening pages, for while there's life there's a possibility of pertness, to her decision to marry a rich man who turns up from her compromised past — 'Of course I am not going into a paradise' — at the end.

Her human truth has nothing to do with *Poor People* as a young and clever book. It encompasses more than her sex. It dilates into the instinctive wisdom of this 'authorless' novel in letters and catches Dostoevsky like a night-creature in the headlights, not manipulating Varenka but brooding alongside her with his lifetime's fiction already astir inside him. His first 'nowhere to go' takes shape in the first of those inset narratives of his which have grown more explosively immediate in memory — flash-outs as well as flash-backs. When Varenka was fifteen her father died, and she tells Mr Devushkin how a remote female relative took her mother and herself to live with her:

To this day I don't see just why it was she invited us into her house. At first she was quite nice to us — but later, when she saw we were completely useless and had nowhere to go, she began to show her real character in full . . . . Day followed day, and each was like the one before. We lived as quietly as if we were in the country. Anna Feodorovna calmed down by degrees as she came fully to recognise her power — though truly no one ever thought of gainsaying her.[28]

The deeper realism, radical but not reductive. The anatomy of sadism in Dostoevsky. But not quite, because I am translating his magazine text of 1846, and when he came to revise it the next year he struck out 'useless' and wrote 'helpless' instead.[29] Helplessness is the stronger, perhaps in the last resort the only mental blood-scent, and the rationale is now complete: she began to torment them when she realized they were helpless, and she began to let up a bit when she enjoyed the full sense of her own power. Think what Dickens would have made of this material. Think of the first quarter of *Copperfield*. Whereas here nothing is fleshed out. Anna Feodorovna tells them they are proud beyond their means,

[28]   Ibid., pp. 153–4.   [29]   *PSS*, Vol. I, p. 444.

but no context is given; and 'at meals she watched every morsel we took, while if we did not eat, there would be a fuss again' — but not a single meal or moment in a meal is described. We are left with the menacing flatness of her 'fuss' matching the monotony, quite unironic, of cruelties endured in a life quiet 'as if we were living in the country'. Being unspecific achieves nothing in itself; it simply offers no obstacle, no hitch, no circumstantial snag for the universal perception about cruelty to catch itself on, and no mitigation of the appalling bareness of 'nowhere to go'.[30]

In the epistolary Double Act of *Poor People* Mr Devushkin plays nobody to be opposite Varenka's nowhere to go. These are the two sides of the single study of extremity which constitutes Dostoevsky's first book. The creative fancy moves to and fro between the almost calm fixity of her sexual-economic exploitation, and the circular fret, the little spurts of self-assertion no sooner essayed than qualified or annulled, of his struggle to sustain the thought that 'I am nevertheless a man, in heart and mind a man'.[31] Both are held in their postures, doomed as Myshkin was to break that vase — but without the blighting schematism of *The Idiot*. Varenka's very question seems to stand still: 'If work does come my way, how am I to work'; while Mr Devushkin chases his tail in the ought-must-can't figure of 'You see I ought to give my landlady more money, in fact I must; but if you consider the whole thing, my darling, and reckon up all my necessities, you'll see it's impossible to give her more, and so it isn't any use talking about it and there's no need to mention it.'[32] She

---

[30]   Constance Garnett and the Everyman translator both provide their own mitigation by rendering the phrase 'nowhere *else* to go' (my italics). The effect is extraordinary.

Dostoevsky's last seamstress, like Varenka his first, has 'nowhere to go'. She is 'a gentle spirit' who gives the title to the short story he published in the November issue of his 'Writer's Diary' for 1876. Her 'nowhere' is her jump from a sixth-floor window, and from the slow torture of her marriage, a jump she makes clutching an icon, a jump to her death on the pavement below.

A Gentle Spirit has rightly been judged one of the most powerful studies of despair in world literature, a banging on closed doors imagined with absolute fearlessness. Dostoevsky read about the seamstress's suicide in a newspaper, and was gripped by the juxtaposition of icon and what was for him the greatest of human sins; but something made him change her way of life, so we lose the livelihood, or non-livelihood, of seamstress in the story.

[31]   *The Gambler*, p. 216   [32]   Ibid., p. 206.

and her question stand still because they have nowhere to go. He and his utterance, both children of men, must keep on the move since they have no place to lay their heads.

This impossibility of rest images a pursuit of identity which is Mr Devushkin's only at the level of attribution.[33] As I remarked about his pain in general, it is not an articulation of selfhood; and that is why we do better to think of Joseph K. and Prufrock than of the characters of the great Realists. Perhaps the strangest thing of all about Dostoevsky is that he worked his way backwards into the nineteenth-century novel during the Siberian years of prison and exile — but without forgetting where he had been, without surrendering his initial proleptic grasp of unborn visions and techniques.

Much has been written about *Poor People* in relation to Richardson, Rousseau, Goethe, and the whole tradition of the novel in letters. It is so much waste paper. The real issues are forward-looking: dramatized chaos and inertia, the Double Act, the Lacuna ('missing' letters and so forth), the resources of 'authorlessness' which Dostoevsky will be exploring all his life. Unlike the other scribblers — so he claimed of *Poor People* — 'I have not displayed my ugly mug';[34] and this, though not entirely true, marks a big and sustained effort and an instinctive modernity which is far more important than Dostoevsky's knowledge of the tradition and his fondness for old-fashioned fictional devices like the mulled-over diary and the discovery of papers in a locked drawer.

More specifically, and closer in time, much has been made of *Poor People*'s debt to Gogol's story, *The Overcoat*. This is a different kettle of fish. People are fond of quoting Dostoevsky as saying 'We have all come out of Gogol's *Overcoat*'. He probably didn't.[35] And even if he did, the remark grows more elusive the longer you ponder it, like many of his apparently straightforward things.

Gogol's hero is also an oppressed middle-aged titular councillor. His name is Bashmachkin which means Shoeman.

[33] p. 18, above.   [34] Letter of 1 February 1846.
[35] The debate is summarized by S. A. Reiser in *Poetika i stilistika russkoi literaturi* (1971), pp. 187–9.

While Dostoevsky is silent about the Girly implication of Devushkin,[36] Gogol makes a point of Shoe, and does this in order to set up the joke that the men in the Bashmachkin family in fact wear boots — 'and why, even the brother-in-law', he adds. That 'even' is the purest Gogol. He leaves his reader to add a second tier to the joke and savour the thought that the brother-in-law's surname will not be Bashmachkin, and that the connection between what people are called and what they wear is nonsense anyhow.

The humour is childlike and zany and has a flitting Irish quality which owes a lot to Gogol's upbringing in the Ukraine — Little Russia as it was called. Nobody who also has the feel of Dostoevsky could confuse the two men for a moment. For example, the joke which dominates *The Overcoat* is also the purest Gogol. Mr Bashmachkin saves up laboriously for a new overcoat to face the Petersburg winter; he buys the overcoat, has it stolen from him, catches a cold and dies. Thereafter he haunts the streets. Who is 'he'? The answer is a *mertvets*, which can only mean a dead man or corpse. I stress this because the translations I have looked at wreck the joke by preferring 'ghost', for Gogol uses the word that cannot mean ghost frequently and consistently until the very end of the story when the troublesome *mertvets* conjures a snug overcoat off the back of his old civil service boss. People wonder if he/it will be satisfied from now on and leave them alone. Then a policeman sees an apparition and timidly follows it, until it turns on him displaying a huge fist and flowing whiskers — quite unlike Mr Bashmachkin. This is somebody/something else. It is a real 'ghost'.

The Overcoat appeared in 1842, the same year as the first part of Gogol's *Dead Souls*. The plot of *Dead Souls* concerns the fraudulent buying up of serfs who have died since the last government census but who remain their owners' liability for tax and other purposes until the next. Humanly dead, the souls are bureaucratically alive. They offer great scope for jokes about real and notional and ambiguous death, and in this central area *The Overcoat* is an overspill from *Dead Souls*.

[36] Conceivably his letting fall the word '*devichesky*' at *PSS*, Vol. I, p. 69, l. 23, is a very glancing reference; but I doubt it. See Mr Devushkin's letter of 1 August (*The Gambler*, p. 200). Mrs Garnett's word is "maidenly".

'Catch that *mertvets*, dead or alive!' is the sort of fooling at the heart of the short story and quarried out of the first part of the novel. They both antedate *Poor People* by four years.

The Gogolian world of dead souls and clerk corpses and real ghosts is by no means trivial, but it lacks the follow-through and coherence, above all the momentousness, of Dostoevsky's nobody to be — as it lacks the different because entirely uncomic momentousness of death and identity in Tolstoy, when Natasha Rostov wonders about her dead Prince Andrew, 'Where is he and *who* is he now?' That Tolstoyan sobriety and directness and obviousness, which nevertheless astonishes: '*Who* is he now?'[37]

Mr Devushkin's version of Natasha's question and Gogol's 'Who/What is Bashmachkin now?' is 'Who can I ever be?' We have caught a glimpse of him, teapot in hand, standing in line with the other lodgers as he waits his turn at the samovar. The lodging-house pecking order and the search for identity are intertwined throughout. To find and keep your right place in the queue is, perhaps, to know who you are — or rather, to believe in who you are. And likewise at the office. He 'does a hedgehog' in his desk very much as he holes up in his 'corner' at home, and he clings to his grade on the bureaucratic scale with unbounded conservative fervour:

One man is ordained to wear the epaulettes of a general, another to serve as a titular councillor . . . . And as there are various grades in the service, and as each grade requires a reprimand which corresponds exactly to itself — so it is natural that the tone of the reprimand should be different in the different grades. That's in the order of things! Why, the whole world depends on that, my darling, on all of us setting the tone with each other, on everybody reprimanding everybody else.[38]

But life, as we say, isn't as simple as that. Both at home and at work an untidy humanity in him and around him makes it impossible to find peace in identity as status. If he knows his station, others do not. He is made to cringe for a loan by a clerk of the fourteenth, the bottom grade. Observe the deeper

[37]   *War and Peace*, Part XV, Ch. 1. Anybody who had been learning Russian for a week could manage '*Gde on i kto on teper*?' Yet the Everyman translator renders it 'Who was he? Where is he?' and Constance Garnett (Pan Books), 'Where is he, and what is he now?' and Louise and Aylmer Maude (Oxford) leave it out. That bottomless simplicity has unnerved them all.

[38]   *The Gambler*, pp. 191, 227.

realism of 'I knew of course this was Markov's house but I asked a policeman' on the brink of their dreaded meeting. Wonderful. But wonderful. Also the elusive presence of religion in this first novel: 'Passing a church I crossed myself and repented of all my sins, then I realised it was low of me to bargain with the Lord God' — again on the way to this meeting.[39]

And his humble yet obstinate 'I am nevertheless a man' keeps chafing against the domestic pecking order and Peter the Great's Table of Ranks. Like Bashmachkin, Mr Devushkin is a copying clerk. 'If all of us became real writers', he asks Varenka in a little rush of self-assertion, 'who would be left to do the copying?'[40] Just as 'the police received orders to catch the *mertvets* at all costs, dead or alive' is the purest Gogol, so that question about real writers and copiers is the purest pre-Siberian Dostoevsky. It certainly did not come out of *The Overcoat*. Its genius is immemorial, one wants to say classical. It flickers between Greek and Latin epigram and Shakespeare and Molière and Pushkin in such a way as to make all talk of Dostoevsky and the tradition seem idle.

Thus Mr Devushkin's job is to copy. His doubling speech is a kind of copying too, often in ways which aren't immediately obvious. In his first letter he urges Varenka 'Now don't you worry about me, my own, and don't imagine there's anything wrong.' That is the magazine text. It is one of Mr Devushkin's innumerable near-iterations or doublets, and it follows the familiar pattern of worrying Varenka by telling her not to worry. At first sight, therefore, it seems odd that Dostoevsky struck it out when he revised *Poor People*. Perhaps he felt there was enough of this sort of thing already. But then it seems even odder that he should substitute for the cancelled sentence, 'My dispositon is entirely such as befits a man of resolute and tranquil soul.'[41] For this is old-fashioned and bookish. It isn't even an impersonal bureaucratic usage such as Mr Devushkin sometimes adopts like a protective colouring. It isn't his voice at all. And this is precisely the point. It is stolen or parroted — copied in a

[39] Ibid., pp. 203-11. [40] Ibid., p. 174.
[41] *PSS*, Vol. I, p. 442; *The Gambler*, p. 136.

different sense. We are tipped off in this same first letter by his apologizing to Varenka for his 'far-fetched comparisons', adding 'I took it all from a book'.[42]

What book was this? We aren't told and it doesn't matter. Mr Devushkin's mind is a junk shop in which second-hand scraps of all sorts float about from books, poems, and newspapers, and what he supposes to be the way smart and clever people talk. 'I was such a bright falcon getting up today!' he exclaims, again in his first letter — verbally close to the heroic simile 'like a falcon'.[43] He and Varenka lend each other books and stories, including Gogol's *Overcoat*. Pushkin's *Stationmaster* rubs shoulders with pulp-literature parodies which Dostoevsky must have had fun concocting — an Italianate Romance and a tale of blood and lust among the Siberian Cossacks. Mild stay-at-home Mr Devushkin sends Varenka samples in the vein of 'all your husband's blood would not quench the frantic surging rapture of my soul'[44] — his hope being that she will admire them as much as he does. This is the youngest side of *Poor People*, and also a reason why the book hasn't travelled well: its literary and linguistic clowning translates unsatisfactorily and sometimes not at all. It is tangled, thickety stuff, especially *vis-à-vis* Gogol. In fact its range of innuendo and nuance has been underestimated by the Russians themselves.

Without naming author or story, Mr Devushkin plunges into a chunnering, chaotic denunciation of the writer who pries into the lives of ordinary people. It gradually dawns on us that the snooping 'he' is Gogol, and that Mr Devushkin, with much mixing up of fiction and real life, is criticizing *The Overcoat*. At the centre of all this literary in-fighting (where, despite Dostoevsky's boast, we catch more than a glimpse of his ugly young mug) can be sensed the protest that no amount

---

[42] *The Gambler*, p. 134.

[43] 'Like a falcon' is formulaic in the national and household classic, the twelfth-century *Lay of Igor's Campaign*; but the 'bright falcon' occurs nowhere in that poem. Nor did 'bright' occur in *Poor People* until Dostoevsky added it in 1847 (*PSS*, Vol. I, p. 441: translated by Mrs Garnett 'gay as a lark' in *The Gambler*, p. 134). Dostoevsky wanted to give Mr Devushkin's discourse a shove towards a humble nineteenth-century rhetoric, and he preferred 'bright' to the diminutive form of falcon he had used in the magazine text.

[44] *The Gambler*, p. 179.

of observation and fine writing will provide 'that clerk' (Bashmachkin, of course) with a new overcoat to replace the stolen one. Nor, says Mr Devushkin explicitly, will reading the story induce anybody to buy him, Mr Devushkin, an overcoat either. Broadening his attack, he exclaims: 'You were going to send me a book of some sort, my darling, to relieve my dullness. What's the good of a book, my darling? What's the point of it . . . ? And if they start talking to you about some Shakespeare fellow, saying "Shakespeare is literature" — well then, Shakespeare is nonsense, it's all utter nonsense and it's nothing but unkind foolery.'[45]

In Dostoevsky's own foolery Gogol's name is never mentioned, but *gogol* means a species of sea duck called golden-eye and the phrase to walk gogol-fashion means to strut, which Mr Devushkin twists into sit gogol-fashion to describe how tail-coats hang on the kind of people he disapproves of.[46] Less ideology and more gathering the threads of this oblique Gogol-baiting by the Soviet editors would have left us all better off. The other *gogol* belongs to a veritable flock of *Poor People* birds: Mr Devushkin's 'little bird' endearments to Varenka, his undereducated 'bright falcon', his touching pomposities about 'the carefree and innocent happiness of the birds of the air', those birds 'created for the solace of men and the adornment of nature'.[47] Then there is Snegirev (Bullfinch), the doorman at the office. When asked by Mr Devushkin for a brush to get the mud off his coat, perky status-conscious Bullfinch, so Mr Devushkin reports to Varenka, 'said no I mustn't, I'd spoil the brush, "and the brush is government property, sir," says he'.[48] And at home, in the lodging-house, so foul is 'our air' — note the quiet horror of the collective — that captive songbirds 'simply die'.[49]

(vii)

Nothing could be more economical in effect than 'simply die', which brings to mind a boast comparable with the one

[45] Ibid., pp. 192, 200–1.
[46] Ibid., p. 221.
[47] Ibid., p. 134.
[48] Ibid., p. 211.
[49] Ibid., p. 143.

Dostoevsky made about never showing his own face in *Poor People*. 'People find the novel long drawn out', he wrote, 'but there isn't a superfluous word in it.'[50] Mr Devushkin's expenditure of over a hundred words in failing to say whether he does or does not live in the kitchen could not be more justly and informatively prefaced than by the claim that not one of those words is wasted. We have here a feat of style that reads beautifully and therefore unsuperfluously free. Study of the four printed texts reminds us that Mr Devushkin's doubling tune did not in fact compose itself.

'If all of us became real writers, who would do the copying?' doesn't require this or any other preface. It carries the stamp of thematic epitome. It proposes the final unity of the copying motif and the search for identity. Comic and agonized, Mr Devushkin's *cri de coeur* gives voice to the Lilliputian battle which is raging on the surface of his mind and at the tip of his pen. If the world needs copiers then to be a copier is to be somebody. Or is it? He cannot find and hold to himself in copying any more than in the domestic pecking order or in office status. 'One has all sorts of dreams, you know', he confides in his first letter.[51] Restive in the role of doer-again, he will argue that he copies other people's work *to please himself*. Or he will produce bizarre scrambled formulae like 'No, I am doing it on my own account, of my own accord, for his pleasure'.[52] Once his rebellious fancy strays a good deal further:

Now then suppose for instance that suddenly, apropos of nothing, there came into the world a book entitled *Poems by Makar Devushkin*? What would my little angel say then? How does that strike you? What do you think about it? I tell you straight, my darling, as soon as my book came out I certainly wouldn't dare show my face in the Nevsky Prospect. Think how dreadful when everyone would be saying Here comes the literary author and poet, Devushkin. There's Devushkin himself! they would say.[53]

But that is a wild extreme in the fluctuations of the quest for somebody to be.

In fact — fact beyond formula — Mr Devushkin is somebody

---

50   Letter of 1 February 1846.   51   *The Gambler*, p. 134.
52   Ibid., p. 178.   53   Ibid., p. 181.

without knowing it. He is self-divided as we all are. Thus, over that 'Shakespeare fellow', he both apes literature and denounces it. He drives himself into the ground, again as we all do, with his ought-must-can't and similar rhythms. He is humble, and the rest of us at least know the feeling. Ranging himself beside a boastful fellow-lodger with literary pretensions, gullible Mr Devushkin asks 'What am I? Nothing. He is a man of reputation, and what am I? I simply don't exist. But he is kind even to·me', adds Mr Devushkin in abject but completely unshaken and unshakable self-identity.[54]

I want to dwell on Mr Devushkin's instinctive self-identity, the thing that can never be undercut. The rare moments when we are allowed to catch him about his daily business, moments of particularity and penetration as when he finishes a letter in a hurry telling Varenka he hasn't shaved yet, he must shave, then 'I will say my prayers and be off' — those moments of the day's routine are psychologically coherent and even peaceful.[55] Unthinking habit brings respite from the pangs of consciousness (yet who dare assume that Mr Devushkin's prayers are themselves unthinking?); and one of the chief explorations of Dostoevsky's next book, *The Double*, will be to deny the grooved self-identity of habit to its hero, Mr Golyadkin. This points the way to the fact that Mr Golyadkin is mad, whereas Mr Devushkin is sane. Without knowing it, beneath his scribble and mental froth, Mr Devushkin finds somebody to be within the frame of shaving, praying, dressing and undressing, eating, drinking, smoking, pen-trimming. Also in his posture of 'hedgehog' self-shelter under external buffeting. When the other clerks tease him or the boss summons him to give him one of those graded reprimands we have read about for a copying mistake, he shrinks down in his desk with his hands over his ears 'as if there was no me in the world'.[56] Self-shelter is tacit self-affirmation and explicit self-collection; it is the most centripetal of responses to stress, and, as we shall see, Mr Golyadkin is denied this area of sane instinct too.

Incomparably the most important revelation of the habitual somebody vouchsafed to us in odd disjunctive glimpses,

[54] Ibid., p. 178.   [55] Ibid., p. 207.   [56] Ibid., p. 228.

shaving and so forth, occurs when Mr Devushkin comes across
a group of his fellow-lodgers roaring with laughter at a rough
draft of a letter to Varenka which they have discovered.[57]
Suddenly, late in the book, the two households facing each
other across the yard are drawn together. Mr Devushkin's
secret is out. It is the first *skandal* scene in Dostoevsky
(*skandal*, given wide currency by the formalist critic Mikhail
Bakhtin, is more rowdy and physical than our scandal but
shares its disrepute and hint of yeasting menace). At a stroke
the twin-based exchange of letters has become a single highly
inflammable structure. We expect a blaze — and here, as with
so many duels, punch-ups, parties, and as with so much sex in
the later novels, the smouldering *skandal* subsides into uncomfortable shamefaced fiasco. For to disappoint expectations is Dostoevsky's frequent way. He likes a duel to add
up to a hat being shot off, and well-advanced motions towards
rape to fizzle out. 'You are ruined along with me, hopelessly
ruined!' Mr Devushkin tells Varenka in token of their newly
entwined fates and the apparently tightening narrative; but
absolutely nothing comes of it. The other lodgers go on
laughing a bit and they dub Mr Devushkin 'a Lovelace' (for
Richardson's *Clarissa Harlowe* with its virtuoso amorist had
swept Russia as well as Europe); and then they just forget.
This gives academic folk a talking point over *Poor People*
and the tradition of the novel in letters, but it leaves the
common reader becalmed in the aftermath of a miniature
Dostoevsky *skandal*. He looks about him, and at this moment
of the story's checked impulse he takes stock. Well, that's
that, he reflects, while Varenka's answering letter reveals
she has burnt herself ironing and life goes on. So there are
rough drafts of the letters, at least of this one and presumably of others It's odd Mr Devushkin hasn't mentioned them
before. But then of course Varenka might be less impressed
by the finished products if she knew about the flotsam of
trial and error lying behind them.

Brooding along these lines, freely as he thinks, the reader
rests in the hollow of Dostoevsky's hand. It is not an altogether comfortable place to be. The aborted climax of the

draft letter's discovery by Mr Devushkin's fellow-lodgers is a foretaste of the seemingly gratuitous crisis-mongering which again and again drives the later novels against the grain of art, at least of art's reposeful virtues. I say gratuitous because nothing comes of it: nothing comes of the holy man's corpse which stinks prematurely, scandalously, in the last novel just as nothing comes of this discovered draft in the first. I say *seemingly* gratuitous because smell proves to be the master-metaphor of *Karamazov*, and the discovery which leads to nothing in *Poor People* is calculated by the young poet to force his reader back upon Mr Devushkin's letter-writing with a certain heavy finality.

For letter-writing engrosses Mr Devushkin as shaving and the rest obviously do not.[58] Here, more than glimpsed, is the habitual somebody, the absorption in routine which means giving up the search for identity without meaning to, Mr Devushkin's fullest self-contact, his ultimate sanity which of course he knows nothing about. He is a copying clerk, a doer-again. The delayed revelation that he also does his own letters again carries with it the primitive, very novelistic satisfaction of an inward 'Of course!' How could it be otherwise with all his fuss about style and getting things right? And as the impending joint ruin of Varenka and Mr Devushkin turns to thin air, so the reader, no longer vexed by aborted climax, finds — or fashions — more than he thought was there, or Dostoevsky shows any sign of intending, in the simple solace of the realization that prim Mr Girly would be bound to make rough drafts of his letters.

Letter-writing, his habit of habits, embroils his creator in parody and other sorts of mimicry, and himself in style. Now style means two things. First, the style which Mr Devushkin is always talking about and seeking to improve, where his literary yardstick is Dostoevsky's parodic opportunity. And second, the style he is unaware of. When he gets trapped in the circle of 'I do but I don't but I do live in the kitchen' he isn't buffing and furbishing his words after some approved model, he is completely lost in his letter-writing habit; but we

---

[58]   That, incidentally, is why it touches off *skandal* after the one earlier reference to gossip about Varenka has failed to do so (p. 200).

catch his mind's voice — style in the second sense — at this juncture, and we also catch Dostoevsky returning to the passage in 1847 and yet again in 1860. Collation of the four printed texts of *Poor People* suggests that here and elsewhere as much work went into the second sort of style as the first.

The second sort is the man Devushkin — the timid, self-contradicting, doubling man, but also the sane man possessed and even tenacious of self. 'My' is the last word of the book, plunging towards oblivion as the final letter to Varenka ends in mid-sentence. 'What does style matter now?' he asks in that last letter; 'I write only to write, only to go on writing to you' — explicitly throwing overboard Style Sense One and tacitly affirming Style Sense Two. Mr Devushkin is losing Varenka to the rich man who will bear her off into the remote steppe 'bare as the palm of my hand', the steppe which is the first emblematic nowhere in Dostoevsky, to be followed by America and other nowheres. When the news of the impending marriage breaks, Mr Devushkin outfumbles even himself in an agony of incoherence, appealing to 'God's will' which is 'inscrutable — and fate too — they are the same'. But in the last letter he rallies and tears into her with the cruelty that feeds off hopeless love: 'Just look at yourself, do you look like a grand country lady?' And then his final floating 'my'. We attach it to Varenka of course ('my dearest, my own'), but equally to himself:

To whom am I going to write letters, my darling? Yes! you must take that into consideration — you must ask yourself, To whom is he going to write letters? —[59]

perhaps the neatest, most economical doublet in the book. And the one whose source is easiest to discern, though here I am not thinking of an ugly young mug inadvertently showing itself now and again, but of the personality of the 'authorless' novel in letters which cannot but show itself all the time. The words are there. They can run, as Joe Louis used to say of his opponents in the boxing ring, but they can't hide.

Mr Devushkin's 'Think of *me*!' as it lies cheek by jowl with

---

[59] *The Gambler*, pp. 240, 246-7.

his 'I only think of *you*!' recalls the selfish selfless rhetoric which informs Marmeladov's *Crime and Punishment* tirade and is a strong trait in personal relations elsewhere in Dostoevsky. But in *Poor People* this rhetoric assumes a specialized aspect: it is projected, as we have just seen, on the epistolary plane of 'You must ask yourself, To whom is he going to write letters?' And the whole love story reflects the constraints which this specialization imposes. It is as if there were a conspiracy between the book's reader and its genius (the authorless device prevents us invoking a novelist, even an absconded one) to make a virtue of necessity, to outface the boredom which love letters hold for third parties by snapping up the pleasures, the pearls of fiction, which bear upon love only remotely or not at all.

The book's genius is the Double Act of nowhere to go and nobody to be stylized as a love affair between a seamstress and a clerk. This stylization is neither a fraud nor a failure, but it strikes very unlike post-Siberian Dostoevsky. Life's lacerations — a word that haunts all the novels — are distanced in *Poor People*; these two lovers claw at each other and at themselves as if observed through glass. We learn that Mr Devushkin has lapsed in his self-denial; he ought in his own eyes to be sacrificing everything for Varenka, but 'I can't live without tobacco, my little angel, and it's nine days since I've had my pipe in my mouth'.[60] He goes on to explain that he would have bought his tobacco without saying anything to her about it, 'but I was ashamed'. And then the backlash: 'So that's why I'm telling you all this, to escape the stings of conscience.' These are the distanced lacerations of *Poor People*. We don't want to call the love affair with Varenka unreal, but it isn't real like that sudden picture of Mr Devushkin and his pipe. He doesn't miss her like he misses it. Although over in a flash, the pipe incident thrusts straight down through the surface turmoil to the 'real' Mr Devushkin of sane habits, instincts, appetites.

But the surface is 'real' too. The zany jinking between shame at the thought of deceiving his beloved and desire for a quiet conscience is of the essence of Mr Devushkin's total tip-of-the-pen instability which the novel is very 'really' about. This selfish selflessness — one supposes Mr Devushkin will sometimes go without his tobacco and sometimes won't, that's life — is Marmeladov country as I've just said, and pervades Dostoevsky's work; but we are never there with Mr Devushkin and Varenka as we are there with Marmeladov and his wife, for example when the truant husband finally returns home and falls on his knees and shuffles forward on them as the poor demented woman tugs his hair and he holds up his arms 'to facilitate her search' while she turns his pockets inside out before their wondering children to make sure there is no money left from his drinking spree.[61]

I am not saying that Mr Devushkin misses Varenka less than his pipe, but that the girl and the tobacco exist on different planes and are incomparable. The simplicity of 'it's nine days since I've had my pipe in my mouth' objectifies itself as an envelope of fond yet cool solicitude surrounding him as it surrounds him while he shaves and prays and trims his pen. At such times the scampering cloud-rack of 'I write only to write' is blown away and he becomes observable and fixed. Herein the pleasures of *Poor People* that are tangential or even irrelevant to the love story.

And the pleasures include, of course, Mr Devushkin's distresses. He can't afford to drink tea, but he can't afford not to drink tea either — lodging-house protocol requires it: one drinks tea 'for the sake of other people, for the look of the thing, for tone'.[62] And the distresses of others too, in a world where charity is double-edged. He tells how a subscription was got up for a destitute clerk. As they handed the money over 'they made a sort of official inspection of every penny. They thought they were giving him his pennies for nothing — but they weren't.'[63] He paid for them in the currency of humiliation.

Chief among these others is the Gorshkov family (the Potsons: the urban poor cling to their potted plants as they do to their sights and dreams of birds), huddled in one room of the lodging house. 'They're poor, dear God they're poor!'

[61]   *Crime and Punishment*, p. 23.   [62]   *The Gambler*, p. 136.
[63]   Ibid., p. 199.

exclaims Mr Devushkin, poverty heartrent by greater poverty. 'It's always still and quiet in their room, as if nobody was living there.'[64] Mr Gorshkov has lost his job over 'some unpleasantness' and is being bled white in a lawsuit. But at last, after years, his honour is vindicated and the court orders his opponent to pay him 'a significant sum of money'. The news spreads through the lodging house.

He came home at three o'clock this afternoon. He didn't look himself, he was white as a sheet, his lips quivered, he kept smiling — he embraced his wife and children. We all crowded round to congratulate him. He was greatly moved by our behaviour, he bowed in all directions, seized each of us by the hand several times. He actually seemed to me to have grown taller and more erect and to have lost that running tear in his eye. He was in such excitement, poor man. He couldn't stand still for two minutes; he picked up anything he came across, then dropped it again, kept smiling and bowing all the time, sitting down, getting up, sitting down again, saying goodness knows what: 'My honour, my honour, my good name, my children' — that's the way he talked. He cried in fact. Most of us were moved to tears too. Ratazyaev [the bumptious fellow-lodger with literary pretensions] clearly wanted to cheer him up and said 'What's honour, old chap, when there's nothing to eat? It's the money, the money's the thing, old chap; that's what to thank God for!' And thereupon he patted him on the shoulder. It seemed to me that Gorshkov was offended — not that he openly showed his displeasure, he just looked at Ratazyaev sort of strangely and removed his hand from his shoulder.[65]

And then, when Mr Gorshkov says he thinks he'll lie down for a bit, and does so, and dies in his sleep unbeknown to his wife who is sitting in their room with him, — then she, as reported by Mr Devushkin, 'was so lost in her thoughts that she doesn't remember what she was thinking about, all she can say is she had forgotten about her husband. But then suddenly she was roused by a kind of anxious sensation . . . '.

She doesn't know what she was thinking about, she only knows she wasn't thinking about her husband. At such moments Dostoevsky and Tolstoy draw close to each other, and away from everybody else. We have left behind the highly stylized love story, and *Poor People* comes across for all its physical smallness as big-boned and suggestive of whole phases of the late, great novels. At the end of the passage I quoted, the 'sort of strangely' with which Mr Gorshkov looked at Ratazyaev has the *strangely* authoritative and awestruck quality of those that are to come, a Dostoevsky epiphany, a manifestation of god in man, or, as we shall read in his own words, a discovery of the human in the human being.

But the love story itself escapes from the tight Double Act routine once and once only:

> Getting to know you, I came first to know myself better and I came to love you; and until you came along, my angel, I was all on my own and sort of asleep, and not really alive . . . but when you appeared you lighted up my whole dark life so that my heart and soul were filled with light, and I found peace of mind and knew that I was no worse than others; the only thing is I don't shine in any way, I have no polish or style, but I am after all a man, in heart and mind a man.[66]

A formal lapse, since one can't imagine this stuff about knowledge and love and humanity shaping itself at the tip of a copying clerk's quill pen. But the noble and mysterious selfish selflessness of 'getting to know you, I came first to know myself better and I came to love you' is no less wonderful for that in the novelist of twenty-four, and unhappy the reader who would be without it.

Everywhere else the lovers and their love are contained by the decorum of style, not the style of Mr Devushkin's 'I have no polish or style', but the other. Unlike the Marmeladovs, Mr Devushkin and Varenka never collide over what he unspecifically calls 'my fearful, fearful lapses'. No doubt these amount to little more than the pipe he can't do without. It's true he goes through a patch of drinking, but this stems from the fiasco of his attempted loan from a fourteenth-grade clerk, and from the humiliation of being thrown downstairs by some young men, one of whom — an army officer — has insulted Varenka and is sought out by Mr Devushkin with the vague intention of calling him to account. These disasters feed that 'reality' of the surface — not of course a superficial 'reality' — which I am trying to shed light on: 'Well, then they turned me out, then they threw me downstairs — that is, they didn't exactly throw me, they only turned me out.' A classic doublet of the living and not living in the kitchen type,

but with the delicious little coda: 'that's the whole story.'[67]
And instead of reaching down to the drinking habit itself,
Dostoevsky gives us a letter which we read as drunken from
its shaky syntax and its inanity and pitiful show of *politesse*,
and its appeal to the following consideration in order to
dismiss the fact that Mr Devushkin's footwear is in tatters:
'The Greek sages used to go about without boots, so why
should people like us pamper ourselves with such unworthy
objects?'[68] Zestfully, Dostoevsky's reader sets about doing
the rest of the work. He conjures a filthy Petersburg drink
shop, and a middle-aged clerk recalling down the years, as
he pens his letter, a dog-eared school Primer with an illus-
tration of Socrates and his disciples disporting themselves
unbooted. And if nineteenth-century Primers lacked illustrations, no matter. The work of imagination still gets done.

And thus the Greek sages are added to the stock of that
mirthful and poignant junk shop which is Mr Devushkin's
mind. And, like the other flotsam there, they advance the
second-hand or copying theme. All this is grist to the mill
of his nobody to be, while its lack of direct bearing upon
Varenka's nowhere to go has already been recognized by
describing *Poor People*'s lacerations as distanced and its love
story as a stylization of the Double Act. If Varenka were a
habit like the tobacco, things would be different; she would
engage directly with the underlying solid self Mr Devushkin
doesn't know he has. But the letter-writing is the habit, the
root habit and craving — not the girl. 'To whom am I going
to write letters?' That is as subtle as the question about real
writers and copiers. It slips through coarse-mesh discussions
of *Poor People* and the tradition of the novel in letters. It
also makes the crucial point about stylization of mode which
naturalistic commentary has been foolish to ignore. Dostoevsky's first novel is not that sort of love story.

---

[67] Ibid., p. 197.   [68] Ibid., p. 214.

Chapter 2:   *The Double*

(i)

In mature Dickens the office messenger tells the office manager of his wife nursing 'as thriving a little girl, sir, as we've ever took the liberty of adding to our family'.[1] Dickens! A giant being very much himself, and also basking in the shared sun of fiction's golden age. The comfort, as reader, of knowing where one is!

In early Dostoevsky the petty clerk meets his boss inopportunely and wonders what to do:

'Return his bow or not? Reply to him or not? Recognize him or not?' thought our hero in indescribable anguish. 'Or pretend that I'm not me but somebody else strikingly like me, and look as though nothing were the matter? Simply not me, not me — and that's all!' said Mr Golyadkin, taking off his hat to Andrey Filippovich and keeping his eyes fixed on him. 'I'm — I'm — it's all right,' he just managed to whisper, 'I — it's quite all right — this isn't me at all, Andrey Filippovich, it's not me at all, not me, and that's that.'[2]

That was Mr Golyadkin, hero of Dostoevsky's second novel, where the young poet asks himself quite calculatedly, apropos the first: will vision and method invert? can doubling be done again yet tighter — more funny, more brilliant, more painful? To which the answer will be a rather complicated yes and no. But certainly there is nothing in *Poor People* as Chaplinesque and as bang on the eardrum of intellect — so visual yet so abstract — as the clerk in *The Double* raising his hat to his boss and saying, Don't worry, it's not me. Not me, but somebody very like me. The thing forebodes the daunting, exhilarating intellectualism of a *coup* in Samuel Beckett. The proleptic twentieth-century smell apparent in *Poor People* has grown stronger.

Dostoevsky's two boasts, that he had not shown his ugly mug nor wasted a word, are more true of this book than its

---

[1] *Dombey and Son*, Ch. XXII.   [2] *The Eternal Husband*, p. 142.

predecessor. Indeed *Poor People*'s relative success — critics loved it, the general public enjoyed it moderately — flowed from readers sensing even if they didn't see their man, and finding extra words to feed on. *The Double*'s discipline was stricter, and it failed; though of course people didn't — and don't — see it like that, they were and are puzzled or bored.

The novel's verbal and formal economy is stated in its first sentence through its hero's name, Mr Golyadkin, Mr Naked (*goli*). But the Russian word also suggests destitution, and since we have here another ill-favoured, middle-aged clerk of the same grade and belonging to the same governmental world as titular councillor Devushkin, Mr Golyadkin has been understood as Mr Poor Man and Dostoevsky's second novel has been duly placed alongside his first in the naturalistic tradition of left-wing protest fiction in the 1840s.

The obvious objection to Poor Man is that Mr Golyadkin is not poor. At the outset he is fondling seven hundred and fifty roubles — ' "a splendid sum! It's an agreeable sum!" ' he whispers to himself 'in a voice trembling and a bit faint with gratification'.[3] This is Dostoevsky money at its most physical and barbaric. Mr Golyadkin strokes it, pinches it, counts it, gloats over it, revels in the different colours of the paper notes. "'I'd like to see the man to whom this would be an insignificant sum'", he concludes ecstatically.

But while the stuff is being flaunted, its sense is being undermined; it is as if some element of an erotic masterpiece — the pubic hair, say, of a Modigliani nude — had obeyed the prompting of a frantically stimulated viewing eye and detached itself from the composition, from all context. Mr Golyadkin's sensual rapture over the notes cuts across their money value. The roll call of colours culminates in the rainbow notes, but these are worth one-fifth of the dull grey ones which come second on the list of 'green, grey, blue, red and rainbow notes' in which colour and worth are jumbled throughout.

And yet what does 'worth' mean to the feasting eye? This question is rephrased when Mr Golyadkin ventures forth with his roubles and drops in at a money-changer's where he pulls

---

[3] Ibid., p. 139.

out his large-denomination notes and exchanges them for smaller ones — 'and though he lost on the deal he nevertheless went through with it, and his wallet became appreciably fatter, which evidently afforded him extreme satisfaction.'[4] The standpoint from which there is now more money in that wallet may not strike the rest of us as rational, but it happens to be Mr Golyadkin's, and *he* is pleased, and presumably *his* money is worth the pleasure it gives *him*. However irrational, his standpoint has its rationale.

Thus only the objective sense of money and money's worth is being undermined; there is some other sense, fanciful, demented, at any rate subjective, being simultaneously affirmed. Slowly, and then only if he is attentive, the reader comes to see how thoroughgoing this dichotomy of senses is. As the book proceeds and Mr Golyadkin begins seeing and hearing and touching things that are unapparent to other people, one recalls the seven hundred and fifty roubles. What was a titular councillor doing with all that money? At the time one assumed the story would reveal in due course where it came from. But the story never does. Dostoevsky is relying on his reader to keep the question alive, and to return to it with the thought that the money may not exist outside Mr Golyadkin's fancy. Only when he does return is the reader likely to notice the completely unstressed scrambling of colour and value, and likewise the single-sentence incident at the money-changer's which must look obvious enough as I have isolated it but is easy to miss on Dostoevsky's cluttered page, particularly since his final version of the novel, in its determination to make a hard text even harder, omits the *Quixote*-style heading to the chapter which directs attention very precisely here: 'Concerning the exact amount for which Mr Golyadkin sold roubles and for which he bought them.'[5]

Dostoevsky's trust in his readers was and remains misplaced. Thus the Soviet editor, the member of the squad assembled in the Dostoevsky Section of the Pushkin House who has been entrusted with Volume I, explains the values of the different colours of tsarist paper money for the benefit of contemporary Russians, and leaves it at that.[6] He has

---

[4] Ibid., p. 154.   [5] *PSS*, Vol. I, p. 344.   [6] Ibid., p. 493.

missed the point. And the initial, more important *aporia* of the money in Mr Golyadkin's hands also proves too difficult. Joseph Frank, for example, in his close and diligent study of the early years, writes that Mr Golyadkin 'has piled up a tidy sum in savings'.[7] Exactly wrong. Nothing could miss the feel of Dostoevsky's hero more completely than the idea of him mindfully *saving* anything.

The Double does not, of course, stand or fall entirely by virtue of Dostoevsky's faith in his reader over this matter of Mr Golyadkin's sourceless roubles. I dwell on it to give a foretaste of the novel's difficulty, and also to explore its hero further. If he really hasn't got any money, Mr Poor Man is surely his right name after all. On the other hand, if he thinks he is rich, who are we to call him poor? And in any case there can be no certainty that the roubles aren't real. (I recall a Charles Addams *New Yorker* cartoon in which two colonial Englishmen are sitting on the verandah of their bungalow, each nursing an enormous drink. Snakes are entwined round the legs of their chairs and one Englishman is saying to the other 'Don't worry, old boy. They bothered me a bit until I discovered they were real.') This is the first of many hesitations — doublings or doublets of a new sort — which generate an overall instability so extreme as to make *Poor People* feel almost rocklike.

But people have odd ways of rationalizing their disquiet. Some of Dostoevsky's early critics stood the truth neatly on its head, complaining that he had carried his adherence to the Natural School too far. K. S. Aksakov noted a rake's progress from being influenced by Gogol to imitating him to direct borrowing from him.[8] A few bright spirits, most notably A. A. Grigorev, were quick onto the Double (*Doppelgänger*) in German Romanticism. Grigorev remarked that if Dostoevsky went on like this much longer he would turn himself into a Russian Hoffmann[9] — which I regard as more insidious than the talk about naturalism, because it offers the handholds which academics find specially comforting: so that the Grigorev approach has flourished with the rise of modern

[7] *Dostoevsky: The Seeds of Revolt: 1821–1849*, p. 300.
[8] *Moscow Literary and Academic Miscellany*, 1847.
[9] *Finnish Herald*, 1846.

literary scholarship and so-called comparative studies. In fact *The Double* and the *Doppelgänger* are analogous to *Poor People* and the novel in letters. Dostoevsky knew and used the tradition, but creative interest lies elsewhere. It rests with *The Double* in itself and in its conscious — hyper-conscious — relationship with *Poor People*; and it belongs to *The Double* in its bearing upon the later novels, especially *Notes from Underground*.

It was not until 1957 that the critic Shklovsky remarked with mild puzzlement that the Double in *The Double* is not after all like the *Doppelgänger* in Kleist and Hoffmann. The German thing is pathological, lurid, buttressed by the pseudo-science of Animal Magnetism, demoniac; while Dostoevsky's Double is *poshli* (trite, commonplace, banal).[10] Although Shkovsky made nothing of his thought, he might have used it to shed light on Mr Golyadkin and his name. For Mr Naked is no less *poshli* than his Double. Indeed one of the pervasive instabilities of the book is the need to distinguish Man and Double in order to interpret and fix what we read, coupled with the impossibility of finding any consistent principle for doing so, except, as we shall see, a formal linguistic principle — Mr Golyadkin's words — which contrive to be lexically consistent and yet humanly unavailing. Mr Golyadkin is Mr *Poshli*, as good a name as metaphorical Mr Naked and much better than literal Mr Poor Man. Mr Golyadkin is *King Lear*'s 'poor, bare, forked animal', no less radical than that, with the featureless heath of the play transposed into the novel's banal urban wasteland of St Petersburg, St Anytown we might call it — yet 'the most abstract city in the world' according to Dostoevsky's Underground Man.[11]

The banal and the abstract, which have no obvious connection in life, were fused at the outset in *Poor People*. Banality — *poshlost* — made and continues to make immediate sense to *Poor People*'s readers. But the banality understood by them as the humdrum existence of an oppressed little clerk, I want to take, and have taken, outside nature into art,

[10] *For and Against* (*Za i protiv*), p. 60. In fact Shklovsky's word is 'paltri-ness' or 'insignificance' (*nichtozhestvo*), but I am sure he would accept my *poshli* and its noun *poshlost*.

[11] *White Nights*, p. 60.

primarily into Mr Devushkin's style sense one and sense two. At the heart of both, that is of the second-hand junk shop and the personal doublet tune, lies that question about real writers and copiers; and the fusion of the banal and the abstract takes place here. I have already stressed the intellectualism of Dostoevsky's early work, but in fact I have under-stressed it because I don't want to try my reader too hard too soon. I have concentrated on those points where the banal and the abstract can be felt to meet in terms of Mr Devushkin's search for identity: the lodging-house pecking order, the graded reprimands at the office, the dream of *Poems by Makar Devushkin* (a real writer!) appearing 'apropos of nothing', the central and recurring thought, rephrased as statement, hope, question, challenge, that to be a copier is to be somebody. The shabby, pitiful banality of these moods and postures is more evident than their intellectualism because they belong plausibly to the very unintellectual Mr Devushkin, though at what I called the level of mere attribution; and so long as he stays in his rat run of lodging-house and office, talk of a search for identity is likely to sound gratuitously cerebral.

But not when Dostoevsky lets him escape. The one moment when the love story itself kicks clear of the Double Act, the selfish selflessness of 'getting to know you, I came first to know myself better and I came to love you', is beyond the copying clerk in its relaxed splendour, not its intellectualism. Contrast, for example, the letter in which Mr Devushkin tells Varenka he has been meditating about Petersburg, wondering 'what goes on in those great black sooty buildings'. As he broods he postulates a shoemaker lying fast asleep and dreaming about some boots he has accidentally spoilt the day before by cutting the leather wrong; 'and in the same house, a floor higher or lower, a very rich man in his gilded halls is perhaps dreaming about those same boots, that is boots in a different way, in a different manner, but nevertheless boots; for in the sense in which I'm meaning it just now, my darling, every one of us is a bit of a shoemaker.'[12] Here is Dostoevsky's schematic, hypothetic, mentally carved-

---

[12] *The Gambler*, pp. 223-4.

up, abstract Petersburg. And here is banality: boots are trash, Mr Devushkin keeps saying, drunk and sober. But the two are not fused. The fumbling tune is unmistakably Mr Devushkin's, but not the thought. We are all sort of shoemakers: this is not his search for identity, it is Dostoevsky's reflection upon identity. Instead of a fusion of abstract and banal we have abstraction from banality, an inference drawn from the *poshlost* of the human condition. We are all sort of shoemakers. This is a free thought. To allow Mr Devushkin to escape is to free his thoughts too, and adroit though Dostoevsky is in manipulating the boot-and-shoe motif (those bootfree Greek sages, for example) as a tethering device, he cannot tie the thought to the man that way. It is not plausibly his.

The source of this free thinking is a young and witty novelist with a strong speculative thrust towards questions of identity. These questions hang over his first two books in a cloud of vaporized comedy. Readers of *Poor People* have scarcely noticed the cloud because there are a lot of things on the ground to look at — unlike *The Double* where it is difficult to speak of the ground at all since the novel's urge is to suck its material upward into total volatility, as with the unaccounted for, dubiously existent money of the opening chapter.

As well as fondling his money, Mr Golyadkin is looking at himself in the mirror — or rather, he is the 'possessor' or 'owner' (*obladatel*) of the 'figure' (*figura*) in the mirror. And thus the Double Theme is launched. Two or one? Or none? Is there *anybody/anything* to possess? Is there anybody/anything to *possess*? The circularity of our thoughts is reflected in Mr Golyadkin's 'round mirror'. Not a word wasted!

Presented like this, the book appears to revolve quasi-literally round an arid little conundrum about a man and his mirror-image. And of all the ways to approach it I think this is the least misleading. *The Double* had and has no significant readership, and the critics get it wrong. It is, as I say, too difficult. It lacks both plot direction and plot substance, privations no less unnerving for being calculated. The outline of its story is that Mr Golyadkin sets off to a dinner party given by his boss whose daughter he is in love with. One's temptation is to say he only imagines he has been invited to dinner because they aren't expecting him there, whereas the daughter and his love for her are real because we aren't tipped off to the contrary by family and friends. And that is how many commentators have proceeded. But, as I suggested with the sourceless roubles, there are ways of unsettling the real/imaginary distinction which undercut attempts to keep it steady by holding 'mad' Mr Golyadkin up against 'sane' other people. And the chief unsettling agent is the Double himself. Mr Golyadkin encounters him on a windy, very abstract Petersburg night; and thereafter chaos reigns. It is no good treating him as the creature of Mr Golyadkin's sick fancy because he goes in and out of focus, now ignored by, now actual and ordinary — indeed *poshli* — for other people. Petrushka, Mr Golyadkin's manservant, pushes the confusion and humour further than anybody else. Sometimes he treats Master and Double as two, sometimes as one. Sometimes he inverts them, dismissing Master impatiently as mere Double. One pleasant incident occurs when Mr Golyadkin sends Petrushka out to discover where the Double lives, and, after pounding the streets, Petrushka returns drunk (for it is cold and wet outside and a man must fortify himself) but securely, complacently possessed of the address — Mr Golyadkin's.[13] 'Why this is hell, nor am I out of it.' The Faustian ordeal of consciousness has been comically reshaped.

And so to the denouement which finds Mr Golyadkin standing in the rain outside the window of the girl he loves, in response to a letter in which she proposes elopement. Or does she? Surely not. The letter is a noveletteish farrago which suggests the escapist reading of half-educated clerks like Mr Golyadkin and Mr Devushkin. But if she did not write it, who did? Dostoevsky's bemused critics behave as if they never read each other's books. Some say Mr Golyadkin has obviously imagined it. Others have no doubt that it is a cruel prank played on him by a fellow clerk.[14]

[13]   *The Eternal Husband*, p. 224.
[14]   Two instances in English are *Doubles in Literature*, p. 105, by Ralph Tymms who takes the first view, and *The Young Dostoevsky*, p. 123, by Victor Terras who takes the second.

I would like to pause over the elopement letter. It constitutes both the climax of *The Double* and our introduction to Dostoevsky's thoughts about this novel spanning more than thirty years. Here it is:

Noble man, sufferer on my behalf, eternally dear to my heart!

I suffer, I perish — save me! That slanderer, that intriguer notorious for his vicious inclinations, has caught me in his toils and I am undone! I am lost! But he is abhorrent to me — while you . . . ! We have been kept apart, my letters to you have been intercepted — and all this has been the work of that vile man who has exploited his one good quality — his likeness to you. A man may always be unhandsome and yet captivate by his intellect, his strong feelings and his prepossessing manners. I am ruined! I am to be married against my will, and in this the chief plotter is my father and benefactor, State Councillor Olsufy Ivanovich, who no doubt wants to secure me a position and connections in high society, but my mind is made up and I protest with all the means bestowed on me by nature. Be waiting for me with a carriage at exactly nine o'clock this evening outside Olsufy Ivanovich's flat. We are having another ball and the handsome young lieutenant will be here. I shall come out and we will elope. Moreover, there are other positions of service where it is possible to be of use to one's country. Remember, in any case, dear one, that innocence is strong in its very innocence. Farewell. Wait with your carriage at the entrance. I shall fling myself into the protection of your arms at precisely two a.m.

Yours until death,

Klara Olsufyevna[15]

First, those thirty years. 'Now I am the true Golyadkin', Dostoevsky told his brother in the late summer of 1845, while work on *The Double* was going swimmingly. And on 16 November: 'it will be my *chef-d'oeuvre*.' And immediately after publication the next January: '*Golyadkin* is ten times greater than *Poor People*.' The ebullience is typical — and not just of Dostoevsky as a young man. So is the volte-face following the book's bad reception. By April he was telling his brother: '*Golyadkin* has become loathsome to me . . . It revolts one's soul, one doesn't want to read it.' Nor does one want to contemplate a writer blown to and fro by outside opinion as Dostoevsky habitually was. But over *The Double* there is a noteworthy saving clause. Long afterwards, when the dust had settled, he wrote in his *Writer's Diary*

[15]   *The Eternal Husband*, pp. 256–7.

(1877): 'This story of mine was assuredly a failure, but the idea itself was rather a splendid one, indeed I have never handled a more serious idea in my career as a writer.' He doesn't go on to say what this idea was. But there is a manuscript notebook of his in the Central State Archive of Literature and Art in Moscow, dating from the early 1870s, which provides the help we need. It calls *The Double* a failure, thus anticipating the published statement in *A Writer's Diary*. But, says Dostoevsky, communing with himself in his notebook, for all its faults *The Double* introduces 'my supreme underground type'.[16] Here, beyond reasonable doubt, is the idea which he never surpassed in seriousness. And so this notebook affords an interesting link between pre- and post-Siberian Dostoevsky, since the underground type does not surface into print until 1864, in *Notes from Underground*.

And next, the separate but convergent path of the elopement letter. There are two versions of the letter. The first is that of the 1846 *Double* published in the magazine *Notes of the Fatherland*. The second, the one I have just given, is that of the 1866 *Double* which appeared in volume form as part of the collected fiction. Between the two we hear of Dostoevsky working on his novel while still in Siberia in the late Fifties, and a couple of very untidy notebooks of the early Sixties witness his return to the charge in Petersburg after the years of prison and exile. Indeed he even contemplated publishing the novel on its own, with a Preface. 'At last people will see what *The Double* means!' he exclaimed to his brother.[17] Nowhere do we find him actually working on the elopement letter. The two versions confront each other across twenty years.

1866 is shorter than 1846, and there is no clue except the totally undependable girl's signature as to who, if anybody, wrote it. So we are back in the *Poor People* groove of no superfluous words and no ugly mug (though Mr Devushkin on living and not living in the kitchen is a reminder that verbal economy has nothing to do with counting words or pursuing ordinary prose sense with ordinary dispatch; and the authorless device did not prevent *Poor People* betraying the man who wrote it).

---

[16]   *PSS*, Vol. I, p. 489.   [17]   Letter of 1 October 1859.

The 1846 version, on the other hand, bears the mark of Mr Golyadkin.[18] I express myself vaguely so the issue shan't be narrowed into his writing or imagining the whole or a part or the gist. The truth is not as neat as that. When Dostoevsky told his brother he was the real Golyadkin he had been busy worming his way inside his hero's skin by means of a peculiarly insinuating mimicry, a sort of inspired ventriloquism. In another of those buoyant 1845 communications he gives his brother Mr Golyadkin, he *is* Mr Golyadkin — that is, 'he goes his own way, he's all right' — that is, 'he's the same as everybody else, he's simply himself, but then just the same as everybody else'.[19] The same but different but the same: this fluttering inanition is Mr Golyadkin's mental and physical voice, which is also the man frantically busy about absolutely nothing, which is also the doubling of image and circularity of thought reflected in the round mirror on the first page of the novel.

The 1846 elopement letter also gives Mr Golyadkin, and the 1866 one takes him away. The one hard fact here is Grishka Otrepev, a sixteenth-century runaway monk who pretended to be the son of Ivan the Terrible. With the Double slipping into his desk at the office and so on and so forth, Mr Golyadkin is naturally preoccupied with ideas of imposture and usurpation, Otrepev has already been mentioned in *The Double*, moreover in a letter of Mr Golyadkin's.[20] The elopement letter of 1846 mentions him twice more, repeating the sentiment that imposture such as Otrepev's is not possible 'nowadays'. The 1866 elopement letter deletes both references.

Another fact, though it hasn't got the almost fingerprint hardness of Otrepev, is the word *povitchik* which is the name for a kind of senior clerk, and therefore, while specialized, likely to be within Mr Golyadkin's ken. *Povitchik* occurs in 1846 and is cut in 1866.

[18] *PSS*, Vol. I, p. 416.
[19] Letter of 8 October 1845.
[20] *The Eternal Husband*, p. 209. By saying that Otrepev has already occurred in one of Mr Golyadkin's letters I mean no more, within this novel of total instability, than that he has just 'plunged his pen into the inkwell and set it racing furiously over the paper'.

Thereafter we are dealing with points of style. The 1866 elopement letter cuts 'my dear sir', a phrase which Mr Golyadkin is fond of and which shuttles to and fro between hectoring and cringing inflections. Also 'for my part', a verbal tic asserting, or at least suggesting, separateness from others ('he goes his own way').

That only leaves the word *deskat*, if not the hardest then by far the richest fact of all. *Deskat* occurs three times in 1846 and never in 1866. Throughout *The Double* this word acts as a bonding agent, encompassing Mr Golyadkin and his world, holding the novel together. It is the very articulation of unsettlement, a verbal *perpetuum mobile* of indeterminacy, because while *deskat* means 'say', the 'saying' — the Russian usage exploited by Dostoevsky — stands in no stable relationship to time or place or person or performance or any other feature of the actual. It shifts in a stirring motion which we are aware of but cannot be sure how to track, between saying out loud and word-framings in the head, between hope and future fact (intend to say, will certainly say), forms of conditional saying (would say, might say), admonition, exhortation, command (ought to say, must say), self-address ('You Golyadkin, you! You'll say'), between saying to somebody, including oneself, and nobody in particular: sometimes *deskat* floats away into a whimsical, drifting, half-questioning, vaguely speculative, hypothetical 'a man might say' where, within *The Double*, banal and abstract meet. That 'man' not only addresses nobody in particular, he is nobody in particular. *Deskat* does not point unequivocally at Mr Golyadkin. At one point, to take a simple example, Constance Garnett and the Penguin translator divide; one has Mr Golyadkin instructing a servant what he must say, the other has him telling the servant what he is going to say himself — and neither is wrong.[21] But however completely *deskat* may fail to point *at* 'our hero', as he is often called, it never ceases to enfold and thus give shape to him. An advancing and retreating coastline, silting up and crumbling away, *deskat* determines the indeterminate Mr Golyadkin. Recall

[21]   *The Eternal Husband*, p. 266; *Notes from Underground* and *The Double* (trs. Jessie Coulson), p. 267.

that Dostoevsky spoke of his novel as *Golyadkin* in the early days. His words are all that we can be certain Mr Golyadkin has and is. We cannot be sure that he is or possesses the figure in the mirror. But we know, for what it's worth (lexically consistent, I said, but humanly unavailing) about his words, and his word of words is *deskat*.

The 1866 elopement letter removes *deskat*, all three occurrences, together with those secondary determinations of the indeterminate Mr Golyadkin. It and he, word and man, are lost to the elopement letter, only (as we shall see) to be restored by a subtle filtering process in the final pages of the novel. I believe this was conceived as a decisive stroke. 'At last people will see what *The Double* means!' In fact they never have. But Dostoevsky's attempt to redeem his 1846 failure is itself a misadventure of genius which makes success, for the moment, rather uninteresting.

We should think of these changes as a ruthless stripping or descaffolding of what was already very bare indeed. The 1846 *Double* presented a Mr Golyadkin who was not developed — whom it is almost profitless to contemplate — as poor or mad or qualitied in any way beyond his words. Mr Naked, Mr Stripped, was already a linguistic ectoplasm distinguished thus, and only thus, from the identical figure in the mirror and all other doubling manifestations: this, indeed, is the form of the novel. And this is the nub of the hyperconscious relationship between *The Double* and *Poor People* which was written a few months and published a mere seventeen days earlier. The love story of the seamstress and the clerk was itself a very linguistic affair, bodied forth as the epistolary Double Act of Varenka's nowhere to go and Mr Devushkin's nobody to be. But bold as Dostoevsky's takeover of the novel in letters was, one cannot say that his lovers only have and are their words. A moment's thought to the inset story of the Gorshkov family, or details like knowing perfectly well this is the right house but still asking a policeman, or being able to afford neither to drink nor not to drink tea, or making a man pay for charity money in humiliation money, or 'our air' where songbirds die, will make clear what I mean. And as for the two principals, Varenka's tetchy smouldering sexuality, though it fails to engage with the love story, swings between 'irritable' and 'bored' — the first of a long line that ends with Dmitry Karamazov's Grushenka (Little Pear: the taste, the texture, those hips); while Mr Devushkin swings, but literally, between his 'corner' and the public places where he meets Varenka,[22] as Raskolnikov will swing between his bedroom and the Petersburg Haymarket.

In contrast with these premonitions, the links between *The Double* and the post-Siberian fiction are underground in that special sense of underground which Dostoevsky will cultivate. There is, though, one exception, one *surface* exception, and it relates to the crucial elopement letter. It is as if — which may be the case — he was staking everything on a juxtaposition of surreal letter and absolute light-of-day credibility of time and place. In the 1846 *Double* Mr Golyadkin goes home, home which is no home, and finds the dubiously existent letter lying on his dubiously existent table; whereas in 1866 he is out in the street and comes on it in his pocket while he is feeling for something else, and goes into an eating-house to read it.[23] Nothing dubious here. This is the first of those cheap food-and-drink shops in Dostoevsky, scenes of shame and violence and destitution tinged with music-hall values ('The waiter shouted down the hall: "You get no bread with one fish ball" '), and enclosing the special sadness of eating alone in public where things are most obviously nothing if not shared. Here is the grinning waiter, the all against one of the other patrons' laughter — faceless, nameless herd-laughter — while 'all at once a retired military man in a red collar asked loudly for the *Police News*'. We have run into something solid. This is not the novel the young poet has been giving us. We might be inside *Crime and Punishment*. Then there is the detail of 'an old man of very respectable appearance who, having dined and said grace before the icon, sat down again and for the life of him couldn't take his eyes off Mr Golyadkin'. Never again, as it happens, do we get anywhere in Dostoevsky an eating-house glimpse of somebody thanking God for a meal he has paid for

[22]   And where, she recalls, he shows her the beauties of Petersburg with pride, 'as though you were showing me your own possessions' (*The Gambler*, p. 172). The riches of the poor!

[23]   *PSS*, Vol. I. p. 416; *The Eternal Husband*, pp. 256-7.

and perhaps can ill afford and which may be poor value anyhow. But I cannot think of a better introduction to religion in his work, or a profounder surface link (so to speak) with Raskolnikov's probing, not quite taunting question to Sonya Marmeladov, and her reply. He asks the girl with the ruined home and prostituted body and wonderful blue eyes,

'And what does God do for you?'
'He does everything.' [24]

Of course there is a spiritual hurricane blowing through those pages of *Crime and Punishment*, whereas the little eating-house scene in *The Double* has to generate what energy it can from the friction of elopement letter and mundane venue. And, one might add, of respectable old man and Mr Golyadkin; for the old man, feet firmly on the ground, thanks God for the meal he *has* eaten, while Mr Golyadkin, distraught at the contents of the letter and glancing down and seeing somebody's dirty plate and assuming he must have had his own dinner without knowing it, tries to pay the waiter for the meal he has not eaten.

' "How much do I owe you, my boy?" inquired our hero in a shaking voice.' The elopement letter has thrown him completely. In the 1846 *Double* we can look over his shoulder and note *deskat* and the secondary signs of Mr Golyadkin's presence in the letter, and tell him to forget about it, it is just his fantasy. 'They'll say such and such' (or 'Let them say' or 'If they say' or 'They may say such and such'), and 'I'll say' or 'What I say is such and such' — that's the 'saying' tune all right. But in the final 1866 *Double* it has been wiped out, and all we can conclude is that the elopement letter is some kind of fantasy. Not Golyadkin's, but some kind of fantasy.

The difference won't seem immediately important because the stuff about Mr Golyadkin being a noble sufferer on the girl's behalf and waiting in a carriage at her door so she can fly into the protection of his arms and so forth, is still obviously his kind of fantasy reflecting his kind of pulp-literature reading.

[24]   *Crime and Punishment*, p. 287.

Everything turns on the force of 'kind of'. The fantasy and the reading are the kind of thing, not the thing itself. Unlike Mr Devushkin's samples from tales of love and lust among the Siberian Cossacks, the elopement letter cannot be pinned to the hero of the novel. And this inability is, on reflection, by no means trivial since Mr Golyadkin (again unlike Mr Devushkin) only is and has his words. The 1866 elopement letter rests, therefore, in a limbo of Dostoevsky's making. This creature of his second thoughts is kind of Mr Golyadkin's. It is also kind of the author's. Instead of the authorless device of *Poor People* we have in *The Double* an unashamed authorial directness, an old-fashioned adventure-story narrative of the doings of 'our hero'; this is one aspect of the question which Dostoevsky is putting to himself in his second novel apropos his first — Will technique and vision invert? And not only is *The Double*'s bluff authorial presence a device, a pseudo-presence, a way of keeping the ultimate ugly mug hidden, it is more guileful than the ploy of authorlessness in *Poor People*.

In terms of content (oh, so that's the kind of junk Mr Golyadkin reads and dreams about!), the elopement letter's interest is secondary, like the fact that Mr Golyadkin is kind of poor and kind of mad. These facts, this secondary interest, attracts a lot of comment because it gives a lot to get hold of. One can talk social and economic (and literary) history indefinitely in relation to Gogol, Dostoevsky, and the spate of poor-clerk stories in the 1840s. The grotesque will yield as many categories as one wants to find, beginning with the following dual parallel: as *The Overcoat* to *Poor People*, so *The Diary of a Madman* and *The Nose* to *The Double*. There is scarcely an end to the potentialities of the *Doppelgänger* and abnormal psychology: we know that Dostoevsky talked to doctors and read the scientific literature as well as admiring Hoffmann's stories, and that he became an epileptic and epileptics sometimes have hallucinations of physical duality. All more or less interesting, but secondary. Whereas the fact that the elopement letter, irrespective of content, is kind of Mr Golyadkin's plays a vital part in the formal economy of the novel.

So does the fact that the letter is kind of authorial. I am

saying both that Dostoevsky wrote it, and that once again everything depends on the force of 'kind of'. Here the *fausse naive* authorial presence which dominates the novel needs elucidating, because the elopement letter suggests in itself the opposite of that feigned directness. It is an oblique, indeed authorless take-off of mannered cheap fiction, done with Joycean relish. And thus it feeds the predispositions of formalist critics between the wars and since, with their heavy stress on parody in Dostoevsky: creative parody, inner parody, *parodie sérieuse*, anti-parody, travesty. Furthermore, it could be argued that the obliteration of *deskat* and other specific (as opposed to 'kind of') signs of Mr Golyadkin fits this pattern too, reinforcing the parody, making it purer.

And no sane man will deny that the letter is parodic, just as the samples of Mr Devushkin's reading in *Poor People* were parodic, and as the discourse of lawyers, monks, seminarists, literary men, Jews, Poles, Germans, revolutionaries, social theorists and gutter politicians in *The Possessed* and *Kara-mazov* will sometimes be parodic. From first to last the question is the function of parody. In *Poor People* I subsumed Mr Devushkin's reading and the rest of his mental junk shop under a meditation about identity. He wonders whether to be a copier is to be somebody. That thought has nothing to do with parody, but it is meat and drink to the parodic talent. Which is not to say it is a mere peg on which to hang the parodic talent. On the contrary, the preoccupation with identity grows and opens out into the book's thematic flower. That is why the spin-off *cri de coeur* 'Who'd do the copying if we were all real writers?' (which also has nothing to do with parody) is so piercing and resonant. So human.

And it is why, outside his job as copying clerk, and in ways which sometimes are but often are not parodic, Mr Devushkin is a timid Second surrounded by Firsts, by the big chaps of the world who certainly are somebodies. And finally it is why our sense of Dostoevsky — his youth, his intellectualism — tends to be strongest when the point at issue can similarly be deployed into First and Seconds. All men are sort of shoe-makers; there are the actual makers of shoes, the Firsts, and then there are the rest, the mere dreamers about shoes, the Seconds.[25] The inset story of the Gorshkovs, which affords the longest and clearest impression of the young poet's own face, contains a death other than the one I mentioned. Mr Devushkin tells Varenka that the beleaguered parents have lost their little boy: 'There's a coffin in their room already — a simple little coffin but rather pretty; they bought it ready-made, the boy was nine.'[26] Of course the point is poverty, but note the carefully careless light punctuation at 'ready-made', encouraging a swift juxtaposition of corpse and coffin. If you are really destitute your child's body must be made to follow and fit; it has got to play Second to its cut-price, reach-me-down First.

The Double proposes Mr Golyadkin as Second to his own First, and First to his own Second, with all the ambiguity injected by Dostoevsky into the German literary mode of the *Doppelgänger*. The result is a sort of drunken dance in which the Double Act of Mr Devushkin's nobody to be and Varenka's nowhere to go gets transposed into a new lyric form. This is the young poet's second venture, and now Belinsky's phrase gains sudden literal force with the alteration of *The Double*'s subtitle, 'The Adventures of Mr Golyadkin' in 1846, to 'A Petersburg Poem' in 1866. And so Mr Golyadkin disappears from the subtitle as he does from the elopement letter.

Getting rid of Mr Golyadkin, except at the 'kind of' level, is the key factor in the evolution of Adventures into Poem. This is an intensifying process, not a change of direction, since the 1846 Adventures were themselves poetic in the astringent fashion of Dostoevsky's first two novels. The altered subtitle neatly makes the point that the 1866 Poem is even more so. The reshaping of the elopement letter demonstrates how it is more so.

Eased of Mr Golyadkin's immediate presence the letter becomes a collective daydream which he vaguely ('kind of') shares. Removed from Dostoevsky — plucked, that is, out of the flow of *fausse naive* adventure story narrative — for the 1866 Poem retains, of course, the mock-robust address of the 1846 Adventures — this same letter resolves authorial stance

[25] p. 52, above.   [26] *The Gambler*, p. 177.

into parodic specimen. Both shifts, both displacements, serve a single and central poetic purpose; hence my concern to show that the formalist stress on parody can be misleading. In which connection it is noteworthy that some of the most deliciously parodic elopement details are not in the elopement letter at all — not in either version. In response to the letter, on his way to the girl's house and standing outside it, Mr Golyadkin thinks about singing her a Spanish serenade, then about a pink ribbon fluttering as a signal and a silk ladder hanging from her window.[27] He thinks about these things as if they were prearranged. Yet none of them appear in the elopement letter — which encourages some people to think Mr Golyadkin has dreamed the whole thing up. And so he 'kind of' has, for the letter is a collective dream. He is not 'our hero' for nothing.

One such detail catches the eye because it is contained in the 1846 letter only to disappear in 1866. Having successfully eloped, according to 1846, 'we will live in a hut on the shore of the Khvalinsky Sea'.[28] This is obviously parodic in some broad romantic sense, and it almost certainly has a specific target, namely the sentiment expressed in a Schiller lyric, that the most miserable poky hut will suffice to make true lovers happy.[29] Its removal in 1866 is an example of the progressive stripping or descaffolding of 1846, and equally of its poetic intensification. These are two ways of talking about the same thing.

Having been removed from the letter, the lovers' Schillerian life of bliss joins the pink ribbon and the other scraps that float through Mr Golyadkin's mind afterwards as he stands beneath the girl's window longing for 'precisely two a.m.' (much pleasure comes from small touches like that adverb). With a further alteration, however. The hut on the shore stays, but the Khvalinsky Sea is cut.[30] Khvalinsky is Old

---

[27] *The Eternal Husband*, pp. 263, 271.
[28] *PSS*, Vol. I, p. 416.
[29] *Raum ist in der kleinsten Hütte*
Für ein glücklich liebend Paar

(from Act iv, scene 4 of *Der Parasit*, performed Weimar 12 October 1803, published 1806).
[30] *The Eternal Husband*, p. 273.

Russian for Caspian, a nice nostalgic–parodic stroke. Its removal is bound to seem odd so long as parody remains the centre of attention rather than the purpose which parody is there to serve.

I have called that purpose the poem, the new lyric form, the drunken dance. In this dance Mr Golyadkin's nowhere to go partners his nobody to be. His nobody has fast been taking shape, and in approaching his nowhere let us compare the parodic collective dream of his hut on the shore with the steppe 'bare as the palm of my hand' which was Varenka's actual destination at the end of *Poor People*. She literally had nowhere to go. Her bare steppe foreshadows the unparticularized but all too actual Americas and Switzerlands which constitute the nowheres of the later novels. That same bare steppe stands in a slightly different relationship to the goalless goal of 'Stepan Verkhovensky's Last Journeying' at the end of *The Possessed*. It corresponds to one half of Verkhovensky's nowhere which is actual, like hers — 'He looked about him sorrowfully; the village's appearance struck him as weird and somehow terribly alien' — but not to the other half of his nowhere, the bodiless half, the feverish dream of his final illness into which the novel draws us all.[31]

Mr Golyadkin's nowhere corresponds to the second, the dream half. Verkhovensky's village is perched on the shore. So is Mr Golyadkin's hut. Verkhovensky is waiting for a real wood-and-metal boat to take him away, as well as forming wishful shapes as death approaches. But Mr Golyadkin's hut stands on the shore of Romance. And Romance is Romance. To localize the dream is to denature it, and the Khvalinsky Sea does precisely that. However agreeable to the parodist-poet of 1846, the Old Russian Caspian has to go.[32] First lift the crucial nowhere of the lovers' hut out of the 1846 elopement letter, then let it filter through Mr Golyadkin's mind but (in 1866) with the Khvalinsky Sea removed: an

---

[31] *The Possessed*, pp. 573–605.

[32] *PSS*, Vol. I, p. 426, pinpoints the Khvalinsky Sea in the 1846 text. In the unlocalized world of Romance, compare Keats's removal of 'the Dartmoor black' from his *Eve of St Agnes*, and substitution of 'the southern moors' (stanza XXXIX).

example of the detail and discipline, above all the direction of Dostovesky's rethinking and rewriting.

(ii)

The elopement letter is as much a trying-on of a chivalric role that doesn't fit as it is an evocation of a happy-ever-after which never will be. This, indeed, makes it *The Double*'s central inspiration. Mr Golyadkin's nobody to be and nowhere to go meet so naturally and easily here, and having met they execute an artful *pas de deux*. Sir Golyadkin to the rescue! Into that carriage and away! Tawdry, prolix fantasy. Yet extreme thematic rigour. A single realization of the nobody and nowhere themes, and equally of the novel's banal and abstract aspirations.

The Double is an uncomfortable book because these two aspirations embarrass each other continually, outside the elopement letter. We are always waiting for Mr Golyadkin's assumption and abandonment of roles to blossom into sustained situational comedy. He sets out for a party, dressed to kill, but loses his nerve on meeting his boss and assures him with a flourish of his hat, 'Don't worry, it's not me!' For sure this is a stroke beyond cleverness, as if the world were about to be blessed with an immortal petit-bourgeois clown. But nothing doing. The narrative tightens its fist into a hard, brilliantly impersonal joke about identity. The abstract Poem (which the joke enhances) doesn't forward the banal Adventures in any way. Nor, of course, will changing the novel's subtitle make it do so. And placing the elopement letter within the first shabby eating-house in all Dostoevsky heightens rather than assuages embarrassment. Nothing, one might suppose, would marry banal and abstract more happily than to position Mr Golyadkin among the familiar clatter and smells of St Anytown, letter in hand, staring down at a dirty plate and wondering if it is his. And yet, though Dostoevsky is a novelist — *the* novelist — of dirty plates, as he is of tousled beds and slop-pails and puddles and candle-ends, the effect is not novelistic at all but as of a film clip or even a still. The narrative freezes. Yet another identity joke is clinched. Mr Golyadkin cannot find himself in the man who ate nor yet the man who did not eat that meal. The thought stands as caption to the picture of the little clerk with his dolorous downward gaze. We acknowledge the picture of the clerk but we don't believe for a moment that the thought is his. He is altogether capable of puzzling over the dirty plate, but miles from conceiving the identity joke. What makes 'Don't worry, it's not me' so magical is that it is a rare, perhaps unique example of Mr Golyadkin blurting out the kind of thing his kind of man might say and leaving us connoisseurs of identity humour to savour its aftertaste. Notice 'kind of'. I made a great fuss about 'kind of' in the elopement letter because it is there, in the *approximate* Janus figure of collective daydream and parodic specimen, that the disjunction of picture and caption is formally healed.

Outside the letter and other less important parodic episodes (notably the girl's birthday party: 'All hearts went out to the fascinating charmer'[33]) Dostoevsky's bluff authorial pseudo-presence roams abroad. He, the pseudo-self, is not capable of these identity jokes either. Nor of observing the other features of Mr Golyadkin's private world in their utter instability, their spareness, and intellectualism. They are as hidden from him as they are from 'our hero', the novel's public protagonist. In that same eating-house scene he won't notice — any more than 'our hero' notices — Mr Golyadkin trying to pay for a meal he hasn't eaten. The reader, however, if he is sufficiently limbered up, does notice this because he is in conspiracy with the young poet behind the backs of 'our hero' and the authorial pseudo-self. This makes for a strenuous partnership, as we have already seen with the scrambling of money value and money colour, and the incident at the money-changer's which left Mr Golyadkin with reduced purchasing power but a fatter wallet. Once alerted, the reader recalls that the money itself came from nowhere, that when he gets outside the girl's house Mr Golyadkin hires a cabby to do nothing — 'If we stand still it's all the same, that's for me to decide'[34] —, that he has the idea of scaring off the Double by requiring him to contribute

---

[33] *The Eternal Husband*, p. 171. You see why I keep thinking of *Ulysses*.
[34] Ibid., p. 273.

half the rent, that he plies a fellow clerk with tips to coax from him information he hasn't got.[35] Different giddy games revolving round money, power, and emptiness. Money is just stuff, you can't even eat it nor, as Brecht's peasant remarks, can you shit it. And money is terribly potent. There was a lot of new yet filthy money flooding through nineteenth-century Petersburg, as there was through Elizabethan London: so another young poet, less precocious in some ways than Dostoevsky, startles us by having his Romeo tell the apothecary 'I sell thee poison: thou hast sold me none' as he pays cash for his death drug in a play which has nothing whatever to do with money.

Dostoevsky, though, does treat purposefully of money, and as with the formalists and parody, so with those whose *Double* is a proto-marxist tract, the question bites back: what is money doing here? At the outset it is more obviously done to than doing: counted, smoothed, fondled, its bulk altered, and value and colour scrambled. And this could well be a prefatory gesture in a sermon on the vanity of Capitalism. But *The Double*'s money also has an active part to play. While Mr Golyadkin looked at the roll of notes in the deepest pocket of his shabby green wallet, the roll of notes 'probably also looked with extreme friendliness and approval at Mr Golyadkin'. We recall the figure returning his gaze in the mirror. Then we notice that the walls and furniture of his room and the clothes on the sofa 'looked at him familiarly' — all in the first paragraph of the novel (a pity that these big paragraphs get chopped up in translation). And in the next we encounter his samovar, or rather it encounters him, threatening to boil over behind the partition where his manservant ought to be but isn't, 'hissing and gabbling, very likely saying' — the first *deskat* in the novel — ' "Take me, good people, I'm completely ready and waiting" '.

So money at the beginning of *The Double*, as well as coming from nowhere, belongs to a world in which mirror-image, walls, furniture, clothes, all look back at Mr Golyadkin, and samovar chatters at, not to, him. Money is both dubiously existent and enmeshed in a complex of totally unstable reciprocities wherein the doubling theme is mooted and matured. The book's *Doppelgänger* motif is thus astir with 'our hero's' waking thoughts. So on the one hand, when Mr Golyadkin eventually meets his Double at midnight out in the Petersburg streets under a wild November sky, 'the stranger' stops him dead in his tracks not just with horror but with absolute, undreamed-of novelty. And yet, Mr Golyadkin 'knew this man through and through'.[36] The flat contradiction is sustained throughout; the stranger is the familiar, the enemy is the friend — indeed the 'oldest friend'.

The burden of this is obvious. *The Double* is a study in selfhood. The affair of Golyadkin Senior and Junior, as they come to be called, can be transposed into the language of self-identity and self-alienation. My preference for nobody to be and nowhere to go (and their opposites) does not deny this, but I think it brings us closer to Dostoevsky — to *Poor People* which precedes *The Double* and to the books which come after *The Double* — closer to Mr Golyadkin himself in his gallant non-role bound for his perfect non-lovenest near the end of the novel, and to Mr Golyadkin looked and chattered at by inanimate objects as he gets ready for a party where they aren't expecting him at the beginning.

If Mr Golyadkin were somebody — an opening gambit cast in the hypothetical form much favoured by Mr Devushkin — inanimate objects would not treat him like that. In fact, throughout the entire novel, Mr Golyadkin only once doubts that he is somebody, and that is when he first meets his Double.[37] He called down this comic doom on his head by telling the boss not to worry, it wasn't him, a single exception proving the rule and throwing light on the way *The Double* inverts the procedures of *Poor People*; because Mr Devushkin fears, and fears obsessively, he isn't somebody but very much is — as becomes *bien entendu* between reader and young poet when Mr Devushkin is glimpsed puffing his pipe, saying his prayers, polishing his prose, clutching his teapot — whereas Mr Golyadkin assumes he is somebody but isn't. It does not occur to Mr Golyadkin to doubt, and his way of not doubting was foreshadowed by Dostoevsky in the ventriloquist letter

---

[36]   Ibid., p. 177.   [37]   Ibid., p. 183.

where he gave his brother the nub of his creation, the veritable Golyadkin: 'he goes his own way', but then 'he's just the same as everybody else'. Quite separate, and one of the crowd. But not nobody. Mr Devushkin's self-annihilating 'I simply don't exist', afloat on the ocean of his unconscious, complacent self-husbanding, is not in Mr Golyadkin to say. The logical contradiction of different and the same is no doubt the human truth, just as (returning to Golyadkin and Double) we are our own worst enemies and oldest friends, bottomlessly mysterious to ourselves and known from the start, before consciousness. Not that their human truth makes these contradictions easy, or in the case of Mr Golyadkin possible, to live with.

He clings to his contradiction about being different and the same. It is a refrain that rattles on and on through the book; and when Dostoevsky found himself moving towards it in that letter to his brother, he pounced. Either way, at the level of the refrain, Mr Golyadkin is somebody — which must be obvious with the assertion of difference, of going his own way, of keeping himself to himself, of being his own man (always *sam po sebe* in Russian). But over sameness it needs to be stressed that to be one of the crowd is not, for Mr Golyadkin, to be lost in the crowd; it is to 'stand on his rights' as a human being, to be 'within his rights', to demand, implore, wheedle — the inflections are endless — just the same treatment and consideration as 'everybody else'; it is Dostoevsky's reworking of Mr Devushkin's declaration, 'I am after all a man, in heart and mind a man'. We are moved by Mr Devushkin because we sense an embattled human condition under the words. But Mr Golyadkin's refrain is mere flat chatter, like his samovar's. Hence the importance of grasping that he only has and is his words. We cannot even speak of a disembodied mind beneath his words because he hasn't the rational coherence *vis-à-vis* present actualities, nor the power of anticipation, nor the memory, to justify that. As to memory and anticipation, the main objection against those who tell us Mr Golyadkin has saved up his roubles is not that they have missed the sourcelessness of the money but that they misconceive the whole book which, like its hero, has no past or future. The midnight when Mr Golyadkin first met his Double was not an hour chimed by clocks; it was the philosopher's midnight in which all cows are black; and *first met*, like all temporal assertions in this novel, must be understood to fall inside invisible inverted commas, the warning sign of the book's ironic intellectualism. One cannot exclude time, of course. What one can, and what Dostoevsky does do, is release the craziness locked up in things we all say about the future, like 'If only tomorrow would hurry up and come'; and he makes time past drift across the narrative sky in broken wisps of warmly tinted luminous absurdity, as when a fellow clerk, no doubt suspecting a tie of blood between Golyadkin and Double, asks our hero 'Where, may I make so bold to enquire, did your mother live for the most part?'[38]

And so we find ourselves getting thrust deeper into the Twentieth Century. After Prufrock and Brecht and Pirandello ('Conscience is nothing but other people inside you') — after these, Franz Kafka. Commentators have judged *The Double* even more Gogolian than *Poor People*, and that is because of the superficial resemblance between Gogol's ghostly Petersburg and the abstract city of Dostoevsky's second novel.[39] The much more suggestive link is with Kafka's Prague, just as Dostoevsky's nobody and nowhere bear more closely upon the Kafkaesque mouse caught between the trap of self and the cat of other people, institutions, the open world.

Then, deeper still, the French. When Mr Golyadkin pays his cabby to do nothing, *The Double* leaps into focus as an absurd fable contemporary in spirit with Camus, and a metaphysical one even more akin to Sartre. 'If we stand still it's all the same, that's for me to decide.' Mr Golyadkin inhabits an existential nightmare in which everything is indeed for him to decide. All I am, said Sartre, is my endlessly renewed choices of what I am to be. But if there isn't even a disembodied mind beneath the words, what does a Golyadkin choice amount to? The essence of this story of a man busy about nothing, this story and this man with no future and no

---

[38] Ibid., p. 185.
[39] I am not denying borrowings from Gogol, among which the manservant's distinctive body-smell is perhaps the most interesting, though this comes from *Dead Souls* and not one of the Petersburg stories.

past, is contextless choice facing not mind but naked (*goli*) will. Contextless choice floods outward, being unframed, into choice without limit, and will stripped of memory, anticipation, rational association, becomes a compass needle which has lost its North. The wild swinging of the needle figures both *The Double*'s directionless plot, the inherent boredom of which defeated Dostoevsky, and also Mr Golyadkin's oddly theoretical agony as he perches on a sharp, forward-tilting personal and cosmic Present. His statement to the cabby falls into two parts, of which 'if we stand still' is as loaded as 'that's for me to decide'. There is no standing still. No repose. Except perhaps in death. (Or in Christ — the one point of substance on which Golyadkin and Double agree is that 'one must put all one's trust in God', Double adding 'there is of course nobody like God'.) Otherwise certainly no repose. Even in his sleep, Mr Golyadkin blushes.[40]

What *moves* him to blush? We don't know. Perhaps we all blush in our sleep; *The Double* has an aura of tentative universality which encourages such thoughts. The proleptic French Existentialism of the novel is incidental to this universality, as is its proto-marxism and all the Freud in it. Likewise, in the empirical shrewdness with which they are observed, its demented aspects. Mr Golyadkin's paranoiac and manic symptoms are all ours, or potentially ours. He reads the ordinary dull routine of the office as a plot against him; so he responds by deciding 'to abstain from the usual interchange of civilities with his colleagues, inquiries after health, and so forth'.[41] If people are nice to him they are feigning, if they are nasty then they are nasty. He buys and eats food he doesn't want in order (one might say) to push the clock forward.[42] He imagines sweeping his girl to safety from beneath that lethal chandelier with a 'Don't be alarmed, madam, it's of no consequence'.[43] He pays a man, as we have seen, to tell him comforting nullities, until the man runs out of ideas and is reduced to waggling his eyebrows to 'earn' more money in a wonderful uprush of aborted cinematic farce.[44] He falls into bed exhausted, and when he wakes up

[40] Ibid., pp. 197, 230.   [41] Ibid., p. 181.   [42] Ibid., p. 155.
[43] Ibid., p. 169.   [44] Ibid., pp. 236-7.

he concludes not that he has overslept but that the sun is in the wrong place.[45] We all perceive our Double in these mirrors, though we change the words a bit; our 'sane' version of pushing the clock forward is killing time. And so on. And with much of Mr Golyadkin's behaviour we don't even change the words. His way of tapping himself on the forehead in fierce anger and calling himself a fool, of communing with himself as 'you and I', and admonishing himself affectionately as 'my young friend', will do for the rest of us just as it stands. It is a non-temporal *long time* since Humanity *first met* its Double.

(iii)

Mr Golyadkin's nobody to be and nowhere to go will transpose into the plight of modern urban man, as they will into the language of self-identity and self-alienation. To do this at all fruitfully we have to move one side or the other of the city in the high Nineteenth Century: either back to the early throes of the Industrial Revolution, to Blake and 'each chartered street' and to Wordsworth brooding from a great height on this false new coming-together where 'neighbourhood serves rather to divide'; or on to *The Wasteland*, Akhmatova's *Poem Without a Hero*, the Kafka novels. Prospect and retrospect, Blake's London before and Eliot's after, share if nothing else an apocalyptic starkness, a bare figuring of the end of the ages, which is missing in the international classics of the City in the Nineteenth Century, and which we still do not find (though we find many other things) if we move sideways out of prose fiction into Baudelaire's verse.

We have to pick our modern examples carefully, of course; there is nothing magical about the year 1900. Thus *Dubliners* looks old-fashioned beside *The Double*, and Saul Bellow's New York and Chicago even more so. But *The Double*, unlike *Dubliners*, is a failure. And here *Mrs Dalloway* affords an interesting comparison while allowing us to stay with Joyce for a moment. I find Virginia Woolf's London half-absent in a way which lies close to — and can be mistaken

---

[45] Ibid., p. 233.

for — her own allusive gift, but which in fact stems from her city's silent colloquy with Joyce's Dublin, this time the Dublin of *Ulysses*. The reader of *Mrs Dalloway* who has finished the book with a sense of something missing, something withheld, and has then recalled *Ulysses* and seen everything fall suddenly into place, will know what I mean. Recalling *Ulysses* doesn't turn London's half-absence in *Mrs Dalloway* into a virtue, but it does shed light on it: this city needs the other one.

The Double's Petersburg needs *Poor People*'s Petersburg. On its own the abstract city of the second novel is impossibly tacit, more than half-absent. Instead of publishing the two books seventeen days apart, Dostoevsky should have produced them together as complementary and contrasting *études*. And even then he should have warned his readers that he was asking a great deal of them.

In separation, *The Double* suffers more than *Poor People* — which is primarily due to what I have called its mode of inversion. Stoves and samovars to the fore! That samovar chattering at Mr Golyadkin in the opening chapter of *The Double* will pass — has often passed — for Gogolian whimsy. The 'huge iron stove' which he darts behind in the entrance to his office building looks, and at one level is, a convenient place to hide.[46] These are the second samovar and the second stove in Dostoevsky. The first are the samovar before which Mr Devushkin lines up teapot in hand with his fellow lodgers, and the stove which sends forth its smells from the kitchen to permeate walls, furniture, clothes. Mr Golyadkin's samovar and stove seem nothing much; whereas Mr Devushkin's, for anybody with eyes to see, are shaping a vision of boarding-house life with economy and assurance. In 'our air' where songbirds die the lightness of phrasing doesn't disguise the new voice. Given time, it will find a lot to say. Dostoevsky did not have to go to prison to imagine *The House of the Dead*, though he needed to have been there to write it.

Solitude and society. *The Double* inverts Mr Devushkin's world of lodging-house and office. For just as we want to

[46] Ibid., pp. 235, 239. 'No, my friend, I — you mustn't imagine — I'm not here to avoid being seen, you know,' explains poor Mr Golyadkin afterwards (p. 240).

speak of aggregation in *Poor People* rather than what we understand by human society, so we hesitate to say Mr Golyadkin is alone as he confronts the samovar and hides behind the stove. 'Alone' does not fit the chatter of the one or the ambiguous flitting to and fro of the Double on the far side of the other. Instead of human solitude corresponding to human society, we have Mr Naked — there seems to be no abstract noun — corresponding to the mere aggregate of *Poor People*.

This may look suspiciously neat. But then I am pressing my view of *The Double* as hyperconsciously related to *Poor People*. Furthermore, while saying that stove and samovar in the first novel are scrupulously inverted in the second, from false or ambiguous society to false or ambiguous solitude, I am also maintaining that in both novels these pre-eminently Russian objects conform to an overall pattern of comfortlessness — there are no 'happy' stoves or samovars in Dostoevsky — which cannot have been premeditated: he was not on his guard against good cheer. And this paradox is a familiar one since calculation and instinct are entangled in all art. Apropos his first two novels, I would call the inversion of stove and samovar deliberate; but their shared creative thrust, the way they press upon, knead, define a tragi-comically beset humanity, must surely run deeper than anything willed by the novelist. The fact that they exert their pressure in opposite directions in *Poor People* and *The Double* is relatively unimportant. Pressure itself and the embattled state are what matter, and while there is no harm in talking about this state as the condition of modern urban man, neither modern nor urban should be heavily stressed. Otherwise we turn a universal genius into the next rarest, the much commoner thing in literature, a great writer.

(iv)

Trapped in his false or ambiguous solitude at the beginning of *The Double*, Mr Golyadkin is neither at peace with himself (as we quaintly put it — and how true to the spirit of this novel), nor is he companionable with his mirror-image. Similar equivocations unsettle him *vis-à-vis* his sourceless money, and next his party clothes which also come from nowhere; they are not exactly new and not exactly not new; they are 'newish'. He betrays no sign of having worn or even seen them before. Our thoughts begin to wander beyond the confines of the text. In retrospect, if we may suppose for a moment that the novel and its hero have a past, perhaps the Double has tried them on for size; this is in tune with his usurping nature, as Mr Golyadkin would confirm. Then the samovar joins in the reciprocity game by 'saying' something. This saying is the first *deskat* in the novel, the first inkling of what will prove not merely the most radical of all its equivocations and by far the most pervasive, but a system, a network of equivocation, at once a technical and an imaginative lynchpin. I cannot improve on my remarks about *deskat* prompted by its removal from the 1846 elopement letter: it is Mr Golyadkin's word of words, he has it and it shapes him, herein is the spirit of indeterminacy at once given free rein and determined.

If *The Double* (initially, *Golyadkin*) appears to be turning into a formalist's paradise under this treatment, let it be remembered that the Russian literary language is almost as young as the novelist. In this respect Dostoevsky writing in the 1840s is much closer to Edmund Spenser and the development of our northern vernacular into a world literature, or to Goethe and the rise of German from kitchen-language status, than he is to Balzac and Dickens. Things are changing fast, much is provisional, experimental, there are many false moves and blind alleys. The positively childish word-fascinations, often untranslatable, of *The Double* should be taken for what they are. 'Friend' and 'enemy' (*priyatel* and *nepriyatel*), 'acquaintance' and 'stranger' (*znakomets* and *neznakomets*), are manipulated throughout as language facets of the doubling theme, Tweedledum and Tweedledee, lexical enantiomorphs without Carroll's story and Tenniel's illustrations to hang on to. Similarly the common root of 'other' and a second word for 'friend' (*drugoi* and *drug*) is naively exploited as if there were something autonomous here, and 'one another' (*drug druga*) becomes a healing dream of mediation and longed-for mutualities, the pathos of which is purely verbal.

Now *deskat* is a different kettle of fish. Who says the samovar is saying? Not Mr Golyadkin. Not the samovar itself. Not — though this only gradually becomes apparent as *deskat* multiplies and the novel's personality establishes itself — not the voice recounting the adventures of 'our hero'. For *deskat* undermines at every point the outward and stable relationship between hero and narrator which this pretend plain tale proposes.

Then who says the samovar is saying? The question leads back to the conspiracy between reader and young poet, and to the alteration of *The Double*'s subtitle from Adventures to Poem which marked, we saw, a process of intensification and not a change of direction in Dostoevsky's work on the novel. The Poem says. Reader and young poet conspire to say. Both answers are correct. Both are as undetermining, as unfixing, as *deskat* in its local manifestations is indeterminate and unfixed. Or, if you prefer, the novel is as mad as its hero. It parades an old-fashioned hero/narrator fixity when in fact, and primarily by means of *deskat*, its discourse slips in and out of Mr Golyadkin's head in ways we sense but cannot track, and a world which is not this 'saying' world of words goes about its business elsewhere. At each stage uncertainty reigns. Not only is the 'saying' world unstable, for example as between what Mr Golyadkin projects for himself and what is projected for him by the pseudo-objective narrator; we may not speak of *the* world busy elsewhere, but only of *a* world — the indefinite article matching mirror image, money, clothes, samovar, then Petrushka the manservant and other human beings in their dubious externality which is also Mr Golyadkin's undependable solitude.

The fact that he is neither alone nor in society reflects, and is reflected by, my two root propositions about language in *The Double*: first, that Mr Golyadkin has and is nothing for certain except his words; second, that *deskat*, his word of words, comprehends and determines him, is bigger than he is, speaks the mind of the novel *alias* Poem *alias* Conspiracy; so that his word of words is also and finally the book's. Dostoevsky pinned down his man once and for all before he had even finished the novel, in that letter about going his own way and being the same as everybody else. Nobody except Dostoevsky ('Now I am the real Golyadkin!') and Mr Golyadkin says this. Mr Golyadkin is constantly saying it. It distinguishes him. We identify him by his refrain. But it effects a poor sort of rescue from his ontological limbo of nobody to be, since through its internal contradiction — the same and different — it is logically self-cancelling, whatever its truth to his and our human condition; and what is more, it strikes to the very heart of his identity malaise by being said not *by* (for it is Mr Golyadkin's refrain) but *about* the Double on Mr Golyadkin's first encounter with him: 'The man was the same as everybody else . . . in a word, he was going his own way.'[47]

Different but the same. So *The Double*'s tiny parable of life extends to — the Double. And in giving Mr Golyadkin something to say, the refrain, the parrot-cry, fails to offer him somebody to be; it is no 'I will never desert Mr Micawber.' The Kafkaesque obsessiveness with which he clings to it ministers to the novel's form, not to a personal distress: lexically consistent again, but without human avail. It's at once remarkable and no use, remarkable and abstract-and-banal, that Mr Golyadkin constantly and the Double never uses the refrain.

The question of *deskat* and Mr Golyadkin and the Double is larger and more subtle. For, while going his own way, or keeping himself to himself, or paddling his own canoe, or not being beholden — however we translate the unvarying *sam po sebe* — and yet being the same as everybody else, is a distinguishing formula specific to the man, *deskat* is a principle of determination common to the man and his world. The first *deskat* in *The Double* is attributed to what would elsewhere be the most securely human and social and historical of things, the ubiquitous Russian samovar. Here, an inhabitant of Mr Golyadkin's world, it shares the dubiousness of money, clothes, and the rest. Is it inside or outside his head? We only know what the story tells us, which is that it confronts him behind the partition in his room, standing untended but at full boil and 'saying' that it is 'ready', yet another thing with no past and no future, perched on a forward-tilting existential present which is no less than the whole of Mr Golyadkin and his world contemplated in their temporal aspect. And *deskat* perches here too, having no past — a narrated 'and then I said to him, I said . . .' is a present 'saying' — and tugged at by a never-arriving futurity of open choice which torments the whole novel. Anything may be in prospect in the 'saying' universe. All over the place, including the 1846 elopement letter, we meet *deskat* with 'such and such' (*tak i tak*) appended to it, a formula at once random and reversible. One of the few linguistic doubling jokes that are translatable in this crazy and childish as well as profound book, is that 'such and such' may be anything and it must be the same anything both ways round.

And just as this restless, questing *deskat* can turn every way except comfortwards on its existential perch, so it can do everything with the speech forms it projects except leave them empty. Say this, say that, say anything. The 'such and such' of that anything can be blocked in how we like, but it must be blocked in, we can't deem it void. It is, after all, not 'nothing' but 'such and such'. Mr Golyadkin himself is often *proposing* to say nothing — which is simply one of the turns his 'saying' takes, even if it stays inside his head. The proposal to be silent occupies a present that has got to be filled somehow, it is as good a 'such and such' as the next. Compare the archetypal 'ready' which is the samovar's 'saying' in a world which itself has erupted at full boil out of nowhere, and where tea never comes. Or Mr Golyadkin's 'So far everything's all right' with which he greets his mirror image, also at the very beginning of the book. 'Ready' and 'so far' are the first of innumerable temporal gestures which mock past and future in *The Double* while affecting to make ordinary assumptions about them and so take them seriously. The present, thus stripped of mental habit, becomes an object of surreal interest for our inspection, as if Time's metaphorical moving finger had been chopped off and laid warm and twitching on a cushion.

Deskat is thus a multipurpose verbal icon held up to life experienced as unremitting stress: the steam in the samovar, the hubbub in poor Mr Golyadkin's head. A world of no repose. I mentioned that Mr Golyadkin blushes in his sleep but I did not add, as the novel does, that he then stifles his blush. Sleep is yet another grim joke, and in isolation it harks back to Descartes's '*cogito*', the light of consciousness which never fails. Overall, though, *The Double* is a saying not a sleeping novel, a novel of will crossing Nietzsche and twentieth-century existentialism, not a novel of consciousness; and will, naked will, is under the saying, impelling it. The chatter of the samovar introduces the turmoil of office relationships (which may all of course be inside 'our hero's' head) where Mr Golyadkin and his colleagues voyage on a merry-go-round they can't climb down from, to which they cling as it thrusts them in a circular figure of nobody's designing and everyone's performing. The thought behind Mr Golyadkin's exchange with the cabby is, in part, that there can be no paying a man to stand still, and the convention of *The Double* is to project a Macbeth-like restless ecstasy on the plane of shared speech forms, of *deskat*. This transpersonal talk, vocalized or in the head, goes to the heart of the conspiracy between reader and young poet, for it is the form of the formless embroilments of Mr Golyadkin and his world.

It is also the Double's one and only but complete discomfiture, a sort of negative unmasking, a revelation of what he is not. The novel which takes his name denies him any part in *deskat*.

And yet how can this be so, since *deskat* speaks the mind of the novel, and the novel contains the Double; or, more simply, since the Double is (as well as is not) Mr Golyadkin? We should look to the 1866 elopement letter from which *deskat* has been removed only to fall like manna on the pages that follow, on the dream of Sir Golyadkin to the rescue and the love nest by the sea. In mounting his climactic double-act vision of somebody to be and somewhere to go, Mr Golyadkin excludes his novelistic Double absolutely. It is a dream, but a healing dream, since to be somebody and have somewhere is to purge all division and become whole.

Elsewhere Mr Golyadkin suffers from the disease of Double Trouble, and the firmest and neatest grip we can get on the fact that he is not (while he also is) his Alter Ego, is to remark that the Double does not suffer from Golyadkin Trouble.

Golyadkin Trouble and *deskat* are inseparable since the latter is an icon of life experienced as unceasing stress, the state of affairs in 'our hero's' head and world. It's fine to give *deskat* to a samovar because, while a boiling tea-machine (but no tea) makes an admirable image of eruptive and vain utterance with nothing except naked human will to shape and go on shaping it, nobody will mistake the image for the human phenomenon. Mr Golyadkin is that phenomenon. But the Double is not, and there must be no *deskat* when he is around.[48]

The exclusion of the Double from *deskat* and a world of total instability, if we ignore the one-man double-act dream, looks more like a kindly dispensation than a witholding. Observing life thus imaged, one might well advise the Double to say no to it if he had the choice. In the event Dostoevsky makes sure he has no choice; while forcing choice on Mr Golyadkin from first to last and down to the level of 'say such and such' and 'say nothing', he removes choice from the Double by creating and maintaining him psychologically void. He does this by casting him in the mould of traditional petty devil or folk-demon with a tightly circumscribed range of skipping and sidling movements and piping, simpering utterances and sudden pranks like pinching Mr Golyadkin's cheek and eating Mr Golyadkin's food and offering his own hand to be shaken and then suddenly withdrawing it. Why shouldn't Mr Golyadkin be imagining all this? Humanly there is no reason. As the novel proceeds and 'our hero' and the

[48] I concede that my assertion is dangerously tidy and embracing. But the fact remains, statistically convincing as it seems to me and of the first critical importance, that of the dozens of occurrences of *deskat* in this short novel scarcely one can be thought to implicate the Double in any way. The handful of doubtful cases are at *PSS*, Vol. I, pp. 150, 1. 11; 172, 1. 1; 185, 1. 25; 201, 1. 39; 202, 1. 11. I offer the rationale that the first is reportage and occurs in the presence of Mr Golyadkin and the absence of the Double; that the second is 'inside' Mr Golyadkin's head and is therefore classically his; that the third is the boldly calculated exception which proves the rule because it is part of a nightmare in which Mr Golyadkin dreams that the Double 'proved clearly' he was the real Golyadkin and Golyadkin was the sham; and that the last two which occur together are an exercise, perhaps ill-judged, in the ambiguity of *deskat*: Constance Garnett translates 'We will have it all out' (p. 250) and Jessie Coulson 'You've talked me over' (p. 250 of the Penguin *Notes from Underground* and *Double*), and neither is wrong.

Double sometimes become Messrs Golyadkin Senior and Junior respectively, Dostoevsky can be felt nudging us towards the conclusion that the two are also one and that the pinching and prodding register the pains of consciousness. 'My own murderer, that's what I am!' exclaims Mr Golyadkin out of the blue, in a sudden premonition of Raskolnikov's mortal self-pursuit in *Crime and Punishment*.[49] But formally the two are never one. Mr Golyadkin and Double, *alias* Senior and Junior, sometimes strangers, sometimes acquaintances, sometimes enemies and sometimes friends — formally, they are divided by the 'saying' line. The Double cannot even propose to say nothing.

' "In one way or another I must explain myself", he thought; "I must say, This is how it is, your Excellency" ' (*deskat tak i tak*).[50] This is the archetypal Golyadkin posture, this is the forward-tilting existential present projected on the 'saying' plane, this is Mr Golyadkin's Double Trouble, this is the line the Double cannot cross. In Mr Golyadkin Dostoevsky realized, as human phenomenon, contextless choice facing naked will. If the Double were allowed to mimic Mr Golyadkin by saying or thinking that he must explain himself and say such and such, the whole internal economy of the novel would be wrecked.

The economy of *this* novel, of course. Things might have been different. Long afterwards, in that *Writer's Diary* entry of 1877, declaring that in his whole career he had never handled a more serious idea, Dostoevsky goes on to say: 'But I failed utterly with the form of the story'; and 'if I took up this idea now and stated it afresh, I'd give it a completely different form; but in 1846 I hadn't found this form and failed to bring the story off.'[51] As we saw, a manuscript notebook also dating from the 1870s identifies the idea never surpassed in seriousness as 'my supreme underground type'. It doesn't matter that the identification is less than conclusive because the link between the underground type and *The Double* is established by the notebook itself. So is the importance of the type in Dostoevsky's own estimation, and so is

---

[49] *The Eternal Husband*, p. 225.   [50] Ibid., p. 268.
[51] p. 56, above.

his judgement that he had failed to realize it in *The Double*. With direct reference to his 'supreme underground type' claim, he writes: 'I hope I will be forgiven this boast in the light of my own admission regarding the artistic failure of the type.' The interest of this can scarcely be exaggerated, especially since a closer look at the notebook reveals that Dostoevsky is not writing in general terms about *The Double* but is restricting his 'underground' remarks to the figure of Mr Golyadkin Junior.[52]

Thus the Double aspect of *The Double* is also its Underground aspect. Of course there's no telling what the novel would have turned into if Dostoevsky had rewritten it in the 1870s. He may have persuaded himself he would now, thirty years on, find the *Doppelgänger* motif tractable, but however he proceeded he would have been returning to the attack within a framework of equivocal difference and identity; meeting Mr Golyadkin and his friend/enemy again, we would again be replying yes and no to the question whether they are two or one. The line dividing them (which is also no line) must be the ground itself, for Dostoevsky would not call the Double his supreme underground type unless he was placing Mr Golyadkin above the ground, with whatever shifts and ambiguities proper to the two-and-one theme. Perhaps the unwritten novel of the 1870s would have switched focus from above to below and become the story of the Double, the Adventures of Mr Golyadkin Junior, with echoes and rumours of life overhead.

If so, Dostoevsky would be following the policy of *Notes from Underground* which he published in 1864. That novel's self-styled 'antihero' is the Underground — literally Underfloor — Man, and its subject is his self-inflicted existence as an honorary rat or mouse beneath the boards. Ground and floorboards are at once the novel's master metaphor and its projection of the Underground Man's blank asserting of will. He is staying where he is, by himself, choosing to say no to what goes on above. The party which the Underground Man refuses to join is the feast of life. Dostòevsky floats this thought. But equivocally. There is a counterthought with which the Underground Man mocks his readers above him in the light and air. This is: 'I may be even more 'alive' than you are. Do take a closer look! Why, we don't even know where the living lives today, or what it is, or what it's called.'[53] We don't know what life is or where it is, above or below. The floor which constitutes the simplest and most clearcut of dividing lines is also no dividing line at all.

The pranks which the Double plays on Mr Golyadkin foreshadow the Underground Man's spiteful whims and fancies directed against his reader. As so often, Dostoevsky is asking himself whether vision and technique will invert. With the Underground Man the power to choose is crucial. Antiheroic flourishes of will which look like silly caprice from above the floorboards are, in the dark beneath, precious tokens of freedom, and the ultimate freedom under which all lesser freedoms shelter is the power to say no to the party going on above.

But the Double, even if he wanted to, cannot join the choosing and saying party in which, to borrow Mr Golyadkin's words and assume his endlessly recurring attitude, 'in one way or another I must explain myself'. Herein we locate the hard core of irreversibility in Senior and Junior roles, and also perhaps of the novel's *formal* failure in Dostoevsky's own eyes. He harps on form and, discussing *The Double* retrospectively in the 1870s, he speaks of Mr Golyadkin Junior rather than the Double. The Senior/Junior nomenclature and the shared surname do justice to the handy-dandy equivocation of his unsurpassed 'serious idea' in a way that is much easier to plan than carry out. In *The Double* that got written Mr Golyadkin is alone on the painful perch of his existential, choosing present, but the Double feeds him back his fears about his job, reflects his self-mockery about his love life — and so on. How to square this with my assertion that the Double has been created psychologically void? By doubling the Double: he who feeds back the fears is, and he who gobbles the savoury patties is not, Mr Golyadkin. This answer is *formally* correct, but it is an extrapolation from the novel, not an achievement of the novel.

[53] *White Nights*, pp. 174–5.

So the Double who is Mr Golyadkin has to be a mental creation which nevertheless must not — and does not — ever say 'in one way or another I must explain myself' and its equivalents. And the Double who is not Mr Golyadkin has to be, and is, mindless. It makes no sense to speak of this Double as choosing to embarrass Mr Golyadkin with a sudden kiss, because Dostoevsky has created him psychologically void. Void not impenetrable. We catch no hint of withheld mentality. This Double is merely impish. And this Double is inverted in *Notes from Underground*. We move from a mindless creation to one that is all mind — and first and foremost irrational, since the Underground Man's power to choose is most conspicuously flaunted by being driven against the grain of reason as understood by the rest of us above the floorboards. 'I agree,' he says, 'that two and two makes four is a splendid thing; but if we are dispensing praise, then two and two makes five is sometimes a most charming little thing as well.'[54] The power and fact of choice are thus stripped of all comforting light-of-day normalcy and made to affront logical and social expectation in a lonely gesture of self-affirmation. Choice is everything — an inversion of the Double's pranks where choice is nothing.

I am not saying that Dostoevsky would have borrowed his own floorboards metaphor if he had rewritten *The Double*; I am only suggesting he would have handled the *Doppelgänger* theme the other way round and produced something much more like the Underground Man's life-rejecting harangue than the novel he did write, even with the 1866 alterations and the change of subtitle — no mere tinkering, as we have seen — from 'Adventures of Mr Golyadkin' to 'Petersburg Poem'. His explicit identification of Mr Golyadkin Junior as the underground type supports this view. So does the proliferation of life-haters and life-deniers in the later novels, of suicides, and of those who present their various alternatives to the common notion of what it means to be alive. Thus *Crime and Punishment* gives us Raskolnikov lying for hours on end with his face turned to the wall, nursing his Napoleonic dream of being different from and more alive than everybody else. And

---

[54] Ibid., p. 86.

while this is happening — one of Dostoevsky's stupendous feats — all the companion in Raskolnikov is dying. And in the same novel Svidrigailov peeps and eavesdrops through literal cracks and crannies, and then says no to the party: he decides on America, that recurring nowhere to go in Dostoevsky, which here means suicide.

And in the final minutes of Svidrigailov's life 'a dirty shivering little dog crossed his path with its tail between its legs'; the rain has been lashing down and the cannon sounds a flood warning: ' "Ah, the signal! The river is overflowing", he thought. "By morning it will be pouring down the streets in the lower part of the town, flooding the basements and cellars. The cellar rats will come to the surface".'[55]

And when Mr Golyadkin first encounters the Double 'a little lost dog, all wet and shivering, attached itself to Mr Golyadkin and ran along beside him, scurrying, with tail and ears drooping'; our hero has heard the boom of the cannon and exclaims 'This terrible weather! Listen! Isn't that a flood warning? So the water has been rising very fast.'[56]

The cellar rats will come to the surface. The abstract city and its apocalypse. All shall be revealed. The abstract city and its flood, its eschatology, its science of ends. Suicide for Svidrigailov. And what for Mr Golyadkin? The death of reason? The rising waters of madness? Perhaps. But it is vital to grasp that he is only *incidentally* mad. Kafka did not need telling this.

Max's objection to Dostoevsky, that he allows too many mentally ill persons to enter. Completely wrong . . . . Their illness is merely a way to characterize them, and moreover a very delicate and fruitful one. One need only stubbornly keep repeating of a person that he is simple-minded and idiotic, and he will, if he has the Dostoevskian core inside him, be spurred on, as it were, to do his very best.[57]

This is a recognizable picture, even in the immature

[55] *Crime and Punishment*, pp. 447, 450.
[56] *The Eternal Husband*, pp. 175, 177.
[57] Diary entry for 20 December 1914. Mr Golyadkin's madness being first and foremost dubious, not incidental, the notebook mention of a lunatic asylum was a mistake and Dostoevsky rejected it (*PSS*, Vol. I, p. 434). 'Shutting somebody else up in a madhouse doesn't prove your own sanity,' says the hero of a late short story: *Bobok*, 1873 — a splendid observation but quite wrong for *The Double*.

Double. Mr Golyadkin, the first incidental madman in
Dostoevsky, is thrust on and on and on to take a decisive
step, to bring matters to a head, to restore things to their
former state, to be completely passive, above all to say this,
say that, say anything, say nothing — his formalistic, *deskat*
version of what Kafka calls doing one's very best. While the
underground Double is almost a nullity, the above-ground
Mr Golyadkin carries the life and character of the book. The
burden crushes him, but he never thinks of putting it down.
He even 'wants to cease to be'.[58] Yet he never contemplates
doing anything about it. He is no Svidrigailov. He denounces
himself, we saw, as his own murderer, but never once in all
his troubles does he consider suicide. Life torments him. He
does not deny life. On the contrary, he affirms life by snapping at it like a teased animal.

Throughout the novel 'our hero' is described as being 'in
indescribable anguish'. This has none of the force of what is
so often called indescribable and yet gets carried straight and
living into the reader's apprehension in the later novels. It's
not that we don't believe in Mr Golyadkin's pain, but that
the pain isn't imaginatively scalding; it is distanced and
inspectable as were the 'lacerations' of the two lovers in
Poor People. In both novels the distancing is a matter of
tragicomic convention: in *Poor People* the Double Act of
nobody and nowhere was stylized as the love story of a
seamstress and a clerk; in *The Double* Mr Golyadkin has to
mount his own Double Act, which is why the elopement
letter is both the novel's climax and its central inspiration,
embracing the nowhere of the hut on the shore and the
nobody of Sir Golyadkin to the rescue.

But in the body of the book this simultaneous nowhere
and nobody has to be sustained on a fragile basis of situational farce. And the grossness of farce must not offend the
intellectual delicacy of the choosing and saying universe
which is *The Double*'s existential present. It proves an
impossibly tall order. Dostoevsky failed to give his public a
good read, and he didn't leave posterity with a great novel,

---

[58] *The Eternal Husband*, p. 173. He is on the point of meeting the Double
for the first time, and busy calling down his doom on his own head.

only a portentous one. In the later books farce will smell less strongly of vaudeville and turn towards fiasco, and the existential present will become less stark and schematic, and therefore altogether less evident, because absorbed into the tissue of those huge narratives.

In terms of Kafka's analysis, Mr Golyadkin has not got much of the Dostoevskian core inside him. Intermittently, though, that core declares itself hard and bright — for example in the opening pages while 'our hero' criticizes his mirror-image and fondles his money and dresses for the party. And the more gleamingly assertive the Dostoevskian core, the more incidental Mr Golyadkin's madness. Incidental to its metaphysical point, and its empirical justice, and its universality. We all do it, as I remarked of small manifestations of 'indescribable anguish' like banging his own head and eating food he doesn't want. The universal human urge towards self-disavowal in 'Don't worry, it's not me' may not be the first thing to catch the reader's attention, but it is there all right. On the grand scale, too, we are all dressed for the party, the feast of life, to which we have been dubiously invited.

Mr Golyadkin has nowhere to go since they aren't expecting him at the party when he gets there, and by the same token he has nobody to be since the role of guest he is trying on will not fit. This two-in-one of *The Double*'s opening gets caught up in the elopement letter and is then thrown open, dilated, poeticized into collective daydream in the letter's aftermath. In these beautiful, not always translatable, pages *deskat* comes into its own, no longer under the lash of the actual, appeased, turned benign. Purged from the 1846 elopement letter it enters with a rush in our received text and entwines the 'saying' Mr Golyadkin plans for himself with what he guesses the girl will say and what he will say to what she says and what others will say about the happy couple. This is a weave we are not curious to unpick, a conspiracy we connive at and therefore in a sense join, a dream we kind of share — that conspiracy and that 'kind of' which *deskat* carries and which are the counterpart of authorlessness in *Poor People*.

Once outside the lighted windows of the girl's house,

waiting for her to come to him, Mr Golyadkin takes up his station behind a dripping log pile. This is described in an old poetic word as a 'canopy'[59] — a statement obviously false and equally, though less obviously, true. He stands there drenched with rain but also canopied by Romance. And also stalked by ruin, as if this late bloom of invulnerability knew its own term. Comparison with Lear's 'birds in a cage' speech to Cordelia is not entirely absurd.

'Aren't you going anywhere at all?' said the cabby at last, approaching Mr Golyadkin with resolute step.

'Yes, my friend, I'm coming at once. You see, my boy, I'm waiting.'

'Very well, sir,'

'I — you see, my friend — what part of the country do you come from, my dear fellow?'

'We are our masters' men.'

'And are your masters kind?'

'Middling.'

'Well, my dear fellow; you stay here, old chap. You see, my friend — have you been in Petersburg long?'

'I've been driving a whole year.'

'And how's it going, my friend?'

'Middling.'

'Yes, my friend, ah yes. You must thank Providence, my friend. Dear chap, you must look out for a kind master. Kind people are rare nowadays, my dear fellow. He'll bathe you and give you food and drink, a kind master will — But sometimes, my dear fellow, sometimes you see the tears flowing even through the gold —'[60]

Though, of course, there is less *Lear* than *Waiting for Godot* here. I take it that Vladimir asking the Boy 'Do you belong to these parts?' and (with reference to Mr Godot) 'Does he feed you well?' are quarried straight out of *The Double*, as is the Boy's answer 'Fairly well, sir'; and beyond these details, rhythm and tone of dialogue in Beckett, spectral yet warm, suggest he is a close student of Dostoevsky's second novel; and beyond again there is the Godot/Master equivocation[61] and the whole waiting theme. The novel's

[59] Ibid., p. 277. 'Canopy' perhaps catches the flavour of *sen* better than Constance Garnett's 'shelter'. It's possible that Dostoevsky is blending the sense of refuge with the fact that *sen*, coupled with *smershnaya*, means the shadow of death.

[60] Ibid., pp. 275-6.

[61] Expressed in Russian by the fact that *Gospod* is the Lord God and *gospodin* is master.

'Aren't you going anywhere at all?' could stand as epitome of the play with its final line 'Yes, let's go' and the stage direction *They do not move*.

But then *Waiting for Godot* and *The Double* are both of them inspired footnotes to *King Lear*: 'I have no way and therefore want no eyes.' And with *The Double* there is also *Don Quixote* astir somewhere, helping to conjure an exploit which is directionless and radiant but full of pain too. I noted the *Quixote*-like chapter headings of the 1846 version of the novel, those pinpointers of jokes like the fatter wallet and the reduced purchasing power. Their removal in 1866, I said, makes a hard text even harder. It is also true that their removal forms part of the development from Adventures into less evidently Quixotic Poem. We lose 'Concerning Spanish serenades and diverse matters not suited to our severe climate',[62] and having lost it can only snatch at the fantasy and the realism as they float intertwined through the head of canopied, drenched Mr Golyadkin.

Another entanglement is that of Mr Golyadkin's ardour with the dishonesty of his manservant. 'Our hero's' elopement plan means, or can be made to mean, rich pickings for Petrushka. Lots of things will have to be bought: 'sheets, pillows, another feather bed, a good quilt'. I am translating 1846. In 1866 Dostoevsky left an intricate paragraph untouched except for adding 'a double one' after 'another feather bed'.[63] Nothing could be simpler. And yet the effect, the real impulse, of this feint towards sexual insinuation is touchingly ludicrous and indeed chaste. The Double cannot get into *that* double bed any more than we can conceive of him coming between Mr Golyadkin and the cabby in their exchange beneath the girl's window.

But the enchantment doesn't last. But again what does, what can the word 'last' mean in this novel? Right back to the opening pages where Mr Golyadkin says so far everything's all right and the samovar says it's ready, time is being mocked. And never more cruelly and comically than when Mr Golyadkin arrives outside the girl's house and the sight which meets his eyes doesn't square with the words of the elopement letter:

[62] *PSS*, Vol. I, p. 416.   [63] Ibid., p. 418; *The Eternal Husband*, p. 261.

'Then it is today?' flashed through his head. 'Is there a mistake in the date? It's possible — anything's possible — that's it, anything's possible. Perhaps the letter was written yesterday and never reached me, and it never reached me because that scoundrel Petrushka took a hand in the game. Or it was written tomorrow — I mean it was tomorrow I'm to do it all — to wait with the carriage, I mean.'[64]

So there he stands in that formulaic 'indescribable agony', experiencing the reality which my image of *The Double*'s razor-sharp, forward-tilting existential present is supposed to depict. By now it should be obvious that Mr Golyadkin is only incidentally mad. And the purpose to which his madness is incidental has also, I hope, been established. My account of that purpose, the purpose of Mr Golyadkin's twenty-four year old creator, is bound to seem implausible unless the beautiful little 'anything's possible' tune is allowed to sink in, and unless details like 'Or it was written tomorrow' are placed and kept before the eye of criticism. An almost random comparison with Victorian nonsense literature serves only to stress Dostoevsky's isolation.[65] This is not a young man amusingly fooling about. It falls within a pattern of dislocation which compels acknowledgement of instinctive and astonishing twentieth-century affinities. The letter that was perhaps written tomorrow belongs, I would say, to the wild end of *The Double*'s temporal spectrum. At the other end, and no less cunningly planted, are commonplaces like 'Why not just stop?' and 'If only tomorrow would hurry up and come'[66] — commonplaces with a grotesque demon lurking inside them. And, at the heart of the time-and-identity tangle, Mr Golyadkin's 'Don't worry, it's not me' turns into the following giddy cerebral boomerang:

'Probably it was some sort of dream, or something else happened and not what really did happen; or perhaps it was me myself walking along, and I somehow mistook myself for somebody else — in short, the thing's quite impossible.'[67]

---

[64] *The Eternal Husband*, p. 272.
[65] 'But really I have been *awfully* busy, and I've had to write *heaps* of letters — wheel barrows full, almost. And it tires me so that generally I go to bed again the next minute after I get up: and some times I go to bed again a minute *before* I get up!' (Lewis Carroll, letter of 30 November 1879).
[66] *The Eternal Husband*, p. 228.   [67] Ibid., pp. 206–7.

Not at all like Gogol or Hoffmann. A morsel of the *Welt-geist* that has somehow got out of phase and swept forward into our own sick times. It doesn't follow, however, that Mr Golyadkin's madness constitutes what Kafka, with his eye on the mature novels, calls a delicate and fruitful mode of characterization. Rather, reverse the thought and say, in terms of pre-Siberian Dostoevsky, and contrasting Messrs Golyadkin and Devushkin, that Mr Golyadkin's madness is a mode of decharacterization. Mr Devushkin is cradled in context, whether alone in his snug den or milling around with fellow lodgers or perched on his rung of the office seniority ladder. No matter that the cradling is often agonized; as John Donne observed, the manger straw may have been no less painful than the crown of thorns; context remains context, and it is this and the grooving of habit that give absolute conviction to Mr Devushkin when he tells Varenka he hasn't had his pipe in his mouth for nine days. It is not a question of believing him, though surely we do; his truth-telling is subordinate to his simple sane appetites — in a word, his humanity. Even if we didn't believe him we would believe *in* him as we believe in so many minor characters in Shakespeare and Walter Scott.

Whereas Mr Golyadkin's pipe-smoking, much more prominent in fact than Mr Devushkin's, is a decharacterizing agent.

Thus feeling his troubles to the full, our hero resolved to adopt a passive role for two hours and wait for Petrushka. For an hour or so he paced up and down the room smoking, then threw aside his pipe and sat down to a book, then lay down on the sofa, then took up his pipe again, then once more began running about the room. He tried to think things over but was absolutely unable to think about anything. At last the agony of his passive state reached the pitch of extremity, and Mr Golyadkin made up his mind to take a certain step.[68]

Mr Devushkin was frantic for his pipe, as we say of distraught but ultimately cohering people like him; whereas Mr Golyadkin is frantic. His pipe, like the book, the sofa, the running round the room, the trying to think, and elsewhere the gulping endless cups of tea with his eye on the clock — all these help to pull him apart. The objection that frantic people

[68]   Ibid., p. 220.

are, in clinical and observable fact, pulled apart, brings us back into the orbit of Mr Golyadkin's incidental madness. Indeed we do have dementia here, but it would be preposterous to maintain the condition is studied, let alone rendered from within. It is used. The pipe and the rest pull Mr Golyadkin apart, shred him, render him unqualitied, decharacterize him to the end that the Mr Naked who makes up his mind 'to take a certain step' shall be neither more nor less than I say he is: naked will facing contextless choice, an abstract and banal figurine positioned in a nightmare existential present. This makes for a very intellectual fiction indeed. And Mr Golyadkin is also decharacterized to the end that the weirdness lurking within everyday notions like resolving to be passive shall come through to the reader unobscured by familiar novelistic selfhood. The 'passive role' won't fit, it isn't anybody to be; the 'passive state' doesn't exist, it isn't anywhere to go. Mr Golyadkin blushes in his sleep. And stifles his blush. There was no paying the cabby to stand still.

(v)

Although Mr Golyadkin holds the same rank as Mr Devushkin the copying clerk, and has the same or very similar duties, the word 'copy' never appears in the whole novel: this is one of the most sensitive points of the hyperconscious relationship between *The Double* and *Poor People*. Both heroes get into trouble over their humdrum clerical work. 'This document is wanted in a hurry,' Mr Devushkin is told. 'Copy it out very clearly, as quickly as possible and with care.'[69] But in his panic he drops a line. Mr Golyadkin is asked: 'Have you finished that document from yesterday?' Whereupon the Double declares the work is spoilt by a huge blot, and while Mr Golyadkin is puzzling over the document unable to see any blot, the Double snatches it up and carries it to the boss and with much simpering and fawning takes the credit for Mr Golyadkin's excellent penmanship.[70]

[69]   *The Gambler*, p. 227.
[70]   *The Eternal Husband*, pp. 202–6. So from my point of view Constance Garnett's 'Have you finished copying out the document you had yesterday?' is unfortunate.

Copying is everywhere in *Poor People*. Mr Devushkin's dropped line is a factual detail in a novel preoccupied with the human (albeit intellectually pointed) question whether to be a copier is to be somebody. In *The Double* copying is nowhere, and Mr Golyadkin's surreal blot contributes its mite to the universal instability of that novel. Pervasive copying, and then no copying: again, this is no accident. Dostoevsky saw that the untethering from the actual he was seeking in his second novel could not be achieved unless the theme of hero as *copying* clerk was totally excluded, and with the effrontery of the great artist he did just that. He was then free to unload all the doublings, all the Firsts and Seconds he was after, upon the *Doppelgänger* motif. Not a word wasted! But: 'What economy of means,' remarked Henry James at the Marionette Show; '— and of effect!' And Dr Johnson who complained of a want of human interest in *Paradise Lost*, what would he have said about *The Double*?

He might have done me the honour of borrowing my words and noting that *The Double*, unlike *Poor People*, is not big-boned — a judgment that has to be qualified only once, in the light of the eating-house scene with the retired army officer in a red collar asking loudly for the *Police News* and the respectable old man saying grace before the icon. It is, I observed, a mark of Dostoevsky's clairvoyance that he switched the tearing open and reading of the elopement letter to the eating-house in his final version of the novel. This was a desperate bid for human interest. We view its failure with mixed feelings. Of course there is a part of us that wants Mr Golyadkin's 'indescribable agony' to bite deep, to *really* hurt. But that mature Dostoevskian *really* will not bed down with the genius of *The Double*. For it is of the essence of the 'agony of the passive state' which we have just been considering that it should be notional and instantly switchable into the agony of the active state: 'Mr Golyadkin made up his mind to take a certain step' — and he found no *real* pain there either.

So the reader must not think Dostoevsky is being lazy or heartless about Mr Golyadkin's 'agony', or about his 'troubles' and his 'extremity' in the same passage, but rather that these fall within his madness and are incidental to the fable at the centre of which 'our hero' stands, as in a waking dream where rational ends are mocked[71] and physical and mental categories are systematically confused, back to the money and mirror-image and on to the savoury patties and the elopement letter itself. And across into language. Dostoevsky seizes on the ambiguity of *zadevat* which means both to brush against and to trouble; his glee in doing so is like that with which Hegel invokes *Aufheben* (to cancel but also to preserve) to express the kernel of the dialectic; and in both cases remember how young the literary language is. The Double repeatedly brushes up against and/or troubles Mr Golyadkin.[72] This is what 'our hero's' agony adds up to, this notional agony which will neither stay inside his head nor take root out in the world. Already in *Poor People* doubling was a master metaphor on which Dostoevsky floated a very private creative unease, probably black as night to himself at the outset. The dead Gorshkov child and his coffin: 'they bought it ready-made, the boy was nine.' Dostoevsky may well have seen no further than the power of money even in death. His sense of the forces stirring beneath his own simple words may have been an unfocused prickling disquiet, an aura.

While the small corpse understudies its coffin, *The Double*'s treatment of Firsts and Seconds is exhaustive and multi-faceted and, we may safely guess, altogether more conscious than *Poor People*'s. At one extreme we have simple visual ploys such as Mr Golyadkin thinking he is looking at himself in a full-length mirror when in fact it is the Double standing in a doorway;[73] and at the other, completely unvisual contortions like Mr Golyadkin wondering whether after all it was really him, just him, walking along and he had mistaken himself for somebody else. To put the thing reductively, Dostoevsky felt menaced by likeness, and the *Doppelgänger* motif presented him with a goldmine of dread if comic

[71] As in the incidental madness of 'With that object he stared at his cuffs' (p. 168).

[72] Thus the first occurrence of *zadevat*, on Mr Golyadkin's first meeting with the Double, is taken one way by Constance Garnett ('crossing my path and provoking me', p. 175) and the other way by Jessie Coulson in her Penguin translation ('crossing my path, he will brush against me', pp. 168-9).

[73] *The Eternal Husband*, pp. 216-17, 268.

semblances. Mr Golyadkin doesn't mind being *identical with* the Double; there might even be money in it as there was for the pair of Siamese twins who had recently been putting themselves on show in Europe and America.[74] The trouble is, if you are identical people tend not to recognize you are separate and yourself alone. To use his own analogy, Mr Golyadkin feels the indignation of one drop of water that has been mistaken for another. Why can't they be seen for what they are, two identical self-respecting drops of water? Here is his 'human' version of this complaint:

He is a different person, Your Excellency, and I am a different person too; he is an individual and I go my own way (*sam po sebe*) too; really *sam po sebe*, Your Excellency, really *sam po sebe*; that's how it is, I shall say. I cannot be like him, I shall say . . .'.[75]

Sam po sebe three times. *Deskat* twice. And Mr Golyadkin's choosing, saying, existential perch — very painful in the abstract. But he is in the abstract! And now consider the strangeness of 'I cannot be like him'. This was implicit at the very beginning, in the letter where Dostoevsky 'gave' Mr Golyadkin to his brother. He is the same as everybody else. But different. But the same.[76] But never like. Like is excluded. Mr Golyadkin gets as far as exclaiming 'What if they get us mixed up!';[77] but he never goes on to say we must do something about it, part our hair on opposite sides or whatever. And yet again this is no accident. If Golyadkin and Double were to do something about it, the novel would have to accommodate the measure of more and less alike. And it must not. 'I cannot be like him.'

To the objection, But this is silly trifling, I reply: Don't underestimate Dostoevsky's intellectualism or the fascination for him, as for all of us, of the paradox of your and my unique and shared humanity. 'I am after all a man,' Mr Devushkin wrote to Varenka, 'in heart and mind a man.' A man among men. But not *like* other men. *Like* is fraught.

---

[74]   Ibid., p. 186. Note, as with the cutprice Gorshkov coffin, the unobvious resonances of money. Also an advance flicker of the mature parajournalistic Dostoevsky. (See *PSS*, Vol. I, p. 494, for his documentary source over the Siamese twins.)

[75]   Ibid., p. 264.   [76]   p. 57, above.

[77]   *The Eternal Husband*, p. 215.

And in *The Double*, that complementary and contrasting study, Mr Golyadkin's parrot cry is 'I go my own way and I'm just the same as everybody else'. Separate and the same but never like — a surreal reworking of Mr Devushkin's solemn 'I am after all a man', the difference pursued into details like that 'hedgehogging' which with Mr Devushkin is natural and self-protective but with Mr Golyadkin is 'to hide from himself'.[78]

So when Golyadkin and Double agree there is nobody like God they are talking about the god in all of us, whom Dostoevsky came to call the human in the human being. Likeness turns communities into crowds, flocks into herds. The epigraph of *The Possessed* is the story of the stampeding Gadarene swine. And no doubt other great texts were running in his head, such as the mysterious gospel injunction to love our neighbours as ourselves, which is silent about our common humanity and yet cannot be an appeal to the yardstick of individual self-love. At least not what we ordinarily mean by self-love. I believe the young Dostoevsky was in this area when the middle-aged Mr Devushkin declared to Varenka: 'Getting to know you, I came first to know myself better and I came to love you.' And even in the fine-boned *Double* where, outside the chivalric–romantic dream of somebody and somewhere, love has been transposed into an astringent doomed mutuality of hunter and hunted, we read:

'They say too, gentlemen, that the gamebird flies of its own accord to the sportsman. Quite true, I'm prepared to admit it. But which is the sportsman here and which is the bird? That is still the question, gentlemen.'[79]

And here anybody who knew Dostoevsky's work well but couldn't place this passage would show perception if he gave it to Dmitry Karamazov under police examination — Dmitry of the raking stride and haunting speech rhythms.

Getting to know you I came to know myself better and then I came to love you. Which is the hunter and which is the prey? Think of these, the statement and the question, as two great globes revolving slowly through the inner space of Dostoevsky's imagination, and think of the surface of his

[78] Ibid., p. 173. [79] Ibid., p. 157.

mind as a clutter of mother's-knee Christianity and student
Socialism and avid reading in four literatures, German,
French, English, and Russian. The false society of Mr Devushkin's lodging-house teapot parade and graded office reprimands, and the false solitude of Mr Golyadkin's Double-
poisoned selfhood, encourage the thought that *Poor People*
is about the pains of status and *The Double*, biting deeper
and much more abstract, about ontological instability — the
dubious being of 'our hero'. And this is true in so far as Mr
Devushkin (in my formulation) is somebody without knowing
it while Mr Golyadkin has and is nothing for certain except
his words. But the distinction between status and ontology
must not be pressed in Dostoevsky. His full comic energy
and his most serious intent are to be found in the grey-
haired soldier who, bewildered by the atheistic chatter going
on around him, stands up in the middle of the room and asks
'If there's no God then what sort of a Captain am I after
that?'[80] The conservative and authoritarian strain in Dostoevsky, boring outside his art and sometimes repellent, here
turns to gold.

And at the outset, in the question whether to be a copier
is to be somebody, status and ontology ought not to be
prised apart, for Mr Devushkin is a copying clerk as well as a
man. So is Mr Golyadkin, and the un-novelistic bareness of
The Double stems partly from the suppression of the copying
clerk, leaving the metaphysical resources of Dostoevsky's
imagination unsupported by the social. 'He is a different
person, and I am a different person too.' This bareness is in
Mr Golyadkin's own mouth. And in his consciousness. First
in a dream, then wide awake, he sees the Double beget more
Doubles until the streets of Petersburg are swarming with
Seconds threatening to engulf Mr Golyadkin's solitary
First.[81] Likeness is undoing him. His cry that he is separate
too is going unheeded.

Less nakedly metaphysical are moments like this:

'My back aches, I've got a cough and a cold in the head; and really I

---

[80]   *The Possessed*, p. 204.   [81]   *The Eternal Husband*, pp. 232, 281.

can't go out, I can't possibly go out in this weather; I might fall ill and perhaps even die; the deathrate's so high, especially now.'[82]

For Dostoevsky has wrapped his brilliant and cunning point, which is Mr Golyadkin viewing himself statistically — 'the deathrate's so high' — inside the sort of fussing about health we all go in for. One of the jokes which reader and young poet share behind the backs of our poor hero and *The Double*'s forthright pseudo-narrator is this statistical or exemplary one. Mr Golyadkin is constantly helping the enemy, abetting likeness in its wiles, by presenting himself as an instance of some familiar human condition. A humble titular councillor hires a smart carriage or eats eleven savoury patties at a sitting or waits for hours in the rain behind a pile of logs — 'and what's so strange about that?'[83] It is statistically unremarkable, lots of people do it (the fact that they don't being yet another of incidental madness's fruits).

This achilles heel of likeness is Dostoevsky's way of maintaining a fantastic, incidentally mad pressure on identity throughout *The Double*, and also on time. 'For example' (*naprimer*) is the nub. Mr Golyadkin's first words in the novel, spoken to himself and/or to the figure in the mirror, are 'It would be no joke if I slipped up in some way today, if, for example, something were amiss — if some pimple had appeared out of the blue . . . '. We recognize the novel and the hero with no past ('out of the blue'), the exposed contextless existential 'today', the overall self/world instability (how is something amiss out there related to Mr Golyadkin slipping up?). And now 'for example' introduces a new factor. It pinpoints the self/world instability since it is precisely as an example of Mr Golyadkin slipping up that we *cannot* find and fix something going wrong in the world. Furthermore, something being amiss is not itself exemplary but a general thought about things going wrong, an example of which would be the sudden appearance of a pimple.

Turning to English versions of *The Double*, we find Constance Garnett omitting this 'for example' and Jessie Coulson (Penguin) transferring it to the genuinely exemplary pimple. Just as these are Mr Golyadkin's first words, so we have

---

[82] Ibid., p. 181.   [83] Ibid., pp. 142, 216, 273.

here the first case of what might be called systematic mis-translation — a resolve, no doubt largely unconscious, to normalize the crazy Russian text. It is always of diagnostic interest, this determination to normalize, since it reveals where the novel's demands are greatest, where most resistance is provoked. The non-exemplary 'for example' is only one point of entry into the world of systematic mistranslation, but a neat one, occurring here at the beginning, and through-out, and especially after the elopement letter. 'What am I, for example, going to do with myself now?' asks Mr Golyadkin. His nobody to be, the non-example, joins the 'here for example' of the chosen poetic haven or canopy, the dripping woodpile, itself ironically unique and non-exemplary. Both translators omit 'for example' on both occasions.[84] Yet again, it can't be an accident on their part any more than the uncomfortable 'for examples' were an accident on Dostoev-sky's in the first place.

The slogan of the Formalists goes: 'The perception of its form reveals the content of the work.' And it can't be denied that study of formal details like *The Double*'s non-exemplary 'for example' leads straight into a dislocated cosmos of the same, the different, and the like. No matter for the moment that the Petersburg Poem marks a youthful climax, that there is less to be got out of *Poor People*, and much less out of the post-Siberian work, along these lines.

From details, we go back to the elopement letter and the two versions which face each other across twenty years. Both versions yield up the gallant role which will not fit and the lovers' destination which no map will find. This nobody and nowhere are of the essence of the letter's parodic form and, simultaneously, of the novel's thematic substance. So far 1846 and 1866 agree. But then the removal in 1866 of all three occurrences of *deskat* together with the other signs of Mr Golyadkin's presence, frees, shares, transpersonalises the

---

[84]   Ibid., pp. 263, 271; *Notes from Underground* and *The Double*, pp. 264, 274. Compare Dostoevsky's text at *PSS*, Vol. I, pp. 212, 1. 24; 219, 1. 32. The very unsettling 'now for example' and 'for example, he might meet the stranger again' at Mr Golyadkin's first encounter with the Double have escaped the instinc-tive censorship of the translator, I suspect because of their subtlety (*The Eternal Husband*, p. 177).

chivalric–romantic dream. As I said, Mr Golyadkin is not 'our hero' for nothing.

And because he is our hero, we still sense the vestigial picaresque Adventures within the Petersburg Poem. At the last the two texts divide. 1846 ends with a no-nonsense, single-sentence paragraph:

And here, gentlemen, we conclude our history of the adventures of Mr Golyadkin.[85]

1866 scraps this ending and replaces it with something drifting, circular, above all surreal.[86] Mr Golyadkin meets up with his physician, Dr Rutenspitz. This is not their first encounter. Early in the novel (both versions) Mr Golyadkin decides on the spur of the moment to visit his doctor. In the spirit of the universal human fable, the footnote to *King Lear*, we aren't told what's wrong with him because nothing and everything is. He notes — a touch of nature — the odd circumstance that his heart always seems to beat on other people's staircases.[87] And so he climbs to the dreaded front door. Face to face with Dr Rutenspitz, struggling to maintain that he goes his own way and is the same as everybody else, Mr Golyadkin flounders in a morass of the merely typical, protesting he is an ordinary man very much *like* other people; while the doctor eyes him, puffing a cigar, and prescribing a new self:

'H'm — I was saying,' interrupted the doctor, 'that you require a radical transformation of your whole life, and in a certain sense a clean break in your character.'[88]

'I cannot be like him', not like this new self, Mr Golyadkin might have said. Instead he flounders. And Rutenspitz tells his patient not to mooch about at home — and 'don't make an enemy of the bottle'. And then another touch of nature:

---

[85] *PSS*, Vol. I, p. 431.

[86] Circularity, masked tautology, pseudo-contrast, are everywhere in this novel. We have met some of them. Here is another in the form of Mr Golyadkin's self-addressed slogan: 'If things go wrong stand your ground, if all goes well hold firm' (pp. 156, 167). Beneath the clowning surface, what is failure and what is success? They will double for each other, as will hunter and hunted and other opposites.

[87] *The Eternal Husband*, p. 143.   [88] Ibid., p. 145.

'I like quiet, Christian Ivanovich,' said Mr Golyadkin, casting a significant glance at the doctor and evidently searching for the words that
would express his meaning most successfully . . . .

A man in pain, and not pain in the abstract. A man who has
been told to go and have a stiff drink. We have all stood in
those shoes in our time. But the search for 'successful'
expression beyond that limpid 'I like quiet' is as true to the
linguistic and intellectual temper of the novel as it is to the
psychology of the moment. And Dostoevsky ensures that the
encounter between Mr Golyadkin and Dr Rutenspitz shall
end with a furtherance of one of *The Double*'s main concerns:
madness that is incidental to denial (through purely deductive
affirmation) of the past, and to a humour of astonishing
rareness:

> 'Tell me, please, where are you living now?'
> 'Where am I living now, Christian Ivanovich?'
> 'Yes — what I mean — I believe at one time you used to live —'
> 'Yes, Christian Ivanovich, I used to live, even at one time I used to
> live. I must have lived, mustn't I!' answered Mr Golyadkin, accom-
> panying his words with a little laugh and somewhat discomposing Dr
> Rutenspitz by his reply.[89]

Though done in a flash, the time-and-identity joke in the
consulting room seems to have more chance of proving a
graft that will take than the elopement letter in the eating-
house; and we await Dr Rutenspitz's return. This doesn't
occur until the end of the novel. In the 1846 version he is a
silent presence, after Mr Golyadkin has been dragged into the
girl's house by the Double, to become the object of general
curiosity and then to be escorted outside and borne off. But
in 1866 Dr Rutenspitz speaks. Next to the elopement letter
this is the most striking of all Dostoevsky's alterations — not
the fact that Dr Rutenspitz speaks, but how he speaks. For
in his first meeting with Mr Golyadkin (both texts) he spoke
rather colourless but correct Russian. Whereas now when
they meet at the end (1866) he speaks the broken Russian of
a member of the Petersburg German colony:

'You vill official quarters haf, vith firewood and *Licht* and service, the
vich you deserf not.'[90]

---

[89]   Ibid., p. 152.   [90]   Ibid., p. 284.

That's all he says. But it is enough to deny God's light to Mr Golyadkin, the light of Holy Russia, the beautiful *osveshchenie*, and condemn him to the hateful German *Licht*. It is also a foretaste of the singular instincts fostered by Dostoevsky's commonplace dislike of foreigners — the parajournalist again. And as to *The Double* itself, that sentence of broken Russian is our final warning, if we need one, not to underestimate the novel's formal-linguistic properties, or Dostoevsky's preparedness to break commonsense expectations on the wheel of his purpose. The changed Dr Rutenspitz behind the changed speech is an embarrassment to those whose critical watchword is Naturalism. The recourse they favour most is to see *The Double* as a careless — yes, careless — book, and to argue that Dostoevsky has forgotten Rutenspitz's early appearance by the time he brings him on at the end. But the thought struck R. I. Avanesov[91] that the second Dr Rutenspitz is a different man. I find that 'different' in this novel extremely piquant.

[91] 'Dostoevsky At Work On *The Double*', in *Tvorcheskaya istoriya*, ed. N. K. Piksanov (1927).

PART TWO: PRISONER

Chapter 3:   The Next Four Years

(i)

Four o'clock one morning in the spring of 1845 Dostoevsky was woken in his bed by two fellow writers who had been reading *Poor People* and couldn't wait to tell him how much they liked it. Four years later, almost to the day, he was again roused in the small hours. This time he saw a lieutenant-colonel in the light blue uniform of the secret police standing by his bed. He was asked to dress. Then the room was searched for further evidence of his connection (about which the authorities knew already) with a circle of literary men, musicians, and political theorists who had grouped themselves round one Petrashevsky, a student of French Socialism. The searchers don't appear to have found anything. But they sealed Dostoevsky's papers and took him off to prison, to solitary confinement in the Peter and Paul Fortress.

His friends had cause to fear then and there for his health and sanity — for his very life — no less than for his ultimate fate at the hands of the secret Commission of Enquiry into the affairs of the Petrashevsky Circle. In the four years between these two early morning adventures his record can have reassured nobody. He had proved himself unstable and morbidly self-concerned — like many another young writer, one might say. But Dostoevsky's psychophysical *faiblesse* was, or at any rate appeared, more serious than that. He showed signs of being really ill. Indeed the main reason why experts still argue about the origins of his epilepsy is that his own letters at this time, and accounts of him by others, are strewn with references to nervous attacks, spasms, seizures, fits, faintings, hallucinations.

When, therefore, he found himself in the so-called 'secret house', the most dreaded section of perhaps the most dreadful political prison in the history of the world, things looked as bad as possible. How they turned out can be very briefly sketched. Prison did not make a nice man of Dostoevsky, but it revealed qualities which no one could have guessed he had. At once he began pacing himself through months of solitude and waiting. He got his brother to send him a Bible and some Shakespeare, and he read *Jane Eyre* — 'an extremely good English novel'.[1] He made a plan of his own work and wrote a short story. His instinct for survival was beginning to manifest itself. While two of the thirty-four men arrested with him eventually went mad and a third tried to commit suicide, he concocted this carefree trifle of a story, *A Little Hero*, and clung mentally to the patch of sky visible through his cell window and to the seventeen trees in the yard outside.

And when eventually he was brought before the Commission and interrogated at length by its five members, he displayed presence of mind, courage, stamina, and loyalty to those who were accused with him of membership of a clandestine group harbouring criminal designs against Church and State. None of this was to be expected, least of all the apparently sourceless resilience of the sick and frail man. He never broke down. Others collapsed and grovelled and implicated friends to save their own skins. But he held firm. One catches a note of surprise in his own reflection to his brother: 'I anticipated much worse, and now I see there is within me such a store of vitality that it cannot be exhausted'; and long afterwards to his friend Baron Wrangel: 'meanwhile it all seems to me as if I'm just beginning to live. Funny, isn't it? The vitality of a cat.'[2] It is a vague notion but a fundamental one, this vitality of which he speaks and which sustained him through his condemnation to death and the often-described mock execution and last-minute staged reprieve which the Tsar took a personal interest in and to which he added some further cruel touches of his own.

Dostoevsky still didn't break down. He allowed himself the agonized cry that he would rather spend fifteen years in prison with a pen in his hand than four years without, but he also wrote that he had never experienced such spiritual energy as he felt within him now.[3] And then he schooled himself through four years of penal servitude with the same instinctive

---

[1]   Letter of 14 September 1849.
[2]   14 April 1865. Letter begun 31 March.
[3]   22 December 1849.

wisdom that he had shown during the months of solitary confinement and interrogation. He saw the crucial importance of work, manual work, the only sort of work he was allowed to do. And finally he emerged from Omsk fortress prison a fitter man, not just a physically stronger man, than he went in. The following passage from his novel about prison life is autobiographical:

I felt that work might be the saving of me, might build my health, my body. Continual mental anxiety, nervous fret, the foul air of the prison, might destroy me completely. I thought: 'Being in the open air more, working till I'm tired every day, getting used to carrying heavy weights — at any rate I shall save myself, I shall make myself strong, I shall leave prison healthy, in good heart, vigorous, and not old.' I was not mistaken: the work and exercise were very good for me. I looked with horror at one of my companions, another gentleman convict; he was wasting like a candle in prison. He entered at the same time as I did, still young, handsome and cheerful; and he left it half-shattered, grey-haired, a broken-winded wreck. 'No,' thought I, looking at him, 'I want to live and I will live.'[4]

Almost, 'I will live because I want to live'. This sheer and featureless vitality sustains his art as much as it does his life. It is both the immediate flickering nervous energy and the staying power of those huge novels. He called it inexhaustible, writing to his brother, which is only a small exaggeration. But before Siberia this had seemed very far from true. As I say, the record was bad. More or less everything was wrong — a nebulous everything which he later described as 'some sort of strange and unbearably torturing nervous illness'; and although he tries to pin the trouble to a time two years before he went to prison, the wider span suggested by 'the period of my various literary harassments and quarrels' in the same conversation squares much better with the rest of the evidence.[5]

(ii)

Let's go back to the spring morning in 1845 when two young men woke up a third to tell him how good his book was. Plenty of encouragement there. But *Poor People's* success

[4] *The House of the Dead*, p. 90.
[5] *F. M. Dostoevsky v vospominaniyakh sovremennikov*, ed. A. Dolinin (1964), Vol. II, p. 191.

with the general public did not, as it turned out, match the critical acclaim of avant-garde literary Petersburg. This might be called the first of the novelist's unspecified 'harassments'. Then with *The Double* came out-and-out failure, and the floodgates of an extraordinary conceit were opened. And of a whining vindictiveness, and hysteria.

Now I believe — it can't be proved, but the first section of my book is meant to encourage the thought — I believe that those two short novels almost broke their author's back. Or if you prefer, when *Poor People* and *The Double* were published almost simultaneously, Dostoevsky felt but only half recognized the very unpleasant sensation of being written out. This is not to explain, merely to gesture towards the psychophysical malaise of the next four years, and, while steering clear of biography, to raise two questions of art.

The first is contentious, or rather I have made it so by arguing at length that *Poor People* and *The Double* are complementary and contrasting studies, works of decisive genius for all their faults, closer in spirit to Eliot and Kafka and Beckett than to Gogol and Hoffmann, and, viewed together, a feat of sustained as well as brilliant application. Incidentally, therefore, I should expect these two novels to leave the man who wrote them exhausted.

The second question won't arouse serious disagreement since nobody sets great store by the ten short fictional pieces and the chunk of a full-length novel which Dostoevsky produced between *The Double* and going to prison in Siberia. This must be reckoned a considerable output in four years, and the novel, *Netochka Nezvanova*, was only interrupted by his arrest. But then he had to write to live, and he was improvident and easily exploited by sharp editors and publishers.

I share the conventional low estimate of this stuff, but holding the view I do of the first two novels I see what follows as largely overspill and aftermath rather than as so many more immature efforts. To my perception, a normalizing or naturalizing process takes place. This is not just a roundabout way of saying that the things written in these four years are less extraordinary than *Poor People* and *The Double*, though that is true of course. I will try to show what I mean.

Mr Golyadkin's 'If only tomorrow would hurry up and come' is indeed normal and natural, the kind of thing we all say; but without denying — while affirming! — this, Dostoevsky brings out the inherent craziness of such remarks. It is a matter of the conspiracy between the young poet and his reader. The reader gets the message and joins in the game because he has been shepherded in the crazy direction by nudges like the letter which was perhaps written tomorrow so Mr Golyadkin never got it. The objection that it is Mr Golyadkin who is crazy brings the rejoinder, inspired by Kafka, that his madness is incidental to the game, and the game does not include him. For example, the moment when he 'had no time' followed at once by 'in order to lose no time he took a cab' catches him in the classic posture of bustle about nothing.[6] But hidden from him, behind the crazy-but-ordinary way of imaging time, a little logical joke is being floated. If Mr Golyadkin had no time, then he had no time to lose. So he could have saved himself that fare.

There are no such jokes in the stories of the next four years. The crazy dimension is missing — not cut out, not suppressed, but simply missing for the reason that craziness is an affair of overall form. There's a certain relief and grateful repose in this new world where a clerk can reject seven hundred uncertain roubles and cling to a secure salary of three hundred 'where every rouble is a friend you can trust', and mean exactly that.[7] If Mr Devushkin or especially Mr Golyadkin were to call a rouble a friend (which they are quite capable of), they would not mean exactly that. Or rather, the 'authorless' novel in the one case and the conspiracy between young poet and reader in the other would conjure a further meaning and hold it hovering above the first.

Craziness may, in some contexts, be too throw-away. Mr Golyadkin's despairing 'Suppose I do know the meaning; but where does that lead?' is not so much crazy as metaphysical.[8] Compare 'What are they going to do with the grail when they find it?' Better still, compare Dostoevsky's own notebook

---

[6] *The Eternal Husband*, p. 212. [7] *White Nights*, pp. 181–2.
[8] *The Eternal Husband*, p. 228.

of the early Sixties where he is considering rewriting *The Double* and we find the following scrap of dialogue:

Golyadkin: 'Allow me to ask what all this means. Here I am straining every nerve. I'd like to have just a glimmer of what it all means.'
Junior: 'Why strain? Relax and everything will come right.'
Golyadkin: 'I'd still like a glimmer.'
Junior: 'But why? And besides, perhaps it means precisely nothing.'
Golyadkin: '*What!*'
Junior: 'As I say. Anything can happen and mean precisely nothing.'[9]

This desolate and comic little exchange brings the Twentieth Century back again with a rush, this time Wittgenstein on things in the world being what they are and happening as they do happen, and the meaning of the world lying outside the world.[10] It also helps to evoke that other shape or second sense hovering over Mr Golyadkin's 'Suppose I do know the meaning; but where does that lead?' But when two men find themselves under a woman's bed in a story of 1848, one of those overspill pieces, and one man complains *sotto voce* to the other that he doesn't even know his name, and the other whispers back 'Would you be any better off if you did know?', we laugh freely, lightly.[11] There is, and can be, no second sense. A second sense would wreck this happy pot-boiling salute to French farce. The young Dostoevsky's avid theatre-going is paying off handsomely. *This* question is just funny. It belongs to what I call a normalized world, where every secure-salary rouble is a friend you can trust.

So do the superficially very different roubles in yet another of these stories, *Mr Prokharchin*. Dostoevsky had read in a newspaper about a clerk who showed every sign of being desperately poor, but when he died he was found to have a thousand and thirty-five roubles, seventy and three-quarter copecks hidden in his mattress.[12] Indulging his quantifying and hyperbolic urge, Dostoevsky changed the sum to 'exactly two thousand four hundred and ninety-seven roubles and a half', but otherwise he put this bizarre circumstance straight into fiction, setting his hero in a rather Gogolian lodging-

---

[9] *PSS*, Vol. I, pp. 435–6. [10] *Tractatus Logico-Philisophicus*, 6.41.
[11] *An Honest Thief*, p. 290. [12] *PSS*, Vol. I, p. 503.

house and devising excellent, rather Gogolian jokes like letting Mr Prokharchin be hoaxed by a fellow-lodger into believing that the head of the office had decided the general deportment of his clerks was unsatisfactory, and that the remedy would be to dock their salaries and with the proceeds hire a hall in which they could be taught to dance.[13]

But French farce and Gogol do not prevent this normalized world of clerks and drunks and philanderers and petty crooks and down-and-outs from being recognizably Dostoevsky's. The banality (*poshlost*) which runs so deep in *Poor People* and *The Double* is itself a strong link. Take Mr Golyadkin's self-admonition, 'If things go wrong stand your ground, if all goes well hold firm'. The novel which contains it has set him abustle in a circular fret since he woke up and consulted the image in the round mirror on Page One — this is the second sense hovering over Mr Golyadkin's words. But it is also true that those words hit off the vapid yet vicious advice columns of the women's magazines, the astrological folly of the daily papers, even the sweet nothings of actual daily intercourse. Such things — masked tautologies, non-sequitur fatuities, and so forth — fascinated Dostoevsky from first to last. They have no obvious bearing on the deeper realism which he later, and insistently, claimed for his writing, but they are very much part of real life.

Moreover, this early work lying between the first two novels and Siberia is not banal in some vaguely Dostoevskian sense, but in a precise one. The story of the miserly clerk with the money in his mattress *is* banal, *is* routine newspaper fodder, *is* the sort of grotesquely dreary episode nineteenth-century urban life throws up all the time. But what is precisely Dostoevskian about it? What caught his eye as he turned over the pages of *The Northern Bee*? The mattress, surely. Just as there are no healthy stoves or samovars in his books, so there are no comfortable mattresses, no beds or couches that are there to be slept on as opposed to throw oneself down on, be ill on, have nightmares on, lie brooding sullenly or frenziedly on, or leap up from. The mattress therefore. And, surely, the money. I spoke of money lying

---

[13] *White Nights* pp. 291–325.

about in Dostoevsky, at the mercy of the first human will to bump into it.[14] One character throws it on the fire, another insults a girl with it. This one stuffs it into his mattress. What Dostoevsky read fitted what he had in him to write. The result is not an important work, but unmistakably his. When Mr Prokharchin dies and the other lodgers trace a mysterious trickle of money to a rent in his mattress, and the room becomes an inferno of flying horsehair and flock and jangling silver and twists of paper containing small change, we know where we are.

So with the two men under the bed, and their Double Act. One has nowhere to go, he is a lover caught under the wrong bed, he is stuck here. The other, also under the wrong bed, has nobody to be, he is a jealous husband who cannot admit himself to be a husband at all — 'I'm not married' — 'I'm not acting for myself';[15] but the reader knows he has nobody else to act for, he is setting himself up as his own stand-in, a new twist to the doubling game. And I mean game. There is nothing to wax solemn about, any more than with Prokharchin and his mattress and money. In a later novel there will be, however; for while the husband standing in for himself under the bed is a lighthearted variant of Mr Golyadkin telling his boss not to worry because he's really somebody else, the same cannot be said of Prince Myshkin, the idiot who gives *The Idiot* its title. Myshkin is Dostoevsky's attempt at an idiot who is also wise — wise not because he isn't really an idiot, but wise as well. It is the earnest, I would say overdriven, aim of the novelist to sustain both the wise man and the idiot in one credible hero.

This Myshkin attempt could itself be described as a normalizing or naturalizing of *The Double*, where it is crucial (though the point seems at first sight dauntingly unnovelistic) that the Golyadkins Senior and Junior should be always separate and always identical but never alike. In real life identical means exactly alike, but in Dostoevsky's 'abstract' fable the category of like is excluded because it not only admits of degree but invokes and positively insists on degree. Two things are or are not identical whereas they are more or

---

[14] p. 7, above.   [15] *An Honest Thief*, pp. 263, 294.

less alike, and inside the fable the fear and fact of getting mixed up mustn't budge as they would budge if the thought that the identical is the exactly alike, and that the exactly alike can be made less so by some such simple ploy as putting a flower in its buttonhole, were to cross the mind of the book. It never does — once Mr Golyadkin has committed his act of hubris in the opening pages by proposing to be not himself but somebody 'strikingly like' himself. Thus he calls down ruin in the shape of the Double who is never 'strikingly like' him, who is always 'another Mr Golyadkin but exactly the same as himself'.[16] And so, true to an immemorial pattern of story-telling, he gets what is coming to him. And at the shock of first encounter with a different but identical Mr Golyadkin he does a Devushkin — that is 'he even began to doubt his own existence' — for the one and only time in the novel. To ask what he has done to deserve such a fate would be falsely to personalize and moralize the tragicomical *Weltanschauung* which I have pictured as nowhere to go and nobody to be. And therefore if we want to speak of Mr Golyadkin's hubris, we must borrow Dostoevsky's adjective once more and qualify that hubris as abstract.

In fact Dostoevsky gave 'abstract' to his Underground Man, the Man who called Petersburg the most abstract city in the world. But, as he tells us, he had already created his supreme underground type in the person of Mr Golyadkin Junior (the Double) long before he wrote *Notes from Underground*.[17] There is thus an explicit underground and abstract link between pre- and post-Siberian Dostoevsky, as we can confirm for ourselves by laying the *Notes* and *Double* side by side. Apprehended together, they hang together; they are thin, theoretical, untypical, and unpopular, for all their genius. Whereas the opening chapter of *The Idiot* is none of these things. Arriving in the train from Warsaw, Myshkin with bundle and inadequate travelling cloak is absolutely 'there', and the mixture of awe and ridicule he brings out in his companions strikes to the heart of one of the great railway-carriage scenes in world literature — even *Anna*

---

[16] *The Eternal Husband*, p. 179 and subsequently.
[17] pp. 56–84, above.

Karenina's are no finer — and reflects the duality of idiot and seer who (the others elicit) has literally nowhere to go, and who (as the novel unfolds) proves literally impotent and in a wider sense powerless to find somebody, anybody, not just Nastasya Filippovna's husband, to be. But none of this comes across at the outset as theoretical. Myshkin is not with us (as we say both of idiots and of seers) which makes him all the more 'there' in the railway carriage on his own dual terms.

The unnamed antihero of the *Notes* is loneliness itself and a powerful underground link with the early work, whereas Myshkin belongs to a whole gallery of above-ground continuities. These are not abstract. They are humanized, what I have called normalized, and normalized on the grandest scale; they are the obvious things to point to when people ask what it means to say Dostoevsky worked his way backwards into the nineteenth-century novel. In breaking new ground for their creator these characters find common ground with their international contemporaries. Apply the yardstick of French, English, and Russian fiction, and you can date within a decade or two the narrative of Myshkin's arrival in Petersburg. Savour the implications of 'Suppose I do know the meaning; but where does that lead?' — and you can't.

Samuel Beckett latched on to *The Double* as others have to the work of Büchner and Kleist; he saw it could help him say his own say. *Crime and Punishment*, *The Idiot*, *The Possessed*, *The Brothers Karamazov*, are not so much formally proleptic as prophetic in vision, prefiguring such pseudo-élites as our media men and terrorists, but equally our inert and superstitious millions, our hedonism, apathy, intellectual vandalism, and a kind of senseless public noise: so that when I first saw the slot in a juke-box into which you put money to buy silence, something in me responded to the madness and terrible humour of it by exclaiming 'Ah, Dostoevsky!' At the same time the four novels I have named are as much novels of their age as *Great Expectations* is. Anyhow, almost as much. Which is not to imply that Dostoevsky's gift becomes tamed; nor that doubling, duality, *dédoublement*, cease to be of the imaginative essence. When Ivan Karamazov tries to nail his alter-ego visitant with 'You are the incarnation of myself', the thirty-five years since Mr Golyadkin met his Double seem a very small span. But that is because we are isolating the paranormal, and indeed abstract and underground, strand in the enormous novel which contains Ivan. When we leave that strand to take its chance with everything else in *Karamazov*, including other sorts of doubling, the gap widens again.

Dostoevsky himself can be found contemplating that gap, that Siberian divide, in two notebooks of the early Sixties where he ponders rewriting *The Double*. He had read and been favourably impressed by Tolstoy's early work — 'Who is this Tolstoy?' — while in exile, and the notebooks propose to render 'the innermost secrets of a bureaucratic soul *à la* Tolstoy'.[18] A tall order. The notebooks give a few scattered hints as to how it might have been carried out. 'Mr Golyadkin looked with hatred at Junior snorting and splashing at the wash-stand' while they shared a room. Dostoevsky was pleased with that detail. He repeated it later in the same notebook, adding that Mr Golyadkin believed the Double 'was snorting on purpose to annoy him'. It's clear he had read Tolstoy's *Childhood* trilogy with profit. But in fact, as we have seen, he moved in the opposite direction, with the result that the 1866 *Double* is even barer and less circumstanced than the text of 1846. The urge towards such promising novelistic country as a man's irritation at another's washing habits was not just resisted but routed.

Yet there remained other, un-Tolstoyan ways of fleshing out the 'abstract' fable. In those same notebooks Dostoevsky sketches a Golyadkin Junior who might be feared to know 'all the secrets of Senior, as though he were his conscience personified'; there are always things which 'each of us has and each of us hides, as secrets, from everybody else'. That is a large and very human thought. Formulated in the early Sixties, it comes to creative fulfilment at the end of the decade in *Crime and Punishment*. It may even have helped Dostoevsky to clinch *The Double* as Petersburg Poem, boldly to sharpen its youthful focus and then leave it alone in the

---

[18] *PSS*, Vol. I, pp. 432–6; letter of 18 January 1856.

knowledge that the realization of 'conscience personified' lay elsewhere; the doubling motif of self-flight and self-pursuit must, if *conscience* is to bear its due human import, be embedded in some rapt, self-engrossed detective story like the first Oedipus play or *Macbeth*. And that is how it turned out — with such success that Dostoevsky decided, not for the first time in his life, that form and vision would invert and that an even more ambitious manhunt might be mounted with an innocent quarry. In Dmitry Karamazov they catch and condemn the wrong man. But also the right one, since in this final doubling phase we are all guilty before each other all the time, whether or not we acknowledge it. The eldest Karamazov brother does acknowledge it.

As I interpret 'conscience personified', Raskolnikov the murderer–hero of *Crime and Punishment* is the relationship of Golyadkin and Double humanized and grandly normalized *à la* Dostoevsky. So is Dmitry Karamazov who hasn't murdered anyone. It matters as regards novelistic ways and means that he hasn't. It is important for a whole range of technical problems. Not, however, for the voicing of self-denunciation, self-repudiation, achieved self-estrangement, because, as Dmitry keeps telling people with raging, blinding simplicity, he hated his father and often wanted to kill him.

The self-division of these two Conscience Characters needs stressing, as it does with the Seer-Idiot Myshkin and Ivan Karamazov *vis-à-vis* his anti-self; but it is equally the case that Raskolnikov and Dmitry are searching for clues to lead them to their single true natures: the detection motif cuts both ways. So does the confessional posture throughout Dostoevsky. At the outset, in *Poor People*, Mr Devushkin comes clean to Varenka about his 'fearful lapses' because, he says, he wants to feel better. The urge to say sorry and feel better doesn't mean he is not sorry; this is the moral universe of 'You first, me first' which we entered with Marmeladov's 'I married her because I could not bear to see such suffering' (and having entered it, we understood that we had unknowingly brought it with us — the deeper realism). As I say, the confessional posture also cuts both ways. Confession is the nub, not repentance, and in this same first novel a remarkable thought, irrelevant to narrative, floating free of character, simply bumps into the reader: 'They say repentance eases the soul. On the contrary!'[19] There, if anywhere, I believe I see the author's ugly mug.

To be more precise, his ugly young mug. In the long term, beyond the general psychological truth that repentance clamours painfully for expression, lies the fact that the inwardness of a contrite heart *à la* Tolstoy is not for this novelist. His idea of projecting conscience on the plane of a busy bustling prank-playing Double is itself a hint that states of mind must be furiously activated in order to be fictionally realized. Dostoevsky and Tolstoy divide here rather as Dickens and George Eliot do, though on first consideration Dostoevsky cannot match Dickens's extrovert flair. His people often appear pointlessly demonstrative, threatening the 'sudden opprobrious act' of the bad child in Auden's poem. Or they bore and embarrass with their wallowing in shame, their self-denigration, and their bowing down before each other and kissing of hands and feet. That they are easing their souls, articulating repentance, adopting confessional postures, will not satisfy the reader who has arrived straight from the joys of Dickens. Still, it is true. And it characterizes a mode of extroversion which is positively Dostoevsky's as well as negatively un-Dickensian.

Raskolnikov's *'It was I who killed the old pawnbroker woman and her sister Lizaveta with an axe, and robbed them'* is the real conclusion of *Crime and Punishment*. The rest is Epilogue. It has taken him hundreds of pages to find, simultaneously, these words and the beginnings of access to himself. He is no Dmitry Karamazov, for Dmitry strikes free and uncringing confessional postures, as we have just seen, and the fact that he does so blazons a certain stupendous affirmativeness which goes to the root of Dostoevsky's way with him, and of his with us. Stavrogin in *The Possessed*, different again, does not confess at all. Many have suggested that he wants to but cannot. The truer thought is that he cannot want. Nothing holds him to life. He has left wanting behind. It is all he can do to summon the will to kill himself.

Indeed 'summon the will' is not quite right either; he

---

[19] *The Gambler*, p. 155.

drifts into it. Then what of extroversion, confessional postures, and so on? Heathcliff, near his end, is like a man who
has to remind himself to breathe. That is a wonderful imaginative *coup*, but it is not for Dostoevsky whose first move was
to compose the chapter 'At Tiknon's' which is often Englished
as 'Stavrogin's Confession'. Then he deleted it, so there is no
confession and a cloud of unshriving hangs over Stavrogin,
the converse of 'faults forgiven' in late Shakespeare and
equally impossible to surpass in power of vision and execution.
Stavrogin leaves behind a letter in which he articulates the
'cannot want' of being neither held by life nor drawn to
death. 'One can go on arguing about everything for ever,' he
writes in sweet-toned and weary rumination which reminds
me of nothing in art so much as 'There are many things I
should like to write to you about, but I feel it is useless' in
the letter found on Vincent van Gogh after he had shot
himself out in the cornfields.

And he has another mode of extroversion, close to the
prank-playing Double: Audenesque and very sudden opprobrious acts like pretending to somebody he has a secret
to whisper to him and then biting the proferred ear, or
responding to the club bore who has just said he won't be
led by the nose by striding up to him and seizing his nose and
pulling him across the carpet. God knows why, but we
tremble for Stavrogin as we laugh. He is sleepwalking, drifting
into death itself, and the well-soaped rope and spare nail of
his suicide don't belie the drift. No doubt he dresses every
morning with the same finicky half-absent care he displays
when he hangs himself, but nobody who has got this far in
The Possessed will suppose he wants to dress.

(iii)

One of Mr Golyadkin's parrot-cries is 'Why not simply give
up?'[20] He never does. And alas, it can't be done — a root-and-
branch impossibility which we easily miss the force of
because, as so often, 'our hero's' little sentence is the kind of
thing we all say. It looks unremarkable. If, though, simply

[20]   *The Eternal Husband*, p. 212, for example.

giving up were coupled with the idea of suicide, we would begin to take notice.

It betokens *The Double*'s formal discipline that this quite natural coupling never occurs; giving up must remain a naked proposal in a speculative void; the abstract character of Mr Golyadkin's despair must not be compromised. We shall meet the same rigour and limitation in *Notes from Underground*. But in the later novels which we have been glancing at, *Crime and Punishment* and the others, giving up and suicide are very much associated, both in the straightforward resolve to make an end of it all, and in the counter-notion that suicide is the opposite of giving up: suicide is the one action a man can put his hand to 'in the full sense' as Mr Golyadkin would say. It is complete and untouchable and perfectly the doer's own, whereas everything else is messy half-affirmation. So the purposive suicides will argue. But not Stavrogin. We don't know what he is thinking; he is entirely perplexing and no less imaginable for that. Because he is so extraordinary he presents the grand normalizing and humanizing process in late Dostoevsky at its most paradoxically satisfying. It's a long way from the spare intellectualism and youthful thrust of 'Why not simply give up?' to 'One can go on arguing about everything for ever', but the road is continuous.

And because of this continuity it is just as futile to try and make Stavrogin's mental oddness the centre of attention as it is Mr Golyadkin's. From first to last madness is incidental, as I keep saying; though only in later Dostoevsky does it become what Kafka called it: a very delicate and fruitful method of characterization.

To characterize is in my sense to normalize, and in the overspill and aftermath pieces of the 1840s a lower, catch-penny normalizing takes place, as one would expect, and as I pictured that solid world where every rouble is a friend you can trust. Madness itself affords an index, since the pre-Siberian fiction rather goes in for studies of derangement which are central, the opposite of incidental, and sometimes, without intention, comically so. 'He is mad!' the hero tells the heroine of *The Landlady*, speaking of her father. 'She is mad!' he soon concludes about her too. That is in the magazine text. When he published the story in volume form Dostoevsky saw what he had done and cut the second exclamation.[21] The perfunctory effect does not make the madness incidental. Nor does the care which he lavished elsewhere on madness make it interesting. *Netochka Nezvanova*, both as interrupted novel and reshaped story, abounds in sick minds dotingly observed, sometimes given straight and sometimes imaged as snapped violin strings or shattered vases, and always nugatory.

But madness in *A Faint Heart* (which is certainly more than mere overspill) gives us the exception which proves the 1840s rule. The story viewed as a whole comprises an obvious amalgam of *Poor People* and *The Double*: poverty and love, a copying clerk, a copying task, a boss to be obeyed, a crisis, a disaster. The crisis is a particularly neat example of catch-penny normalizing; there's a deadline to be met over the copying; it's a real deadline though it and the copying itself turn out to be unimportant. The hero fails to meet the deadline and goes mad.

Now the interesting thing is that he doesn't go mad through his striving and failing to complete a job which he believes to be of great moment. All this is to one side. We are faced at the beginning with a total and unexplained collapse of will which prevents him getting down to the copying, and we have to proceed from there. Gradually *A Faint Heart* shapes the paradox that the trouble with its clerk is his good fortune. He is going to be married, he loves and is loved, and everything appears set fair. There is just this little copying job; but he's not worried, he's got plenty of time to do it. Yet something stops him. This something is the point of the story. It can be given a familiar look by remarking that he feels he doesn't deserve his happiness, he is too happy, it hurts to be so happy when the whole world is not happy with him. And indeed these things do get said. The distinctive twist comes with his experiencing the sense (to be rendered famous by D. H. Lawrence through Tom Brangwen early in *The Rainbow*) that 'I did not belong to myself'.[22] To whom then does he

---

[21]   *PSS*, Vol. I, p. 454; *The Gambler*, pp. 294, 306. Constance Garnett gives us the cancelled 'She is mad!' (p. 306) because she is translating from one of the bad posthumous editions which print the magazine text.

[22]   *White Nights*, p. 179.

belong? He rationalizes this question, and his own malaise, in terms of a debt of gratitude. He asks the friend who shares his flat:

> 'Now what if gratitude, thankfulness, is asked of one — and one can't give it?'
> 'Vasya, I don't understand you at all.'
> 'I have never been ungrateful,' Vasya went on softly, as though speaking to himself, 'but if I'm incapable of expressing everything I feel, then it's as if — it works out as if I really am ungrateful, Arkady, and this is killing me.'[23]

It doesn't kill him, it sends him mad, and thus the denouement of the story bends back upon its title: there is some frailty of spirit that disables Vasya, first of all causing him to put off and put off the copying job, and then to terrify his friend who sees him, as he thinks, at last getting down to it — but no, his dry pen is flashing over sheet after sheet of blank paper.

So the sense of not belonging to himself culminates in a burden of gratitude which crushes him, sending him off his head. I say this is more than mere overspill from *Poor People* and *The Double*. My real reason is my start almost of fear at ' "I have never been ungrateful," Vasya went on softly . . .'; this is the very clasp of Dostoevsky's hand. In *A Faint Heart* and some other stories in the late 1840s the novelist is beginning to open up the relationship between society and single human beings in new and surprising and potentially important directions.

Once again our warning sign is Dostoevsky's act of conscious limitation and stern artistic self-discipline. His first significant alteration to *The Double* was to cut a passage in the magazine text introducing Mr Golyadkin as a man who makes 'certain romantic assumptions about himself', who lives a make-believe life by burrowing inside an unwritten 'most fanciful novel' where he overcomes all difficulties, wins honour, magnanimously forgives enemies and shines in every way.[24] This gets cut as part of the overall stripping process which leaves Mr Naked barer than bare in the final version and allows the Elopement Letter (Sir Golyadkin

[23] Ibid., p. 199.   [24] *PSS*, Vol. I, p. 335.

to the rescue) to leap out of nowhere bearing its full creative charge.

Of course Mr Golyadkin's fantasy existence, first evoked, then cut out, is a business of *The Double*'s internal organization. But the way we are looking at the excised passage now is from the standpoint of 'the dreamer', a figure who crops up repeatedly in the stories which follow. He is somebody who either fails to cope with life or else opts out of it. Vasya in *A Faint Heart* is overtly the first type, though his friend lets fall the thought — again purest Dostoevsky — that he is 'simply trying to find an excuse to go off his head'.[25] Also, while he presents himself as the frail spirit of the story's title, he is equally and insistently 'a dreamer, and that's a bad thing too'.[26]

Dreaming in these stories is always what Vasya's friend succinctly calls 'a bad thing', though the dreamer may be in two minds about the viciousness of dreaming and his own shaky state. One part of the dreamer hero of *White Nights* thinks he is fine as he wanders through the streets of 'his' Petersburg, humming to himself 'like every happy man who has no friends or kind acquaintances with whom to share his joy', holding phantom conversations with the houses he passes and living inside the books he reads.[27] *The Landlady*'s dreamer hero had been completely wrapped up in 'the first ecstasy, the first fever, the first delirium of the artist' — until he was forced to change his lodging. And then real life began 'to weigh on him, to inspire in him a sort of involuntary dread and awe'.[28]

Real life, reality, means other people. Vasya doesn't belong to himself, he belongs to the human family, that is where his debt of gratitude is lodged. The hero of *White Nights* ought to be in touch with other human beings instead of, or anyhow as well as, house-fronts. The *Landlady* man is, in Wordsworth's phrase, 'housed in a dream, at distance from the Kind'. The first-person narrator of *Netochka Nezvanova*, a little girl born into the classic no-home nightmare of a Dostoevsky household, holds her own hand (so to speak) in

[25] *White Nights*, p. 212. [26] Ibid., p. 208.
[27] Ibid., pp. 2–6. [28] *The Gambler*, p. 251.

her dreaming, to ensure *that* much companionship: and here's a bad state of affairs too, though we aren't meant to blame her for it.

The late 1840s produced these studies in solitude and society, tending in their opting-out aspect towards the Underground Man in *Notes from Underground*, and in their portrayal of failure to cope towards Raskolnikov the murderer-hero of *Crime and Punishment*. 'A weak man cannot stand alone' rounds off *The Landlady* (as it might *A Faint Heart*) like a motto which will blossom into Raskolnikov's discovery that we all prove ourselves weak in the very attempt to stand alone. And *The Landlady* continues: 'Give a weak man freedom — he himself will shackle it and hand it back to you.'[29] The Grand Inquisitor's drift in *Karamazov* could not be summarized more neatly. But *Karamazov* is bigger than the Inquisitor; it enfolds and completes those thoughts about freedom and weakness in a revelation of universal frailty like but distinct from that of *Crime and Punishment*. We are all weak with the weakness of mutual guilt, all of us before each other, so in our weakness is our human solidarity. The novel shows forth silently (the words aren't said) what Vasya had intimated more than thirty years before. We do not belong to ourselves.

A Faint Heart gets little mileage out of this thought, but that doesn't prevent it being more than overspill from *Poor People* and *The Double*. The same is true of *The Landlady*'s weakness and freedom motto. And, of course, to be more than overspill is not to lose connection with what went before. A circumstantial terror of freedom might supply, and in the mature novels will supply, the concrete human filling which needlepoint Will facing contextless Choice in *The Double* is without. From the start, though, a single apprehension was astir.

So it was when the young poet guided Mr Devushkin's quill pen, and formed the words 'I am after all a man, in heart and mind a man'. A clear glimpse of the authorial face; and it comes as no surprise many years later, in the throes of gambling disasters, bills unpaid and unpayable, himself

<hr>

[29] Ibid., p. 313.

prisoner in a cheap hotel bedroom with clothes, watch, even wedding ring bound for pawn, when Dostoevsky emerges from a raging passion of self-abasement to remind his wife 'But surely I too am a human being! Surely there is something human in me too.'[30] This is idiosyncratic and central; it means more than that he is not altogether a brute; the lifelong search for 'the human in the human being' is here self-directed; and moving sideways into the fiction of the previous year, 1866, we find Raskolnikov rallying himself to acknowledge his crime:

Again the same rubbish, the same eggshells on the spiral staircase, again the doors of the flats wide open, again the same kitchens with fumes and stench coming from them. Raskolnikov had not been here since that last time. His legs were numb and were giving way under him, but they kept moving. He stopped for a moment to take breath, to collect himself, to enter *as a man*.[31]

On the surface Raskolnikov is trying to summon a minimal human dignity and self-possession. Underneath, as Dostoevsky's italics indicate in a typographical gesture embracing the whole novel — compare the italics of the confession itself — underneath there is more to being, or rather becoming, a man than that. Raskolnikov is striving to rejoin the human family. The struggle is agonized. He must pay his debt of guilt acknowledged and proceed to punishment in its public aspect.

Then is Raskolnikov not a man until the debt gets paid? This kind of question divides the mature novels which never voice it from the stories of the late 1840s which play with it incessantly. The hero of *White Nights* makes a show of being forthright with the girl who brings him into painful contact with reality, with herself that is, with another person, or persons, as always: 'A dreamer — if you want a detailed definition — a dreamer is not a human being.'[32] It's typical of him that he should proceed negatively in this way, and typical of Dostoevsky's youthful Gogolian humour that nothing 'detailed' should be forthcoming. Typical proves a

---

[30] Letter of 24 May 1867.   [31] *Crime and Punishment*, p. 464.
[32] *White Nights*, p. 15. The thought of the dreamer not being a human being reappears almost word for word in a piece of Dostoevsky's 1847 journalism, as do a number of *White Nights* witticisms like the dreamer being reduced to celebrating the anniversary of his own sensations (*PSS*, Vol. XVIII, pp. 11–34).

word to hang on to. Instead of giving details, the *White Nights* hero keeps reiterating that he is 'a type', the type of 'the ridiculous man' or rather non-man, 'a sort of neuter creature'.[33] We recall that Vasya was a type too, the faint-heart type, and that his crushing debt of gratitude to humanity very dimly foreshadowed Raskolnikov's struggle up the spiral staircase to acknowledge guilt, and Dmitry Karamazov's acceptance of Siberia for all the innocent suffering of the world. And apart from the dreamers and faint-hearts and ridiculous men, Polzunkov is thrust before us very insistently in the story which bears his name as the type of 'the voluntary buffoon',[34] and Mr Prokharchin joins the oppressed little clerks of the first two novels as the type of 'man-rag' — though all three resist the typification, and Mr Golyadkin adds the characteristic rider that even if he were nothing but a rag he would still be a special sort of rag, 'a rag with feelings'.[35]

And what is more he would be a rag 'possessed of pride', says Mr Golyadkin, meaning the status-seeking pride (*ambitsiya*) he likes to attribute to himself.[36] This is the social equivalent of the private self-loving vanity (*samolyubie*) which Mr Devushkin takes upon his head again and again in *Poor People*. The distinction between the two words, their separate apportionment to the two novels, is much too systematic to be fortuitous. Dostoevsky may have been thinking his way towards a paper called 'Individuality and Egoism' which he later read to members of the Petrashevsky Group. The text is lost, but we have a summary given by him in the course of interrogation by the Commission of Enquiry: 'I wished to show that there exists among us more pride (*ambitsiya*) than true human dignity, and that we ourselves tend to reduce our own stature, to detract from our own individuality, by falling into petty vanity (*samolyubie*) and egoism . . .'.[37] Potentially a grand theme. Vasya's thought about not belonging to himself begins to open out hugely — only in our minds, though, and perhaps in the young Dostoevsky's, but nowhere in the fiction of the 1840s. The

[33] Ibid., pp. 14–15.   [34] Ibid., p. 234.
[35] *The Eternal Husband*, p. 210.
[36] Translated 'dignity' by Constance Garnett (p. 210).
[37] *Dostoevsky v protsesse petrashevtsev*, by N. F. Belchikov (1971), p. 107.

central poetic and novelistic realities of *Poor People* and *The Double* were nobody to be and nowhere to go. And now in the follow-up stories we have this odd fussing about types in relation to not being, or not fully and truly being, a man. One who is a type resembles others of the same type. Overspill again, this time from Mr Golyadkin's dread of resemblance and from the whole elaboration, so unpromisingly, implausibly theoretic on first encounter, of separate and identical but never like. 'I cannot be like him' is a bodiless cry from *The Double*'s abstract heart.

Chapter 4:   The Dead House

(i)

I want to begin with a large and lucid sequence from *The House of the Dead* which is also technically interesting. The convicts have decided to release a wounded eagle they have captured and tried and failed to tame:

One day after dinner when the drum had sounded for work, they took the eagle holding his beak because he began to fight savagely, and carried him out of the prison. They got to the rampart. The dozen or so men making up the party were filled with curiosity to see where the eagle would go. Strange to say, they were all somehow pleased, as if they themselves had received a share of freedom.

'Look at the brute, you're good to him and he keeps biting you!' said the man who was holding him, eyeing the fierce bird almost with affection.

'Let him go, Mikitka!'

'So it's just pie in the sky to him, everything else is. Give him freedom, real free freedom.'

They threw the eagle down from the wall into the steppe. It was a cold, murky day in late autumn. The wind whistled over the bare steppe and sounded through the yellow, withered, tussocky grass. The eagle set off in a straight line, flapping his injured wing as if in a hurry to get away from us no matter where. The convicts followed his head with curiosity as it flitted through the grass.

'There he goes!' said one thoughtfully.

'And he's not looking round!' added another. 'He hasn't looked round once, boys, he just runs on!'

'Did you expect him to come back and say thank you?' remarked a third.

'It's freedom, bet your life. He smells freedom.'

'Sure it's freedom.'

'Can't see him now, boys.'

'What are you standing for? March!' shouted the guards, and everybody trudged on to work in silence.[1]

That passage begins with a 'they', then has an 'us' tucked away in the middle, and ends with 'everybody'. Were it not for the 'us' one would assume that Dostoevsky is using

---

[1] *The House of the Dead*, pp. 230–1.

conventional third-person narrative. This 'us' causes a percep-
tible if slight disturbance, turning the final 'everybody' into
an all of us as well as an all of them. It insists that the narrator
is somehow inside his story; he must be one of the 'us' as
well as external to the 'them'.

Constance Garnett writes of the drum sounding for 'us to
go to work', and she continues that 'we got to the rampart'.
Neither the 'us' nor the 'we' are in the Russian text, but it's
easy to see how she came by them. Immediately before the
sounding of the prison drum is an 'I' who tries to make
friends with the eagle and who describes the attitude of 'the
convicts' to the fierce bird. Both the 'I' and 'the convicts' do
occur in the Russian, and if we had taken this passage instead
of the one I translated, everything would suggest first-person
narrative at its most untroubled. Faced with such a scene, no
wonder Mrs Garnett added — and elsewhere subtracted —
'we' and 'us' when she felt like it.

The freeing of the eagle happens near the end of the book,
but this I/We/They/Everybody flexibility goes back almost
to the beginning and pertains to *The House of the Dead*'s
fictional substance no less than to its narrative mode, as the
'dozen or so men' of the translated passage will illustrate.[2]
They are simultaneously 'us' and 'them'. They are not,
however, the 'everybody' at the end, because the hitherto
unmentioned guards are also in the party that moves off to
work beyond the perimeter rampart, thus closing one of the
finest chapters in the novel. Looked at one way this is a
matter of dry technique, of calculated authorial stance.
Looked at another, the same object of scrutiny reveals an
abiding aspect of prison life. 'Of course! Those everpresent
guards!' the reader thinks as he suddenly comes upon them,
and turns the page and reads on.

With this narrative flexibility in *The House of the Dead* the
now not so young poet made perhaps the biggest single step
of his writing career. *Poor People* was an 'authorless' novel
in letters, and *The Double* a conspiracy between reader and
poet behind the backs of 'our' incidentally mad hero and the

[2]   Mrs Garnett's 'twelve' introduces a false precision. She has forgotten that
when a numeral follows the noun it governs, as here, it suggests an approximate
number.

pretend plain tale. The stories which follow in the late 1840s show an extreme restlessness which boils down to disquiet over straightforward first-person and third-person narrative: the obliqueness, the distanced or removed procedures, of the first two short novels pointed the right road for Dostoevsky, but he couldn't be sure where it was going; and he seems to have regarded the *deskat* device as both crucial to *The Double* and not to be repeated, except in one merest bagatelle which he wrote in collaboration, and where the formulaic 'our hero' also recurs.[3] He hesitated. He began *Netochka Nezvanova* in the third person, then scrapped that plan and put the story in the mouth of a female narrator engaged in long childhood retrospect.[4] The hero of *White Nights* actually asks permission of the girl he falls in love with 'to tell my story in the third person' — to escape his feeling of shame, he says, but we know better.[5] *A Novel in Nine Letters* (in fact a very short story) makes a perfunctory return to authorless-ness. *Polzunkov* adopts the device of a story within a story, and the 'I' who introduces the main narrative then stands rather oddly to one side of it, at the elbow of the chief characters. Nothing comes of this peripheral 'I' in *Polzunkov*, but one recalls the mature novels, and especially the dilating and contracting 'I' who is the elder Verkhovensky's friend in *The Possessed* and the most flexible, most resourceful of narrative vehicles, now keyhole vantage-point, now from an upper window, now metropolitan news, now provincial gossip: and one is conscious of things to come. *Polzunkov* seems to have suggested to Dostoevsky the idea of a slot-round narrative frame which he could use as often as he wanted. Certainly he planned a cycle of stories 'From the Diary of an Unknown Man'; how many we don't know, but by the time he was arrested he had completed four (two of which he later ran into one), and the fragment of a fifth survives.[6]

When a novelist tells you he is a mere middleman purveying the contents of a stranger's diary he distances himself from his narrative by feigning helpless unaccountability; he can't

[3] *PSS*, Vol. I., pp. 321–33.   [4] Ibid., Vol. II, p. 495.
[5] *White Nights*, p. 18.   [6] *PSS*, Vol. II, pp. 479, 482, 519.

be asked to justify what he says he didn't write, and, honest man that he is pretending to be, he can't bring himself to meddle with somebody else's work, however obscure or offensive or plain boring it may strike the reader. In itself an obvious and wooden ploy, the stranger's diary device does not look promising. Being pinned to a text like this looks the opposite of flexibility. In fact the seeds of flexibility, of the unprivileged standpoint and the inspired guess, of seeing through chinks but now and then totally as if the sky had been ripped open, of things dipping and ducking amazingly, out of control, then folding their wings in lucid stasis — these seeds are carried in the very business of feigning helplessness. Its outcome will be the foaming prose of those huge exhilarating Dostoevsky paragraphs which open 'We were all astonished when we heard . . .', the fitful but fierce gusts of Rumour, half-personified like Vergil's *Fama*, blowing through the sidestreets and back-alleys of 'our town'.

(ii)

The framing, introducing peripheral 'I' of *The House of the Dead* writes jauntily, with frenchified irony, about his miserable hole in Siberia as a paradise of girls and food and drink, a town where, on Page One, 'game-birds fly about the streets and positively thrust themselves upon the sportsman'. Here he gets to know a gentleman ex-convict, an enigmatic fellow, a recluse who dies leaving a basket of manuscripts. The tale buried in this mound of papers is the story within the story — the equivalent of the stranger's diary in the pre-Siberian fiction.

This inner story makes up the substance and often the detail of Dostoevsky's own recent past, his prison years. It is far more autobiographical than the early stories, even the 'dreamer' group where we often get a long clear look at the young writer and fast-fading star of Belinsky's literary set, mooching about 'his' Petersburg thinly disguised as lover or scholar. 'Talent needs sympathy, it needs to be understood' could be straight from the lips of the man still smarting under *The Double*'s bad reception.[7] ' "How painful it was!"

[7] *The Friend of the Family*, p. 218.

I said in a frenzy of joy. "It broke my heart!" ' reads like parody — not the creative parody that goes back to Mr Devushkin's Cossack Romances and Mr Golyadkin's silk ladders and Spanish serenades, but the ordinary spiteful parody someone might concoct who was out of patience with Dostoevsky and wanted to get across the messy convoluted sadomasochistic way people are (not what they say; they do not in fact talk like this) in his famous novels.[8] And indeed part of the unsuccess of the early stories is the author-betraying way people do talk like this.

So it must be reckoned a strange thing about *The House of the Dead* that its author kicks clear of himself creatively while staying with himself in actuality, in personal history, to an extent hard to match in the world's elect fiction. Here is a great novel which could also be thought of as not a novel at all. It stands as close to personal record as *War and Peace* does to national — 'not a novel', as Tolstoy says of his own book, and he goes on to make something like my comparison, remarking that Dostoevsky's narrative also doesn't quite 'fit into the form of novel, epic, or story'.[9] One sees roughly what he's getting at here, though of course there must be something wrong with a view of novelistic form which excludes *War and Peace* and *The House of the Dead*, whatever else they may be as well as novels.

As to form and *The House of the Dead*, my first step is from the I/We/They/Everybody flexibility of the eagle episode to the initial feigned discovery of a tale in a basket of papers. The discoverer, the peripheral 'I', does all he can to cast doubt on the text he is offering the reader. He calls it

[8] Ibid., p. 300. I am not including *The Insulted and Injured* (1861) among the famous novels. This is self-portrayal at its most silly and melodramatic — on balance a poorer book than *The Gambler* which Dostoevsky knocked off in under four weeks. Ivan Petrovich in *The Insulted and Injured* 'is' Dostoevsky seen as sick young writer and defeated idealist of the 1840s, and 'the critic B.', of course, 'is' Belinsky. Here and there the book has mordant zest, as in the thought that the dead Ivan Petrovich's manuscript will be useful to keep the draught out when the hospital gets its winter window frames (p. 11).

The most impressive sentence in *The Insulted and Injured* runs: 'They say the well-fed do not always understand the hungry, but I would add that the hungry do not always understand the hungry' (p. 262).

[9] 'Some Words about *War and Peace*', published in Vol. XVI of the Soviet Academy's edition of the Complete Works.

fragmentary, unfinished, interspersed with stuff 'from another story', unbalanced, indeed sometimes so wild as 'almost' — a frequent trick in mature Dostoevsky, that exasperating, fudging, life-simulating 'almost' — as almost to suggest insanity. Even his own decision to publish the tale is provisional and unsettled; he proposes 'to pick out two or three chapters to begin with as an experiment'.[10]

The reader soon discovers that these fears and warnings are grossly exaggerated, and that the narrative before him is more or less stable. He still can't feel comfortable for a number of reasons, one of which is that the peripheral 'I' has cast himself in the role of preparer and publisher of the ex-convict's tale, and may at any moment intervene, cease to be peripheral and start throwing his weight about editorially. This threat materializes immediately after the eagle episode. Without altering his received text, the peripheral 'I' moves in and turns the dead ex-convict 'I' and narrator of the tale into a 'he', and what is more a deluded 'he' because the object of this intervention is to set his record straight over an important matter of fact. In a sudden reaching back across almost the whole span of the novel we are told that the narrator had been wrong about a fellow prisoner who was doing twenty years for murdering his father.[11] The narrator had presented this man as one of those Iago-like monsters whose mentality is so baffling that one supposes there must be some simple but hidden explanation like a missing chromosome. He was cheery, feather-headed, garrulous, quite happy to reminisce about his father who, he would say, 'never complained of any illness to the end of his life'. He didn't admit to the crime, but the other convicts heard him cry out in his sleep 'Hold him, hold him! Chop off his head, his head, his head!' And in any case the evidence against him at the time of the murder was accepted as absolutely conclusive. But now, after the narrator's death, the real criminals have confessed and the man wrongly convicted of parricide has been released, and the peripheral 'I' interrupts the tale to put us in the picture.

Not that there is any final certainty in this picture either.

---

[10] pp. 4–5. [11] p. 231, back to p. 14.

The 'now' of the peripheral 'I's' intervention is just life outside the life of the tale, with more life outside it again, all bottomlessly chancy as life is: I mean, yet further news might come from remote Siberia any day, disclosing let's say that the 'real' criminals aren't real at all, but were indulging a typical Dostoevsky exhibitionist whim when they confessed. And that picture wouldn't be certain either, because there is no such thing, certainty is always beyond. One feels an urge to give up. But again there is no such thing — Golyadkin country. We have to live as we can, relying on the peripheral 'I's' intervention as a Stop Press which we have no present means of improving on.

Its effect is to make the case of the wrongly convicted man more strange still. His relaxed chatting about the father he didn't murder but is in here for murdering becomes unimaginably weird without losing its human fascination, its power to grip. And the audacity with which Dostoevsky has him shout 'Chop off his head!' in his sleep suggests to me a shaping up towards the young man who will roar out to all and sundry that he *wanted* to kill his father (the parricide link with *Karamazov* is obvious and has often been noted at the level of theme). Elsewhere in *The House of the Dead* we encounter a man who seems to enjoy torturing children, that is how he is made, apparently; and a husband who said to his wife one day 'I'm sick of you' and cut her throat.[12] But the cry in the night of 'Chop off his head!' is something else, the voice that strikes at once utterly fantastic and quarried out of four years' experience in the fortress prison at Omsk.

(iii)

I remarked apropos lodging-house life in *Poor People* that Dostoevsky did not need to go to prison to imagine *The House of the Dead*. The office in the same first novel points to the same conclusion; a clothes-brush in the custody of a zealous doorman — ' "and the brush is government property, sir," says he' — conjures up the special salty desolation with

[12] pp. 43, 204.

which this fiction flicks into the recesses of the barracks state, onward to *The House of the Dead*'s prison furnishings, clothes, rations, bedding, fetters, flogging paraphernalia.[13]

I added that he had to have been to prison before he could write his prison novel, meaning that life there gave him facts with which to furnish his intuition of collective hell, and, less obviously and with an eye to a grossly forced young talent and the overspill syndrome in the stories of the late 1840s, that prison stopped him writing. It halted the flood. It also gave him new words. Obviously this is another way of saying it gave him new facts, but it is the way I prefer, and I will try to explain why.

The only book convicts were allowed to have with them was the Bible. On arrival in Siberia Dostoevsky was given a New Testament by the wives of a group of political exiles. He kept this through the prison years and for the rest of his life, and he asked to be handed it when he was dying. It is preserved in the Lenin Library at Moscow. His underlinings and other scorings show that he made straight for Jesus' 'hard' sayings, and had a special interest in the Book of Revelation.[14] These were not strictly new words but old words grown new again for Dostoevsky, and he had plenty of time to ponder them.

Against the rules, he had a second book with him in prison. This was (and is, for it too survives) a home-made notebook consisting of sheets of ordinary writing paper roughly stitched together. It must have been a dangerous enterprise; prisoners were flogged into unconsciousness for smaller offences than that, and though at least one of the doctors or doctors' assistants in the prison hospital seems to have been kindly

---

[13] pp. 36, 75, above, 'I'm government property now,' joked the radical Pisarev when he was put in prison in the early 1860s.

[14] Contrast Tolstoy: 'The Book of Revelation reveals absolutely nothing' (*Introduction to a Study of the Gospels*). The difference between the two men could not be more neatly pointed, nor that between *The House of the Dead* and *Resurrection* which was written after long and loving study of Dostoevsky's novel.

While the general tendency of Dostoevsky's markings and occasional annotations of his New Testament is clear enough, we have no way of distinguishing the early (Siberian) entries from later ones. Also, since the book stayed in the family, his widow and children may have added items of their own, but this is unlikely.

A scholar now working in the United States possesses microfilm of the whole book, part of which he has allowed me to see. He asks me to say no more until he publishes his own conclusions.

disposed, that might well not have helped him if he had been caught.[15] Anyhow, he used the notebook to record words, turns of phrase, jokes, oaths, songs, jingles, proverbs, saws and sayings, speech rhythms, scraps of conversational exchanges — anything that was new to him or caught his attention in some other way. His fellow convicts came from all over Russia and beyond. There were educated Poles and wild frontiersmen. The notebook records many Siberian usages unknown in European Russia. Its main concern is with the talk of tramps, vagabonds, robbers, soldier-convicts, army deserters, Little Russians (Ukrainians), Jews, religious dissenters, prostitutes and others who hung about the prison, queer folk generally. There are 522 entries in all. The Soviet editor of Volume IV of the Complete Works, flanked by his colleagues in the Pushkin House's Dostoevsky Section, tells us that over two hundred of these entries are used in *The House of the Dead*.[16] The true figure is 306. Some are easy to miss through slight alteration or being so inconspicuous in themselves that one needs to know the novel more or less by heart to pick them up. Others catch the eye readily enough. It's surprising, for example, that the editor has failed to spot the quaint phrase which I englished as 'pie in the sky' in the eagle episode, especially as Dostoevsky draws attention to it himself by writing 'NB' against this entry in the notebook.[17] He had it ready, and at one of the great 'folk' (*narod*) climaxes of the novel, he used it fondly.

With the editor's handling of the convicts' attitude to religion, ideology becomes entangled with the neutral question of competence. Thus there was a man doing time for despoiling churches of their furnishings, and among his specialities were icon settings of John Chrysostom, the Golden Mouth, the eloquent saint. Dostoevsky records that this man's name for Chrysostom was Johnny Bawler, and the Soviet editor comments that we have here a typical example of the convicts' negative and mocking attitude to religion.[18]

---

[15] *PSS*, Vol. IV, pp. 275, 310.

[16] Ibid., p. 275, also reminding us (p. 296) that the novelist Saltykov–Shchedrin gave *The House of the Dead* the alternative title of *Essays in Comparative Etymology*.

[17] Ibid., p. 238 (entry number 103).

[18] Ibid., pp. 311–12 (entry number 76).

No doubt Johnny Bawler is indecorous, but it is not disrespectful at heart and in no sense irreligious. It is free, familiar, buoyant, striking to meet for the first time — that is why Dostoevsky recorded it in his notebook, and no matter that it never comes to the surface of his novel. It illustrates what I mean by saying prison gave him new facts in the shape of words. And surely to join issue with editors over such matters amounts to more than an academic squabble. While *narod* occurs all over the place in this novel as 'the common people' or simply 'the people', and while 'pie in the sky' is a morsel of folk talk heard in prison, noted down, slipped into the convicts' chatter about their eagle, Johnny Bawler is a bigger affair altogether. He haunts two letters which Dostoevsky wrote to his brother. In the first, a mere week after his release, he writes: 'People are everywhere people. Even in prison, among robbers, in four years I finally distinguished people.' The man who used the fond diminutive Johnny (Ivanushka) of Chrysostom was at once a robber and a distinct person. And nearly six years later, when the novel was well under way and he was anticipating its impact: 'My personality will disappear. These are the notes of an unknown man.'[19] The first letter resurrects the question which engaged him in his pre-Siberian fiction: what is it to be a man (as opposed to a man-rag, a faint heart, a voluntary buffoon, a dreamer — and so on)? The second returns to the problem of authorial stance which he had solved one way in *Poor People*, another very different way in *The Double*, and had fumbled with in the stories that followed.

It makes immediate and encouraging sense to think of a novelist's prison sentence and denial of privacy as a four-year exercise in distinguishing human beings, in discovering what it really means to be a man among men. On the other hand the 'notes of an unknown man' inspires no confidence at all because it harks back to the feeble device of the stranger's diary — 'an unknown man' are the very words — in the stories of the late 1840s. But taken together the disappearance of the second letter is no ordinary absconding manoeuvre but

[19] Letters of 22 February 1854 and 9 October 1859 (the second quoted in *PSS*, Vol. IV, p. 289).

a dying into the life of the novel, and the life of the novel is the distinguishing-and-discovering process of the first letter. I have already mooted the paradox that keeping closest to his own life afforded Dostoevsky the cleanest creative get-away; and here is another one: the second letter's disappear-ance is the first's discovery, and I append the observation that Dostoevsky doesn't talk about *self*-discovery, writing to his brother, any more than he does when Raskolnikov climbs the filthy spiral staircase and girds himself to enter '*as a man*'. But there is a powerful sense of *self*-loss, of Raskolnikov's personality disappearing, as he moves towards admission of guilt. Now he sheds the prickly antinomian intellectualism we knew him by and for, and which appeared to make him what he was. It is as if the novel had come full circle and the unnamed 'young man' of its first sentence had walked out of his own front door — which he does — but then had climbed straight up those police-office stairs. We have lost Raskolnikov and found *a man*.

To speak (as I did) of a struggle to rejoin the human family sounds glib and reductive. But that's the fate of critical extrapolation; one has to carry the thing back into *Crime and Punishment* and see how it sounds then. And herein the relevance of Johnny Bawler to *The House of the Dead*. He is a detail in one entry of the Siberian Notebook, as specialists call it. The same specialists, nearly all of them, regard the notebook and the novel as an extraordinarily solemn finding out how the other half lives. This misses the point both of prison as collective hell and of prison life as human com-monalty: of the counterthrust in which there is no other half: of the I/We/They/Everybody flexibility which (I also said) pertains equally to narrative mode and fictional sub-stance.

Johnny Bawler is a step back from reflection, into the life of the novel. The unknown convict who gave John Chrysos-tom this name was a church despoiler, a robber. To Dostoev-sky, a political prisoner and a gentleman, he will have been unsentimentally one of 'them'; there's plenty of observation, sometimes revolted and horrified, of the common criminals at their drinking, fighting, gambling, smuggling, whoring, or just plodding about their daily — but so alien — business.

They are very much 'they'. How the narrating 'I' and the Johnny Bawler convict also fall inside a coherent 'us' of people and circumstance is an I/We/They/Everybody affair, as when the prison population goes to church in the town at Easter. The narrator remembers his own childhood church-going when he would look over his shoulder towards the peasants crowded at the back, near the door:

> Now I too had to stand at the back — and not just at the back; we were fettered and branded, with our heads shaven; everybody avoided us, even seemed afraid of us. We were always given alms, and I remember I found it in a way actually enjoyable, there was a special subtlety in this strange pleasure. 'So be it!' I thought. The convicts prayed very earnestly, and each of them brought his mite whenever he came to church, to buy a candle or for the collection. 'Why then I too am a man,' he thought, perhaps, or felt, as he gave it; 'before God we are all equal.' We took the sacrament at the early mass. When the priest, with the chalice in his hands, recited the words 'Accept me, Lord, even as the robber', almost all of them prostrated themselves with a clanking of fetters, each one apparently applying these words literally to himself.[20]

To a reader who comes straight out of the cold into this one-paragraph scene, Dostoevsky's claim about authorial disappearance must seem the purest effrontery. The prefacing childhood memory, and the educated man's observing of his companions in their naive literalmindedness at the close, suggest the stranger's diary device at its most mechanical. And in the middle, it isn't just any gentleman convict who savours the mental taste of finding himself the recipient of charity, and who puts into the head of a fellow exile from society the thought that he too is a man. This is somebody we know, somebody we first met through Mr Devushkin in *Poor People*.

The reader who moves into and through this tiny episode from within *The House of the Dead* will also, of course, recognize Dostoevsky, and he will hastily add that it doesn't matter, it positively enhances, and flashes of temperament like 'why then I too am a man' should and do surprise the novel itself. The novelist's talk of his disappearing personality was a quick reckless gesture towards the fact that he can afford to show, and even to be, himself within the flexibility

[20]   p. 209.

peculiar to *The House of the Dead*. To put it another way, he has no need to create and sustain a convincing narrative persona so long as he can slip at will between solidarity with the 'us' and externality to the 'them'; and it won't be denied that the I/We/They/Everybody juxtapositions of the scene in church are even more stark, in extract, than those at the release of the wounded eagle. But again, what looks awkward or even impossible in a small lump sample on my page comes with ample august nature in the course of Dostoevsky's novel, and with a towering probity which recalls Tolstoy's companion piece about prison life, the still widely undervalued *Resurrection*. *Resurrection*'s royal freedom of observation — Keats's 'indolent and kingly gaze' fits Tolstoy better than Shakespeare, to whom he was applying it — runs back to the earliest work, to the stories about childhood, the Caucasus, the Crimea. Because free, it migrates and flourishes outside the fiction: that is why Tolstoy's greatness remains with us all the time whereas Dostoevsky's comes back as a shock, almost a reproach, each time we read him. If Dostoevsky had conceived the lawyer in *Anna Karenina* who absentmindedly snatches at moths when in conference, that character, however minor, would be entangled in the terrible bureaucracy and the forms; he would take us back to the barebones exchange between Mr Golyadkin and the clerk senior to him:

> 'You will be officially informed about everything today.'
> 'What does officially mean, Anton Antonovich?' —[21]

and the ghostly strands enmeshing him would make him what he is, would define him, and yet they would lack all force and sense outside the claustrophobic *mise-en-scène*. Whereas Tolstoy's divorce lawyer, the lamp, the moths, can be apprehended neutrally without special regard to *Anna Karenina*, as if God had put them in the world, our world, overnight.

And even in *Resurrection* which drives hard towards

---

[21] *The Eternal Husband*, p. 245. When Spassky lost the world chess title to Fischer, Alexander Kotov, the journalist and grandmaster, wrote in *Pravda* that Spassky 'made vexatious miscalculations of both a practical and theoretical nature, and in complex matters of the psychology of so testing a contest'. Kotov was writing more or less officially. Spassky may well have asked himself 'What does officially mean?'

predetermined moral and religious ends, the observation is free. Tolstoy will note the sweet lilting sound made by fetters on a walking man. Dostoevsky would never do that. The noise of fetters in the Easter church scene is of the occasion and of the group activity. So is the noise audible under the frock-coat of a convict dressed up to act the part of a dandy in prison theatricals. So is the sound of 'a hundred chains dragging along the floor' as the naked convicts — naked except for their fetters — take their communal bath.[22] The narrating 'I' both observes and participates in churchgoing, theatricals, bath-house session; these are the very stuff of the novel and the ground of my insistence that *The House of the Dead*'s I/We/They/Everybody flexibility is as much fictional substance as narrative mode. Of course this flexibility can be presented as a solution to the problem of authorial stance which had bedevilled Dostoevsky in the late 1840s. But one must add that the problem had not taken this form before and would never take it again; the story of prison life is a singleton in which to succeed in articulating the problem is to have solved it; the 'what' of the tale and the 'how' of the telling are only formally distinct.

(iv)

Tolstoy made two extracts from *The House of the Dead* which moved him deeply and which he loved to read aloud. One he entitled 'Death in Hospital' and the other 'The Eagle'. We have met the eagle. He appears at the end of a chapter called 'Prison Animals', the centrepiece of which is the choosing by the convicts themselves of a horse to bring water into the prison and take rubbish out. This is another of the novel's group activities, with the narrating 'I' unable to match the experts in knowledge of horseflesh and veterinary jargon, and therefore very much an observer, but still with his small part to play making friends with Sorrel, the new horse, gazing into his handsome face and enjoying the feel of his soft warm lips on the palm of his hand: the horse 'they' have chosen becomes 'ours', and 'I' grows fond of him too.[23] The

[22]   *The House of the Dead*, pp. 112, 145.   [23]   pp. 220-4.

idiosyncratic flavour of it all, the flexibility, is unmistakable; which is not to argue that the choosing of Sorrel is finer than the eagle episode, but that it lies even closer to the heart of the novel, and, incidentally, that it lacks the Tolstoyan directness of the eagle's release, the heroic simplicity, the very grand and unified vision of freedom. It is easy to see why the younger man was moved.

Likewise with 'Death in Hospital'. The narrator's sojourn in the prison hospital takes up almost a fifth of the novel and is more of a sequence with digressions than a single scene or episode. Only one death gets described, that of a young consumptive, and it is all over in a couple of pages.[24] But again they are noble Tolstoyan pages. The wasted body fights for air, and the hands pluck at the wooden cross on the chest as if even that was too much weight to bear; and when the duty sergeant appears with two guards to collect the corpse, a grey-haired convict looks down at the form on the straw mattress and says 'He must have had a mother, too', and walks away.

The death is not quite the end. A loud clanking resounds through the ward. 'We could hear the sergeant in the corridor sending someone for a smith. The fetters were to be removed from the dead man.' So the chapter closes. And the noise of hospital fetters is no more free, no closer to Tolstoy's observed lilt, than the noise of church and play-acting and bathhouse fetters. The unparticularized clanking bends back upon the narrator's earlier puzzlement that fetters are never removed from a living convict, even in hospital. The doctors are kind men. 'They're as good as a father to you' (literally, 'You don't need a father') is a favourite convict exclamation about them, quarried out of the Siberian Notebook. The doctors don't make the rules. But neither does it occur to them to petition 'the authorities' (*nachalstvo*, a collective singular neuter noun) that the sick should be allowed to lie or even die unfettered.[25]

So Tolstoy's calm attention upon death is not for Dostoevsky, whose gaze keeps flickering, whose eye will not settle. And this introduces a general truth about *The House of the*

[24] pp. 164–6.   [25] p. 163.

Dead. It has nothing to do with squeamishness that the narrating 'I' cannot look straight at an excrement tub. The tubs of *Resurrection* — how and why they leak, when if at all they are emptied, the different problems they pose for men and women convicts, strike home as if Tolstoy had been appointed to undertake an independent inquiry into the running of government prisons and had come up with a severe but fair report. *The House of the Dead* is not thus informative. We learn merely that a tub remained all night in the ward where there were patients suffering from 'certain illnesses which compel one to retire'.[25] The narrator observes 'It is both terrible and disgusting to imagine *now* how pestilential it *must have been*' (my italics) even without the excrement tub. This sudden momentary shift to retrospect is the unsettlement I am speaking of, it is the dragging of the narrator's eye away from the fact and nightlong presence of the tub, once again towards the rules and forms and 'the authorities'. The gravamen, the abiding nag, is the existence of an ordinary privy two steps down the corridor which *nachalstvo* will not allow the convicts to use. Thus while the reader, like Mrs Garnett, expects and perhaps wants to hear about dysentery and other immediate horrors of the ward, he has to put up with fussy, peripheral stuff about the grating on the privy window and its double frame in winter, the armed guard, the ward attendants — everything that makes escape impossible and the rule unreasonable. 'And where can a man run to in winter, in stockings and slippers, in a hospital dressing-gown and a nightcap?' demands the narrator in what comes through as slightly comic indignation.

I suspect a lot of artifice here. This, by far the most documentary of Dostoevsky's novels, may be also in some respects the most contrived — which is another approach to his kicking clear of himself creatively while staying with himself in personal history. It doesn't matter in the least that Dostoevsky and the narrating 'I' have, and are felt to have, the same experiences so long as something, whether it be a death or an excrement tub, sustains the thrust towards

---

[25] p. 162. Rather than 'diseases which were intolerable without some outlet' (Jessie Coulson's Oxford translation). And Constance Garnett's mention of 'dysentery' is unwarranted.

the realization of the life of the Dead House, *Notes* (or *Memoirs*) *from the Dead House* being the book's literal title. Nor does it make sense to enquire about the documentary truth of this realization, because the end-product is imaginative, the creative kicking-clear has happened, the book is a novel.

Prison life, imagined and realized, sometimes contracts into absolute embattled solitude. Dostoevsky is capable of turning his back on the defeated recluse he has set up as narrator, in order to acknowledge he was 'terribly alone' and yet to bless the chance of 'self-judgment' and 'stern scrutiny of my earlier life'.[27] Or, ' "A dead house!" I said to myself, gazing intently from the steps of our prison . . . '.[28] That is early days, in a chapter called 'The First Month'. But even here the prison is *ours*, and by the end of the chapter the narrating 'I' has made common cause with the prison dog, 'my friend, my only friend', the two of them making the smallest 'we' in the novel, a 'we' capable of dilating into the whole dead house and its occupants, simply and physically when the eagle leaves the perimeter wall for the steppe, humanly and socially when the townsfolk look askance at, while they give alms to, the prison party in church. Even the prison major, a monster of drunken sadism, Dostoevsky's first grand essay in a comic ferocity and terror he was to make perfectly his own — even he is *our* major. He can evoke an elsewhere which 'we' (which includes him) are all and equally bounded by. He rubs his hands at the sight of his newly-painted quarters and declares he really must get married. He removes his spectacles in deference to the general who inspects the prison.[29] Visionary humour, enfolding the mirthful and the mirthless: the bride from outside who will never come; the general from outside who does come and as surely leaves again.

Then there can be sensed a menacing and perversely mystic elsewhere of imposed rules and forms and never identified *nachalstvo*. It's stressed that *our* kind doctors had nothing to do with forbidding access to the privy, just as the fettered sick and dying are not their fault. The novel doesn't pursue the question of who is to blame, and Soviet

[27] p. 262.   [28] p. 77.   [29] pp. 219, 259.

commentators have made much of the restraining force of tsarist censorship. Of course Dostoevsky had to watch his pen; there is plenty of evidence that he did so. But the prudential argument is misconceived. Who or what, I ask, sustains the pecking order and endless petty tyrannies of Mr Devushkin's lodging-house and place of work? Where does one start to look for an answer to Mr Golyadkin's lethal Kafkaesque question, 'What does officially mean?' The fact that it *is* Kafkaesque should be enough to relax all tight literalisms. Equally, the social circumstances of Mr Devushkin are an emphatic and early warning that to concentrate on government and public life is to miss the main point. So then who is to blame? Already in *Netochka Nezvanova*, the thought that we are all guilty in relation to each other had been given a lengthy airing, and it was reinforced by a clear reference to 'He who is without sin among you, let him first cast a stone at her' in the Gospel text about the woman taken in adultery.[30] I can't think of a better example of a theme that is at once the purest Dostoevsky and completely inert in the pre-Siberian fiction. *The House of the Dead* prowls stealthily round this question of blame because Dostoevsky is still examining and imagining its terms, not because he is afraid of the government censor. In any case, being spiritual in that broad sense of *Geist* which makes blame itself a misleading word, the question cannot be answered as a literalist would demand, but only rephrased, its terms illuminated and transfigured in the way of art.

Punishment by flogging illustrates *The House of the Dead*'s circular prowling in relation to what I have called the mystic elsewhere of imposed rules:

Men being punished absolutely must cry out and beg for mercy. That was the accepted thing: it was looked upon as proper and necessary, and when on one occasion the victim was not prepared to scream, the flogging officer whom I happened to know and who might perhaps have been reckoned a good-natured man in other respects, took it as a personal affront. At first he had meant to let the convict off lightly, but when he didn't hear the usual 'your honour, my own father, have

---

[30] *The Friend of the Family*, p. 330. The Gospel reference is even more insistent in a manuscript fragment of the story which antedates the 1849 magazine text; *PSS*, Vol. II, p. 495.

mercy, I'll pray to God for you all my life' and the rest of it, he got furious and gave about fifty extra lashes in the desire to elicit screams and supplications — and he did elicit them. 'Can't have that; the man's a pig' he explained to me most earnestly.[31]

'The accepted thing' — at its most dreadful and inspired this novel develops a kind of fleck where we expect the centre of vision to be. It doesn't follow that we are looking in the wrong place. On the contrary, having noted how death in the hospital sequence refuses to settle into focus and dominate attention in the Tolstoyan way, I now add that we cannot but want to engage with death, that at *our* end, the receiving end, the Tolstoyan way is the only way, and that it is natural to the stressful relationship between Dostoevsky and his reader — and to the very odd form which the joy conjured by all art assumes in his — that this should be so. Something like inadvertence possesses the flogging vignette, so a reader cannot be sure to what extent the horror of a brave man's broken will, and of a mentality that presses on with fifty more lashes, is his own evocation. It can't be his *invention*. He didn't put the horror there. But a blind spot, a fleck appears when he tries to concentrate upon it, and the colour-less *eliciting* of screams and supplications doesn't help him decide what he is trying to do (every reader of every real novel is doing some of the work) and how he stands in relation to his author. The *eliciting* gives nothing away. It has no smell of craft. It may be beyond, or it may be simply to one side of, another writer's calculated laconicism. 'The accepted thing', the communal attitude enclosing flogger and flogged, frustrates the eye as it seeks to rest on what is being done, in this case *elicited*. Perhaps the attitude is the greater horror, as the accepted thing of the convict's fetters in hospital might be thought more dreadful than his death. But sometimes, in the dead house, the attitude isn't a horror at all. It may be a positive mitigation or salve, as another flogging vignette will illustrate.

The prison housed a certain Lieutenant Smekalov who supervised punishment. They would bring a chair for him, and he would sit down and light his pipe — 'he had a very

[31] p. 183.

long pipe'. The convict about to be flogged would begin the usual supplications and entreaties, but Smekalov always broke in with 'Oh no, brother, lie down, it's no use'. And when the convict had lain down with a sigh, Smekalov would ask him if he knew the Lord's Prayer. 'To be sure, your honour, we're Christians, we learnt it when we were children.' 'Well then, repeat it.' So the convict starts, and Smekalov bends forward in his chair, raises his hand, leaves off smoking, and waits for the familiar word. And at 'Thy kingdom come' the lieutenant shouts 'Stop!' and with an ecstatic gesture commands 'Now give him some!' — and the flogging is under way and Smekalov roars with laughter as if he had just thought up this rhyme for 'come' and was overjoyed at his own wit. But in fact it is an old joke, a very old joke, Smekalov's 'one and only joke', the whole prison knows it including the man being flogged, and everybody loves Smekalov.[32]

The lash 'cuts like a razor' just the same. There are no half measures about the flogging. The horror remains. What has changed is the periphery, the surrounding attitude, the shared joke, perhaps pseudo-joke, anyhow some elusive spirit of human kindness is abroad, even for the reader who has no patience with the Christianity and the carefully placed folk 'we' of the convict's answer to the question about the Lord's Prayer. Smekalov is no enemy of the lash, yet punishment from him is easier to bear; so in half an hour the flogged convict can be seen going round the prison telling his mates what a splendid fellow Lieutenant Smekalov is. It *is* mysterious, this benign surround, and in its fascination just as unsettling as the terrible 'accepted thing' within which the eliciting of screams and supplications is played out.

Thus the eye which can't help wanting to rest upon the interesting prison institution of flogging, equally can't help being frustrated. Frustration here is nearer the truth than distraction because these surrounding attitudes and accepted things aren't so much an alternative focus, a competing centre of attraction, as the presiding spirit or genius of *The House of the Dead*: and no reader wants to be told that instead of trying to concentrate on flogging (or death in

[32]   pp. 176–8.

hospital for that matter) he ought to be attending to the quintessential book. Nor should he be told this. The 'not X but Y' of it is wrong. The truth is 'X *and* Y'. In any case, as I say, the reader cannot help trying to concentrate on what fascinates. He has in front of him a most readable yet fretting tale, an agent of self-division holding something in common with the television documentary whose interest seems to be positively goaded by the urge to switch it off, and with experiences like resolving to turn away from the sea after watching the next wave break. While *The Double* is metaphysical and difficult, *The House of the Dead* is anecdotal and restless, and it has moved so far lifewards as to put its fictional status at risk. Tolstoy, we recall, brought himself to the brink of denying it was a novel, but stopped short, or ducked to one side, with the observation that it did not quite fit the form.

As to form, the untidy life of the dead house has this envelope of communal attitudes round it, colouring it, and colouring it differently as attitudes themselves differ. Often a Nobody seems to be added to the I/We/They/Everybody of the story and its telling, for example when the reader attempts to trace 'the accepted thing' of a flogged man's screams and supplications to a responsible human source. Nobody is to blame. But this Nobody proves a dubious addition, a sort of counting the same thing twice perhaps, because the same facts yield the inference that Everybody is to blame, and Everybody needs no introduction; this Everybody has been a familiar though shifting and imponderable presence, back to the Everybody that sets off for work after the freeing of the eagle in our first encounter with prison life. Of course an existence compulsorily shared is bound to breed its collective standards and decorums like 'the accepted thing' over flogging, but this doesn't give the lie to what I said just now about a mystic elsewhere of imposed forms; to reject 'elsewhere' because the forms are in varying degrees self-imposed is as literalistic and diminishing as to see the Tsar behind every reference to the authorities, that singular neuter noun *nachalstvo*. The man who persists until he elicits his screams may be perfectly good-natured except when in the grip of this highly specialized yet all-confronting evil spirit. The narrator knows him and says so. Equally mysterious, the revered Lieutenant Smekalov is 'far from averse to the lash'. The first man — the first phenomenon — prefigures *The Possessed* with its Gadarene swine epigraph. The second compounds the lash with the Lord's Prayer and folk values, though the reason Smekalov is loved turns out to be more personal than this mixture suggests; he has a gift which he never thinks about of making the convicts feel he is *'one of them'*; when he asks something it is *'because he really wants to know'* (Dostoevsky's italics). The first condition is aggregate ritual hell, the second human community. Both are life, prison life. And Smekalov and the elicitor of screams both say it cannot be helped.

At the chapter-end, as the novel bids farewell to Smekalov sitting at his window in a dressing-gown watching the world go by, his 'it' that cannot be helped also will not be cornered. 'He'd laugh to himself,' one convict recalls dotingly without knowing or caring what had amused 'our' lieutenant. No sadist and no enemy of the lash, he has everything and nothing to laugh at in the dead house's *comédie humaine*, and he is equally elusive in himself as an object of fond regard. The reminiscing convict's sense of fellowship with Smekalov is certainly not egalitarian; he takes his hat off as he passes the window, and when he hears his own surname spoken by the figure in the dressing-gown drinking tea and smoking the very long pipe, he answers respectfully with christian name and patronymic. One can only say that Smekalov reaches out to the bare-headed convict in front of him; as the narrator puts it, *'he really wants to know'*; or, in Dostoevsky's habitual formulation, he finds the human in the human being.

Where does that get us? Precisely as far as the Nobody and Everybody engrossing the question of blame. The thing that cannot be helped but can be laughed at by some (though not by others) bears too closely upon better hap and worse for novelistic comfort. The book feels defenceless against huge aimless pressures, wide open to the winds of the merely actual, to contingency itself. 'Peerless!' exclaimed Lenin. But he wasn't reading *The House of the Dead* to get the joy of art from it. He was propagandizing on the platform of a great documentary text, as was Tolstoy before him; and Tolstoy was simultaneously pointing up its potentiality of rational, available art — his own ideal. 'Give him freedom, real freedom' in the mouth of one of the convicts provides a sharp focus for the eagle episode. Other prison animals feel and fare differently. Sorrel the horse thrives in the bondage of work he is good at, like a healthy human being. Vaska the goat plays at butting heads with the convicts. Happy Vaska! Perhaps happy convicts! Where outside prison — ? Byelka, the abject dog who rolls on his back when man or beast approaches, doesn't want to be free, he wants to get by.[33] We have all met him.

Nor is it true that the eagle projects some nobler and ultimately coherent vision; he is a savage solitary bird, neutrally observed. One might quote 'The aim of us all was freedom', but this is the dilating and contracting 'all', the non-absolute 'all' which has such a crucial bearing on the book as fiction and not documentary; because if one demands a stable factual 'all', then trouble ensues — for example over those who deliberately commit crimes in order to be put inside and get away from 'the incomparably harsher servitude of being at liberty'.[34]

And what is freedom? That convict's 'real free freedom' looks a Cartesian idea, clear and distinct, rendered *à la* Tolstoy. But the narrator observes how daydreaming and long sojourn in captivity make prisoners think of freedom as 'somehow freer than real freedom, the freedom, that is, that exists in fact, in real life'.[35] Of course our dreams may be clear and distinct, and they may vouchsafe us the freer than free, the freest, even the realest freedom. Who knows? Anyhow we have them. And then elsewhere, and repeatedly, a notion appears which seems to undercut freedom itself, the notion of 'changing one's lot', an expression which fascinates the narrator as 'rather bookish' (so no wonder it got recorded, twice in fact, in the Siberian Notebook).[36]

[33] pp. 225–8.
[34] pp. 46–7, 234. Constance Garnett omits 'all', perhaps sensing it can't be the documentary truth.
[35] p. 275.
[36] Entries 38 and 53. The Soviet editor fails to note 53, and he records only the second and third of the expression's five occurrences in the novel (pp. 49, 73,

Changing one's lot covers all assertions of will made in the desire to conjure anything, but *anything*, for a change; and therefore it includes not only rational behaviour like a carefully planned escape, but wild outbursts, murderous assaults, actions that can only lead to flogging or even the death penalty. We have already encountered will-assertion, the Audenesque sudden opprobrious act, and we will meet it again in the later novels, in suicide and the search for a deed that is truly one's own. From *Crime and Punishment* onward this becomes familiar territory. But in the novel of prison life its familiarity is not so much that of a mapped area as of furniture about the house, the furniture of the dead house, imaging desultoriness.

We sometimes get flat contradiction as well as untidiness, following the pretence of a scrappy unrevised manuscript found among a dead man's effects. The frame narrator's suggestion of chaos is a calculated exaggeration, but Dostoevsky does want to unsettle us in ways which recall *Poor People* with its 'missing' letters and other loose ends. Authorlessness in that novel, and a dead man's rough autobiographical draft in this one, license much the same life-simulating postures. There we had the letters — or some of them. Now we have a narrator unreachable in death, hushed in that privacy, and when he was alive seldom certain of his facts, or of reasons for and consequences of his facts, often thinking aloud as if making a telephone call somebody else is paying for, hesitating whether to tell this or that anecdote, airing his views on the Russian soul, darting about in time, more or less repeating or contradicting himself[37] — the whole story proceeding by way of apparently artless overlapping cumulation.

207, 263, 267): see *PSS*, Vol. IV, p. 313. Moreover his 'escape' (*pobeg*) is too narrow an account of 'changing one's lot', as I indicate above.

[37] Things tend not to square from the start, even at the elementary level of the number of convicts at the prison which is stated as an almost constant 250, then as 200, on successive pages (pp. 8–9). Inadvertence can be ruled out. *The House of the Dead* is a carefully considered work, as variants through the printed texts show, and Dostoevsky is never more conscious and finnicky than over figures and dates. Thus, in the same short paragraph where the number of convicts is given as 200, our earliest text states that the narrator entered prison in December, the next changes December to January, and the third goes back to December again; *PSS*, Vol. IV, p. 260. Similar patterns are observable with numbers of lashes inflicted, distances walked, weights carried. It doesn't follow that one fact

The dead man can't be blamed for an unsatisfactory job, and the frame narrator, despite his one intervention late in the novel, assumes no responsibility for what we read. And behind them, nothing — the nothing of ultimate authorial unaccountability which puts us back at square one as regards form in Dostoevsky. The urge not to be caught and brought to book, the boast that he hadn't shown his face, were there at the start, in *Poor People*. And one step on from the start he declares himself the real Golyadkin and invites the question — then who in terms of authorial identity and stance is Dostoevsky? For Mr Golyadkin, 'our' third-person 'hero', did not write *The Double*, and the thought that he is not the real one, not the real Golyadkin, points once again to a nothing behind him. My answer was that Belinsky's young poet wrote *The Double* in collusion with an ideally perceptive reader, but of course that answer recognizes the same public unaccountability as in *Poor People*, only wearing different clothes.

And now the third major work in the canon shields its author behind dead autobiographer and frame narrator. This has struck people as mere coyness special to the circumstances of *The House of the Dead*; the prison experiences are in substance Dostoevsky's, but he is recounting them as fiction and so he proceeds as he does. Well yes. Evasion is forced on him, and we all agree, back to Tolstoy, that the result is a maverick. Equally true, though, and much more interesting: this is from first to last a self-inflicted trouble, it is his own hand he is forcing. Dostoevsky had no need to write a novel at all. He was a prompt journalist and could have made what he wanted of the prison years that way — while walking warily of the censor, which he had to do in the novel too. And not any old novel in this case, not a mess like *The*

rather than another is the documentary truth, but that Dostoevsky knows what he is doing when he feeds contradiction to his narrator. Nor is it plausible that we are supposed to regard the difference between 250 and 200 as insignificant; that goes dead against the grain of the book; handfuls of men are *meant* to *seem* to count. Finally, government records establish that the total at Omsk on Dostoevsky's arrival was 158 (*PSS*, Vol. IV, p. 279), so there is yet another side of his deliberate tinkering to be reckoned with. There's no saying why this fussy exactness and pseudo-exactness should be. The strangest things help to get imagination stirring.

Insulted and Injured or a rush job like *The Gambler*, but a work astir in 1856, being read aloud, bits of it, in some form during the next year, and mulled over on and off until magazine serial publication began in 1860.[38] So the root thought is that the need for evasion in *The House of the Dead* matches a desire to evade. And this is not a local difficulty but a new, acute, in some ways uniquely stimulating phase of the thing he had been living with in the two important pre-Siberian novels, neither local nor a difficulty, but his creative fate.

(v)

Considering Dostoevsky, one kept bumping into the idea of a deeper realism. He started it himself by staking his claim in that form. And it is natural (and I have followed nature several times already) to seize on the psychology that emerges in the teeth of nineteenth-century assumptions, and emerges so coherently and convincingly: accidental men and accidental families, love as hate, sex as power, destruction as making, sensual self-despite indulged by way of basking in humiliation and other luxuries. 'Changing one's lot' is an early example of Dostoevsky putting his finger on a phenomenon that would have made sense to Kierkegaard and Nietzsche but not to the world at large, including the novelists.

And just as *The House of the Dead* is not any old novel, so Dostoevsky cannot see the human self new and grab any old narrative fictional blanket to throw round its naked original-ity, leaving everything else to take care of itself. The proposal to set down the vision was also and equally a quest for form, and no matter that this makes him sound a bit like Henry James; all novelists, through-and-through novelists, are the faintest bit like *ce cher maître*, however little they discuss or consciously ponder the demands of art. The hard and funda-mental work may seem to be going on elsewhere, or the whole thing may look easy. In Dostoevsky's case we have his throwing down the gauntlet of a deeper realism. He wanted

[38] Letters of 18 January 1856 and 9 October 1859. See also *PSS*, Vol. IV, pp. 275–6.

to direct his public, specially his unborn public, towards the overall thrust of his books; a hived-off psychology is interesting, it is the stuff of much commentary, but it still isn't what he meant; and pressed to say what he did mean he could only have talked in a circle, appealing again to the experience of reading his novels.

The deeper realism, the real thing. When we are lost (there is no other word) in the early chapters of *Copperfield*, it never occurs to us that the little boy and the people and things round him were made up by a man called Charles Dickens. Dostoevsky's real thing, as it has shaped itself so far, maintains no settled illusionist front of any kind, and it seems to prefer a highly idiosyncratic cross-bench position in the alignments of nineteenth-century naturalism. When I made play with Kafka, Brecht, Pirandello, Eliot, Beckett, in relation to the two pre-Siberian novels it was to remark a mysterious proleptic flair, not to unfold a strategy. What may look calculated was, I am sure, an instinctive response to un-analysed and largely negative promptings. The same is true of that authorial unaccountability which also distinguishes the two early works, and which reappears in *The House of the Dead*. It's hard even to give a name to authorial unaccountability without bringing in train sophistications which were surely, in fact, not Dostoevsky's: deliberate novelistic, or anti-novelistic, compromising of the old plain tale, and obfuscation of the teller. He wasn't like that. He was calculating and devious, untiringly devious, but not like that. History to the fore and even to the rescue as we contemplate him in the middle decades of the century, finding his own voice while reading and admiring Dickens, Charlotte Bronte and before them Scott from one country, Balzac and Hugo from another, Turgenev and the young Tolstoy at home. To us these are big settled stars in the sky, and also obviously in a tradition — so obviously it scarcely seems worth noting the robust narrative confidence which they share and which goes to the root of attitude and method and is the hallmark of fiction's golden age. We take the cardinal thing for granted. Ours are the valuations of retrospect. We are looking and judging when the tradition has shaken itself out and may be almost exhausted, asking ourselves with hyperconscious regard to theory and technique, and feeling near the end of time: what have the mighty dead left for us to do? In fact there's always something for talent to do, but that is not at all the same as working at the height of the storm, like Dostoevsky, when no dust has settled, in an international creative bedlam which throws up the most extraordinary juxtapositions. Thus Mr Pickwick gets seized on during the writing of *The Idiot* as a type of fictional hero beautiful in his goodness, beautiful and absurd, a less great creation than Don Quixote, but comparable and 'enormous all the same'.[39] The letters and notebooks swarm with surprises like that. It is not our Dickens, but this Russian knew what he wanted.

That was when he was on the track of Prince Myshkin, his own idiot-seer hero. Whereas with the tradition at large it was more a question of knowing, or rather sensing, what he did not want. The availability of the others was not for him; and that is just as true of masters with whom he had no special rapport, Stendahl say, as of those he felt in one way or other close to, some of whom I have just named. But I left out Gogol. Gogol burst through availability itself, into an intense inane gone comic and pseudo-cluttered, 'a wonderfully uneasy immediacy': into 'a kind of Russian hilarity and dishevelment, that majestic dishevelment that runs riot in *Dead Souls*'.[40] The negative impulse, the shying away, which in Dostoevsky's case led to an unaccountable authorial persona, with Gogol produced an irresponsible one. 'If all of us became real authors, who would be left to do the copying?' 'Don't worry, it's not me.' There is no Gogolian equivalent to the thematic follow-through, the responsibility, of these unaccountable identity jokes.

Those, and they are many, who typify Dostoevsky's vision and execution as dramatic have felt the breath of the deeper realism. The trouble with dramatic analogies, the writing, staging, watching, and reading of plays, is that they shed least light on matters of greatest interest. Certainly it appears impossible to make a boring play or film or television series of

[39] Letter of 1 January 1868 (*Pisma*, ed. Dolinin, Vol. II, p. 71 — at this very crowded letter-writing time for Dostoevsky).

[40] John Bayley, *Times Literary Supplement*, 22 February 1980. As Hazlitt remarked of another comic and cluttered work, *The Rape of the Lock*, 'it is admirable in proportion as it is made of nothing'.

Crime and Punishment, but that novel possesses unmatched availability, as we shall see. Mr Golyadkin, hat in hand, is cinematic. His joke is not though, and film and theatre have no bearing on *The Double*'s climax in the elopement letter and aftermath, any more than they have on the takeover of eighteenth-century epistolary novel in *Poor People*. The paradox here is that the direct, unmediated, 'real' quality which leads people to call Dostoevsky the most dramatic of novelists first shows itself in two painstakingly arcane works whose multi-layer intellectualism and linguistic self-absorption in parodic and other areas would seem to work actively, even purposefully, against drama.

Then comes *The House of the Dead* which gave Janacek an idea for his last opera. That is not the same thing as crying out for translation into another medium while succeeding triumphantly in its own, like *Crime and Punishment*, but it does mark an obvious shift towards openness and availability. The story of prison life often reads easily. Think of Lieutenant Smekalov leaning forward on his chair, pipe in hand, arm raised, waiting for 'Thy kingdom come'. What's so very unlike Victor Hugo about that? Why not call it dramatic?

Why not indeed? Hence my fear that talk about authorial unaccountability will stick in the gullet of common sense. Then I also pictured Dostoevsky working his way backwards into the nineteenth-century novel. That idea may not appeal to common sense either, but if more bizarre it also appears less pompous and theoretic than the other, and the job of vindicating it is already half done; for if my account of the pre-Siberian fiction is accepted, then we agree that Dostoevsky had a position to work backwards from. The second half, the establishing of a position he was working towards, is easier in that the instinctive resistance of expert and layman to the idea that Mr Golyadkin's Petersburg is more Kafkaesque than Gogolian has no counterpart when Raskolnikov's Petersburg gets assimilated to the nineteenth-century literature of the city, particularly in Balzac and Dickens.

But common sense will still protest that an authorial unaccountability which suits Dostoevsky's pre-Siberian deviousness runs dead against the grain of a candid tale. So attention turns and returns to that dead man's scruffy manuscript. The candour of *The House of the Dead* depends on it. For if this simple evasive device is not just meeting a simple need to evade, to fictionalize actual happenings, but is gratifying a far from simple hunger after evasion, then we have not left unaccountability behind, but only its pre-Siberian modes, and the prison novel is only skin-deep candid.

It is no less readable for that, no less easy after *Poor People* and especially *The Double*. It has arrived in the Nineteenth Century. And the role of unaccountability is to get and settle it there — without, of course, playing its author's genius false. This is the distillation of the problem, the essence of the quest for form. Properly called *Notes from the Dead House*, the title directs attention, sets the tone, looks forward, and harks back. Mr Devushkin's lodgings were a dead house, so was his quasi-military place of work, houses within which that first novel found room to ponder what it is to be a man, a man among men. Such rumination strikes us as preternaturally, biblically bare, but no barer than Dostoevsky's statement to his brother on leaving the dead house of prison, that 'in four years I finally distinguished people'. The latter is the bareness of immediate retrospect, and it is voiced by an 'I' who, if the letter-writer novelist is correct, cannot be carried across from his letter into his novel because it is the nature of the novel to cause this 'I' to disappear.[41] The retrospect remains true, but a truth about the novelist, not the truth of the novel.

In fact the successful distinguishing of people — bare, clear, an achievement — is exactly false to *The House of the Dead* and just what doesn't happen. The novel counterfeits the jumbled actuality of a dead man's memoir, life as he lived and recorded it. And the result is the art of the remiss, of provisional assessment, gossip, idle conjecture, contradiction, uncertainty above all. A lot goes on but nothing is accomplished — except a novel; and then the credit goes, so Dostoevsky says, to the 'unknown man' who wrote it.

The true and unaccountable author, at no point unrecognizable, parades and promotes his dearest values, as when there is a clanking of fetters at the back of the church because

[41] p. 138, above.

the convicts have taken Basil the Great's prayer to themselves, 'Accept me, Lord, even as the robber', prostrated in simple literalness which is the heart of hearts of Russian folk Christianity. There's no sense of the novelist being caught out as there would be if the disappearing 'I' were a straightforward absconding manoeuvre, and if the 'unknown man' betokened an attempt to advance a convincing *alter ego*. Instead, the flexibility of I/We/They/Everybody establishes itself, which is both the presence of the author and the substance of his tale. In other words, the effect is of four prison years simultaneously experienced and narrated, and far from being a rather silly paradox, the dead house's life is the novel in a nutshell. Naturally in loneliness and despair this life shrinks back to the root, as at that moment in the very early days when ' "A dead house!" I said to myself, gazing intently from the steps of our prison'; but even here the breath of something shared and human and redeemable is stirring in that unobtrusive yet slightly surprising 'our'. (Constance Garnett omits 'our': recall the telltale phenomenon dubbed by me systematic mistranslation.)

(vi)

And next the manuscript evidence. Only one fragment survives, apart from a very short passage which was cut completely in all printed versions, so no word-by-word comparisons can be made there.[42] This fragment covers seven pages of the hospital sequence.[43] Here at last we are looking over the composing author's shoulder as nowhere else in the novel; and our inquisitiveness is at once rewarded. The first eight lines reveal that 'in our ward' is missing in manuscript, that 'the ward doctor' becomes 'our ward doctor' in all printed texts, and that the manuscript reading 'ill at ease' is elaborated into 'ill at ease with us'. And so on. The focus is unmistakable, and the direction of change clear almost beyond

---

[42] *PSS*, Vol. IV, pp. 250–2. In 'I want to say my prayers but they are singing obscene songs' we may suspect a move to appease the censor which Dostoevsky later thought better of. But the brooding on freedom in the same discarded passage, and on the convicts being called 'unfortunates' by those outside, has a different flavour and gets assimilated into the novel at various points.

[43] pp. 166–73; *PSS*, Vol. IV, pp. 255–9.

the dreams of a commentator with a case to argue. Some time between penning this fair copy and printing his first magazine text Dostoevsky decided that the integrity of the hospital scene, the solidarity of the 'I' with the 'they', needed strengthening. A typical change is from the doctor 'respected by the patients' to 'respected among us', and the same phrase shows a further rush of confidence and clinching of the final view in that this doctor who is 'even' respected for his severity in manuscript becomes 'specially' respected for it in print.

At the same time a restless hand, not easy to placate, hovers over the other terms of I/We/They/Everybody flexibility. 'The common people' gets rather fussily elaborated into 'all the Russian common people'. The convict-patient who gossips while 'sitting on my bed in the evening before the candles were lighted' comes as an addition to the manuscript itself, a second thought, an enlarging touch; 'sitting on my bed' leaps off the page with extraordinary tender affirmation after one has just read a draft which is without it; in the midst of all this holistic 'among us', 'our fellows', 'our ward', it is the narrative voice of the novel fined down to a first person singular that brings the hospital sequence within a hair's breadth of pure documentary recall.

Therefore to set the manuscript fragment over against the printed texts is to indicate something statistically compelling; it can't, as we strangers to the theory of probability say, be an accident. What it amounts to is another matter. Changing 'patients' to 'us' and so on throws no magic switch unless there is magic in the air already, just as the overall stratagem of pretending to purvey the contents of a dead stranger's memoir remains inert at the level of a formula to be followed like a cooking recipe. These must engage with each other and with the central energies of the book. In other words, the formal properties which have gone under the names of flexibility and unaccountability in our discussion should not be thought of as separable from theme and inspiration and the other terms of old-fashioned humanist criticism. Indeed if they won't translate into these terms, flexibility and unaccountability are a worthless coinage. Equally, since they are both meant to go to the heart — the single heart — of the matter, they must translate into each other. And so, I hope, they do. To make that marvellous little episode in church: it is the case that the shifts, dilations, contractions (flexibility) of I/We/They/Everybody happen before our eyes, and it is also true that the narrative remains uncommitted to the events narrated (unaccountability) in ways which a traditional commentator might grope after by noting a certain obliqueness, a working to one side of or even all round the Orthodox liturgy and the convicts' response to it, round religion itself, faith, the world of the spirit, in a procedure bearing the clearest stamp of Dostoevsky's genius.

And then towards the edge of his vision, in Tolstoy's 'Death in Hospital' extract, a calm presence emerges momentarily, a level voice addressing the event which eases the whole burden of a man's life, the gift which comes, like life, once in eternity. We should not disown the passage for Dostoevsky, or even be unwilling to judge *The House of the Dead* by it — so long as we remind ourselves that the chapter closes with the removal of fetters from the corpse, and that the rule about fetters in hospital belongs to a ghostly collective fabric of imposed forms which is the walls of the dead house enclosing those who live and die and everything that happens there. But to make an extract and call it 'Death in Hospital' is to drag a piece of furniture out of the house; and then it does cease to belong; whereas left where it is it exemplifies the book's nineteenth-century prodigality, the tumult of goings on within the walls which make it so unlike the two pre-Siberian novels, while obviously by the same hand.

This death bears the same relation to the hospital sequence as the released eagle does on the chapter on prison animals. The two Tolstoyan extracts are the only motifs not projected socially, which is a way of saying that death is solitary for everyone and that the bird is even more alone than Varenka disappearing into the bare steppe at the end of *Poor People*; he has even more keenly and poetically nowhere to go than she; the earth is in no sense this creature's element. But Sorrel the horse is suitable '*for the house*' (Dostoevsky's italics). Vaska the goat not only butts heads with convicts, he marches in front of them as they return from work. And the dog Byelka addresses the whole world lying on his back, which is his statement of unconditional surrender at, or near, the centre of the novelist's vision and field of operation.

Drawing in towards the middle of the hospital sequence, like a mist in a valley, is the impenetrable social mystique of enforced fetters and forbidden privy, continuous with lodging-house mores in the young poet's earliest fiction. Again the simplest question has its use: what happens? The narrator arriving in hospital is issued with a dressing-gown. He puts it on and thinks no more about it. Everything strikes him as shiningly clean after the rest of prison. Then he goes to bed in his allotted ward and begins to take note of things round him. An old convict-patient with a heavy cold and a habit of cramming his nostrils with snuff catches his attention. He too wears a hospital dressing-gown, and he uses it to keep his own handkerchief 'comparatively clean' by transferring his snot from handkerchief to dressing-gown when he blows his nose. The narrator suddenly remembers his own dressing-gown:

Then I realised it had been soliciting my attention for a long time by its powerful smell; it had become warm on me by now and was smelling more and more strongly of medicines, plasters, and, I thought, some kind of suppurating matter . . . .[44]

He learns that these dressing-gowns have a long, confused history. One reason for their state is their contact over the years with the torn and bleeding and festering backs of convicts brought to hospital after being flogged. And so the narrative turns to these convicts and their affairs, to the tricky business of getting rod-splinters out of their wounds, to how they behave on admittance after flogging, and the tricks some of them get up to in order to avoid or at least postpone punishment. One convict who is due to be flogged seeks and obtains admission to hospital with inflamed eyes. Once he arrives his eyes mysteriously stay red. The doctor suspects him of malingering, and eventually discovers he is rubbing plaster from the ward walls into his eyes at night. So the doctor threatens him with what is literally a form of horse treatment unless he 'consents to recover'. The convict doesn't consent, and the treatment proceeds. It works like this: the loose flesh at the back of the neck is pinched up

[44] p. 159.

and transfixed with a knife, and through this wound a linen tape is passed. And once a day at a fixed time the tape is pulled to and fro in the wound so the man's neck has no chance to heal. Finally, unable to bear it any longer, 'he agreed to take his discharge'.[45]

The narrator's dressing-gown and the malingering convict's linen tape are *House of the Dead* furniture at its most characteristic and belonging. What is one to say about the stench called forth by 'my' body from the 'government' (*kazenni*) and communal (our/their/everybody's) garment? How to get a purchase on the convict's *agreeing* to go, when he can be turned out any time, and punished, for faking his condition, and when the doctor administering the horse treatment is the very one respected by the convicts for his severity — 'even' respected for it in manuscript, 'particularly' respected for it in the final text? Potent stuff. These are the inward energies without which manuscript alteration would be mere tinkering. And very mysterious stuff. Man's inhumanity to man is far too tidy and confined a view of it, just as the novelist's 'I finally distinguished people' must not be carried across into his novel. The dressing-gown incident is no help in sorting human beings out, however tactfully one tries to handle fictional 'message'; but it does release an effluvium, some vital further thing which others might call a subtext but I am happy to leave as a smell. The evocativeness and the conceptual opacity of this blended human taint of ages are inseparable. The same is true of the dabbling interplay of wills — the psychic stink — surrounding the horse treatment, out of which there emerged a consent to get well. And true also of those fifty extra lashes we read about earlier. They elicited the screams and supplications required by a decorum for which everybody and nobody was responsible: another smell and yet also the same smell because the life of the dead house is one as well as manifold.

And then in the novel's most famous scene this pervasive opaque element becomes literal and physical again in the form of bath-house steam. Impressed by the hellish murk of it, Turgenev wrote to Dostoevsky saluting another Dante and a modern miniature *Inferno*.[46] Again this is too neat, too

[45] pp. 168–70. [46] *Pisma* (1961–8), Vol. IV, p. 320.

literary and domesticated, the sort of reaction Thackeray or Matthew Arnold might have had, true but far from the whole truth. Even the simple linen tape and the extra lashes refuse to settle into focus as sadism, refuse categorization, hover between the involuntary and the accidental; whereas the bath-house encompasses a whole world grotesquely askew but not tampered with, and therefore still ours. 'Making it strange', another formalist pearl, never enriches Dostoevsky at his best. It *is* strange! The bath-house routine is as circumstantial as a skirmish in *War and Peace*, yet its economics are as stark and schematic as any of Brecht's little allegories of capitalism. Convicts pay to squat on the higher benches so the dirty water runs off them onto those below who can't afford to 'buy a place'. Bureaucracy and the forms intrude their madness even here. Soap — a thin sliver — is government issue although peasants have very little use for soap; but every bucket of water after the first has to be paid for, and the profit goes to the entrepreneur keeper of the bath-house.[47]

A world to weep over and even more to wonder at on its Dostoevsky tilt, to struggle for balance in while recognizing our own there. Isaiah Fomich, the only Jew in the prison, a terrific capitalist, steams himself towards unconsciousness on the very top shelf, and in order to intensify the experience he hires a relay of men to thrash him.[48] Is this hell or heaven?

[47] pp. 105–113.

[48] Tsarist records give his religion as Russian Orthodox, but Dostoevsky makes him Jewish in faith. There is no sign that he does this to indulge his spite against non-Russian ways (compare the Mohammedan Tartars who are lovingly dealt with: pp. 55–60). I suspect he wants to give one of his sidelong glances at the convicts' rough childish religion as they taunt Fomich with 'You sold Christ' (p. 107), but also to guide the novel yet again into the area of imposed forms, this time in relation to prescribed ritual conduct. Fomich's Sabbath devotions require him to indulge in lamentation followed by rejoicing. 'I once asked Fomich what the sobbing meant and then the sudden solemn transition to happiness and bliss. Isaiah Fomich hugely enjoyed such questions from me. He at once explained that the weeping and sobbing stood for the thought of Jerusalem's loss, and that the Law prescribed the most violent possible sobbing and breast-beating at this thought. But at the moment of the very loudest sobbing, he, Isaiah Fomich, *must suddenly*, as it were by chance (this suddenness was also enjoined by the Law), *must suddenly* remember that there is a prophecy concerning the return of the Jews to Jerusalem. Then he must immediately burst out into rejoicing, song, laughter, and recite the prayers in such a way that his voice expressed the greatest

I suppose neither. A sensual extreme of savage animal torpor. But there are human things here too. The narrator is nursed through the occasion by Petrov, his self-appointed servant, who sometimes steals from him, 'as it were *by accident*', while loving him dearly.[49] And now Petrov tends his master's 'little feet' (the untranslatable Russian diminutive), and a Biblical resonance is surely calculated because this bath is the first stage of preparation for the festival of Christmas, four days before the Day, a bowing the head to the prophet's admonition 'Wash you, make you clean'. Their wounds from rod and lash glaring crimson in the steam as though freshly inflicted, the naked bath-house convicts are a community furthering a purpose which unites them with each other here and now and with lives and a history outside.

They are also fettered and brutally herded. The novel has it both ways, as great art can. And it continues to do so through the holiday, which is both a time of gorging and drunkenness, and Christmas:

At the kitchen door I was overtaken by a convict from the military division with his sheepskin thrown over his shoulders. He had caught sight of me in the middle of the yard and shouted after me: 'Alexander Petrovich! Alexander Petrovich!' He was running towards the kitchen in a hurry. I stopped and waited for him. He was a young lad with a round face and a gentle expression, very taciturn with everybody; he had not spoken a single word to me or taken any notice of me since I entered the prison; I didn't even know his name. He ran up to me out of breath and stood looking straight into my face, gazing with a vacant but at the same time blissful smile.

'What is it?' I asked with some surprise, seeing him standing there, smiling, staring wide-eyed at me, but saying nothing.

'Why, it's Christmas,' he murmured, and apprehending that there was no more to be said, he left me and rushed into the kitchen.

I may mention here that he and I had nothing to do with each other afterwards and scarcely exchanged a word from that time until I left prison.[50]

possible happiness and his face the greatest triumph and nobility' (pp. 108–9). It's noteworthy that while Dostoevsky alters Fomich's religion, the *House of the Dead* account squares with the official record over his trade of jeweller and other details (*PSS*, Vol. IV, pp. 283–4).
[49] p. 93. The italics are Dostoevsky's, showing once more his fascination with the involuntary/accidental idea. Compare 'as if by chance' in Isaiah Fomich's ritual switch from sorrow to rejoicing.
[50] pp. 123–4.

The holiday that began in a bath-house ends in an equally crowded makeshift theatre. The pitiful inadequacies of staging and performance turn to gold: 'There was no criticism, and indeed there could be none' — at one level a sly evasion since it doesn't follow there was nothing to criticize (as in everyday expressions like 'One can't blame them'), and at another level the very voice, the life, of the house united in creative joy and admiration of 'the tremendous show' put on by 'our fellows': the novel's holism at its most powerful, but also the narrating 'I' at his most separate since word has got about that he had to do with books and suchlike in the big city before coming inside, and so 'they' call on 'me' to help. For once 'I' am deferred to. A beautiful example of that flexibility which is at once narrative mode and fictional substance.

And so the narrator who was very much on the fringe of communal activities like the purchase of Sorrel the horse now finds himself at the centre, and also alone. As expert and critic he can deviate; for example he can judge the scenery to be 'very poor', in flat contradiction of the holistic voice; and the reader who has a moment ago been attending to that voice feels a rush of defensive solicitude on behalf of the convicts and their theatricals — an involuntary tribute to the novel's power to convince and move.[51]

The reader feels torn. That is to say *The House of the Dead* thrives by contradiction, though here again it couldn't do so but for those inner energies we have been speaking of. And contradiction (are the theatricals good or bad?) translates into flexibility and unaccountability, just as those two translate into each other. Much remains unspoken. Thus the narrator who, as expert, openly contradicts the voice which says there can be no criticism, is himself, for the time being, a silent contradiction of the solemn and repeated statement that the gulf between the gentlemen convicts and the rest can never be bridged. But so he was at that moment of 'Why, it's Christmas' under the morning stars.

This impasse over gentlemen convicts and the rest is as blunt, and as central to the novel's interests, as the confrontation

[51] pp. 134-52.

of the statement that everybody in prison longs for freedom by the counterstatement that some are here to escape the even greater servitude of life outside. And the case of Z—ki is more extreme than that of the narrator at the theatricals, an even bolder naturalizing of the thought that leaps like a spark from *The Double* to Beckett's *Molloy* — the thought that freaks are common. Z—ki is alienated from the ordinary run of convicts on three counts. He is a gentleman, but he is also a Pole and a political prisoner, and Poles and political prisoners are specially hated. Z—ki is even disliked by his fellow Poles. But an accident can overset everything. 'Our' major accuses Z—ki, who is unshaven, of looking like a tramp. Z—ki's Russian being bad he only half understands the drift of this and replies with dignity that he is a political prisoner, not a tramp.

'Wh-a-at? You're insolent, are you? Insolent!' roared the major. 'To the guardroom! A hundred this instant, this very second!'
The old man was flogged. He lay down under the lash without protest, he bit his hand and endured the punishment without a cry, or a moan, or a movement . . . . He would have to come back straight from the guardroom where the flogging had taken place. Suddenly the gate opened: Z—ki, without looking at anyone, his face pale, his lips white and trembling, passed through the convicts who were gathered in the yard and who already knew that a gentleman was being flogged. He went into the barrack hut, straight to his own berth, and without saying a word he knelt down and began to pray. The convicts were astounded and even touched.[52]

Dostoevsky has a way of making amends for his extreme but still fundamentally commonplace xenophobia with gestures of the rarest splendour. We will be considering his treatment of Herzenstube, the old German doctor in *Karamazov*. Here, with Z—ki, a documentary source is traceable in the memoirs of a fellow Pole in the prison which were published long after he had been released.[53] These disclose that the old man of our text was middle-aged when he was flogged and never lived to be old, and that while he had been a Professor of Mathematics, as in the novel, the 'somewhere' of his chair was in fact the world-famous university of Warsaw. Altering Z—ki's age makes for an obvious heightening of effect, whereas that apparently lazy 'somewhere' works more subtly, recalling the careful carelessness which was so important in the earliest fiction. Dostoevsky can scarcely have been cooped up with Z—ki and failed to hear about Warsaw. The narrator makes the clear implication that Z—ki is one of the Poles with whom he 'associated quite intimately'. Substitute 'Warsaw' for 'somewhere', or even leave 'somewhere' out (as Constance Garnett does),[54] and the whole thing goes a bit wrong. The detached, bright, so to say euphoric, scrap of information about mathematics gets tamed and tethered by the Warsaw of maps and history and personal knowledge; or, when 'somewhere' is omitted, the sense of our prison being more than just out in the sticks becomes very slightly weakened, for it is by innumerable such touches as this elsewhere, anywhere, 'somewhere', of life outside, that the apocalyptic remoteness of the dead house is evoked and sustained. Figures tend to loom out of nowhere — which must mean somewhere — in spectral solitude. A girl selling bread rolls comes up to the narrator when he is out at work, and cries 'Not so dandy!' at the sight of his convict clothes. Dostoevsky conceals the fact that she is not alone by the simple device of cutting out the word 'Girls!' with which she addresses her companions in the Siberian Notebook entry where he records her exclamation.[55]

Thus he can be caught playing with the facts to suit his purpose, though it isn't always possible to prove that he was not himself deceived and swept along on the tide of rumour and false opinion. The Gazin who 'made a terrible and tormenting impression on everyone' and was held in horror as a child-murderer, had been sentenced, the official record shows, for 'frequent absence from barracks, drunkenness and theft'. The Old Believer who is in prison for burning a church down in the novel, and who gets to know the narrator well and talks about his crime, is actually there for much smaller demonstrations of religious dissent such as failing to be present at the ceremony of laying a church foundation stone.[56] (Soviet commentators point at the censor. I prefer

[54] p. 248.   [55] p. 10; Entry Number 32.
[56] pp. 35, 43; *PSS*, Vol. IV, p. 283.

to recall that Dostoevsky loved conflagrations.) But if not this Gazin and this Old Believer, then others. Children will always be getting murdered and churches burnt. Freaks are common.

The memoirs of the Pole who writes about Z—ki also state that Dostoevsky was invited to direct the Christmas theatricals.[57] There's no whisper of this in the novel. The theatricals chapter moves from 'the rest of us' in the dark and curious about what is going on, to the narrator knowing 'in outline' what will be performed, to his being 'consulted' because he is reckoned 'a connoisseur'.[58] The novel doesn't give an inch over the kind and extent of help this leads to. If it did, the narrator would be in some measure pinned down, accountable, and the swing between undifferentiated group joy and expert comment would not be the sheer and flexible thing it is. The joy is literally unconfined. The comment, though, is fact-bounded, loyal to a documentary trust which expects circumstances to be noted for what they are. For example, the stage curtain is made of old leg wrappers and shirts and paper. If 'I' were director, 'I' might be expected to do something about it or at least wring 'my' hands. But no, this is the narrator at the observing extreme of the observer/partaker swing, and his voice is to one side, almost bodiless, on the verge of third-person narrative. So removed is this voice during long stretches of the sequences of Christmas and hospital that we almost forget about it as a single destiny. I don't suppose many readers are bothered by the fact that although the narrator has gone to hospital we are never told what's the matter with him. He spends a lot of time there, on and off, but in effect we have lost him; so it comes as an inordinate surprise when the communal 'government' dressing-gown begins to grow warm on *this* back. Of course he's here too — in the flesh! we suddenly recall.

Being the recipient, under a frosty Siberian sky, of 'Why, it's Christmas' is scarcely more voluntary than warming a dressing-gown. Narrator as captive one-man audience and as human radiator hits off the novel more amply than fetters and shaven heads and the other immediate passivities and compulsions of prison. The feel of Christmas in the air, a garment's mounting stench, are forms which shared life assumes, the house's endlessly shifting ways. Sometimes we take these forms and ways directly to ourselves, as with the patterns imposed by 'the authorities'; and sometimes we use imagination — for example over the joy of 'the rest of us' in the play put on by 'our fellows', and the envelope of bath-house steam with water flowing from body onto lower body, and the consent that emerges from the linen tape treatment. And only a very literalistic or sanguine reader will deny that the decorum recommended by fifty extra lashes is everywhere too.

Thus with the applause at the theatricals, or even the gale of unmalicious group laughter following Lieutenant Smeka-lov's 'Then give him some!', prison becomes residually rather than radically prison. And so, when the convicts return from work with Vaska at their head, his stout figure garlanded with flowers, are they going home? The question reveals how the very terms of Dostoevsky's art were delivered into his hands by circumstance. There are no homes in his books, but prison allows him inexhaustible play with shadows and semblances of home. The dead house is a sort of home for those who found life outside unbearable. It is always more like home for peasants than for gentleman convicts. The heart of the Russian home is the stove, and I remarked that there are no healthy, functioning stoves in Dostoevsky. The prison bread-oven is a sort of exception; the bread it bakes is so beautiful that its fame has spread beyond the prison and through the town. A visiting priest praises it. The novel digs its heels in with the very bold mystic assertion that the convicts 'blessed the fact' that the bread was not weighed and served out to them in rations: 'if the bread had been served by weight, a third of the people would have gone hungry; but served in common there was enough for everyone.'[59]

This matchless and sufficient bread discovers *The House of the Dead*'s integrity at its most spiritual, and its most tacit. There are no kitchen scenes. We never see that bread-oven working: hence its being a *sort of* exception. The nearest

[59] pp. 20–1, 125.

the novel takes us to it, and to the other prison ovens, is a glow through the window and the smoke 'puffing in clouds from the kitchen chimneys'.[60] Once again it is Christmas, dinner is being cooked, and the narrator awakens a half-promise of home and human identity — of somewhere to go and somebody to be — with another bold expression: 'it was the same in prison as everywhere else.'[61] Convicts drink. Balalaikas are got out. Songs are sung:

> *The owl upon the roof will call*
> *And grief my heart will tear;*
> *His voice will echo in the woods,*
> *And I shall not be there.*

But also:

> *We behind these walls are hidden,*
> *No man sees us, counts the cost;*
> *But God who made the world is with us,*
> *Even here we are not lost.*[62]

---

[60] p. 123.
[61] p. 121. Constance Garnett translates *u lyudei* 'amongst other people' and Jessie Coulson (Oxford World's Classics) rationalizes it into 'among real people'.
[62] p. 128.

Chapter 5:   Under the Floor

(i)

Dostoevsky excluded *The Double* from his 1860 Complete Works because he wanted to rethink and rewrite it. The result was the transformation of the 1846 'Adventures of Mr Golyadkin' into 'A Petersburg Poem' published in 1866 — two years, that is, after the magazine version of *Notes from Underground*. The *Notes* reappeared in volume form with few but significant changes in 1865.

So the final *Double* and the *Notes* are chronologically very close. That isn't sufficient reason in itself for treating them together. Dostoevsky was capable of writing unrelated things at more or less the same time, and of course the *Notes*, unlike *The Double*, has no earlier text linking the middle-aged man who was back from exile and living in Petersburg with his Siberian or pre-Siberian self.

He also claimed that in Mr Golyadkin Junior (*alias* the Double) he had found his supreme underground type.[1] But again this isn't decisive on its own. He often said things that weren't true; the more grandiose the more suspect, as a general rule. Those two short novels, *Notes* and *Double*, must speak for themselves.

(ii)

The underground man describes his state as one of 'assiduously constructed yet somewhat dubious hopelessness'.[2] That is the novel's voice, absolutely its own, inconceivable in *The House of the Dead*, impossible in the later books of the Sixties and Seventies. So what about the 1866 *Double*? Its voice is

---

[1] pp. 56–83, above.
[2] *White Nights*, p. 65. Mirra Ginsburg's Bantam Books translation of this novel is excellent, and so is Donald Fanger's Introduction — though he subscribes to the orthodoxy that the *Notes* is the 'first essay' representing a 'sudden mastery' of the 'new kind of fiction' of Dostoevsky's maturity (pp. ix, xiv).

different again, but cognate. Those words could not be said about or by Mr Golyadkin, and yet they have an urgent bearing on him and on the formulaic 'indescribable agony' of his abstract lacerations. Precisely those words could be said, though, by Samuel Beckett. And herein lies the kinship of *Double* and *Notes*; for very much as the first gets plundered to further the action (or rather inaction) of *Godot*, so the collocation of assiduous construction and dubious hopelessness might be extended thus:

The niches or alcoves. These are cavities sunk in that part of the wall which lies above an imaginary line running midway between floor and ceiling and features therefore of its upper half alone. A more or less wide mouth gives rapid access to a chamber of varying capacity but always sufficient for a body in reasonable command of its joints to enter in and similarly once in to crouch down after a fashion. They are disposed in irregular quincunxes roughly ten metres in diameter and cunningly out of line. Such harmony only he can relish whose long experience and detailed knowledge of the niches are such as to permit a perfect mental image of the entire system. But it is doubtful that such a one exists. For each climber has a fondness for certain niches and refrains as far as possible from the others. A certain number are connected by tunnels opened in the thickness of the wall and attaining in some cases no fewer than fifty metres in length. But most have no other way out than the way in. It is as though at a certain stage discouragement had prevailed.[3]

In other words, Dostoevsky is back in the Twentieth Century. The young poet rides again, though — and in the same breath — art never repeats itself any more than men win their spent years back. Sameness with difference presents itself in the 1860s notebooks like this: Golyadkin Junior is to be reworked as Senior's 'conscience personified', and he will know things which Senior, like all of us, wants to keep to himself and hide from everyone else.[4] How will he know them? The *Notes* were originally advertised, before publication, as 'A Confession'.[5] The underground man will and in the event does try, fitfully, to reveal all. His diatribe has a confessional aspect which nothing in either text of *The Double* can match. And yet Dostoevsky had spoken of the 1846 *Double* in its day as a confession, which is some

[3] *The Lost Ones*, pp. 11–12.   [4] p. 117, above.
[5] *PSS*, Vol. V, pp. 374–5.

measure of the intertwining of *Notes* and *Double* through the years.

Conscience, in these same notebooks, points onward to *Crime and Punishment* later in the decade, as indeed does confession in its familiar and contained sense. Both get excluded from the 1866 *Double*. In *Notes from Underground* they burst their banks and flood out in an orgy of mental exhibitionism. The book in its overall mood is an indecent exposure of consciousness, not a confession, not an un-burdening of troubled conscience. Dostoevsky was right to abandon his proposed title, and it's no accident that the word consciousness pervades the *Notes*, whereas conscience appears only once.[6] It is the case, one should note, that consciousness was much to the fore among writers and intellectuals in this period. *Hamlet* was endlessly discussed. Turgenev's 'Hamlet and Don Quixote' and 'A Russian Hamlet' are the most famous among many studies, and the Shakespearean motif sometimes gets blended with that of the indigenous 'super-fluous man' — the Russian of good will and reflective talents who cannot find a part to play in the barracks state. What separates Dostoevsky in the *Notes* from other people and general trends is the twentieth-century quality I have been remarking. While his contemporaries used *Hamlet* to expatiate on thought and action along Goethe's and Coleridge's lines, Dostoevsky took to himself the Prince's miraculous throw-off about being too much in the sun and had his own hero do something about it, take himself out of the sun, underground, beneath the floor.

(iii)

The underground man chooses to say no to our human party, the feast of life. Choice is crucial to the assiduous construction and dubious hopelessness of this willed solitude, and to the relationship between *Notes* and *Double*. Choice appears to be everywhere in *The Double* but is in rational truth nowhere.

---

[6]   *White Nights*, p. 154. 'Confession' (*Ispoved*), the abandoned title for the novel, does not appear at all; the word at p. 90 (*priznanie*) is better translated 'declaration' or 'avowal' than 'confession'. The verb to confess occurs once, at p. 91.

Golyadkin Junior's pranks and antics — stealing pies, for example — are not choices, decisions, manifestations of mind made up, because he has been created psychologically void, merely impish. It's not a case of withheld mentality but of no mentality. And here Junior and Senior divide. Senior's mentality has been withheld — which is another way of approaching his incidental madness. The form this withholding takes is to deny him and the novel itself a past, to perch him and it on the razor edge — that formulaic 'indescribable agony' — of a forward-tilting existential present. And one of the ways the young poet reveals what he is up to is to visit his work with the very faintest breath of intrusive normalcy, when Senior consults the doctor who tells him to be more sociable and have a stiff drink when he feels like it. The doctor asks him where he has been living. Senior's answer, 'I must have been living', completely unrelated to personal memory, points up the absence of a real past. Senior's thought, as if from outside himself, as if coughed up by a computer, is that he can't have come from nowhere, any more than his sourceless roubles and newish clothes; but for the purposes of the novel that is exactly where he and they do come from. And for the purposes of the novel, at the intersection of time-joke and withheld mentality, Senior's empty echoing declarations that he is about to adopt a passive role or take a decisive step or say such and such are not full and rational choice but verbalized twitchings of the will.

Whereas the underground man's long stay beneath the floorboards is truly, sanely of his choosing. That doesn't make his choice whole-hearted; the elaborate rationale — assiduous construction — whereby he expounds and defends his positon is self-divided throughout since he also envies those above his head. He's not sure the feast of life is no good. His hopelessness is indeed somewhat dubious. In the 1860s notebooks, when Senior says he'd give a pretty penny to know what it all means and Junior replies that perhaps it happens as it does happen and means precisely nothing, his 'perhaps' is double-edged; the meaningful possibility remains open.[7] Once more the importance of not allowing consciousness to narrow into conscience asserts itself, and the

[7] p. 112, above.

metaphysical, pre-Siberian flavour becomes unmistakable.

The *Notes* are a fable of consciousness and choice, and of absolute contradiction — duality or doubling in a new guise. The underground man calls himself an antihero.[8] He has an urge to stick his tongue out at logic, science, and society. This sticking out the tongue recalls Junior's impish tricks, but with the difference that the underground man's rude gesture is his emblem of considered choice. It is the opposite of mindlessness. You can't win but you need not assent to losing. You can't make two and two add up to five but you can stick your tongue out at $2+2 = 4$. You can't refute Darwin but you can stick out your tongue at *The Origin of Species*. You can't stop people designing sociopolitical utopias, but —.[9] And so on.

You can't win *vis-à-vis* yourself either, but again you need not be reconciled to losing. The equivalent of sticking out your tongue at yourself is telling 'the loathsome truth' in a riot of self-betrayal and denigration.[10] There is plenty of this in the *Notes*, which is why commentators like to call them a confession. They are wrong, I maintain, because the confessing is no more singleminded than the sticking the tongue out, and it's of the essence of the fable of divided consciousness that this should be so. Then what of going underground and staying there? However halfhearted his decision, the novel's antihero surely stands by it? This question touches the relation of *Notes* and *Double* at its most sensitive. In the 1860s notebooks Junior is proposed as the one to whom Senior will reveal the things he conceals from everybody else. The 1866 *Double* turns its back on this proposal, intensifying Junior's mindlessness and sharpening yet further Senior's one-man Double Act of nobody to be and nowhere to go. *Notes from Underground* not only embraces the proposal, it expands and colours it to the point where the novel might properly be subtitled 'Consciousness Personified'. Beyond that there's no conclusion one can reach about the book which doesn't engender its own opposite or contradiction in a shuttling nightmare of unprogressive dialectic. A new turn

[8]   *White Nights*, p. 174. From now on unattributed page numbers refer to *White Nights*.
[9]   pp. 66–7, 77, 87–8.   [10]   p. 169.

to Macbeth's restless ecstasy. Not only does the underground man want to belong to the world he is rejecting and to justify the self he is vilifying; his very staying underground, his holding to his choice, confronts the counter-circumstance that he has no alternative to sweating it out down there. We have, then, among other things, a drama of determinism and free will. Choice is no more than what we call choice. It is also no less. Choice is the right and only word because we have nothing else to call it. (Why call it anything? — a lurking thought, waiting to pounce.)

To settle attention upon this 'it' of choice is to consider authorial stance. Dostoevsky introduces the *Notes* in his own person, saying that their author is fictional but that people like him 'not only may but positively must exist in our society', and that in his work the author 'attempts, as it were, to elucidate the reasons why he appeared and was bound to appear in our midst'.[11] Thus the 'it' of the underground man's choosing to be who and where he is has been trapped in a deterministic web at the outset. But dubiously so. Dostoevsky's lending the authority of his own name to this introductory statement is a device like any other. And it is itself afflicted, unostentatiously yet undeniably, with a familiar pre-Siberian instability because of the way it slides from the social type ('He represents a generation') to the very man (this man and no other: 'he appeared and was bound to appear') who wrote *Notes from Underground*. Moreover, if he himself was bound to appear, in what sense is he a fiction? The notional representative of a class becomes, or becomes also, an actual man among men, and the signature Fedor Dostoevsky merely gives a new twist to the old ploy of frame narrator.

The introductory note seems to forebode an editorial role like that of the finder of the tatty manuscript in *The House of the Dead*. In fact 'Fedor Dostoevsky' never moves in. And not only does he keep out, he disappears — again dubiously. He melts into a 'we' which is how the book is brought to a stop. The underground man who has been showing no sign of flagging suddenly says he has had enough,

11 p. 57. 'Author's Note' is Constance Garnett's rendering of 'Fedor Dostoevsky'.

and his discourse breaks off. Another voice informs us 'However this isn't yet the end of the *Notes* of this para-doxist. He failed to keep to his resolve and went on writing. But it seems to us, too, that we may well stop here.' And that really is the end of the novel, and yet again a dubious 'really' since the underground man is carrying on without his readers. Readers! Here is more dubeity in that the under-ground man alternates a hectoring address to his readers with the assertion that he has not and will never have any readers, he is writing for himself alone.[12] And who is this 'we' em-erging from nowhere, in dubious complicity with the author over the equally dubious business of stopping? The little touch of 'us, too' exemplifies the novel's unrelenting and detailed assid
uity.

So the intellectualism of *Poor People* and specially *The Double* is back with a vengeance. In terms of authorial stance, Dostoevsky never pushed elusiveness as far as he did in *Notes from Underground*; an all-pervading dubiousness — the word suggested by his text — recalls flexibility and unaccountability in *The House of the Dead*; but that was a free novel about unfree yet real, and therefore also un-circumscribed, people, while this has the tight grip of theory on it. The inhabitants of the dead house had been sent to prison. The underground man sends himself there, notionally. His solitary confinement follows a disembodied addressing of himself to the human condition; it is a consequence no less purposed than Petersburg itself, 'this most abstract and intentional city on earth' created out of nothing in the north-eastern marshes of Russia by Peter the Great's fiat.[13] His opting out of life is a counter-fiat to Peter's. He has made himself one against all. Rational awareness of what he has done, of context and circumstance, is crucial here. Mr Golyadkin was also one against all, but he didn't know it. Excluded from the party, outside the festive house ablaze with light, 'in his agony he began at last staring resolutely and directly at all the windows at once; *that* was the best thing to do'[14] — physical, incidentally mad, dubiously

<hr />

[12]   pp. 90–2.   [13]   p. 60.
[14]   *The Eternal Husband* p. 277. Mrs Garnett (systematic mistranslation!) omits 'all' and 'at once'.

possible (it may be the best thing, but can one stare at all the windows at once?); whereas the underground man reflects 'And there was another thing tormenting me in those days: the fact that no one else was like me, and I was like no one else. I am alone, I thought, and they are *everybody*.'[15]

We have all thought that in our time; the *Notes* would not be the parable of consciousness I take them for if we hadn't. Each of us bears traces of the underground world, but only traces, we aren't underground men — a fact projected by the novel on the plane of consciousness: 'any consciousness at all is a disease', whereas the underground man suffers from 'excessive consciousness'; 'we all limp, each one of us, more or less', while he is a dubiously hopeless cripple.[16] His troubles are self-inflicted in that his isolation is willed like Peter's city, and equally they are determined *ab extra* since to be conscious is to be penned within the walls of a single given life: he didn't ask to be born. This duality mirrors the universal human lot, the difference between him and us being that the solitude of conscious self-identity is not, the rest of us find, always tormenting, we sometimes want to be ourselves; and secondly that the underground man's 'they are *everybody*' — though we know its desolation well enough — has a way of benignly resolving itself into family, friends, neighbours, colleagues, enemies, strangers, and so forth.

The underground man cannot simply will himself out of existence. Or be released from willing. Nor can we. Schopenhauer asks too much. But we can at least blow our brains out. My polemic regarding the pre-Siberian ambiance of the *Notes* finds support in their absolute exclusion of suicide. The underground man seems to leave no possibility unvisited in his mind's restless ecstasy, but he never turns in this direction. 'Why not simply give up?' asked Mr Golyadkin, and reader and young poet share the grim Cartesian joke about consciousness: there is no such thing as giving up, even in their sleep men find some shameful thought to blush at. 'Our hero' doesn't laugh with reader and poet because in his state of withheld mentality or incidental madness he can't know what he is saying. The underground man also talks about giving up, and he can and does

[15] p. 95.   [16] pp. 60-1, 174.

know what it is all about. This all excludes suicide because he is the self-proclaimed antihero of a fable of disembodied consciousness, and you can't kill consciousness without doing violence to the body.

And he has no body. We are examining Dostoevsky's strict terms of reference, *alias* the tight grip of theory on this novel, *alias* the kinship of *Notes* and *Double*. Commentators, east and west, have seen the pre-Siberian work as much more socially and psychologically orientated than I do, and have regarded the *Notes* as marking, for better or worse — better in the west, worse in the modern east — , the emergence of a metaphysical novelist in the 1860s. A particularly close link has been asserted betwen the underground man rejecting the world and its values, and Raskolnikov kicking herd morality in the teeth by murdering the old moneylender. I don't want to loosen this connection so much as to shed light on it. *Crime and Punishment* and the *Notes* both figure a lonely bending of the will, the one driving forward into the deed that cannot be undone, the other, a narrative levitation or Indian Rope Trick, hovering over the point of wilful pressure, discovering the antihero already underground and leaving him there scribbling on when the words of the novel stop. The two books would be closer than they are if *Crime and Punishment* ended with Raskolnikov still addressing — but *addressing* — himself to the murder. And if Svidrigailov had been left likewise in mid air, alive at the close but suicide-bent, suicide-intent, the two books would be brought even nearer together.

In *Crime and Punishment* suicide enters Dostoevsky's fiction for the first time, and in a big way, and with suicide come solid human phenomena like the longing for oblivion and the withering of the ties that hold a man to life. Contrast the bodiless affair of giving up. The underground man is returning to Mr Golyadkin's joke about consciousness, but consciously. In fact hyperconsciously. It is central to the *Notes* that the whole business should admit of degree, that the underground man should have the disease of consciousness worse than other people, that whereas his state has been positively willed like Peter's city, the same is true of others only in so far as they are tainted with the underground.

Therefore the impossibility of giving up is itself, so to say, relative. Dubious hopelessness once more. The underground man pictures 'simple, direct people', minimally conscious people, who 'will sincerely give up' if a blank wall confronts them when they are pursuing some crude unreflective aim; whereas for him life's blank walls are 'a pretext for turning back'. There is a sense, of course, in which he himself gives up in the face of these same simple direct people; they do at least (or at most) get things done, and in his Hamletish paralysis of will they make him feel a mouse — but 'a hyperconscious mouse' and therefore incapable of sincerely giving up.[17]

This is the hall of mirrors, the infinite regression of being conscious of being conscious. The hyperconscious mouse chimes with the literal sense of underground (*podpole*), which is under the floor, and in doing so it awakens the man/mouse duality, or doubling, of our antihero's state. It is not just that he admires what he despises. He cannot really, sincerely, despise or admire anything, any more than he can give up. Further, he cannot mean a word he says, not in the full sense as Mr Golyadkin would express it, though the underground man is conscious of being unable to mean anything. He is his own antihero, totally undependable to himself, and his discourse amounts to no more than a prolonged howl or moan. And even moaning is undercut and its sincerity (we would nowadays be invoking the idea of authenticity throughout) poisoned by consciousness. He had toothache for a whole month once, and in his pain the thought came to him that 'these are not candid moans, there's malice in them, and the malice is the whole point. The enjoyment of the sufferer finds expression in these same moans; if he didn't enjoy them he wouldn't be moaning.'[18] And of course he cannot mean that either.

Complete authorial elusiveness and instability of content make the *Notes* potentially, and sometimes actually, a boring as well as a difficult novel. The common reader has never been enchanted. Not for him subtle but very real distinctions like the one between giving up and finding a pretext for turning back. Nor the queasy twentieth-century equipoise of

[17] pp. 63–4.   [18] pp. 67–8.

dubious hopelessness. Nor a whole gallery of tacit internal contradictions like 'conscious inertia', nor logical absurdities like the second half, in relation to the first, of being unable 'either to begin or to finish anything', nor self-cancelling assertions like being 'at fault through no fault of one's own'. Nor the weirdness of the thought that however much you wanted to effect a change in yourself 'you would probably do nothing about it because, in fact, there is perhaps nothing to change to'.[19] In some of the novel's more accessible moments a spent and tender luminosity of spirit discloses itself, Hamletish again and gesturing towards Stavrogin in *The Possessed*. 'This sets their minds at rest,' says the anti-hero talking about the unreflective bustle of 'all direct and active men' — 'and that, after all, is the main thing'. The common reader knows what peace of mind means, and what it's like to be without it, and he is down there for a second with the underground man as he continues, 'And how am I, for example, to set my mind at rest?'[20]

But the common reader probably won't experience more than a faint mental hiccup at Dostoevsky's carefully planted 'for example'. It isn't quite the expected thing. It deflects what would otherwise be an urgently personal question away from the here and now of nature, towards a self un-selved by being proffered as a human case. Playing the same trick with the terrible self-focus of Macbeth's first person singular produces the same effect in a more obvious and gross form: 'But wherefore could not I, for example, pronounce Amen?' This is Golyadkin country — the non-exemplary 'for example' which, like viewing himself statistically ('the deathrate's so high'), undermines the abstract struggle to assert identity ('He's a separate person and I'm a separate person too'), and inflicts those distanced lacerations which resolve themselves in the poetic motifs of nobody to be and nowhere to go.

Golyadkin country with a difference, though, in that *The Double*'s non-exemplary 'for example' becomes in the *Notes* dubiously exemplary. In so far as the underground man is fiercely and wilfully himself, himself and no other, himself sticking his tongue out, and equally in so far as he laments

[19] pp. 62-3, 71, 89.   [20] p. 70.

the singularity he cannot help ('I am alone and they are *everybody*'), there is no class or group for him to be an example of. But once, only once, he speaks of 'we underground men',[21] and the whole novel is shot through with that relativism which is the more or less virulent poison of consciousness, the taint of underground, so that the themes of nobody to be and nowhere to go get smeared across all humanity in the form of 'We even feel it's too much of a burden to be men' and, even more bare and formidable, 'But where is man to go?'[22]

(iv)

The total instability of the *Notes* being just that, we cannot even rest upon consciousness as deformity and disease. To be human is to be conscious, and 'Consciousness, for example, is infinitely more exalted than two plus two makes four':[23] life above logic, though life has got to be bled of *life* by another denaturing 'for example' before it can enter this novel. It is true that the antihero introduces 'living life' in the closing pages as if to put blood back into the life of the *Notes*, but in doing so he throws inverted commas round the phrase to show its special, borrowed status. It has had to be imported. 'Living life' is not indigenous to the fable of consciousness, and its last-minute arrival in the book raises questions of overall intention and achievement.

Dostoevsky complained that his grand design for *Notes from Underground* had been frustrated. The original manuscript, now lost, contained, so he told his brother, a Christian answer to the underground man's tirade. The Christian part was deleted by the government censors. 'Those swine the censors approved the passages where I mocked everything and sometimes blasphemed *for effect*, but where I deduced from all this the need for faith and Christ — that they prohibited.'[24] This smells all wrong. Deducing the need for Christianity is preposterous in relation to the text we have. In fact all deducing, all light-of-day rationality, works on the

[21] p. 88.
[22] pp. 85, 175.
[23] p. 86.
[24] Letter of 26 March 1864.

side of disbelief in Dostoevsky, and it is also to be noted that he took no steps to get the cuts restored, either while he was altering the magazine text for publication in volume form, or later when he was a national figure with some power. He won't have been telling lies in the letter to his brother, but it would be in character if the complaint about the censorship were grossly exaggerated and the whole issue melodramatized.

I believe the underground man's imported 'living life' tells us all we need to know about Christianity in the *Notes* — I mean it tells us about such Christianity as has any business being there. Living life was indeed life in Christ for Dostoevsky. But until *Crime and Punishment* there was not much he could do to evoke it creatively. One recalls moments in lodging-house and even prison — 'It's Christmas!' — when the horrors of a godless human comedy are more than mollified. Otherwise there is the journalism and the letters, and a narrative which ought to have been translated but hasn't, called *Winter Notes on Summer Impressions*.

Dostoevsky published *Winter Notes* alongside his fiction despite its documentary and philosophic nature. The piece came out the year before *Notes from Underground* and records a brief visit to France and England. It is a critique of 'the European spirit', a spirit complacent, bourgeois, decorous in Paris, drunk and reeling with Bacchanalian capitalist frenzy in London. The vision of Victorian London aflame with getting and spending — industry, trade, exploitation, drink, food, sex, sullen gaslit revels *à l'anglaise* — is specially memorable, and Dostoevsky's eight days there left him with a sense of the 'terrible force which has united all these countless people' and has united them 'into one herd' — a false unity, the unity of Antichrist, of Baal as he calls it.[25] Herd stands in tacit contrast to the true flock, his own ideal of Russian and ultimately world society:

Understand me: voluntary, fully conscious self-sacrifice, free of outside constraint, sacrifice of one's entire self for the good of all is in my view a sign of the highest development of individuality . . . . What would brotherhood consist in if we were to transpose it into rational, conscious language? It would consist in each separate individual saying to society,

[25] *PSS*, Vol. V, p. 69. We meet the phrase 'herd enthusiasm' in the *Double* notebooks of the early 1860s (*PSS*, Vol. I, p. 432).

without compulsion, without advantage to self: 'We are strong only when we are together . . . '.[26]

The pre-Siberian theme of our not belonging to ourselves is being picked up again, and the other pre-Siberian thought that a weak man cannot stand alone has broadened into the conviction that it is not the terrestrial nature or Christian destiny of any man to stand alone.[27] Both themes will become matters of great fictional moment when Raskolnikov collects himself to enter the police station *'as a man'* and declare what his self-will has led him to. It is also true, as he climbs the winding staircase of the police station, that his ascent is towards the living life of *Notes from Underground* and the brotherhood of *Winter Notes on Summer Impressions*. But *Winter Notes* is not fiction, it is Dostoevsky airing his views, and the living life of which the underground man speaks has, I am arguing, been imported from elsewhere.

The brotherhood of the one discourse may be used to elucidate the living life of the other. Thus the antihero hears a voice from above ground, 'through a crack in the floor', telling him 'You hunger for life yet you yourself tie up life's problems in a logical tangle'.[28] The voice must be referring, however broadly, to his reasons for going and staying underground, to the stance of the no-sayer to what goes on above; and the token of that stance is sticking his tongue out — which covers refusing to assent to $2 + 2 = 4$, wishing harm for himself instead of advantage, choosing to do stupid and aimless things 'because at any rate this preserves for a man the most important and precious thing, his personality, his individuality'.[29] This reading of selfhood, of what it is to be a man among men, runs dead counter to that in *Winter Notes*. And to explain what the voice from above means by saying that the underground man wants life but has misapprehended and misrepresented what he wants, we should oppose the self-surrender of *Winter Notes* to the self-assertion of *Notes from Underground*. The antihero locates selfhood in the solitary human will. His starting point is the proleptic existentialism of *The Double* in which the classic substantial self of the

[26] Ibid., p. 79.   [27] pp. 122–5, above.
[28] pp. 89–90.   [29] p. 81.

Cartesian tradition has collapsed into a vertigo of unqualitied willing. Will this, will that, will anything — but will. In *Notes from Underground* the withheld mentality of Mr Golyadkin's incidentally mad contextless willing has dilated and been normalized into conscious choice. And, one may add, rational choice in the sense that when the underground man elects to do crazy things or things in his own despite he is flaunting the ultimate rationality of his unreason. 'I have carried to the limit', he tells those above the floorboards, 'what you have never ventured to carry even half way.'[30]

But of course the flaunting and carrying to the limit are riddled with internal contradiction. All-pervading dubiousness ensures this, just as it makes any single-minded, let alone clinching, argument for living life and Christianity impossible in the context of the novel we have in front of us. Even the words about hungering for life while entangling life's problems are 'invented' by the underground man himself (so he says) as well as, or in contradiction to, being heard through the floorboards.[31] Nothing is dependable, nothing persists, except the naked burning light of consciousness.

(v)

This doesn't sound remotely like a nineteenth-century text; and nor would it have come out like one if Dostoevsky hadn't deployed his material the way he did, dividing the *Notes* into two distinct parts. The first, so to say the twentieth-century part, is the antihero's furious but unprogressive harangue, his polemical weaving and ducking; it constitutes a one-man Double Act of self-divided consciousness, an abstract tragedy which is also sometimes witty and glancing in the way of nonsense and the absurd, as when the antihero remarks that every man has things on his mind which he will not reveal to anybody 'except to himself, and then only in secret'[32] — leaving the reader to savour the unspoken alternative of revealing things to oneself publicly.

The second and longer part is a retrospect which pulls the novel much more into line with conventional narrative. The

---

[30] p. 174. [31] p. 90. [32] Ibid.

antihero describes an incident that happened long ago, when he was twenty-four, before he went underground. We recognize this young man from the stories Dostoevsky wrote in the late 1840s. Or rather, we recognize the type. He is the dreamer, the solitary moocher, the night-walker, the 'artist of his own life', and his Petersburg has the poetic atmosphere we encountered in *White Nights* and *The Landlady*. The argument is that the dreamer of the 1840s has become the underground man of the 1860s (and incidentally that the atmospheric city has been stripped to its abstract and intentional origin in the whim of Peter the Great). We are told in the introductory note by 'Fyodor Dostoevsky' that this process was bound to happen. The inevitability asserted here is two-stranded. One strand relates to talking points of the 1860s, to burning even if now forgotten issues, most notably the utilitarian determinism and optimistic secular rationalism of the novelist and critic Chernishevksy. The underground man's polemic along the lines of 'Who wants to want according to graphs?' advances the counter-argument that men will always prefer to go their own way rather than fall within some overall scheme of enlightened self-interest.[33] So an antiheroic determinism confronts Chernishevsky's: men are *bound* to rebel. But — and this is the second strand — the dividing line of ground-level or floorboards in the *Notes* also images timeless questions of solitude and society.

These questions emerged very early for Dostoevsky in the shape of the paradox that your and my humanity is at once unique to you and me, and shared. Separate and identical but never like, becomes Mr Golyadkin's cry. By pretending to his boss that he is not himself but somebody strikingly like himself, he brings on his head a tragicomical doom in the form of the Double who is, unrelentingly, separate and identical but never like. There is nothing corrective about this doom, merely the sense that like is fraught. In the same way the preoccupation with types, with people, that is, who are like each other — dreamers, rag-men, faint hearts, and so on, in the stories of the late 1840s: types which aren't or aren't fully, human — in the same way this cannot be called

[33] p. 79.

corrective, despite the portentous thought that we do not belong to ourselves. In prison Dostoevsky 'finally distinguished people'. But that occurs in a letter, and the great novel itself, *The House of the Dead*, rests on the edge of documentary. And then comes *Winter Notes on Summer Impressions* which, though classed with the fiction, is reflective journalism.

There the pre-Siberian motif of separate and identical but never like has developed into a vision of mystic brotherhood. The link between separate and identical on the one hand, and achieving the highest individuality (separateness) through the completest self-surrender (identification with all) on the other, will be obvious enough. Then for the idea of never like we have to turn to the false unity of the herd, again in *Winter Notes*. Falseness resides in unity being achievable only by ignoring the human (which is the divine) in the human being; and as well as promoting a Russian ideal of brotherhood Dostoevsky is engaged in a running fight against western and western-inspired orderings of society, both capitalist and socialist, variously depicted as Kingdom of Baal, Crystal Palace, False Paradise, greenhouse, anthill and hen-coop. These constructions are not for real men to live in, but what *Notes from Underground* calls aspiring 'generalhumans',[34] notional creatures, mankind trying to envisage itself as a type, as *like*.

Thus a corrective element has entered. *Like* is no longer merely fraught. There is now an alternative to seeing people as crystal-palace or hen-coop types, as like each other — and no doubt the censored 'Christian' argument in *Notes from Underground* dwelt on the brotherhood and organic commonalty which we encounter in the *Winter Notes* and elsewhere in Dostoevsky's journalism. Once again the issue is two-stranded. Talk of a true non-herd unity, both rooted in the soil (*pochvennost*) and religious (*sobornost*), belongs to the 1860s as much as does the polemic against Chernishevsky and the quarrel with other positivists and materialists and champions of rational self-interest. *Pochvennost* and *sobornost* are more or less where Dostoevsky's wayward sympathies

[34]   p. 175.

lie in the politico–theological debates of the time. His creative gift is another matter. 'Living life', I maintain, has no role in *Notes from Underground* beyond that of a flourish towards the romantic conservative values of soil and church. The Russianness of these values is of the age, of a mental map drawn by a few outstanding men in the middle decades of the Nineteenth Century; whereas Dostoevsky's attitude to like and the type is both highly idiosyncratic and Russian from the beginning of civilized time. An icon is never *like* the Saviour or the Mother of God. Then if it is not *like*, what is it? This question, over which the Greeks spent enormous effort and time, almost passed the Russians by. They took the icon from Byzantium untroubled about speculation, criticism, apologetics. They historicized and humanized the Bible. They fed their souls on the Lives of the Saints, on story and precept — not dogma. They loved the human Jesus, the naughty boy of the apocryphal gospels. 'Christ stands here' in the Russian Confession, not in the Greek. This belongs with a paucity of allegorical and symbolic forms, with a simplehearted unfanciful typology, with direct experience of heaven in the liturgy and of God in Christ, the god-man. It underlies the fact that Russia, with her seers, mystics, 'thinkers', holy men, has not produced a single philosopher as that word has been understood in the West since Heraclitus and Parmenides.

Dostoevsky's creative idiosyncrasy resides, of course, in the way his immemorial Russianness is deployed. The question, what am I like? arouses in him the fear that there is no such thing. In his work the theme of nobody to be goes back to the very beginning, to Firsts and Seconds, to Mr Devushkin wondering whether to be a copier is to be somebody. And if like is fraught, how is the birds-of-a-feather of human community to be attained? How does one reach it? And again, perhaps there is no such thing. Perhaps there isn't a haven to reach. Thus nowhere to go also begins at the beginning, with the girl seamstress setting off for the bare steppe — the same 'bare' as in the name of the second novel's hero, Mr Golyadkin, Mr Naked.

The dubiousness and relativism of *Notes from Underground* give a special twist to the nobody and nowhere themes, and indeed unite them. What is separate in 'We even feel it's too much of a burden to be men' and 'But where is man to go?' becomes one in the image of mankind 'eternally and incessantly building a road for itself'. To be a roadbuilder is, dubiously, to be somebody, and it is also to be going *'some-where, no matter where'*.[35] The underground man, who has the disease of consciousness worse than other people, cannot even claim to be a roadbuilder. Nor, in failing or refusing to build roads, in 'doing nothing', can he claim to be a lazy man:

Ah if I were doing nothing simply out of laziness! Heavens, how I would respect myself then — precisely because I would be capable at least of laziness, at least of one personal and so to say positive quality which I myself would be certain of. Question: Who are you? Answer: A lazy man. How very pleasant to hear that about myself! It would mean that I was positively defined, it would mean there was something to say about me. 'A lazy man!' Why, that's a title and a vocation, it's a career.[36]

Roadbuilders and lazy men. Once again, with my mind running back to the copying clerk and on to the soldier who asks, if there's no God what sort of captain can he be?, I urge the interdependence of status and ontology in Dostoevsky.

This still doesn't sound like a nineteenth-century text. So let me observe that just as, from first to last, nobody and nowhere constitute the radicals of his narrative impulse, so his master metaphors of the human condition are Prison and Party, opposed foci of constraint and celebration. The underground man's self-imposed solitary confinement occupies the first part of the *Notes*. The second and longer part is built round a dinner party of young men at the Hôtel de Paris in Petersburg. Part Two's title, 'On the Occasion of Wet Snow', augurs the atmospheric city familar to us from the stories of the 1840s: the city of winter fogs and twilight summer nights. And what I said about overspill and normal-izing or naturalizing when I discussed those stories in relation to *Poor People* and specially *The Double* has an even more direct bearing on Part Two of *Notes from Underground*. *The Double*'s surreal climax finds Mr Golyadkin standing outside

---

[35] p. 84. Dostoevsky's italics.   [36] p. 72.

in the cold and wet, contemplating the lighted windows of a house where a party is going on. In Part Two of the *Notes* the young dreamer-hero, not yet antihero and not yet underground, invites himself to dinner with some former school companions. The mixture of French bravura Romanticism and Germany and Pushkin and Gogol, further compounded by Dostoevsky's private normalizing process, doesn't make this a comfortable nineteenth-century text, but at least a recognizable one. The hero's rudely wishing himself on the others for dinner — a party in honour of one of the group who is leaving Petersburg — is itself a fleshing-out of the theoretical courting of insult and humiliation which the underground man goes in for in Part One. So is the passage where he tries to get himself thrown out of a window and then, having failed, contemplates provoking a duel and writes a letter of challenge which he never sends.[37] Equally, these absurdities are a narrative dressing-up of Mr Golyadkin's cry, naked as himself: 'If only *something* would happen — even a catastrophe.' Equally too we are in the area of fiasco and *skandal* native to Dostoevsky's fiction, early, middle, and late.

In a word, Part One, naturally called 'Underground', is a fable of disembodied consciousness which has been granted personal and social extension and an urban context in 'On the Occasion of Wet Snow'. None of this amounts to much. The genius of the *Notes* belongs almost entirely to Part One, and that genius (as I keep insisting) is pre-Siberian in spirit and particularly intimate with *The Double*. As to overall design, it's not easy to say what has gone wrong. Dostoevsky's alterations to the magazine text concentrate on deleting references in the opening pages to a long novel lying ahead, and the postponement until *Crime and Punishment* of this big confessional project must have set him problems of narrowed scope and shifted emphasis. Then there is the censor's intervention. Then there is the fact that his wife was

---

[37] pp. 98–101. The *Double* notebooks reveal Dostoevsky toying with the idea of an elaborate duel scene (*PSS*, Vol. I, p. 432). In the event, as elsewhere, he took the opposite course; the duel theme which is lightly touched on in the 1846 *Double* becomes in 1866 lighter still, the merest hint (*The Eternal Husband*, p. 234).

dying. And two days before her death, on 13 April 1864, Dostoevsky wrote to his brother about a plan for a three-chapter story; so that if by chapter he meant part, we have a contemplated Part Three of the *Notes* to allow for. And three months later his brother died too. It was a calamitious time. And yet haste and harassment are doubtful considerations with this writer; thus the weakest of his late novels, *A Raw Youth*, is the one over which he had most leisure and health and peace of mind.

The text is the thing — and in the *Notes* I would put my finger on the schematic and skimpy way the master metaphor of Party in 'On the Occasion of Wet Snow' is opposed to Prison in 'Underground'. The prison aspect of lodging-house and office in *Poor People*, and the party which Mr Golyadkin's incidentally mad aspirations centre on in *The Double*, come through as large instinctive shapings; whereas in the *Notes* Dostoevsky seems to be playing with these terms of his art, not unseriously but more consciously than is good for him. This suspicion gains strength from two short stories, one before and the other immediately succeeding the *Notes* — the only short stories he published during the entire decade. In *An Unpleasant Predicament* a bureaucrat blunders upon the wedding party of a subordinate and gatecrashes it with shallow liberal philanthropic intentions, and gets what's coming to him.[38] The unfortunate human hero of *The Crocodile* approaches the exotic monster on display and is swallowed. His wife, now 'a sort of widow', reminds him that 'a husband ought to live at home and not in a crocodile'. He spends his time 'devising a complete system' of society. Everything seems clearer to him here — as no doubt it would in a Crystal Palace. The crocodile's inside (note the Beckett taste returning) is 'an empty expanse enclosed by something of the nature of india rubber, probably really india rubber'.[39] This, unlike the *Notes*, is not serious, at least not tragically inclined. It is calculated satirical farce. And it is also prison.

The image of life under the floorboards is too close for comfort to life inside a crocodile. In other words, the prison metaphor in both cases invites crisp comic treatment which,

[38] *An Honest Thief*, p. 194. [39] Ibid., p. 320.

in the *Notes*, it doesn't get. Similarly the young dreamer-hero's existence in 'On the Occasion of Wet Snow', being a travesty of life, a substitution of reading and reverie for the real thing, a living out of books, has obvious literary-parodic possibilities. And these are exploited, but not satisfactorily. Overspill from *Poor People* and *The Double* — from Mr Devushkin's pulp-fiction pleasures and Mr Golyadkin's elopement dreams of silk ladders and Spanish serenades — appears at its most inert in the all too predictable clash between a fantasy life where 'I am a famous poet and a courtier, and I fall in love' — and 'reality'.[40]

The big word reality is matched by an ambitious attempt at creative parody. Part Two of the *Notes* has as its epigraph some lines of a famous poem by Nekrasov, again from the 1840s, in which a prostitute is made to see the error of her ways by the narrator's compassionate eloquence. Our *donnée*, therefore, is a moral and spiritual rescue operation. This stands in a parodic relation to what follows in that nature ('reality') — the dreamer-hero's retrospect — mimics art (Nekrasov's poem). But only up to a point. The drunken aftermath of the dinner party in 'On the Occasion of Wet Snow' is a visit to a brothel. The dreamer-hero goes with the other young men, spends the night with one Liza and then in the sober morning gives her his address, urging her to visit him, which she does. All is set for a grand redemption scene. But because he is the underground man in embryo, self-divided to the root, he cannot go through with it. Art and nature part company.

This separation recalls the elopement letter and its sequel in *The Double* where art (Quixotic Sir Golyadkin and Schillerian love nest) fails to stay with nature and the fact of the matter. But *The Double*'s art is Dostoevsky's: the absurd and delicate and intellectually taxing substance of 'our hero's' dream; whereas art in the *Notes* is Nekrasov's poem. In consequence the parodic art/nature relation in the *Notes* is on the one hand tidy and unresonant, and on the other boringly impenetrable. I am returning for the last time to the floorboard image which is the neatest of dividing lines,

[40] pp. 107, 129.

and to the 'living life' of the *Notes* which has been imported
and tells us nothing.

What does Dostoevsky mean to evoke by the parting
company of Nekrasov's poem and the events of 'On the
Occasion of Wet Snow'? On the dreamer-hero's side, when
Liza comes to him, there is the anguished cry 'They won't
let me — I can't be — good!'[41] Something is going on here,
something as deep and persistent as solitude and society in
Dostoevsky, as being a man among men; but he hasn't made
fiction of it. And on her side,

What happened was this: Liza, insulted and humiliated by me, understood far more than I had imagined. She understood from all this what
a woman, if she loves sincerely, will always understand above all else.
She understood that I was myself unhappy.[42]

The lifeless didacticism of this writing is not fiction either.
As the brotherhood passage in *Winter Notes* expatiates on
'living life' in *Notes from Underground*, so Liza paraphrases
the relationship between Sonya Marmeladov and Raskolnikov,
but with the difference that the living life shared by the
murderer and the prostitute has not been imported into *Crime
and Punishment*. It is the achieved fiction, the stuff of the
book. Or if you like: Sonya not only sees the human in the
human being as Liza does, and as Dostoevsky did when in
prison he 'finally distinguished people'; she touches the
very thing.

[41] p. 169.   [42] p. 168.

PART THREE:
PARAJOURNALIST

Chapter 6: *Crime and Punishment*

(i)

In the mid-1860s Dostoevsky developed a marked tendency to fuss about the relation between real life and fiction, between the goings-on in the newspapers and what he was saying or wanted to say in his novels. I stress the newspapers. He was altogether more interested, on the surface at any rate, in what he found there than in what he could observe of people and events around him. A draft letter to his publisher Katkov — the fair copy is lost — discusses the plot of the as yet unwritten *Crime and Punishment*. It states defensively:

You'll find in our newspapers many signs of an extraordinary mental instability leading to terrible deeds (that theological student who killed a girl he had arranged to meet in a shed, and who was arrested an hour later eating his breakfast — and so on). In short, I'm convinced my theme is partly justified by contemporary life.[1]

For once he was underplaying his hand. *Crime and Punishment* did not merely reflect or even confirm that strange and removed elsewhere, the world journalists write about. It anticipated that world. Readers were settling down to the novel's opening instalment — not a venture to be recommended for 'people with weak nerves' remarked Strakhov, the gifted critic[2] — when a murder story broke in the newspapers. Danilov, a student who had tried to live by private teaching, intelligent, handsome, dark-haired, solitary, killed and robbed a money-lender and his maid. In the course of the trial one Glazkov made a false confession which he later retracted. The newspapers themselves leaped on the parallel with Raskolnikov and his crime and with the innocent Nikolai's declaration of guilt. Nature had followed art. Danilov, *The Voice* observed, had probably not even begun to contemplate his murder when Dostoevsky was shaping Raskolnikov's.[3] The

---

[1]   September 1865.   [2]   Cited in *PSS*, Vol. VII, pp. 349–50.
[3]   Issue of 8 March 1867.

two cases were laid side by side, and likenesses and differences were solemnly analysed as if we had here before us two 'real', directly comparable objects. All this brought joy to the novelist. He often spoke to Strakhov of his 'pride as an author' in his creative foreshadowing of facts, and to A. N. Maikov he enlarged:

Oh my friend, I have completely different notions of reality and realism from our realists and critics. My idealism is much more real than theirs [meaning 'than their realism'] . . . . Their realism won't help you explain a hundredth part of the real events which have actually occurred. But we by our idealism have even prophesied events. It has happened.[4]

We are on familiar ground, since this idealism is none other than his deeper — sometimes he called it deepest, sometimes highest — realism; but with new implications in that he is beginning to show a sensitiveness to the actual which no doubt existed before but was rarely evident, a sensitiveness which is now coming out like a bruise. This is an important aspect of the process I have called his working his way backwards into the Nineteenth Century. *Crime and Punishment* takes its place in a perfectly obvious and open fashion among the international classics of naturalism (or realism), and it is the first of his novels to do so: the earlier and great book *The House of the Dead* walks so close beside personal history as to rule itself out in this connection; formally it is a freak, so I argued, a quasi-novel; and as regards fact and fiction, since he is recounting not 'prophesying events', Dostoevsky cannot have found much in the Dead House to get excited about.

Whereas in *Crime and Punishment* and in the novels which follow he can, though his narrow glee over being ahead of the fact is unworthy of his art and of what 'idealism' and 'deeper realism' intend. Shrewd guessing at tendency is not the jewel in his casket. The interest of how things are resides in their figuration, discernible and expressible by the deeper realist, of how things will be only in so far as that futurity is the truth and the end of how they are and always have

<hr />

[4]   Letter of 11 December 1868.

been. His naturalism is apocalyptic. The social and psycho-logical trends that were bound to produce Raskolnikov/ Danilov are the mere phenomenology of a transcendent mystic and Biblical cryptogram. The Book of Revelation, which Tolstoy said 'reveals absolutely nothing', is more heavily marked than anything else in the New Testament which Dostoevsky took to prison with him, and we know that huge overarching shapes like Baal, the Kingdom of Antichrist, are beginning to appear in his writing from the early 1860s. Danilov's double murder looks small beer in comparison. Indeed it is pertinent to ask what scope of revelatory prophecy *Crime and Punishment* is aiming at.

An ambitious impression is created by Raskolnikov's delirium and nightmare:

In his illness he dreamt that the whole world was condemned to fall victim to some terrible and unknown pestilence that was coming upon Europe out of the depths of Asia. All were doomed to perish except a chosen few, a very few. There appeared a new strain of trich-inae, microscopic creatures parasitic upon the bodies of human beings. But these creatures were spirits endowed with intelligence and will. People who were infected by them immediately became as men pos-sessed and out of their minds.[5]

A grand and dread apocalypse. But this occurs in *Crime and Punishment*'s Epilogue. It is aftermath rather than the novel itself. And the Epilogue also points forward in its closing words to 'a new tale', because 'our present one is ended', and the narrator says he has in mind the slow regeneration of Raskolnikov, now in prison, through love and suffering. No such novel ever got written. But Raskolnikov's nightmare calls to mind one that did, namely *The Possessed*, while the specific link between 'as men possessed' (*besnovatimi*) and *The Possessed* (*Besi*, literally *The Devils*) is inescapably obvious — just as the word 'Socialism' which Dostoevsky has written against the beast in Revelation coming out of the earth with horns like a lamb and speech like a dragon shows the general way his thoughts are tending.[6]

[5] p. 479.
[6] Ch. 13, v. 11. And there's another link here with contemporary journalism. At the end of 1865 and early in 1866 Russian papers were carrying alarming stories of microscopic creatures unknown to medical science: *PSS*, Vol. VII, p. 399.

And again this is the way of *The Possessed* rather than *Crime and Punishment*. However, a second marginal comment in his New Testament both latches on to *Crime and Punishment* and provokes a backward thought. His note on the beast of Chapter Seventeen of Revelation, the beast which doesn't exist and still has to appear and is destined for perdition, is 'generalhuman' — the word he coined for *Notes from Underground* and incidentally never used again in his fiction. At the end of the underground man's tirade 'general-humans' appears as the notional creatures we are trying to turn ourselves into because 'we feel it's too much of a burden to be men — men with real bodies, real blood *of our own*'.[7] How can we have any other bodies and blood than our own? We can't. We can only think about it. And *Notes from Underground* is precisely such a fable of disembodied consciousness.

But in the opening paragraphs of *Crime and Punishment* consciousness has found a home in the unnamed and very physical young man who leaves his stuffy little top room and slips downstairs like a cat, out into the street. This young man is also very mental. His being is riddled with theory and hypothesis. He has a plan. Rather, he has a plan of a plan: the plan being to murder an old money-lender, while the plan of that plan is to embark here and now, out of doors, in the glare and summer stench of Petersburg, upon a rehearsal of the murder.

The question of motive hangs over these first pages, and over the whole novel. Dostoevsky's letter to Katkov asserting that crimes like Raskolnikov's can be found in the newspapers also discusses motive. The old money-lender with her 'Jewish' interest rates is to be murdered because her life is worthless and her hoarded wealth can be put to good use; when the unimportant deed is done the doer will launch himself into something that really matters, a large-scale

[7] *White Nights*, p. 175. Dostoevsky's italics. The burden of being flesh-and-blood men, of sharing in living life, is of course the burden of each other's humanity as much as our own, whereas 'in abstract love of humanity one almost always loves nobody but oneself' (*The Idiot*, p. 446). *A Raw Youth* returns to the 'generalhuman' issue (while not using the word) with the argument that any love we may entertain 'for humanity' can only be for the idea of humanity we have created within ourselves (p. 210).

philanthropic exercise. But *Crime and Punishment* didn't work out like that. The letter to Katkov belongs to the autumn of 1865. Between then and the end of the year Dostoevsky put aside every word he had written and began again. And in this new version the philanthropic rationalist and utilitarian Raskolnikov has almost completely disappeared.[8] And in his place we have a murderer fascinated by the Napoleonic idea.

Repeatedly, he says that to brush a vicious old woman aside like a swatted fly and get on with life is to prove oneself a Napoleon — not Napoleon himself who lost whole armies and forgot about them, but *a* Napoleon. He finds out that there is no such person. In *a* Napoleon he cannot discover anybody to be; *a* Napoleon is a projected, dreamed-up, aimed-at type, a 'generalhuman'. Dostoevsky's home-made word doesn't appear in *Crime and Punishment*; it has been left behind (unlike the mind that coined it) in the much more theoretical *Notes from Underground*. With Raskolnikov the issue has been naturalized into a restless and greedy discontent. 'Mere existence had never been enough for him; he had always wanted something more.'[9]

And it follows from this calculatedly vague 'something more' that the Napoleonic idea doesn't settle the question of motive either. Its domination of the final text only means that it is Raskolnikov's favourite way of rationalizing his malaise. Nothing in him matches his deed. Dostoevsky exhorted himself in his notebooks to 'explain the whole murder *one way or another* and make its character and relations clear',[10] but the artist in him wouldn't allow it. On one occasion, lashing about for reasons after the event, Raskolnikov cries out 'I simply wanted to dare, Sonya, that was my only motive'; and next to 'I just did it' this must be

---

[8]   His only straightforward affirmation of this motive is at p. 457. Dostoevsky makes us bump into it obliquely at pp. 369 (where Raskolnikov himself calls it 'nonsense'), 432 (where Svidrigailov tells Raskolnikov's sister that the reason her brother made no use of the things he had stolen was 'simply that he didn't dare to'). At pp. 58–61 the argument for philanthropic murder is put into the mouth of a student whom Raskolnikov overhears, and he wonders how he came to listen to it 'at the very moment when *exactly the same ideas* were just beginning to stir in his own mind'. The last of course occurs before the murder.

[9]   p. 476.   [10]   *PSS*, Vol. VII, pp. 141–2.

reckoned his least untrue account of himself and his deed.[11] Wanting to dare is his opposite number to the underground man's wanting to want, because whereas wanting to want holds fast to the earlier novel's metaphysical spareness and abstraction, wanting to dare opens up the whole huge circumstance of the murder itself, the thing that in fact gets done.

(ii)

Though Conrad's *Narcissus* runs it close, *Crime and Punishment* remains for me the most accessible and exciting novel in the world. It is the king of murder stories. And of detective stories. And of thrillers. Its atmosphere and suspense are nursed by locality — Petersburg — in ways which can't be escaped but which often get misreported. Commentators are fond of discovering and praising a guidebook clarity in the novel. They have been deceived by the plethora of street-names, bridges, islands, and so forth. All these topographical details are there and are correct. But they don't cohere, don't add up. You couldn't find your way round this city any more (and here is a strange thought) than you have got the practical hang of the little fortress prison at Omsk by the end of *The House of the Dead*. To compare Raskolnikov's haymarket with Kim's bazaar is to see that Kipling has done all the work so that you don't have to go there to know what it's like at the level of vivid and varied description, whereas Dostoevsky leaves his reader with an impression which hovers between smell and vapour and dream.

In fact the street names and the rest belong with the extremely important disjunctive flotsam of the book: paint-pots, old rope, the odd sock, boots that once belonged to the Secretary at the English Embassy, twists of paper, egg-shells, fish-guts, frayed blood-soaked strips torn from trouser-bottoms and coat-pockets, an axe-sling in ribbons ('Little bits of torn linen cannot possibly arouse suspicion!'[12]) half-eaten meals, small change, miscellaneous pawned objects, candle-ends, trousseau-stuff ('fancy boxes, dressing-cases, ornaments, dress material, and all that sort of junk from

[11] pp. 368–9.   [12] p. 81.

Knopf's and the English Shop'[13]) broken crocks (*cherepki*), and skulls (*cherepi*). And what the commentators are really paying homage to, what prompts their sense of coherence and a world revealed, is a feat of illusionist sorcery. In a notebook, beneath the underlined word 'tone' and 'NB' penned three times, Dostoevsky has written among other jottings 'summer, dust, mortar'; and in this case the man and the artist are at one.[14] *This* is the city which readers of *Crime and Punishment* carry with them for the rest of their lives. The novelist stayed away from 'stinking Petersburg' during the unbearably hot summer of 1866, to avoid his creditors but also on his guard against what he called 'false inspiration'.[15] He relied on his mind's eye and ear — and nose. The result is a townscape of 'terrible despairing cries' which mean, and mean more than, that the drunks are leaving the pubs between two and three o'clock in the morning, the pubs that reek of alcohol and cucumber and fish.[16] A townscape of nightmare yellows: sky, buildings, furniture, wallpaper, faces — the colour of age, heat, pestilence, bile and jaundice, bruisings and stainings, with a stronger connotation of dirt in Russian than in English; the colour of the tickets of identification which prostitutes were required to carry; the colour of Raskolnikov's 'cubbyhole' of a room; and the colour which greets him when he comes to after fainting at the police station and sees a man 'holding a yellow glass filled with yellow water'.[17]

Looking over Dostoevsky's shoulder, we find him first writing 'small yellow glass', then deleting 'small'; and writing 'water' then adding 'yellow warm' to the water, then deleting 'warm'[18] — the final text uniting an apocalyptic starkness of yellow meets yellow with the topicality of Petersburg's notoriously filthy water supply, a subject of much comment and complaint in the newspapers. At such moments we come

---

[13]   p. 319.
[14]   *PSS*, Vol. VII, p. 149. Compare 'again the dust, bricks and mortar, again the stench from shops and pubs' and 'a smell of mortar, and dust, and stagnant water' on pp. 85 and 245 of the novel itself.
[15]   Ibid., p. 324.   [16]   p. 80.
[17]   pp. 36, 95. One extraordinarily bold stroke is Raskolnikov's displeasure at finding the yellow wallpaper has been changed to white when he returns to the scene of the murder (p. 153).
[18]   *PSS*, Vol. VII, p. 27.

as close as it is possible to get to the spirit of *Crime and Punishment*. Having, as I say, abandoned everything he had done, he sat down and wrote a six-part novel within a year which included a twenty-six day break in which he threw together and dictated *The Gambler*, itself not a small book nor a negligible one, to satisfy the terms of a contract he had made with a shyster publisher. 'The very thought would be enough to kill Turgenev,' so he told a friend,[19] and posterity salutes a marvel of concentrated effort. He wrote month after month with fearful haste, and yet the Soviet editor only exaggerates slightly when he says that the manuscripts reveal 'immense, most rigorous work, literally over every phrase'.[20] This combination of speed and close attention may have a lot to do with the narrative thrust and atmospheric coherence and intensity that make this the most gripping of his novels.

Then there's the energy generated by frustration. The thing had refused to come right. His notebooks show him hesitating between reminiscence ('It was exactly eight years ago') and testimony during trial ('I am on trial and will tell everything').[21] Note the 'I'. He was thinking in terms of first-person narrative — Raskolnikov's own story. This proved unmanageable. Much of what the novelist wanted to say lay outside the murderer's ken, and, as we shall see, Raskolnikov's consciousness was in other, subtler ways too confining.

Also, Raskolnikov's narrative was to have been 'A Confession' — Dostoevsky's own title — and this wouldn't work either. We recall that the confessional idea has a long history. First the pre-Siberian 'confessions'. Next the unrealized plan for a full-length novel, *Confession*, which got switched to the short *Notes from Underground*. And now another failure. And still, after *Crime and Punishment*, the idea of a confession novel or story tugs at the edge of Dostoevsky's vision, and continues to do so for the rest of his life in the form of *The Life of a Great Sinner* which he planned on the scale of *War and Peace*, but which never got written though it fed previous material into his novels of the seventies, and

---

[19] Letter of 17 June 1866.   [20] *PSS*, Vol. VII, p. 314.
[21] Ibid., pp. 96, 144.

especially *Karamazov* at the turn of the next decade. (Dmitry didn't kill his father but he keeps baring his breast to people about how much he wanted to.)

So the idea of Raskolnikov's 'Confession' ran into the ground. But there it encountered another ruined project, a work to be called *The Drunks* of which only a tiny fragment survives, and the marriage of these two constitutes the success of *Crime and Punishment*. The drink theme too, broadly understood, goes back a very long way. Behind the truant husband Marmeladov, perhaps the greatest feat of instant creation in all Dostoevsky as he buttonholes Raskolnikov in the pub with hay sticking to his clothes and vodka at hand[22] — behind that immortal Russian drunkard stretches a long line of urban dropouts and psychological cripples, of paupers and other victims of the ravages of early capitalism (think of Petersburg as several decades behind Manchester), of the 'insulted and injured' in the novel of that title and elsewhere, back to the beginning, back to Mr Devushkin with his teapot and pipe and his 'fearful lapses' over the bottle.

Why does Marmeladov drink? The *Crime and Punishment* notebooks expend considerable effort trying to establish an overarching reason or at least an empirical scatter of factors, and failing. Compare Dostoevsky's attempt, frustrated by the good angel of his genius, to explain Raskolnikov's motive for his crime. In the novel itself, where we might expect Marmeladov to speak of solace, respite, forgetting, companionship, he grasps the paradox that he drinks because he is in search of suffering, of 'tears and tribulation'. And, he adds, 'I have found them.'[23] This has the same free, metaphysical bearing on his being a drunkard that Raskolnikov's wanting to dare has on his being a murderer. Moreover, as always in Dostoevsky, the search for suffering refuses to settle into coherent masochistic focus. Marmeladov's wife, he says, 'has a consumptive tendency, and I feel it. How could I not feel it? And the more I drink the more I feel it. Indeed that's why I drink, to find compassion and feeling in drink. It's not happiness but sorrow that I'm looking for. I drink because I want to suffer more and

[22] pp. 18–22, above.   [23] p. 20.

more.'[24] So his intensified sorrow is the intensified compassion and feeling for his wife which drink whips up. This is the Marmeladov who married his present wife — not that that did any good either — because he could not bear to see such suffering. We have here the grand selfish selfless non-logic, the deeper realism, of his drinking.

And so the drunkard wants to suffer, while the murderer wants to dare. The one is the passive and the other the active form of a single human truth, as Dostoevsky sees it and realizes it fictionally. The singleness of this truth is what I called the marriage of the *Drunks* project and the 'Confession' project in *Crime and Punishment*. The novelist is now of course in middle age, but right back in his teens he wrote to his brother 'Man is a mystery', adding that a lifetime spent trying to unravel the mystery would not be wasted. On its own this reads like a perfectly ordinary youthful Europeanized sententious romantic flourish. But now comes the idiosyncratic twist. 'I am devoting myself to this mystery because I want to be a man.'[25] He doesn't mean that he wants to become mature or to quell the beast within or anything else comfortable to the understanding. It's a very personal way of thinking and writing which we have encountered several times already, and which now, twenty-seven years after that letter to his brother, appears most insistently with Raskolnikov as he 'paused for a moment to take breath, to collect himself, and to enter *as a man*' and tell the police who it was killed the old money-lender and her sister. But since *Crime and Punishment* encompasses the drinking as well as the confessional theme, we can approach Dostoevsky's abiding human question — what is it to be a man? — also by way of the minuscule *Drunks* fragment:

'The reason we drink is we're at a loose end.'

'Nonsense. We drink because we've got no morals.'

'Yes, and the reason we've got no morals is that for a long time (150 years) we've been at a loose end.'[26]

---

[24] p. 13. The sentence 'It's not happiness but sorrow that I'm looking for' got dropped in some inferior Russian texts of the novel after Dostoevsky's death, and so it is also missing in translations (including those of Constance Garnett and Jessie Coulson in her Oxford version) which follow them.

[25] Letter of 16 August 1839.   [26] *PSS*, Vol. VII, p. 5.

And that's all. Put most simply, being at a loose end leads men to the vice of drunkenness and the crime of murder; and the jobless Marmeladov and the ex-student Raskolnikov are both very pointedly at a loose end. But to say that the devil finds work for idle hands to do is misleading because hyper-moralistic or (if meant literally) hypertheological. In that little exchange which is the entire *Drunks* fragment the 'loose end' idea undercuts the moral and every other aspect of the matter, and once again there's a link with journalism, this time Dostoevsky's own. He specifies 150 years because he has in mind the social and political reforms of Peter the Great in the early Eighteenth Century. This subject had interested him, both as contributor to and editor of the magazines *Time* and *Epoch* in the years immediately before he wrote *Crime and Punishment*. He believed that Peter's reforms had disrupted society by creating a Western-type bourgeoisie and separating the educated class from the common people. What Peter had damaged, and what one might hope to restore, was the natural soil-based unity of Russia. And so, as in *Winter Notes*, Dostoevsky is really talking about *pochvennost*, his own brand of romantic conservatism, half history, half dream.

In *Crime and Punishment* itself the Petrine reforms get the merest glancing reference, and only one, when Raskolnikov's friend Razumikhin speaks of 'us' (compare the 'we' of the *Drunks* fragment) as 'divorced from practical affairs of every sort for nearly two hundred years'.[27] This is a hasty throw-off in the middle of a wide-ranging argument, and it has no particular bearing on drink. Nor for that matter on crime. Nor has it any more to do with Peter's reforms than might perhaps justify an editorial footnote.

But the underlying idea of being at a loose end, or out of the practical swim, is a different matter altogether. It is the very clay out of which Dostoevsky shapes his fictions of solitude and society. And while it might be said that his version of *pochvennost* comes from this same source, and while it is certainly true that *pochvennost* deserves a longer footnote than the Petrine reforms, a footnote is all it should

[27] p. 132.

be. For the novelist works to one side — hence parajournalist — of the writer busy with magazine polemics in *Time* and *Epoch*, just as his novel exists to one side — parajournalism — of the double murder in the newspapers and of scary science-fictionish forewarnings about microbes.

This to-one-side posture of novelist and novel explains how it is that Raskolnikov and Marmeladov are pointedly at a loose end while *Crime and Punishment* is anything but pointedly sociological. The thrust of their loose end, as of details like the murderer's yellow cubby-hole — coffinlike, his mother calls it[28] — and Marmeladov's greenish-yellow face and the mortal yellow-black bruise over the heart after he gets run over, is metaphysical and apocalyptic, not documentary. 'Every man must have somewhere to go,' Marmeladov tells Raskolnikov who has dropped into the pub after his 'rehearsal' of the murder. 'For there comes a time when he absolutely must go somewhere.'[29] Raskolnikov is young, preoccupied and merely puzzled — 'young, abstract and therefore cruel', the severe voice of the novel describes him elsewhere[30] — but the reader attends in tragic wonder, for he understands that Marmeladov has indeed nowhere to go, a nowhere which is the finality of his loose end, at once in character, at once personal to the selfish selfless rationale of one man's marriage and his other circumstances, personal to his 'destitution' or 'extremity' or '*misère*' (*nishcheta*, which he is careful to distinguish from his poverty), and at the same time an objective and transpersonal theme running through all Dostoevsky's work.[31]

From the novelist's journalism and notebooks and letters we glean the almost comically unresonant information that being at a loose end leads men to drunkenness and murder.

---

[28] p. 205. Raskolnikov recalls her words at p. 212, an intensifying device Dostoevsky is fond of. It is also a device — one of dozens — binding the confessional to the drinking motif since Raskolnikov is put in mind of his mother's remark by a discussion of the plain cheap coffin that will be provided for Marmeladov's funeral. (A pity, therefore, that Mrs Garnett renders coffinlike room as tomblike.)

[29] p. 12.   [30] p. 286.

[31] p. 10. The novelist makes doubly sure that his reader shan't miss the transpersonal nowhere to go theme by isolating it, for no *apparent* reason, as the only thing in Marmeladov's discourse which Raskolnikov remembers afterwards (p. 41).

His novels, though, suggest a mental movement not unlike Vergil's thought to the effect that bees are working animals and don't retire and spend their sunset years playing golf: being at a loose end is not the condition of us spiritual and working animals, it is not being a man among men. Marmeladov doesn't think of a drunkard as a human being but as a brute, a beast, a swine. He lives a swine and he dies a swine. But on the Last Day certainly God will call the drunkards of the world to Him:

He will summon us also: 'Come forth,' He will say, 'ye also! Come forth ye drunkards, come forth weak ones, come forth children of shame!' And we shall all come forth, and yet not in shame, and we shall stand before Him. And He will say: 'Ye are swine! ye are made in the Image of the Beast and bear his mark; yet come ye also!' And the wise ones and the men of learning shall say: 'Lord, why dost thou receive these?' And He shall say: 'I receive them, O ye wise ones, I receive them, O ye men of learning, inasmuch as not one of these has deemed himself worthy.' And He will stretch forth His arms to us, and we shall fall down before Him and weep, and we shall understand all things.[32]

So the swine — swine in God's eyes too — will appear on Judgment Day immortal souls capable of penitence and knowledge. This tirade, carried on vodka-laden breath, is a classic instance of Dostoevsky's apocalyptic naturalism working on two levels at once. Marmeladov projects the Christian Revelation on the church-slavonic plane of his and every Russian's Bible and liturgy, remoter from everyday usage than the English Authorized Version; and he indulges a maundering drunken account of himself. The second is an untidy surgical exposure, the more convincing and moving for its incompetence, of the first's withheld human inwardness, while the first is a theological drama in which the *must* of 'a man absolutely must go somewhere' gets tortured on the rack of faith. The one point on which Mr Golyadkin and Double were agreed was that there is nobody like God, but it follows pat and false that if a man has nowhere to go God will look after him. In the notebooks of *Crime and Punishment*, Marmeladov (at this stage called 'the civil servant') is made to argue that 'if only a man is *really alive*, then he suffers, and therefore he needs Christ,

[32]   pp. 20–1.

and therefore Christ will come.'[33] Such explicitness would be
a disaster in the novel, but it underlies the final text of the
pub tirade like a geological substratum, and it reflects the
great and growing importance of mystic suffering in Dostoevsky's post-Siberian work.

Even more damaging would be the inclusion of the following thought about Raskolnikov: 'NB. With the crime itself
begins his moral development, the possibility of those questions which didn't exist before. In the last chapter, in prison,
he says that without the crime he would not have found within
himself *such* questions, desires, feelings, needs, strivings, and
development.'[34] Were he to say any such thing we would be
left with a therapeutic murder. But again Dostoevsky is
fumbling after a creative or regenerative suffering, because
it is of the essence of Raskolnikov's questions, desires,
feelings, and so forth (which of course do appear in the
novel) that they should be agonized. The fictional morphology
of this suffering is more aptly suggested by the novelist
and critic Akhsharumov, writing the very year *Crime and
Punishment* appeared in hard covers, who observes that
Raskolnikov's mental torment, which *is* his punishment in
all but its public aspect, begins with his first promptings
towards the crime.[35]

Thus Akhsharumov directs the reader to something that
makes him certain he holds a masterpiece in his hands before
he has read half a dozen pages: a single pre-natal life, a foetal
stirring and growth, no ordinary robust narrative sense of
something afoot. Raskolnikov's first thought on slinking
down the lodging-house stairs is one of surprise at himself
that he should be 'simultaneously' in terror of his landlady
and planning a murder. The mental suffering and the evil
intent won't be separated. Raskolnikov doesn't put it to
himself like that. We do. He is just surprised. On the surface
of his mind lies the contrast between a trivial though tormenting fear and a monstrous scheme; and beneath that
contrast appears a positive contradiction: for a few sentences
earlier we have been told 'He was not really afraid of any
landlady'.

[33] *PSS*, Vol. VII, p. 87.   [34] Ibid., p. 140.   [35] Ibid., p. 353.

The question, who tells us?, recalls the most important of Dostoevsky's many changes in the course of writing *Crime and Punishment*, his switch from first-person narration — the murderer's story — to what is formally third-person but proves so supple, so volatile, that the distinction between the inside and outside of Raskolnikov's head disappears when his creator wants it to. The solution to 'He was not really afraid of any landlady' might appear to be that we have here a masked first-person avowal, and that it is simply an indication of Dostoevsky's boldness that it should be surrounded by authorial statements which are firmly outside and (so to say) on top of Raskolnikov in the classical omniscient third-person mode: for example, information about his poverty, irritable frame of mind, withdrawal from society, his 'not naturally timorous and abject' disposition. But masked first-person narrative turns out to be deflected stream of consciousness — 'He was not really afraid' will only transpose into 'I'm not really afraid' flitting through his head as he passes the landlady's open kitchen door — so that the past tense collapses into the present, and we find we have put our finger on something pertinent to the novel's urgency and attack and (to borrow Andrew Forge's ugly but useful key-term for late Monet) its frontality.

That Raskolnikov is not by nature timorous is the author's assurance to his readers, dependable through nineteenth-century novelistic convention. That Raskolnikov is not really afraid is, in its latent truth and force, what he tells himself. The two narrative modes walk side by side in bold yet relaxed society, and support each other in the face of the fact that Raskolnikov is shaking in his shoes. The author knows (even if Akhsharumov has to remind him) that the natural man in his hero has been laid low by the combined psychic onset of crime and punishment. Raskolnikov knows (but leaves us to infer) that his present state of mind renders chatter on the stairs intolerable, which looks like fear of his landlady but 'really' isn't. As to state of mind, Raskolnikov lives with his own continuously but inspects it only intermittently, like the rest of us; whereas the author surveys the whole truth the whole time, so that we never find him wondering whether perhaps Raskolnikov is thinking this or perhaps he is thinking that: a fact which isolates *Crime and Punishment* among the mature novels, because elsewhere Dostoevsky loves the unsettled and unsettling narrative posture of 'perhaps', particularly with his contracting and dilating collective voice, the 'we' swept by rumour and speculation which arrives in *The House of the Dead* and reaches its full flowering in *The Possessed*.

While *Crime and Punishment*'s author (or omniscient narrator) knows the truth, he picks his moment to tell it. He bides his time. Then he moves in, for example to reveal that the young hero-murderer, once the deed was done, had a completely new experience 'of infinite loneliness and estrangement'; and that this experience 'was most agonising in that it was a sensation rather than knowledge or intellectual understanding, a direct sensation, the most painful sensation he had ever experienced in his life.'[36] Raskolnikov could never have said that — which introduces the deeper issues involved in the switch from first-person to a nominal third-person narrative. Raskolnikov lives with his pain, but most of the time he doesn't focus on it. He rubs it absently, accosting strangers in the street, seeking out a friend and within minutes exclaiming that he wants to be by himself, watching children wistfully, accusing wellwishers of persecuting him with their kindness; until at last he explodes on the brink of confession in a terrible universal cry: 'Oh, if only I were alone and nobody loved me, and if only I had never loved anyone!'[37]

Of course he doesn't really want to be alone. He is still just rubbing his pain when he says that. What he *really* wants is a business of the inside and outside of his head, in this case of his 'alone' juxtaposed with the authorial 'loneliness and estrangement': a rich relationship, not a flat contradiction or dead end, a relationship which evokes and nurses a distinction established as far back as *The Double*, between false solitude ('loneliness and estrangement') and true solitude which is the obverse of true society and meaningless without it.

[36] pp. 93–4.   [37] p. 459.

But occasionally, as I say, Raskolnikov contemplates the pain he lives with:

> The conviction that everything, even memory, even the simple power of understanding, was deserting him, began to torture him unbearably. 'What if it is beginning already, what if my punishment is already beginning? Look, over there — I thought so!' And indeed the frayed scrappy edges he had cut off from his trousers were lying strewn on the floor, in the middle of the room for everyone to see! 'What on earth can be the matter with me?' he cried again like a man utterly lost.[38]

And this in fact, not in theory, is how crime — the bloody evidence on the floor — and punishment — Raskolnikov's agony — intertwine in the novel. A wonderful moment. It sets one hesitating between general admiration and the attempt to give point to frontality or some such term: anything to obtain leverage on a narrative mode which sweeps up event and idea, fictional past and stream-of-consciousness present, into a single impulse of this immediacy and power.

(iii)

For a moment Raskolnikov wonders if his punishment has already begun. Now the reader met a suffering young man on the first page of the novel. And having met him, he at once began studying him and suffering with him: observing him *ab extra* and sharing the inside of his head; hence his sense that he is both witnessing and experiencing the 'strange smile' which accompanies Raskolnikov's surprise at his own dread of meeting his landlady. That 'strange' which would be a lazy gesture in another novelist is indeed strange to the reader, strange as the feline, supremely *observed* young man himself; and yet he feels the very muscles and skin-surface of Raskolnikov's smile — a prelude to the way in which the book's entire action is simultaneously read about and lived through.

Common sense may deem this a highfalutin account of a quality possessed by every exciting story. Well yes, in so far as it's a question of degree, though if *Crime and Punishment*

[38] pp. 81–2.

really is the king of thrillers then there's something unique to remark in it and even to wax a bit pompous about. For in a monarchy, as Beethoven remarked of Handel, one knows to whom one must bend the knee.

But also: well no. Sometimes there's no question of degree. The wrath of Achilles doesn't work like Dostoevsky's novel at all, and not because it's an old tale. The ship *Narcissus* in her fight to the southward doesn't work like this either. The truth is, not all exciting stories are properly thrillers. Being gripped by a narrative is an altogether wider notion than what is presaged by the two-in-one of being outside yet inside Raskolnikov's 'strange smile': the rehearsal of the murder, the murder sequence itself, the three long duels with the detective Porfiry, the suffering, the hesitation, the final climb up the police-station stairs. Dostoevsky's own attempt to suggest how he disposes his reader in relation to these events goes as follows: 'Narration by the author, a sort of invisible but omniscient being who nevertheless doesn't leave him [meaning 'his hero'] for a moment . . . . '[39] So, after appearing to settle for third-person narrative, he doubles back on himself and leaves us to make what we can of an omniscient author who is bound hand and foot to a far from omniscient protagonist.

That he succeeds in having it both ways is our experience of reading his novel in its dominant and thriller aspect. His Petersburg counts for an awful lot. The illusionism which conjures a complete and natural (I would prefer apocalyptic–natural) city out of materials as unpromising as the colour yellow, also yields up Raskolnikov like a natural secretion, and this vouchsafing process encompasses and transcends the resources both of first- and third-person narrative. To stay with yellow for a moment: we noted a paring-down to the bare bones of yellow water in a yellow glass when Raskolnikov comes to after fainting on his first visit to the police station. An opposite movement occurs with the elements of oppressive heat and smell on that same momentous fourth floor. In the first draft of the scene neither are mentioned. Then, as an afterthought, Dostoevsky wrote 'the air was

---

[39] *PSS*, Vol. VII, p. 146. The grammar of this note is tricky.

terribly stifling' and 'in addition, a smell of wet paint assailed the nostrils'.[40] Our final text elaborates this to 'the nauseating smell of fresh paint which had been mixed with rancid oil'.[41]

Rancid oil is simply right. Hundreds of such details mark Dostoevsky's year-long burst of composition, hour upon hour 'without straightening my neck', he said. Thus he caught the police station and the whole city during those few fictional July days when everything except the Epilogue happens. And he caught his hero too since a man is (among a million other things — but art concentrates attention) the yellows he sees and tastes, and the evil rancid oil he smells. Also, and perhaps to a greater extent, a man is what he *has* smelt: later in the novel Raskolnikov gives the police-station smell as the reason for the suspicious circumstance of his fainting, which is neither the whole truth nor a straight lie but the blending of the guilty man with the poison of the city.[42]

Crime and Punishment's Petersburg does not produce the murderer with the inevitability shown by the 'abstract' city in the novel immediately preceding it, where the underground man 'was bound to appear in our midst'. The draft letter to Katkov merely claims that crimes like this fictional one can be found in the newspapers, and that the fictional murderer has come under the influence of certain half-baked ideas which happen to be in the air at the time. Here, despite life following art with Danilov's double murder, we have an ordinary modest contingent naturalism, and in this area the novel bears out the letter to Katkov. Inevitability, at once psychological and religious, enters (so the letter goes on) after the crime has been committed, in the shape of 'the truth of God and the law of nature' which compel Raskolnikov first to be exiled from the humanity he has outraged, and then to confess and accept the public consequences of confession as the only way to become a man among men again. Here we have the apocalyptic naturalism which marks out Dostoevsky absolutely, and in this area too, though we shall find an overreliance upon the Epilogue, *Crime and Punishment* follows the Katkov letter while breathing life into its dry and sketchy determinism.

[40] Ibid., p. 15.   [41] p. 86.   [42] p. 171.

Moreover the novel takes up the remark to Katkov that the criminal *'himself morally demands'* his punishment (which on its own might mean no more than that Dostoevsky had been reading Hegel or popularized Hegel), and builds some marvellous effects upon it. Raskolnikov has of course outraged the human being in himself too; the pad pad pad of the hunter and hunted relationship with Porfiry is intertwined with self-pursuit to the point where the murderer actually makes the running in the second of the three long interviews, arriving unsent-for and demanding interrogation 'according to the rules', if interrogation there must be; which leads Porfiry to exclaim: 'Good heavens! What do you mean? What is there for me to question you about?'[43] And in the third interview, the net now drawn tight about him, when Porfiry makes a sudden little feint which suggests he won't be accused after all, 'Raskolnikov felt a rush of a new kind of fear. The thought that Porfiry believed him innocent suddenly began to frighten him.'[44] The reader is both astonished and utterly convinced, as he is later on in the interview when Porfiry plays the dangerous game of saying he has got no real proof, he's going on hunch and 'psychology' — so Raskolnikov had better confess.[45] It's up to you, he's saying, to satisfy the hunger which the letter to Katkov and the *Crime and Punishment* notebooks rationalize as the criminal's moral demand.

Porfiry is also asking Raskolnikov to recognize his hunger for what it is. Both he and Sonya Marmeladov, in their separate areas of the novel, impress the need to accept suffering. Now suffering is a vast and many-sided fact of *Crime and Punishment*, as of all mature Dostoevsky — larger than the 'loose end' idea of *The Drunks* which produced Marmeladov the marmeladey wallower in abasement and humiliation,[46] the man who seeks suffering and finds it (and so finds satisfaction too) at the bottom of his vodka jug, who screams 'I'm loving this!' when his wife pulls him across the room by his hair;[47] and larger than the 'out of the practical swim' idea of 'A Confession' from which emerges the murderer, the man with something to confess, who doesn't seek

---

[43] p. 297.   [44] p. 397.   [45] p. 403.

[46] 'Marmeladov — such a sugary surname' (*PSS*, Vol. VII, p. 186).

[47] p. 23.

suffering but learns, though only in the Epilogue, to accept it. Prostitution is the hardest labour in the world, Dostoevsky thought, and Sonya of the yellow ticket who sells her body to buy her family's bread has no loose-end aspect to her suffering. Nor has her consumptive step-mother, Marmeladov's wife, endlessly busy with children and no-home. One can only regard them as victims of other people's loose ends, just as the terrible sustained anxiety of Raskolnikov's mother and sister on his account is the measure of his power to make others suffer as well as himself in that limbo which his friend — his only friend — Razumikhin calls being out of the practical swim. Nastasya, the general maidservant at Raskolnikov's lodging-house, finds him in bed, where he often is nowadays:

> 'You used to give lessons to children, so you say. Why are you doing nothing now?'
> 'I am doing — ' Raskolnikov began reluctantly and grimly.
> 'What are you doing?'
> 'Work.'
> 'What sort of work?'
> 'Thinking.'
> Nastasya fairly shook with laughter.[48]

Murderous and anguished work — the thinking that goes on between the rehearsal and the deed itself. This thinking is the mental pulse which registers the single prenatal life of his crime and his punishment. Razumikhin would not have laughed like the jolly Nastasya. Nor would Raskolnikov's poor mother and sister: 'but I'm afraid, afraid — oh God he's so strange. He speaks kindly but I'm afraid. What am I afraid of?'[49] We recall that in the notebooks Dostoevsky has Raskolnikov reflect upon his crime and declare he had to commit it to achieve moral development and get himself out of the mess he was in. A comically facile conclusion. Nevertheless he *was* in a festering condition, and the murder *did* induce a crisis. In his exchange with Nastasya he reveals himself an underground man who has wandered into a nineteenth-century naturalistic novel, a bohemian Hamlet. The point of contact with the fable of disembodied consciousness is that thinking has become Raskolnikov's work, it has almost become Raskolnikov, and if he did and were nothing but this work we would have the first part of *Notes from Underground* repeated.

And of course committing the murder is an act of perverse self-assertion, like the underground man's notional sticking his tongue out — with the difference that the anti-hero's mind movement breaks no bones, and hurts no feelings except his own. With the murder Raskolnikov erupts into the full glare of the actual, and parts company with his predecessor. But Dostoevsky did not want to surrender the tract of suffering bounded by the sense of being and doing nothing but one's thoughts. The result is Svidrigailov. The notebooks show Svidrigailov developing from a minor into a major character while *Crime and Punishment* was being planned and written, and they show his growth as interdependent with Raskolnikov's final definition. In some early drafts Raskolnikov commits suicide, and the striking thing here is that it's never suggested he does so out of remorse or because he thinks he's going to get caught or even from some vaguer, larger self-loathing. He appears to lose interest in life. He is bored. Sonya asks him, 'I don't understand: how will things be for you, how will you marry and have children?' — of course thinking about his estrangement from human kind; and he replies (Dostoevsky's italics): '*I'll get used to it.*'[50]

During the year in which the final version was written it became clear that Raskolnikov must be freed absolutely from suicide and blanket boredom and ripostes like the one about family life which issue out from beneath that boredom.[51] All these are inconsistent with 'living life', the two words which are placed between inverted commas and imposed at the level of mere idea upon *Notes from Underground*, but which truly drive Raskolnikov, which are his need to become a man

[50] *PSS*, Vol. VII, p. 187.

[51] At one point in the notebooks Raskolnikov's boredom and suicide are explicitly linked: 'A bullet in the head because his future was suddenly illuminated and he saw himself a family man, father, husband, good citizen and so forth' (Ibid., p. 136). Then added in brackets are the words 'Awareness that he doesn't respect people', which may show Dostoevsky's focus beginning to sharpen on the Napoleonic idea and false self-assertion.

again. Mere existence had not been enough for him, in the Epilogue's diagnosis; he had always wanted something more. This wanting teased him on as it happened — contingent naturalism — to murder. Then murder led him inexorably — apocalyptic naturalism — to confess and accept suffering, and acceptance of suffering took him back to mere existence which is living life, neither more nor less. Life is life. It has no outside to it (hence Dostoevsky's ready acceptance of Christ the complete man and his difficulties with God). To theorize about life is not to live. But on the last page of the novel 'life had taken the place of dialectics', and Raskolnikov is on his way home.

Meanwhile Svidrigailov has taken over the suicide role, which is to say the blanket boredom has become positively terminal. 'You know, I take no particular interest in anything,' he tells Raskolnikov musingly on their first encounter; 'especially now, I have nothing to occupy me.' In his time he has tried a lot of things: card-sharping, prison, wife-thrashing and perhaps wife-murder, child-violation, even good works. He contemplates balloon-travel and a journey to the North Pole. 'All my hopes rest on anatomy now, goodness me they do!' 'On anatomy?' asks Raskolnikov, understandably mystified. But Svidrigailov ignores the question and starts talking about politics.[52] He puts in a word on behalf of debauchery because 'it's an occupation of a sort'.[53] Yes and no. The notebooks are beginning to pull him into shape with their 'NB. Not an *occupied* man.'[54] In fact nothing binds him to life. He pictures eternity as a filthy Russian bathhouse with spiders in the corners, and yet he blows his brains out to send himself there.

It's difficult to avoid making his suicide sound too purposeful. Again the notebooks can be seen moving in the right direction with '*Svidrigailov*: I'm happy to go to America at once, but somehow nobody really wants to.'[55] America is his favourite way of talking about the undiscovered country, and it shows that as well as suicide and blanket boredom he has taken over the flavour of Raskolnikov's joke about getting used to family life. Dostoevsky's notebook word 'tone'

[52] pp. 251–2.   [53] p. 415.
[54] *PSS*, Vol. VII, p. 162.   [55] Ibid., p. 204.

amounts to more than dust and mortar and summer smells; it catches up human beings and entangles them with the city. It's no accident that Svidrigailov is the only one in the novel to handle yellow paper money, just as it's no accident that children are frightened of him and run away 'in indescribable terror' because (so we understand in our bones) they smell death on him, or rather the unattachment to life which defeats even Sonya Marmeladov.[56] The girl who has reached the human being in Raskolnikov the murderer is left for the last time by Svidrigailov 'bewildered and frightened, and filled with vague and oppressive suspicions'. He has just walked out into a spectacular summer storm. As he leaves, she asks him 'How can you — how can you go now, in such rain?' 'What! All set for America and afraid of the rain!'[57]

America is his bleak private fancy, the loneliest of witticisms. He shares the rain, though, which comes evenhandedly to city and inhabitants, a psychological force like the heat it dispels. The rain brings him an end-of-time vision, solitary as his sense of humour, of flooding cellars and emerging rats.[58] To others it brings relief from the merciless summer heat. Raskolnikov is one of the others, though it's only through the long crime-and-punishment process that he comes to understand this: he had 'wanted something more' — more than our mere-existence rain. He had wanted to be a Napoleon and special. In the closing moments of their final interview Porfiry wonders if there's a storm coming — 'and it would be no bad thing', he says, 'to freshen the air'; which is a literal rephrasing of the metaphorical 'All you want now is air, air, air!' with which he presses home his argument for confession and acceptance of suffering, and for life.[59]

Porfiry's words have a heightened transpersonal effect because Svidrigailov has just told Raskolnikov the same thing. 'Ah, Rodion Romanovich,' he says completely out of the blue, 'what every man needs is air, air, air! That above all!'[60] He doesn't exclude himself. Balloon-travel, debauchery,

---

[56] pp. 410, 440. [57] p. 441.
[58] p. 87, above. [59] pp. 405-7.
[60] p. 387. A few pages later (391) in his usual intensifying way Dostoevsky has Raskolnikov pick up Svidrigailov's remark: 'Yesterday somebody said to me that what a man needs is air, air, air! I must go to him at once and find out what he means by that.' Of course he never does.

card-sharping and so forth are frustrated struggles for air, and he knows it. When eavesdropping (a vicarious ghost-life he goes in for), he hears Raskolnikov tell Sonya about the crime, and later, without openly referring to it, the potential suicide twits the actual murderer: 'Well, you can certainly do a lot.'[61]

The irony of murder as doing a lot — doing *anything* — bears the stamp of Svidrigailov. He is probably a murderer himself; the lightmindedness of his retrospective half-confirmations and half-denials is oddly disgusting; and for him killing people is no more doing something than sleeping with little girls or setting off for the North Pole. It's just another struggle for air, for living life. He recognizes in Raskolnikov a fellow-struggler, and repeatedly he says that the two of them are birds of a feather; but he also bids him farewell with a pointed 'You to the right and I to the left, or the other way round if you like' towards the end of their final meeting, because setting off for America, unlike the North Pole, while it may or may not amount to doing anything (*Crime and Punishment* doesn't raise the question) marks a parting of their ways.[62] In Svidrigailov's America there is no air to struggle for, and no rain to soften hearts and freshen cities and give the excluded (or self-excluding) man occasion for jokes about fear and death.

Most people breathe naturally, they don't struggle for air. In the underground man's sick yet piercing analysis, most people are roadbuilders, instinctively being somebody, doing something, going somewhere. Not so the antihero himself paralysed by the disease of hyperconsciousness in abstract Petersburg. And not so Svidrigailov and Raskolnikov, both hyperconscious men, and both (as we shall see) linked by their condition to the city which Peter the Great pondered over and then ordered to be built. Svidrigailov's answer, when Raskolnikov asks him 'Why don't you see a doctor?' is that he doesn't need to be told he's ill.[63] It doesn't follow that he knows what the matter is — 'honestly, though, I don't know what's wrong with me,' he adds. He hasn't got the underground man's bodiless analytic clarity. He only knows that he needs air and can't get it; a state evinced by his terminal boredom, and by single sovereign descriptive strokes like the fact that his eyes are 'a little too blue', leaving the reader to imagine a pair of empty summer-sky souls, very bright and staring in pain.[64]

One of the marvels of *Crime and Punishment* is its clear distinguishing, untainted by clinical knowingness, of Svidrigailov's and Raskolnikov's ways of being (as the saying is) not with us. Svidrigailov appears not to notice insults and rudenesses. Nothing signifies for him, yet he seizes on details with a toneless precision, almost pedantry: when Raskolnikov calls him a gambler he says he is actually a card-sharper. Observing Raskolnikov wince at the idea of eternity as a bathhouse, he murmurs 'with a vague smile' that he would certainly have made it like that himself. He suggests that behind Raskolnikov's sister's loathing of him there lurks attraction, and he states flatly that she and his own wife were once in love with each other; and perhaps he is right. Ghosts visit him, he says. He frequents a seedy restaurant — 'You see this wretched tavern I spend all my time in, and I enjoy it, or rather it's not that I really enjoy it, but one must have somewhere to perch': this is the form which the Dostoevsky no-home takes with him, likewise the transpersonal motif first voiced by Marmeladov in this novel, that a man must have somewhere to go. He is absent yet meticulous, paying for a missing drink-shop teaspoon which has nothing to do with him, and spending a long time in the 'interesting occupation' of trying to catch a fly.[65] (Recall 'not an *occupied* man' from the notebooks. And recall Kafka on incidental madness in Dostoevsky; it's not just the children whom Svidrigailov terrifies.)

Raskolnikov is not with us either, but in the novel's final text he could not have done or said any of the things I have just mentioned. Even his way of throwing his money about, what he has of it, is immediately distinguishable from Svidrigailov's, while with both of them money is the very image of merely imputed and therefore reversible value in a loose-end world: 'You to the right and I to the left, or the other way round if you like.' Cocooned in false-Napoleonic narcissism

---

[64] p. 412.   [65] pp. 253-6, 413-18, 439, 450.

he reads about his own deed in the newspapers. He goes in for a sort of hall-of-mirrors self-impersonation, telling people how he would have done the murder if he had done it (which he has). His crime-and-punishment existence is a process of endless self-monitoring:

> What Razumikhin had just said about Porfiry also disturbed him.
>
> 'I'll have to play the sick man act with him too,' he thought, white in the face, his heart pounding, 'and I'll have to do it naturally. But the most natural thing of all would be to do nothing. *Make a point* of doing nothing. No, *making a point* would be unnatural again. Oh well, it depends how things turn out — we'll see — soon enough — is it a good idea to go there or not? The moth flies into the flame of her own accord. My heart's pounding, and that's bad!'[66]

A normalizing and fleshing-out of Mr Golyadkin deciding to adopt a passive role.[67] And the details of Raskolnikov's alienation show Dostoevsky at his most unrelentingly careful and sensitive. In another passage our final text reads 'His words were as if meant for himself, but he spoke them aloud, and he continued for some time to look at his sister like a man perplexed.'[68] The first draft has 'he thought to himself' but nothing about the sister. The second draft introduces the sister and cuts the thinking to himself. The magazine text brings in the paradox of public and yet *as if* private utterance: 'His words were as if spoken to himself, but he spoke them aloud, and he continued for some time to look at his sister like a man perplexed.' And that is how the passage appeared in volume form, in the editions of 1867 and 1870. But in 1877, the last text overseen by the novelist, 'as if spoken to himself' becomes 'as if meant for himself', shifting and refining nuance while involving the change of a single word in Russian, and enabling the artist to get at last the effect he had been working towards.[69]

The naturalness of doing nothing. The unnaturalness of making a point of doing nothing. These are underground and pre-Siberian thoughts. But a new sort of humour has arrived: witness the exquisite dew-drop exchange between Svidrigailov and Raskolnikov:

---

[66] pp. 142, 147, 219, 239.   [67] pp. 93–4, above.
[68] p. 207.   [69] *PSS*, Vol. VII, pp. 254, 277.

'Incidentally, do you believe in ghosts?'
'What kind of ghosts?'
'Ordinary ghosts, of course.'[70]

And with the young doctor who tries to help Raskolnikov, the voice of the underground man has become more accessibly funny: 'I admit there's scarcely such a thing as a normal human being. You might find one in tens or perhaps hundreds of thousands, but even he will turn out a rather feeble specimen.'[71]

We all limp, more or less, was the antihero's way of putting it, and for him all consciousness was a disease. His own hyperconsciousness, the disease in an acute form, he considered a product of nineteenth-century civilization, rendered yet more virulent by the 'abstract and intentional city' he lived in. This tight argument becomes relaxed and humanized in *Crime and Punishment*. The hyperconscious Double Act in which Svidrigailov's terminal boredom plays opposite the greedy, theoretical self-assertion of Raskolnikov's wanting 'something more' than 'mere existence', becomes grounded in suicide and murder; and the Petersburg where these things happen gains a fuzzy-edged documentary aspect which never comes anywhere near dominating the novel, but which is there. Once and once only a finger is placed, by Svidrigailov appropriately, on the fact that Peter's city turns people odd. He mentions the climate, but without filling in the summer smells of this novel, or the fog and white nights and wet snow of others. And he observes in a flat parajournalistic way that Petersburg is 'the administrative centre of all Russia'.[72] This makes it a city of arrivers. Some come like Marmeladov to get a job on the appropriate rung of the bureaucratic ladder. Others are in search of justice, 'with a petition to some Minister'.[73] Others again, like Mr Luzhin, Dunya Raskolnikov's middle-aged suitor, want to make a lot of money: there's a Dick Whittington side to Petersburg. Speaking for himself, Svidrigailov says he is after the women, which isn't untrue but we know what it's worth. Raskolnikov

[70] p. 253.
[71] p. 201. 'Feeble' is a hair's-breadth improvement on 'mediocre' in the manuscript (*PSS*, Vol. VII, p. 245). Mrs Garnett omits the whole clause.
[72] p. 411.   [73] p. 425.

has been here three years. He arrived from the deep country to attend university. His friend Razumikhin, a truthful witness, has known him for eighteen months. Razumikhin himself may or may not have come from the country, but he is certainly a member of the floating, unbelonging population of students and ex-students, and he records in simple puzzlement that Raskolnikov has been growing increasingly moody and suspicious and introverted; 'he has no time for anything, people are always in his way, and yet he lies about and does nothing'[74] — a confirming echo of Raskolnikov on his bed telling Nastasya the maid that he is working, by which he means thinking. His mind's not right. Petersburg encourages his vicious loose-end tendency, as it teases Svidrigailov with phantom images of what it would be like to be an occupied man. Raskolnikov's 'incomplete smile' is the index of those 'half-baked' (literally, 'incomplete') ideas which Dostoevsky writes about in the letter to Katkov.[75]

(iv)

Among *Crime and Punishment*'s major characters only Porfiry the detective is in no sense an arriver. It will appear mechanical, when plucked out of the huge and vital narrative flow, that Dostoevsky has given him 'a sickly dark yellow complexion' as a mark of his belonging to Petersburg.[76] Nevertheless he does possess a yellow face as opposed to lodging in a yellow room, or handling yellow money, or being issued (the bureaucracy!) with a yellow ticket. He also belongs for the reason suggested by Svidrigailov; Petersburg is the administrative centre of Russia, and Porfiry occupies his position there as an official examining magistrate within the metropolitan and national legal system.

Therefore he has a public front and function as well as an unhealthy yellow human face. It's his job to bring the murderer of the old money-lender and her sister to justice. The job occupies him, as Svidrigailov would say; it involves

[74] p. 190.   [75] p. 359.
[76] p. 222. Marmeladov has the jaundiced face of a 'confirmed drunkard', but it gets pushed slightly to one side of yellow by the fact that it is 'greenish, even' (p. 9).

both the man and the salaried magistrate, and it defines the part played by Porfiry in the apocalyptic naturalism of the crime-and-punishment process. But what is there for Porfiry to do? We have just caught Raskolnikov saying to himself that the moth seeks the candle-flame, and Porfiry says similar things aloud; while behind both of them Dostoevsky is telling Katkov that the murderer demands punishment and bends to an inexorable divine and human law when he gives himself up. At one level, as in all picturings of God's rule and man's free will, there is nothing for Porfiry to do; he just has to sit and wait, which he is good at. And at another level he has to know and play every trick of the detective's trade, which he is good at too.

Cat and mouse has no less force, in this fated relationship, than moth and candle-flame. 'I won't allow myself to be tortured,' Raskolnikov tells Porfiry, but our sense of their three long encounters is that there's nothing either of them can do about it.[77] In a single serpentine sentence Porfiry seems to dissolve into his own prose, showering Raskolnikov with a patter of tiny verbal blows as if exercising the Russian particle for its own sake (*nu da uzh*), telling him that he considers him 'quite incapable' of committing suicide, and in the same breath to leave 'a short circumstantial note' if he does.[78] This, in the blood and bone of the novel, is how the doubleness — the two levels — appears, in which all is destined and anything can happen. It might be objected that the doubleness is just a trick of Porfiry's. But this wouldn't match up to the greatness of the Porfiry–Raskolnikov scenes. It isn't *just* a trick. And it isn't just *Porfiry's* trick. Life in the guise of the crime-and-punishment process snatches up hunter and hunted into the contradictions and cruelties and deceits and frailties which are, in a word, life — not the whole of life of course, but life. Porfiry misquotes Raskolnikov back at himself. He commends him for the wit and wisdom of things he hasn't said. He tacks on tendentious continuations to things Raskolnikov has said. He suggests that he's got no evidence, then that he's got some evidence, then both at once: 'There's nothing here, precisely nothing,

[77] p. 308.   [78] p. 407.

perhaps absolutely nothing' — the torture tune.[79] Surrounded by 'government furniture of polished yellow wood', he proffers blandishing diminutives; 'how about a spot of open window?' (*okoshechko*) he asks the ready fainter.[80] He drops, or there happen to be dropped, sore words like 'Napoleon' and 'axe' into his discourse. He scrambles his own identity as a man and magistrate: 'Do you suppose I didn't come to search your room at the time? I did, I did — ha, ha! — I was here when you were lying ill in bed. Not officially, and not in my own person, but I was here.'[81]

What is Raskolnikov supposed to make of that? Or the reader? Or Porfiry himself? *Crime and Punishment* is a ghostly book in which all three — murderer, detective, reader — tiptoe mentally round dubitable presences and absences, and create between themselves strange large silences. Again and again the murder of Lizaveta is ignored. And yet Raskolnikov's greater enormity is that having forgotten to bolt the door after killing the money-lender he is surprised by her half-sister, the woman who mends linen and has mended his in her time, apparently always pregnant, through simplicity, not waywardness, meek-eyed though 'she looks like a soldier dressed up as a woman'[82] (who but Dostoevsky!) and Raskolnikov kills Lizaveta too. Since Porfiry wants to break Raskolnikov, why doesn't he exploit Lizaveta's murder? Raskolnikov is no moral idiot. He recognizes an atrocity when he commits one. Equally, why is it not pointed up that philanthropic murder and the Napoleonic idea and all other theorizing come unstuck here?

There seems no reason, and the very business of raising such questions is itself part of a widespread collusive conjuring of absences and of whole worlds of what might have been. The fact remains that Porfiry does break, or tame, Raskolnikov, and that an enterprise lucid in prospect becomes fogbound by the chance which brings Lizaveta home unexpectedly. She, the simple mender and dealer in second-hand clothes, happens to return as she happens to keep getting pregnant — and what fuller and neater manifestation of chance than that, than conceiving and being conceived?

[79] p. 398. [80] pp. 295, 303.
[81] p. 398. [82] p. 59.

Lizaveta's final outrage is inflicted by a man who almost cleaves her head in two. Raskolnikov uses the blade of his axe on her, whereas he has just used the back of it on the older woman, crushing her skull. Again these things happen as they do happen, the magic narrative containing spur-of-the-moment impulse within trancelike inevitability. Readers are at one, levels of sophistication vanish, in those cinematic sequences on stairs and landings, where footsteps echo and distant doors slam, and in a flat below two workmen fool about and daub each other with paint. We all see with one pair of eyes, Raskolnikov's, when the visual field narrows upon the back of an old woman's head, her hair 'thick with grease, twisted into a rat's-tail plait and gathered up under what was left of a broken horn comb which stuck out at the nape of her neck'.[83]

That broken comb exemplifies the apparently inexhaustible strength of the novel's flotsam, its disjunctive detail which makes nevertheless for tonal coherence. The painters downstairs, skylarking on the fringe of the main action, celebrate (though they would be surprised to hear it) the living life which was, I said, merely imposed on *Notes from Underground*, but which now surrounds both crime and punishment and makes the whole novel responsive like a touched spider's web. Nastasya the maid has only to hand Raskolnikov a bowl of soup for his mental structures to be set trembling in their unrealism. Lizaveta once mended his clothes: when we puzzle over the chance-induced actuality of her murder being so largely left to *speak for itself* we are creating a false problem by the inertness of our own metaphor. 'Didn't I live just now?' Raskolnikov asks himself after he has helped the Marmeladov family and been in contact with little children.[84] Other existences rub off on him, as can be shown at the grammatical level when he overhears a student

---

[83]   p. 70.
[84]   p. 168. Note the moment immediately before (p. 167) when somebody remarks that Raskolnikov has blood on him after carrying the injured Marmeladov home. ' "Yes — I'm all covered in blood," Raskolnikov answered with a peculiar look, then he smiled, nodded and went downstairs.' The blood of *Crime and Punishment*, the reds surrounding the murderer (including the 'huge, round, copper-red moon' of his nightmare immediately before he first meets Svidrigailov: p. 245), are in their way as wonderful as the yellows.

and an army officer discussing the money-lender. 'I would kill that damned old woman without a single twinge of conscience,' says the former, and proceeds to give his reasons. 'Here you are talking and holding forth,' says the latter, 'but tell me this: are you going to kill the old woman *yourself*?'[85] Translators have 'would you kill?' here, but Dostoevsky uses the future tense for the officer, whereas the student's 'I would kill' is genuinely in the conditional. This distinction should be preserved (even though the Russian verb is not quite square with the English), since it belongs to the novel's overall life-against-logic argument: in theory the student would kill her, but in fact he won't. 'Of course not!' he tells the army officer, and that's the end of it.

Acting by theory, Raskolnikov does kill her, and life impinges. The two painters downstairs impinge — directly through their crazy behaviour arousing suspicion against themselves, and indirectly through Porfiry. Porfiry uses them to try and catch Raskolnikov out. They were working in a flat below the old money-lender's at the time of the murder, but not at the time of the 'rehearsal' three days earlier. Raskolnikov has admitted to visiting the old woman on the first occasion but of course not on the second. Pretending to be worried about the painters and the incriminating evidence against them — 'It's very, very important for them!' — Porfiry asks Raskolnikov if he has any recollection of passing an open door on the lower landing and seeing two men at work inside. For a split second Raskolnikov is thrown. His attention has been decoyed. He gropes mentally, 'straining every nerve in an agonised attempt to divine as quickly as possible where the trap lay'. And then he sees it, and the moment is successfully negotiated.[86]

Porfiry's bait for Raskolnikov ('a precious question' Dostoevsky calls this dangled interrogative hook in his notebooks[87]) holds a different but equally potent fascination for the reader, instancing the story's inexorable grip and the virtuosity of the examining magistrate at work. Porfiry is, as we say, very human. He smokes too much and is overweight, altogether in poor physical shape. This simply goes along with his being the archetypal great detective, and even with Dostoevsky making him a vehicle for the airing of central thematic issues. In their third and last encounter Porfiry tells Raskolnikov that what he needs more than anything is somebody to be — 'life and a definite position'. This echoes the statement in their second encounter that he, Porfiry, has no intention of making an immediate arrest because by doing so he would give the murderer somebody to be: 'I'd give him, so to say, a definite position, I'd give him psychological definition and peace.'[88] Peace! The out-of-the-practical-swim ex-student, ex-teacher, the worker at thinking in bed, would be able to call himself an arrested man! We think back to the antihero of *Notes from Underground* lamenting that he can't even call himself a lazy man, and we think sideways to Svidrigailov: 'Believe me, if only I were something; a landowner, say, or a father, a cavalry officer, a photographer, a journalist say — but I'm nothing, I've no speciality.'[89] He too ('birds of a feather') has nobody to be, and the ice-cold comedy of his father/photographer/landowner *mélange* projects the disjunctive genius of *Crime and Punishment* on yet another plane.

In any case, says Porfiry, there is no need to lock Raskolnikov up, because 'you won't run away'. He has nowhere to run to, nowhere, absolutely nowhere, to go. His crime has brought him to the extremity which Marmeladov was telling him about and tasting at the bottom of his own vodka jug in the opening pages of the novel. Moreover, Porfiry adds, 'what will you run away with?'[90] An amazing stroke. Raskolnikov is Mr Naked done again. Porfiry means that he doesn't really believe in his theory; to wonder if he is a Napoleon is to prove to himself that he isn't. It is to steal his own clothes, and by the time he comes to Sonya to confess, the Napoleonic idea is already crumbling into wanting to dare or something even vaguer.

And nobody else can be a Napoleon either. A Napoleon is a non-person, a 'generalhuman'; and although the word doesn't appear in *Crime and Punishment* itself, the notebooks

---

[88] pp. 300, 406. Observe status and ontology going hand in hand.
[89] p. 414.   [90] p. 406.

make the point that one can't just live 'the general life of humanity'.[91] In this general-human life there would be 'nothing whatever to do', the notebook continues. Napoleon himself had plenty to do, but *a* Napoleon is a member of a conceptual class of people who are like each other; and likeness, the 'unseemly likeness' of *The Double*,[92] is fraught throughout Dostoevsky. When Raskolnikov goes to Sonya to declare himself, she implores him to tell her 'straight out — without examples'.[93] She doesn't want to know what he's *like*. She wants to know *him*, in his unique humanity.

Which also means his shared humanity. 'But how,' she cries, 'how can you live without human society?' (literally, 'without a human being').[94] She knows he can't, as does Porfiry who will soon rephrase her question in statement form: '*You can't get on without us.*'[95] His typically unspecific and floated '*us*' is the human family which Raskolnikov must rejoin, and he can't rejoin it without accepting suffering. Both Sonya and Porfiry tell him so.

The words come easier from Porfiry who speaks for public justice than from Sonya on whom falls the main and mystic burden of creative, regenerative suffering. Marmeladov's huge notebook gesture towards Christ and the Russian people and suffering constitutes one warning that Dostoevsky was, at one stage, after something too big or too difficult or perhaps simply wrong for *Crime and Punishment*; and Sonya's declaration, again in the notebooks, makes a second: 'The Russian people have always suffered like Christ, says Sonya.'[96] In the novel itself we meet the Russian people, the folk, only once, and then as inflictors of suffering, in Raskolnikov's half-dream (which is also half-memory) of a little mare being tortured and finally clubbed to death by drunken peasants. Mrs Marmeladov's death is very like an animal's, like this mare's: 'Her bloodless, yellow, wasted face dropped back, her mouth opened, her legs straightened convulsively. She heaved a deep, deep sigh and died.'[97] The

---

[91] *PSS*, Vol. VII, p. 165.
[92] *The Eternal Husband*, p. 210.
[93] p. 366.
[94] p. 370.
[95] p. 406.
[96] *PSS*, Vol. VII, p. 134.
[97] p. 383. Compare 'The wretched animal stretched out her muzzle, drew a labouring breath, and died' (p. 53).

whole novel reeks of pain. We mustn't think of its Petersburg crowds as the folk (*narod*); they are a medley of exploiters and exploited, above all of arrivers and non-belongers. When, on his final journey to the police station, Raskolnikov kneels down in the middle of the Haymarket and kisses 'the earth, the filthy earth' (*zemlya*) as Sonya has bidden, it is entirely calculated by Dostoevsky that a tipsy artisan should laugh at the strange young man who 'is bowing down to the whole world and is kissing the capital city of St Petersburg and its soil' (*grunt*, the German *Grund*).[98] This has no more to do with Christ and regenerative suffering than Dr Rutenspitz telling Mr Golyadkin that *Licht* will be provided for him where he's going at the end of *The Double*.

But in the Epilogue, as opposed to the body of *Crime and Punishment*, people don't torture animals or bear the mark of Peter the German. We are back in the world of the Dead House, of simple Russian convicts and Sorrel the horse, their pride and joy. In effect Dostoevsky is revisiting his own fortress prison at Omsk. Raskolnikov is here, serving an eight-year sentence. He has got off lightly: we learn with mildly comic surprise of mitigating circumstances: he had been good to a consumptive fellow student, and he had saved two children from a blazing house, getting burnt himself while doing so.

More important, and very surprising, we are told that 'he did not repent of his crime'.[99] So his rallying himself to enter the police station '*as a man*' and confess was not the acceptance of suffering which Sonya and Porfiry both — but separately — urged him towards. Or rather, it was not yet that acceptance, something in Raskolnikov remained obdurate. Prison finds him longing to feel contrite, to feel he deserves his punishment, but only able to believe he has committed 'a simple *blunder* which might have happened to anybody'. Then, as the notebooks put it, 'Sonya and love broke him'.[100] On the same page we read about a vision of Christ and a seeking forgiveness of the common people — two ideas which were abandoned. And it should be noted that the actual breaking point for Raskolnikov in the novel is the

illness which induces his apocalyptic science-fiction nightmare of germs and *Possessed*-type madness and destruction,
bringing him literally to Sonya's feet and both of them to
'the dawn of a new future, of a full resurrection into a new
life' which will be the subject of another story.[101]

So having laid the weight of mystic, creative suffering on
Sonya, the novel proceeds to hive it off into its own Epilogue
where all strains and difficulties are waved away. What the
Sonya of the novel has to do with Christ and resurrection and
creative suffering remains fleeting and indirect, though no
less wonderful for that. In the original version, now lost, of
the chapter in which she reads to Raskolnikov the gospel
story of the raising of Lazarus, Dostoevsky intended and
wrote a head-on debate about Christianity; but his publishers
refused to print it. The novelist was very distressed. And yet
he took no steps to reintroduce it in later editions. I believe
he came to see it would not do. As with the censored Christian argument in *Notes from Underground*, I believe an
unfathomable good luck wearing the face of bad luck was on
his side at the start. If Raskolnikov was to have mounted an
assault of something like Grand Inquisitor proportions, if
he was to have expatiated on the whole God business not
being worth the pain of one misused child, then the time
wasn't ripe; we must wait for Ivan Karamazov. And if Sonya
was to have replied to him, what could she have said? No
more than the answer she gave in the *Crime and Punishment*
which did get printed, to the not quite taunting question
'And what does God do for you?'

'He does everything,' she says, but there is no debate.
Sonya is the church-slavonic 'daughter' (*dshcher*) whom
Marmeladov introduces in his pub tirade. God will call her to
Him on the Day of Judgment, asking 'Where is the daughter
who had pity on her earthly father, the filthy drunkard, and
was undismayed by his beastliness?'[102] There must be many
who are touched to the heart by that phrase 'earthly father'
and yet who don't believe a word of the novel's religion;
just as, and more obviously, Raskolnikov's kissing the dirt
in the middle of the Haymarket doesn't stand or fall by

[101] p. 201, above.   [102] p. 20.

Dostoevsky's Soil Philosophy. For the earth and the filth are
the realized human stuff of the book. Not, of course, all its
human stuff; when Dostoevsky told his biographer that the
task of his own deeper realism was 'to find the human in
the human being', he meant there is more to us than filthy
earth, and this 'more' must be found.[103] In extremity, with
nowhere to go, and not even a believed theory to wear or
hold his mind's hand ('what will you run away with?'),
Raskolnikov turns to Sonya; 'it was to her, Sonya, that he
first went with his confession; when he felt the need of a
human being, he sought the human being in her'[104] — which
does indeed isolate for a moment, and emphasize, the mystic
business of his alienation from the human family; and for
this moment the dross (as it were) of Sonya and of Raskolnikov is withheld; the god in his humanity is looking for the
god in hers.

But the Raskolnikov of the notebooks who joked grimly
about getting used to being married and having children will
do that average and earthy thing, though in a different
spirit;[105] and in another story, as the Epilogue tells us. The
Raskolnikov of *Crime and Punishment* has got *unused* to
everything; all the calm pressures of habit are denied him,
his punishment has begun. And the Sonya of the novel is
very slightly indicated. She is little more than her blue
eyes and green shawl, the blue and the green undismayed
by the yellows and reds of the book,[106] as the girl is by her
father.

He, the loose-end, filthy-earth drunkard, introduces the
shawl as he does so many motifs. He describes how Sonya
is driven out onto the streets by her step-mother's gibe —

[103] p. 373 of the *Biography* printed in the first volume of the posthumous
Complete Works of 1882–3.
[104] p. 459. All translators flinch from this spareness and strangeness of
phrase.
[105] Dostoevsky saves the notebook joke about acquiring familiarity by having
him reply 'I shall get used to it' after Sonya has expressed horror at his suggestion
that he will just live on after confessing to her, and not give himself up to the
police (pp. 370–1). She of course is still talking about estrangement from humanity, while his terminal boredom of the notebooks has been switched to
Svidrigailov.
[106] See n. 84.

'Why not? What is there to preserve so carefully?' — and returns and lays thirty roubles on the table.

'She looked at her step-mother but uttered not a single word; she simply picked up our big *drap-de-dames* green shawl (it's a shawl we all use, a *drap-de-dames* one), and covered her head and face entirely with it and lay down on the bed with her face to the wall, and her little shoulders and her whole body were trembling.'[107]

His 'which we all use' is authorially bold. We are never told what use Marmeladov might have had for the shawl. But, 'We are one, we live as one,' says Sonya in the Lazarus chapter, and that is much bolder.[108] Greater disunity than that of the Marmeladov non-home can scarcely be imagined. I've just mentioned the taunt that drives Sonya to prostitution. Members of the family are sleeping in three different places. Even the father's funeral feast explodes in chaos — the classic Dostoevsky *skandal*. And yet, while God doing everything for Sonya remains shielded by her faith, the green shawl keeps cropping up through the novel for all to see. She puts it on to follow Raskolnikov on his final journey to the police station, and through his mind flashes the thought that this is the shawl Marmeladov referred to in the pub as 'the family one'.[109] Actually Marmeladov said 'which we all use'. Dostoevsky will have remembered that; it is one of those overlapping cumulations, sameness with difference, which reveal simultaneously the closeness of his workmanship and his imagination's bias.

Our last sight is of the shawl flitting about among the convicts in Siberia: not altogether happy, like many things in the Epilogue. Again it should be seen as close and calculated that the shawl which wraps the head in shame at first, becomes at last a green emblem of mercy. And yet the effective place of this life-soiled object is in the body of the book, nourishing the reality of the whole Marmeladov set-up, like the children's washed day-clothes drying overnight. For there are no spare things. On second thoughts there is nothing surprising in 'which we all use'; how could it be otherwise in a *family* like the Marmeladov's?

And Sonya's 'We are one, we live as one,' while it remains

[107] pp. 15–16.   [108] p. 282.   [109] p. 461.

authorially bold, has nothing to fear at the hands of readers quick to sniff out dogma. *Crime and Punishment* naturalizes the mystic brazenness of Sonya's statement, as it does Porfiry's '*You can't get on without us*'. Parajournalism, creating to one side of the actual, seems to me the nub here. When Svidrigailov and Porfiry, who never meet — bold again — and who have nothing to do with each other, both tell Raskolnikov that a man needs air, my business is to try and suggest how it is that Dostoevsky's reader finds himself in immediate dual touch with a Petersburg July day and a universal truth.

He senses, too, that the actual has more than one side to it. Thus when the girl secretary who was to become Dostoevsky's wife rang the bell of his flat for the first time, the door was opened by an elderly woman servant with a green shawl thrown over her shoulders. Anna Grigorevna had been reading *Crime and Punishment* in the magazine *Russian Herald*, and she thought she recognized the object 'which played such a big part in the Marmeladov family'. No doubt she did. And soon afterwards, in the first week of their marriage, Dostoevsky showed her the stone under which Raskolnikov hid the stuff he had taken from the old moneylender. She asked her husband what had brought him — Dostoevsky — to this deserted yard. He replied, 'The reason that does in fact bring people to secluded places.'[110] Now that's our man.

---

[110] *PSS*, Vol. VII, pp. 365, 370-1.

Chapter 7:   *The Possessed*

(i)

In the 1860s Dostoevsky was spending a lot of time abroad. That made the tie between him and journalism even stronger than it had been. From his letters and his wife's memoirs we picture him in cheap cafés hunched up in his greatcoat over a cup of coffee, with Russian and European newspapers spread about him. Or spending his evenings in public libraries.

The scene is Dresden Library. He is picking his way through the *Moscow Record* of 27 November 1869, and there he reads about a murder which had occurred six days earlier. An unnamed man had been killed and his body dumped in a pond in a park. The alarm had been raised by two peasants who, as the first sentence of the newpaper story recounts, were walking in the park and noticed a cap lying on the ground, together with a hood and a cudgel.

Dostoevsky had no use for the two peasants or for the hood and the cudgel, but he wanted the cap. In *The Possessed*, the conspirators have enticed their victim to a dark remote spot where nothing will be seen or heard, and have done the deed and tied two heavy stones to the body so that it is sure to sink, and have carried it to a pond and thrown it in: then, 'with extraordinary carelessness' they overlook that cap which has no doubt fallen off in the struggle, and which the police will soon find.[1]

The carelessness cuts as much creative ice as the cap. It interknits with that world of chances and mischances, improbable or absurd or grotesque or just neutrally happening as they do happen, which we meet everywhere in later Dostoevsky and specially in *The Possessed*. The conviction carried by how things are in his fiction cannot be separated from the sense that they might be otherwise. The cap that

---

[1] p. 608. Having got his lead from the newspaper Dostoevsky ignored the continuation of its report where it turns out that the cap did not belong to the murdered man.

happened to get overlooked returns the reader's gaze blankly yet unavoidably, like the bill from a restaurant abroad which the conspirators find when they turn out the dead man's pockets, and like the child's clay whistle which one of them has provided himself with to give the agreed signal — for he has lost so many teeth that he can't trust himself to produce the sound naturally.[2]

The cap, then, falls within an overall grand vision of chanciness and risk; Liputin's teeth are by no means the only things that hang by a thread. But, I repeat, Dostoevsky wanted the cap for its own sake. The *overlooked* hood in the newspaper scanned by the parajournalist would not have done equally well, nor would the cudgel. The cap is comparable with, while absolutely distinguishable from, the broken horn comb and other odds and ends — the disjunctive flotsam — of *Crime and Punishment*. On one level it is yet another accident, and on a second level it is inevitable, it must be so because it belongs here and nowhere else, as the foreign restaurant bill belongs to a novel about human birds of passage, and as the whistle belongs to a novel, in fact the only late Dostoevsky novel, with no children in it but haunted by the toys of absent innocence and peace: the governor of 'our province' where these crazy terrible events take place was disappointed in love as a young man and consoled himself by making a paper theatre with curtains, actors, audience, orchestra, conductor — the lot. Then he wrote a novel and sent it to a magazine which rejected it.

On the other hand he constructed an entire model railway, and again the result was most successful. Passengers came onto the platform with their trunks and bags, their children and dogs, and got into the carriages. The guards and porters walked about, the bell was rung, the signal was given and the train started off. He spent a whole year over that clever toy. But he still had to find a wife.

And at last, and most imprudently, he married an ambitious tyrant who drove him up the career ladder, and when things began to get too much he set to work on a toy church with pastor, pulpit, congregation, organ and so forth. But she discovered what he was up to and confiscated the church. So that when Von Lemke came to 'us' as governor and felt himself overwhelmed by 'our' troubles and scandals, he had no toy-making to turn to, he had nowhere to go — his version of the abiding Dostoevsky extremity — and in fact he went mad. He sent for his carriage and jumped in, and after telling his coachman to drive fast he ordered him to stop. They were now miles out of town. Von Lemke got out and crossed the road and went into a field. The coachman thought he wanted to relieve himself. But he just stood still and gazed at some withered autumn flowers. The narrator can't be sure but guesses he wasn't even aware of the existence of the flowers. On the other hand the Police Inspector of the district found him standing with a bunch of yellow flowers in his hand.[3] That is typical of *The Possessed*'s speculative openness, within which a reader is entitled to his own view. The flowers caught Von Lemke's fancy as ruined but at least not forbidden toys, perhaps.

But back to that dropped and overlooked cap. The word in the *Moscow Record* story is *shapka*. The name of the murdered man first appears in the *Possessed* notebooks as Shaposhnikov.[4] What's in a name? There is no simple answer with Dostoevsky any more than with Dickens.[5] Certainly, while he is alive, Shaposhnikov the cappy man refuses to be parted from his headgear; he grabs it when he determines to leave, and he drops it when he is persuaded to stay.[6] It is a mark of his abrupt nature. However, in the novel's final text the *shapka* becomes a peaked cap (*kartuz*) and Shaposhnikov's name gets changed to Shatov which has nothing to do with caps or hats at all.

It doesn't follow that the cap/name link disappears but

---

[3]   pp. 280-2, 400-1.   [4]   *PSS*, Vol. XI, p. 66.

[5]   The Veneerings are flashy snobs and all surface; Steerforth steers his sensual selfish way forth on the voyage of life and dies by drowning; Lammle, Noggs, Chollop, Smike, Squeers, Slurk, Cratchit, Gurnock, Drood, Guppy, Mowcher, Boffin, appear to be observations on the weirdness of English word-forms; in life Fagin was a kindly childhood companion in the blacking warehouse, but the name fits the fiction as neatly as Scrooge and Pecksniff and Gradgrind fit theirs; then there are double-barrelled effects like Uriah Heep, and escapes from conventional naming like Pip and Mr Dick, and jokes like M'Choakumchild; while it seems a matter of untendentious history that Dickens should have, as he said, 'a favourite child, and his name is David Copperfield'.

[6]   At p. 31, for example, when he first opens his mouth in the novel.

that it becomes so to say transpersonalized. *Kartuz* itself is pinned to a Captain Kartuzov who appears just once in *The Possessed*, and then only by name.[7] We learn not a thing about him. But this Captain is prominent in the notebooks: a chivalric Don Quixote figure of absolute non-compromise in matters (as he sees them) of virtue and truth, in effect an overspill from *The Idiot* — which Dostoevsky seems to have recognized, for he abandoned the positive and sublime venture, and hived off the comic material he had accumulated into the drunken buffoon Captain Lebyadkin who grows into a substantial second-rank character in *The Possessed*; and as to Kartuzov, the novelist left us with nothing more than his cappy surname.

At the same time the final text propagates caps like overnight mushrooms. We begin with Shatov. The object goes, as I say, with his impulsiveness; he is the man who roars 'Shatov is out' when an unwelcome visitor knocks at his door.[8] The cap also goes with Shatov as migrant, as a railway-station man, a traveller between Russia, Switzerland, and America, a man with an old foreign restaurant bill in his pocket. It also goes with the people he moves among, the 'circles' and 'sets' of *The Possessed*, many of whom are travellers too, and with the 'quintet' which he doesn't belong to but is entangled with, which he tries to kick himself clear of, and which dumps him in that pond and leaves his cap behind.

Peter Verkhovensky, the real murderer, who manipulates the members of the quintet, whose dupes they are, travels more than anybody. The novel's atmosphere is thick — sticky! — with news and rumours from abroad, and we learn that Shatov once spat in Verkhovensky's face in Geneva. Taxed with this incident as his reason for contriving Shatov's murder, Verkhovensky replies: 'For that reason, and for something else, too. For many other things. But without any hard feelings.'[9] But on the next page he speaks of 'that swine Shatov'. And in any case what can it mean to murder a man for spitting in one's face and yet feel no spite towards him? A breach of objective decorum? And what are the many other reasons? And so on.

[7] p. 26. [8] p. 187. [9] p. 557.

Such questions begin to evoke the crumbling processes of *The Possessed*, the instability which flushes its entire structure. To ask them, and equally (or even more) to wave them away absentmindedly like circling insects, is to greet the novel, to respond to its personality which is the same thing as the tonal area colonized by the novelist for his present purpose. He gives us a murderer whose 'words pattered out like smooth large grains' — clear and distinguishable, and yet somehow there is nothing to get a purchase on.[10] It's no great surprise that a lecture on *Othello* is mooted in the *Possessed* notebooks, and that 'O, Iago, the pity of it' gets quoted in Russian.[11] While Dostoevsky was interested in the noble Moor and the jealousy question, he will also have been pondering ghost-reasons for his own villain. That Shatov spat in Verkhovensky's face is one. That the members of the quintet will be 'bound' to each other in secret guilt by the cement of blood, having been tricked into thinking Shatov is a danger and must be removed, is another and a promising rationalization which reveals a local shrewdness like Iago's.[12] I stress local: Verkhovensky's group psychology is plausible enough but it doesn't engage with anything wider or further that he proposes to do. He postures as a political activist, and the solidarity forced on the quintet by Shatov's murder might be expected to make them a more effective instrument. But the notion of an instrument turns out to be as empty as his posturing. There is nothing he wants to use the quintet for. Having entangled them in crime, he catches a train and goes away. And he takes a travelling rug with him — another of those fussy bag-and-baggage objects which assert the novel's tonality.[13] For he is an eternal traveller.

As well as a rug he takes a book, author and title unspecified; the eternal traveller is also the eternal student, and it is as 'the student' that Verkhovensky first appears in the manuscript drafts. From the start, as in *Crime and Punishment*, Dostoevsky is projecting a theoretical murderer, the difference being that Raskolnikov was an ex-student, only potentially an eternal student, because in the event he got pulled back out of theory into living life. Murder brought

10 p. 162.   11 *PSS*, Vol. XI, pp. 142, 162.
12 p. 570.   13 p. 573.

Raskolnikov to see that he didn't believe his reasons for committing it. Now the other young man never believed any of his professed and contradictory reasons in the first place. That last fact carries with it an unjust overall valuation of student status, eternal or otherwise, and one which Dostoevsky was not prepared to stand by; which is why 'the student' becomes Peter Verkhovensky in *The Possessed*.

His argumentation is diminished and made much less coherent through successive drafts of the novel, while the sheer rattle or patter of those smooth large grains which are his discourse gets carefully worked up. It's not that he ceases altogether to be the eternal student, but that he becomes reshaped and misshaped into an aberration. Nor is the consecutive argumentation — the theorizing — lost. It gets parcelled out among the society he moves in, or rather flits in and out of, while himself belonging elsewhere, which means nowhere. This is a novel of talk and opinions got out of books, and at one stage Dostoevsky proposed 'NB. *A Title*: PAPER PEOPLE', which survives as a phrase in Shatov's mouth, tossed up twice by the polemical flood.[14] A paper person is a walking theory, and one which may not even believe in itself; and then the paper person will not merely have nobody, he will have no theory to be. He belongs to a paper society which goes through the motions of life, in the air, notionally. Many a reader of *The Possessed* will have smiled at Von Lemke's paper cut-outs — the conductor waving his baton, the bustling railway porter, the hell-fire gesticulating preacher — and at the same time he will have wondered why the microcosmic animated toys feel so supremely right for this novel.

Shatov directs his paper-person thrust against himself too. 'Since I cannot be a Russian,' he says, 'I became a Slavophil' — an articulator, that is, of romantic church-and-state conservatism in the debates of the time: indeed a walking, talking theory.[15] In the notebooks Shatov (as Shaposhnikov) calls Slavophilism 'a gentleman's fancy'.[16]

[14]   pp. 122, 124; *PSS*, Vol. XI, p. 170.

[15]   pp. 229, 519. 'I'm a luckless, boring book, and nothing more so far, so far.'

[16]   *PSS*, Vol. XI, p. 66.

We are back in the area of Peter the Great's reforms. Peter tried to rouse his countrymen from their aboriginal stupor and turn them into Europeans; but a Russian isn't and can't be a German or a Frenchman, and the result of Peter's efforts was to produce an educated class who can't be Russians either. They can of course call themselves Slavophils, but that is to try and wish away Peter, to perform an act of mental regression, not to be a Russian.

It is a paper act in a paper situation, inflammable and precarious. The dangerous consequences of Peter are much canvassed in the notebooks: 'the social unsteadiness (*shatost*), as Shatov says'.[17] Thus the cappy man has become the shaky man, the waverer. And once again the motif is trans-personalized, for in the novel Shatov proves himself more than ordinarily resolute; his paper Slavophilism doesn't touch his human courage as husband and friend — and enemy. Events and tendencies are bigger than he is, and while not shaky in himself he gets dealt the final shove of murder.

(ii)

So on first consideration it seems odd that in the early days of planning *The Possessed* Dostoevsky should write to his friend Maikov and describe his new venture as 'like *Crime and Punishment* but even nearer to reality, even more urgent, and directly concerned with the most important contemporary question'.[18] 'Like *Crime and Punishment*' — another murder story — is obvious enough. What falls less easily into place is the judgment about relative importance, urgency, contemporary relevance, nearness to reality; because Raskolnikov comes over as a very grand and accessible conception, a nineteenth-century bohemian Hamlet was one way of putting it, whereas Verkhovensky is just a wrecker.

That is our starting point. It could be said as brusquely of Iago that he is just a wrecker. And of a terrorist in today's headlines: one of those inscrutable middle-class Germans, for example. Thus what I called *Crime and Punishment*'s

[17] Ibid., p. 148.   [18] Letter of 12 February 1870.

apocalyptic naturalism is its most vital link with *The Possessed*; I mean, when Dostoevsky read about that gang murder in the *Moscow Record* his mind's eye was caught not by a bizarre and therefore very newsworthy incident but by the seed of a foul commonplace: the seed in eternity, in the deepest realism, though also in the mere mundane future, for Dostoevsky did imagine a time when only the most spectacular acts of terrorism would get headline treatment. Shatov's murder, in the world of this novel, is momentous because it is potentially unremarkable.

Crime and Punishment was different in that Dostoevsky never supposed lots of people would begin committing Raskolnikov-type murders; Danilov doing so was enough to produce from him the exclamation 'It has happened!' For Raskolnikov is incorrigibly patrician and rare at heart (which is one reason why the Epilogue does not convince), even if I have overstressed the Hamletish side to him. Nevertheless his crime, like the tawdry footloose elimination of Shatov, springs from unsteadiness (*shatost*). The word appears twice in Dostoevsky's letter to Katkov outlining *Crime and Punishment*, in the phrase 'unsteadiness of ideas' — which is natural since a drama of reflection is about to unfold: thinking is Raskolnikov's work, as he tells the maid Nastasya. Unsteady work, we might add. Moreover the surname Shatov appears once in the notebooks relating to *Crime and Punishment*.[19] But nothing further. It's as if the name were waiting for the man, and for the novel which will transpersonalize or socialize the murderous concept: 'social unsteadiness, as Shatov says' and as we read in the *Possessed* notebooks.

And in his definitive text the novelist voices social unsteadiness as empty groupings and vapid motions. Von Lemke's cut-outs are phantom human concourses (theatre, station, church), and they are mobile. The quintet is Peter Verkhovensky's plaything. He tricks its members into thinking they are part of a revolutionary network extending across Russia, and at the local level he generates pseudo-purposeful activities which culminate in Shatov's murder. There's a littleness about it all: again it must not be seen as mere

chance that we encounter Swift's Lilliput on the first page
of the novel.

This littleness is at once paltry and menacing and never in
repose. One of the members of the quintet bears the quaint
name of Tolkachenko. Dostoevsky followed the trial proceedings closely, and I think the Soviet editor is right to put
his finger on the verb *tolkatsya*, to loaf or lounge about,
which occurs in a speech by the prosecuting lawyer.[20] The
editor might also have noted the colloquial sense of roaming
around which the verb *shatatsya* carries, for this may perhaps
have encouraged the switch from Shaposhnikov to Shatov
as the novel began to define itself. Loafing and roaming
cohere into a larger whole, together with such imaginative
furniture as hats and travelling rugs and passports and foreign
restaurant bills and trashy pamphlets printed abroad and
incompetently circulated. This novel seems, but only seems,
but does seem insistently, to come from a man who knew
nothing but was very opinionated, who checked no facts and
guzzled rumour scraps, whose mind was uncouth, raggity,
raucous, florid. For it is a condition of Dostoevsky's art to
arouse our longing for the settled and the normal and the
beautiful itself.

The Possessed swarms with amateurism and with fooling
about and make-believe just as childish as Von Lemke's, but
dangerous. And if not immediately dangerous, then wanton
and sinister in its curious evil comedy. Another member of
the quintet, one Lyamshin, a post-office clerk, gets himself
asked to parties where 'he would give imitations of a pig, a
thunder storm, a confinement, with the first cry of the baby,
etc., etc.; that was what he was invited for'; and later we hear
of him 'mimicking, when requested, various types of Jews,
a deaf peasant woman making her confession, or the birth
of a child . . . '.[21] Note the single common element, Lyamshin's confinement act. Masked by the apparently careless
tumble of examples ('etc., etc.') is a calculated insistence on
the sore spot, on what Shatov in the notebooks calls social
unsteadiness, a small but virulent secular profanity standing
over against the noble, perhaps the noblest sequence in *The*

[20]   Ibid., Vol. XII, p. 207.   [21]   pp. 27, 293.

Possessed, where Marie Shatov returns to her husband to give birth to another man's child.

Peter Verkhovensky can't be fitted into this picture because his *raison d'être* is outside it, manipulating. He plays with the quintet in a quite different sense from that in which they play at revolutionary politics; though, bemused by him, set at odds, their purposes deflected and their fantasies fed and coaxed along, it doesn't seem like playing to them. One of the quintet not only means business but high-minded, selfless business. Virginsky — the surname once more points the way — is a utopian socialist of 'rare purity of heart' and 'honest fervour'; Horace would have called him *candidus*. ' "I will never, never abandon these bright hopes," he used to say to me with shining eyes. Of his "bright hopes" he always spoke quietly, in a blissful half-whisper, as it were secretly.' And of the tribulations of his personal life, which were in fact grievous: ' "It's of no consequence. It's just one particular case. It won't interfere with the 'cause' in the least, not in the least." '[22] One senses a rush of creative warmth as this lonely rapt figure is conjured in a few sentences. Virginsky will always belong to the Petrashevsky Circle of Dostoevsky's own youth, as well as to the ill-assorted group that dances to Verkhovensky's tune in the late 1860s.

How to describe that tune? I called Peter Verkhovensky a wrecker. I might also have said a nihilist. Nihilist is the case but it risks confusion between Dostoevsky and Turgenev who may not have invented the word but certainly gave it very wide currency. In his novel *Fathers and Children* which (as the title suggests) is about the generation gap, Turgenev pinned 'nihilist' to the son Bazarov. The heart of this new word and new conception is a humane, scientific, and Germany-focused enlightenment, a delayed *Aufklärung* hitting Russia's young élite of the 1860s. Bazarov is an idealist and a brave man, and his aims are rational. Verkhovensky has courage (though in its lower forms of which Plato speaks), but otherwise there is nothing in common between the two young men except the times they live in.

After the non-fictional *Sportsman's Sketches*, *Fathers and*

[22] pp. 25–6.

Children is Turgenev's best book, and the best thing in it, apart perhaps from the bereaved old couple at the end, is the sensitive give-and-take marriage of its hero's idealism to his scepticism, a questing, generous idealism and an undestroying scepticism. So the novel strikes me, and at one time Dostoevsky thought so too. At least he said he did. One can't be sure. He was at his most two-faced in his dealings with Turgenev. Anyhow, he praised *Fathers and Children* to its author, and in his own *Winter Notes* he remarked Bazarov's 'greatness of spirit, in spite of all his nihilism'.[23]

Then later, in the *Possessed* notebooks, we read: 'Bazarov was created by a man of the 1840s, and was created as a figure without affectation, which means that a man of the 1840s could not create Bazarov without violating the truth.'[24] A remarkable statement, and a difficult one. It needn't mean that Dostoevsky had been telling lies and is now telling the truth in the privacy of his own notebooks. He may very well have changed his mind. But if he has, I don't think it follows that *Fathers and Children* has become a bad book in his eyes, but rather, it is now not all that good. A rift has opened between realism and something beyond, and at the same time a link has been forged between Dostoevsky's favourite phrase, the deeper realism, and my own apocalyptic naturalism.

If Turgenev is a man of the 1840s (which he is), what is he supposed to do about it? And if Turgenev were to object that one could not find a more typical product of the 1840s than the Petrashevsky Circle to which Dostoevsky belonged, how would the other man reply? Over both questions, and over all plausible answers to them, I see hovering those common Dostoevsky ideas of split and break and rent. The *raskol* of Raskolnikov means split with a further specialized religious sense of schism. Raskolnikov is self-divided and also separated from the human family in a way which for Dostoevsky is both social and religious. But, as Porfiry tells him, '*You can't do without us*'. Nor can he do without his undivided self. And that is how the body of the novel leaves the matter. It's only in the *Crime and Punishment* notebooks that we read 'Love and Sonya broke him'. Confusion — the

[23] *PSS*, Vol. V, p. 59.   [24] Ibid., Vol. XI, p. 72.

sundering of *raskol* — was thus itself confounded; and the crisis or breaking point of his illness followed by his 'regeneration' (*voskresenie*) and his 'passing from one world to another' and his 'acquaintance with a new and hitherto unknown reality' are merely affirmed at the end of the Epilogue.

Just as *raskol* means split and religious schism, so *voskresenie* means regeneration and theological Resurrection. Both areas, breaking and mending, engrossed Dostoevsky from the time when the shared convict existence of prison snapped him like a dry biscuit yet also made him new, so that in the closing words of *The House of the Dead*, with the knocking off of his fetters, the narrator greets 'a new life, *voskresenie* from the dead'. Of his attempts to realize this experience over again in his post-Siberian fiction, the bald Epilogue to *Crime and Punishment* is an early and unpromising instance. We have here perhaps the most delicate of all points of contact between his life and his art: hence the impression that further and very private issues are involved in, even shielded by, the assertion that 'a man of the 1840s could not create Bazarov'. As I suggested apropos the Petrashevsky Circle, one feels an urge to smoke Dostoevsky out with the question, who's talking?

'The epileptic' makes a neat reply, again touching life and art simultaneously: the author and hero of *The Idiot*. I have in mind the experience of being suddenly thrust outside time, which constitutes in *The Idiot* and elsewhere the epileptic aura.[25] When this and the regeneration/resurrection theme are brought to bear upon the remark about Bazarov and the 1840s, what seemed a difference of degree turns out to be one of a kind. The criticism of Turgenev is only incidentally that he is stuck in the 1840s and not far-sighted enough. New-sightedness, the timeless standpoint, 'hitherto unknown reality' — these have an air of mystical hubris when dragged

---

[25] First, the suffocating lull, tense and unsafe, before the thunder storm, an external correlative to Myshkin's inner state. Then the premonitory and unbearable extremes of darkness and light. 'Then suddenly some gulf seemed to open up before him: an extraordinary *inner* light flooded his soul.' We are told that this timeless 'half-second' before the fit was 'full of understanding and the final cause' (pp. 219, 228). Translators are understandably daunted by that 'understanding and the final cause'.

into the open, but they are what Dostoevsky is really talking about.

And so while he sat in a German public library and the story of the murder in the park unfolded before him in the newspapers, a novel began to stir. Or, in mystic vein, an order of being was glimpsed in which the 1840s, the 1860s, nihilism, Bazarov, found themselves apocalyptically and teleologically disposed — those two polysyllabic adverbs embracing and transcending all nature, including futurity. As one would expect, pre-existing material got sucked into this new world. First, the murdered man: he turned out to be a student at the Petrine Agricultural Academy, and his name was Ivanov. It so happened that the novelist's wife had a younger brother at this Academy who knew Ivanov. Now the remarkable circumstance, recorded by Anna Dostoevsky in her memoirs, is that her husband had a foreboding of political disturbances at the Academy, and fearing that his brother-in-law 'because of his youthfulness and weakness of character might take an active part in them', he persuaded Anna's mother it would be a good thing if the young man came to them in Dresden: which he did in October of 1869, the month before Ivanov was murdered.[26]

Next the murderer, the original of Peter Verkhovensky. He was Sergei Nechaev. In defensive mood, and not with complete truth, Dostoevsky wrote to Katkov: 'I do not know and never have known either Nechaev or Ivanov, or the circumstances of the murder, except from the newspapers. And even if I had, I would not have begun copying them.'[27] He had reason to be touchy about Nechaev. This ascetic, strong-willed young man, dominating yet dull-toned in personality to the point of satanic flatness, captured as if in his own despite the imagination of the day. Ordinary people talked about him. He even disquieted the hardened revolutionaries he moved among, most notably old Bakunin. His *Catechism of a Revolutionary* is a classic in the tactics of terrorism, and it came with an agreeable click of fittingness

[26] *PSS*, Vol. XII, p. 162. L. Grossman has cast doubt on some aspects of Anna's account (*Zhizn i trudi*, 1935, pp. 184–5).
[27] Letter of 8 October 1870.

to learn recently that this work earned a place on the book-shelves of Stalin.[28]

Dostoevsky wanted to stifle the thought that he was riding on the back of Nechaev's perverse glamour. Thus Nechaev forms the most important part, but still only a part, of the perennial parajournalistic debate about actuality and fiction. In the same letter to Katkov Dostoevsky also claimed that the murder was itself the merest peg; 'I am only taking the accomplished fact'; and he went on to assert that the human type 'which corresponds to this crime' was the creature of his imagination. At one level, he got there first. At another, we are still getting there, and the man whose bomb explodes at Bologna railway station one summer day in 1980 while I am pulling this page into shape falls straight back inside *The Possessed*. At yet another, we will never get there since a stream of tendency has been caught and held in new-visioned (as opposed to far-sighted) iconic stasis, and there can be no movement on out of the world we live in into the book we read.

Katkov, therefore, is being asked to accept that 'my Peter Verkhovensky may in no way resemble Nechaev'. This of course won't do. The identities need switching and the whole statement inverting, thus: 'The historical wrecker and terrorist, whether in Petersburg or Bologna, must bear the mark of the fiction and thereby confirm it.' For the moment Dostoevsky has been sidetracked by his immediate anxieties. As I say, he had reason to feel touchy about Nechaev.

It is also important to note the time gap of nearly a year between the murder and the letter to Katkov. Initially, a swift, artistically rough job was contemplated, a 'tendentious piece' which would take a few months to write and would enrage 'the nihilists and Westerners' and set them 'howling about me that I'm a *retrograde*. Well, to hell with them, but I will say everything to the last word.'[29] It was to be topical and polemical, and among other things a direct challenge to *Fathers and Children*. The enlightened Bazarov had inherited, was continuous with, took a stage further, the liberal and

[28] Reference mislaid.   [29] Letter of 25 March 1870.

Westernizing impulse of the 1840s which itself followed the Decembrist uprising of 1825, an aristocratic bid for reform by men who had chased Napoleon out of Russia and had later felt the civilizing influence of Paris. But Verkhovensky the wrecker is unrelated to anything that had gone before, except in the new-seeing eye of his creator. He articulates the Dostoevsky split (*raskol*) in terms of a generation-gap story. Obviously the other side of the gap had to be blocked in, and to represent the 1840s the choice fell on Timofey Granovsky, in his time a renowned liberal professor and public speaker, and to a lesser extent a man of letters. Dostoevsky wrote for Stankevich's published critical study of Granovsky — 'material absolutely indispensable for my work', a life-and-death necessity 'like air'.[30] All was bustle and confidence. In the earlier *Possessed* notebooks Granovsky appears under his own name, and Peter Verkhovensky (it must be recorded) is often Nechaev. The 'tendentious' story would soon be out of the way, making possible a return to what Dostoevsky thought was much more important, the *Life of a Great Sinner* project. But it didn't come out like that. He found he had taken on more than he bargained for.

(iii)

Painfully — for no work cost him more or perhaps as much as this one — Dostoevsky came to see that *The Possessed* wasn't a sideshow. In its essentials it wasn't a diversion of any kind. It proved in due course, and in its own degree, the *Life of a Great Sinner* itself. Looked at another way, *The Possessed* and the two remaining novels he had in him to write, *A Raw Youth* and *The Brothers Karamazov*, are all generation-gap stories, and for Dostoevsky the generation gap is only subordinately topical and tendentious and mixed up with Turgenev. How much of the great-sinner project remained unachieved and how much dissolved itself into the books that

[30]   Letter of 26 February 1870. The urgency may be due to the odd flavour of Granovsky's religion, which was in the mould of eighteenth-century sentimental deism. Most Westerners were ordinary nineteenth-century atheists. This link between the historical Granovsky and the fictional Stepan Verkhovensky gives light and air and pathos to *The Possessed*, and a hint of timelessness.

in fact got written, can be debated endlessly. His own discussion of the project tended to be vague and large. In any event the last three novels juxtapose fathers and sons in an effort to gain access to or leverage upon some further thing.

The October letter to Katkov envisages this world beyond *The Possessed*'s initial scope in forthright great-sinner terms. Nicholas Stavrogin has arrived during the summer months of 1870s, and has established himself as the one 'who might really be called the chief character of the novel'. He is 'a villain', but 'tragic', and Dostoevsky continues in his most pushy vein, anxious that Katkov shall take notice, 'I have taken him from my heart'.

He means the heart of his creative instinct. There is nowhere else to take Stavrogin from, no other link between the middle-aged overdriven novelist and his idle young well-connected 'chief character'.[31] Dostoevsky also calls him his 'real hero' and his 'new hero', and I think he might not object to 'anti-hero' if the suggestion were put to him. For Stavrogin reaches back, or rather Dostoevsky reaches back in himself, brushing against Raskolnikov and Svidrigailov as he does so, and makes common cause with the underground man. Let me try and bring this out by means of a single phrase in Stavrogin's suicide letter. The final text has 'When all's said and done I've got the habits of a decent man'. Five drafts of the relevant passage survive, the first reading 'When all's said and done I'm a decent man'. The simple end-product arrives only at the fifth attempt.[32]

With hindsight one can point to the underground man complaining that if he could manage even to loaf and idle around wholeheartedly he would be able to call himself a lazy man. This is the rationale of the movement from 'a decent man' to 'the habits of a decent man'. Stavrogin can't, and in our definitive text doesn't, claim to be a decent man or to have any other thing to be; all his letter indicates is a death-like mime or sleepwalk within behaviour patterns determined by upbringing, class, and kind.

[31] The vast secondary literature offers us, inevitably, 'prototypes', but these cut no real ice.

[32] p. 614; *PSS*, Vol. XII, pp. 105–6. A yet earlier sketch for the letter in a notebook (Vol. XI, p. 304) has the bald 'I'm a decent man' with no 'when all's said and done'.

This must appear implausibly neat. But so do many things once the dust of composition has settled and the builder's yard of notebooks and rejected drafts can be studied at leisure. The neatness comes afterwards; it gets imposed when a long and laborious and very untidy process is shortcircuited by the observation (which Dostoevsky himself may never have made) of a direct link between Stavrogin and the underground man. Fumbling after phrases in the suicide letter and a thousand other places, the novelist strives to clarify an idea, but also to purge his understanding of great-sinner preconceptions and ambitions which the developing *Possessed* refuses to accommodate. It isn't because Stavrogin is *not* a decent man that the form of words has to be changed; he also says 'I'm bored' in the earliest draft of the letter, and this assertion goes completely. The reason is the underground one I have just stated. Stavrogin acts bored, other people call him bored: he *is* bored! But he lacks the minimal ontological ballast to call himself bored. Or anything else. He writes in that same letter 'I can't hate anything', and he admits he can't even own to 'despair'. And so he drifts towards vanishing point: 'One may argue about everything endlessly, but from me nothing has come but negation, with no magnanimity and no force. Even negation has not come from me.' Only negation. But really not even negation. Nothing.

Which leads one to ask what becomes of the sinner — let alone the great sinner. What counts as sinning greatly? Or, what does sinning greatly count as? One recalls Svidrigailov and Raskolnikov, the potential suicide twitting the actual murderer with 'well, you can certainly do a lot'. Stavrogin writes: 'I've tried the depths of debauchery and wasted my strength over it; but I don't like debauchery and never wanted it.' It doesn't and didn't amount to anything. There is nothing (so to say) deedy in his actions. This crablike sidling away from all he is and does catches the tune of the achieved, fully formed Stavrogin; unlike Svidrigailov, who incidentally makes great play with the fact that he's bored, he would — could — never call himself a debauchee. He is a different sort of great sinner, or essay upon the great-sinner theme, which is why I stress the aspect of return to the vicious and tragic antihero who can't even call himself lazy. The underground man's heart is no more in being idle than in anything else, however much, as he himself puts it, he 'wants to want'. Stavrogin naturalizes this thought by observing 'My desires are too weak'. But the suicide letter also keeps a foot in the abstract world, the world of metaphysics in my extended sense. Between them Stavrogin and Dasha Shatov, Shatov's sister, the girl to whom the letter is addressed, have conjured the word 'nurse' which is a term of art as metaphysical as anything in *Notes from Underground* and impossible to match in the other post-Siberian novels. 'Nurse' is a sort of code between them. She invented it and he picks it up. He has promised that in extremity he will send for her, and she will come and be his nurse. He is perching on the railway, six stops down the line, with a stationmaster he got to know somehow when he was on the town in Petersburg — the Dostoevsky no-home at its most stripped and strange in this novel of aimless movement. She never comes because he hangs himself, she has nobody to be nurse to, but her journey — were she to have made it — would prove as nugatory as his. The letter declares Stavrogin's fear of killing himself. It comes no closer than that to threatening suicide. Nor does it have to: we know his fears are as weak as his desires. Nature is likely to follow art, art here being the pure abstraction of Stavrogin's remark that even negation is more than he can manage.

Svidrigailov would never have said that; he would have gone on making jokes about America. And how different the tone of the two men and their two suicides! The nurse trope, I admit, shares America's power to open human doors the further side of whimsicality, but that is because the suicide letter has only one foot in the completely flat uncomic abstract world of negation talk. The other foot remains in Dostoevskian nature. Dasha actually wants to come and look after Stavrogin, as actually as Svidrigailov is bored — 'especially now', he says, as America looms. The two worlds of nature and abstraction meet when Stavrogin asks Dasha whether by coming to be his nurse 'you hope to set up some aim for me at last'. This thought combines the antihero wanting to want and Svidrigailov trying sex, balloon-travel, good works even, in his struggle to latch on to life. As nurse, Dasha's *aim* would be to give Stavrogin an *aim* — simultaneously an underground and an American idea. In the *Possessed* notebooks Dostoevsky tries a snatch of dialogue in which Stavrogin is asked 'Why don't you just simply live?'; and he replies 'Ah, that's the hardest thing of all'. The novel itself foregoes many such touches which aren't quite true because they betray a teasing Svidrigailov-like zest, or, if you prefer, counterzest; just as, on the secondary plane, Lebyadkin's reply to the man who tells him to stop getting drunk is wonderfully funny but wrong. 'What a strange demand!' says Lebyadkin with an effrontery beyond the man we have been given, though not of course beyond old Karamazov.[33] The long disciplining process of notebooks and drafts reduces Stavrogin to a state very near automatism: the *habits* of a decent man. In rejecting drafts he is constantly saying he's bored.[34] In the book we have in front of us — and it is a long one — he never does. But, as I say, he acts bored. Peter Verkhovensky is telling him about a religious conversation among some army officers. The mood of the party, according to Verkhovensky, was atheistic. As a group 'they gave God short shrift'. But

One grey-haired captain, a rough old chap, sat and sat not saying a word, mute as a mackerel, then suddenly got up in the middle of the room and, you know, said aloud as if speaking to himself, 'If there's no God then what sort of a Captain am I after that?', and seized his cap and threw up his arms and went out.

'He expressed a rather sensible idea,' said Stavrogin, and yawned for the third time.[35]

A wine-breath intellectualism hangs over the sturdy little comedy of the captain who has found his own words for declaring God to be the ground of his being. And if there is no God? That brings us to Stavrogin's third yawn. He has grasped the neat theological and ontological crux implicit in the captain's statement, and has acted bored at it. If he

[33]   *PSS*, Vol. XI, pp. 130, 253.

[34]   At one point a complete rationale of boredom seems to be contemplated. When Stavrogin (at this stage 'the Prince') tells Dasha ('the Ward') how bored he is, she asks him: ' "What is this boredom like? I've heard about it, but I don't understand it." The Prince explains — sincerely, as best he can' (Ibid., p. 137).

[35]   pp. 203–4.

could help himself this would be mental vandalism; but he can't; Stavrogin's are yawns that refuse to be stifled; automatism and involuntarism are finally one, and the tragic villain-hero who at once apprehends the 'sensible idea' and yawns at it betrays a high but helpless intelligence recalling Raskolnikov as well as Svidrigailov.[36]

Stavrogin is no more an atheist than Raskolnikov was, but his belief — all his beliefs — are weak, as the suicide letter to Dasha Shatov makes plain, and their weakness corresponds to the instability (*shatost*) of Raskolnikov's. Equally, to yawn is to act bored, to admit and even to flaunt kinship with Svidrigailov, and the evil-omened word listless (*vyali*) that dogs Stavrogin, though he never uses it himself, corresponds to the other man's terminal boredom. This is what it means to say that Dostoevsky brushes against Raskolnikov and Svidrigailov as he reaches back towards the underground man.

The object of the reaching exercise is of course to arrive at Stavrogin. It holds more true of some of us than of others, that in the struggle to make it new we are writing the same book all our lives; and with Dostoevsky this truth is very true. His post-Siberian great-sinner project won't convincingly disengage from his interest in the confessional form, and, as we have seen, the Dostoevsky Confession was afoot before Siberia. With Stavrogin, confession and the great sinner come together in the chapter 'At Tikhon's', often referred to as Stavrogin's Confession. Dostoevsky set great store by this chapter which marks the acutest phase of his tribulations over *The Possessed*, because his editor Katkov refused to print it. We recall the same editor's objection to the debate about Christianity between Raskolnikov and Sonya Marmeladov in *Crime and Punishment*, and, before that again, the censor's blocking of the positive Christian counter-affirmations in *Notes from Underground*. But this time the rejected text survives: we have the galley proofs of 'At Tikhon's' submitted to the magazine *Russian Herald*, and Dostoevsky's alterations to those proofs, and his widow's list of further variants.

[36] And Hamlet. The *Possessed* notebooks contain 'To be or not to be' in Russian, as well as 'O, Iago, the pity of it' (*PSS*, Vol. XI, p. 204).

Therefore it becomes possible at last to read and evaluate what was earnestly planned, executed, fought for, tinkered with in a vain attempt to propitiate Katkov (but also, as we shall see, for another reason), and finally surrendered. Furthermore, 'At Tikhon's' provides the chance to get a look at the figure named by me Dostoevsky's good angel, because here again, as in the two earlier cases, the novelist took no steps to restore the deleted material at some future date when he was his own master; and I think he was right. My proposition, embracing *The House of the Dead*, *Notes from Underground*, *Crime and Punishment*, *The Possessed*, *Karamazov*, and, negatively, by way of relative failure, *The Idiot*, is that Dostoevsky could only promote his dearest values by creeping up on their blind side: in other words that he had an urge towards crisis and clarity which he could only satisfy by yielding it to the enemy — to the horror of the flogging routine in the 'Thy kingdom come' episode in the Dead House at one chronological extreme, and to Ivan Karamazov's showdown with the Religion Swindle at the other.

Clarity appears in those self-directed exhortations of the novelist to elucidate Raskolnikov's motive for murder. The novel itself ignores them. Crisis introduces the word *podvig*, translated 'exploit' or 'feat', though Jacques Catteau remarks that *avancement* sometimes renders it best.[37] *Podvig*, also prominent in the *Crime and Punishment* notebooks, gets relegated in the final text to the Epilogue where it is seen at its simplest in the mitigating circumstance that the murderer is discovered at his trial to have burnt himself rescuing two little children from a blazing house. With both the motive for the murder and the brave rescue *Crime and Punishment* sets the pattern for later Dostoevsky; his post-Siberian notebooks swarm with admonitions like 'Decide the matter definitely one way or the other', and with the X marks the spot of 'Here a *podvig* is achieved'; and in the other novels, as in *Crime and Punishment*, the actual outcome of such promptings makes an interesting study.

Crisis and clarity are notebook froth whipped up by a single hidden energy. I ask, what does Dostoevsky's gambling

---

[37] *La Création littéraire chez Dostoevsky*, p. 296.

mania aspire towards? And I answer, breaking the bank of all banks, busting Plato's very Idea of a bank; and also being cleaned out absolutely — but absolutely: body, mind, immortal soul: in fact the Dostoevsky apocalypse where all shall be revealed, where crisis *is* clarity. And obviously the novelist's apocalypse is by no means identical with his received Christian one; hence, in part, the divergence of his art from the things his notebooks show him wanting to say. It's a reflection on sadomasochism, and on negation, and on the Underground throughout these novels, that the true gambler's urge to lose is as strong as and not ultimately separable from its opposite.

All this bears closely on Stavrogin and his so-called confession. In 'At Tikhon's' he goes to the holy man with a document which he gives him to read, and which he does read, and which Stavrogin next proposes to publish. I see the whole chapter as a subtle but misconceived footnote to *Crime and Punishment*; in these pages, instead of brushing past Raskolnikov and Svidrigailov in his return upon the underground man, Dostoevsky has allowed himself to be obstructed by them, and the result is a Stavrogin who compounds Raskolnikov's bracing himself to enter the police station '*as a man*' and confess with Svidrigailov's reaching out in all directions, including the far extremes of moral and physical debauchery, in the hope that something, it doesn't matter what, will make him unbored.

After a sleepless night Stavrogin sets forth. Then outside the monastery where Bishop Tikhon lives, 'he stopped, hastily and anxiously felt something in his side pocket and — smiled'.[38] That is Raskolnikov's smile. We know it well. And the gesture is Raskolnikov's too, for example when he feels for the axe slung inside his overcoat.[39] Even the sudden stopping is tell-tale. Stavrogin would never stop in the street like that, his psychophysical being is other. This is not a *Possessed* moment, not a *Possessed* sentence. At the outset we are aware that the chapter 'At Tikhon's' is going wrong. Not bad but wrong.

When, driven by unbearable mental torment, Raskolnikov

enters the building and climbs the stairs, a splendidly ample and imaginative *podvig* seems to be in prospect, *un avancement spirituel*. It's only afterwards, in the Epilogue, that we learn with surprise and perhaps some vexation that repentance and acceptance of suffering come to him not then but much later, in prison; his confession was not the decisive moral feat we took it for. It was not a heart-and-soul confession but an admission of guilt. And what about Stavrogin as he stands smiling, not of course a happy smile, no kind of unambiguous smile, about to enter the monastery, fingering the pages in his pocket? The man as I say is all Raskolnikov. The document which Bishop Tikhon will read puts Raskolnikov in Svidrigailov's shoes because it is a record of the excesses a mortally jaded palate has got up to.

And as Stavrogin describes his search after new and ever stronger and more bizarre sensations, and as he laments his boredom, and as suicide is touched on, tracts of *Crime and Punishment* open up again: but without the astral, feathering humour of America, anatomy, and ordinary ghosts. And as he mulls over his reasons for behaving as he has and for writing and publishing this record, the footnote status of 'At Tikhon's' causes it to embrace a wide range of familiar themes. To loose them off together, scatter-gun fashion: Stavrogin says 'I am making this statement, incidentally, to prove I am in full possession of my mental faculties and understand my position'; 'I want to forgive myself, this is my chief aim, my whole aim'; 'I want everyone to look at me'; 'I fall back on this as my last resource'; 'The thing about me then was I felt bored with life, sick and tired of it'; 'I am seeking boundless suffering'; 'I took it into my head to mutilate my life somehow' (not necessarily the same thing as seeking suffering, any more than seeking suffering need entail accepting it).[40]

Let us pause for a moment over 'I want everyone to look at me'. And I would also like to add yet another 'reason' to the already formidable pile, which is that Stavrogin intends a 'challenge to society'. Now the first is one of Dostoevsky's alterations to the galley proofs of 'At Tikhon's', and the

[40] *PSS*, Vol. XI, pp. 20, 23, 27.

second is a variant recorded by his widow.[41] I draw attention
to their provenance because commentators have focused on
the family-magazine question, on the attempt, that is, to get
the chapter past Katkov in some shape or form, and I think
this is only half the story. I think in all this textual fussing
Dostoevsky was also — and increasingly — troubled by the
chapter's footnote status and by the problem which I picture
as obstruction by Raskolnikov and Svidrigailov in his backward groping towards the underground man. The sharpened
exhibitionism of Stavrogin's wanting everybody to look at
him will not have helped Dostoevsky with Katkov, but it
does mark a step away from *Crime and Punishment* and
closer to *Notes from Underground*. The 'challenge to society'
seems to fit Raskolnikov's Napoleonic idea — until we read
on in Anna Dostoevsky's manuscript where it is at once and
directly linked to 'the governor's bitten ear', that is to one
of those sudden sallies of Stavrogin's elsewhere in *The
Possessed*, sallies hovering between outrage and prank. The
instance here is of Stavrogin pretending to the provincial
governor that he has a secret to communicate to him, and,
when the unsuspecting old man 'hastily and trustfully'
inclines his head, seizing his ear in his teeth and holding on
to it, biting hard.

'Nicholas, what kind of joke is this?' moaned the governor mechani-
cally in a voice unlike his own.[42]

It is a *Possessed* kind of joke, inconceivable in *Crime and
Punishment*, and there was no reference to it in the version
of 'At Tikhon's' submitted to Katkov initially. Once again
the change can have nothing to do with making the chapter
more acceptable. This incident of the bitten ear, presented
explicitly as 'a challenge to society', has no tonal affinity
whatever with Raskolnikov's murder, its home is with the
underground man sticking his tongue out; the hesitant backward movement towards the world under the floor is also a
forward fumble towards Stavrogin and *The Possessed*.

And what of the document itself? Since 'At Tikhon's' is
constantly referred to in Russia and the West as Stavrogin's

[41] Ibid., Vol. XII, pp. 108, 128.   [42] p. 42.

Confession, it occurs to me to note that the word confession does not appear anywhere in the chapter. That the written statement and its publication add up to a true Dostoevsky confession, to repentance and acceptance of suffering, to 'a wonderful *podvig*' in Tikhon's words, is one possibility among many.[43] Stavrogin's prodigal scattering of reasons does more than leave the question open. It leaves all questioning behind. It muddies the waters of speculation utterly. If we take wanting everybody to look at him as the 'real' reason, then the case of Stavrogin is (in the lawyer's phrase) on all fours with that of the underground man's indecent exposure of consciousness. However, 'I invite nobody into my soul' he declares, as if to banish the exhibitionist thought.[44] And then if the search for suffering is allowed to eclipse the rest, we are back with Marmeladov squinnying into the bottom of his vodka jug; whereas Stavrogin saying he wants to forgive himself might be Raskolnikov pondering retrospectively, self-critically, on his admission of guilt at the police station.

To Marmeladov, Raskolnikov, and the underground man, I now add Svidrigailov, because the chief enormity which is being confessed, or merely admitted to, or flaunted, or feigned, binds Stavrogin to the America-minded debauchee no less tightly than does the boredom theme of the 'At Tikhon's' chapter. As with the highly misleading phrase Stavrogin's Confession, critics and commentators behave as if they had got into a huddle. Everybody, including the present Soviet editor, talks about Stavrogin's forcing or rape of a young girl.[45] So to sort the thing out: Stavrogin has designs on the child; he kisses her hand, puts her on his knee, whispers to her. She is in terror. Then

At last there occurred, suddenly, a most strange event which I shall never forget and which astonished me: the little girl flung her arms round my neck and in a rush began kissing me frenziedly. Her face expressed complete rapture. I nearly got up and went away out of pity, I found this so unpleasant in a slip of a child. But I overcame my immediate fearful feeling, and I stayed.[46]

---

[43] *PSS*, Vol. XI, p. 24. [44] Ibid., p. 11.
[45] Ibid., Vol. XII, pp. 241, 244. He also writes of Stavrogin's 'confession' throughout. Neither confession nor sexual violence are mentioned in any of the manuscript variants of the 'At Tikhon's' chapter.
[46] Ibid., Vol. XI, p. 16.

And that's that. The next sentence begins a new paragraph: 'When all was over, she was covered in confusion.' Therefore no rape occurs. The child is sexually responsive and perhaps dominant. Hence her smile 'as if ashamed, a kind of twisted smile' after her terror and immediately before the passage I have just quoted. Hence, later, her words 'I have killed God', and her suicide. Getting this right obviously matters in itself, but also for its bearing on two further issues.

First, it drives Stavrogin even closer to Svidrigailov than I have suggested so far. The episode with the child is a reworking of Svidrigailov's nightmare immediately before his suicide, in which he finds an abandoned little girl and carries her upstairs and puts her in his bed, and goes back later to see how she is.

Now, without any further concealment, she opened both her eyes; they turned a blazing, shameless glance upon him, they invited him, they laughed . . . . 'Damn you!' Svidrigailov cried in horror, raising his hand to strike her. But at that moment he woke up.[47]

Second, it discredits those — and again the Soviet editor is among them — who seek to explain Dostoevsky's failure to reinstate 'At Tikhon's' solely by the prevailing conditions of censorship.[48] He got Svidrigailov's nightmare past the censor, and there is a good deal more to that horror than I have quoted; and 'At Tikhon's' could have been got past him too. It is unsound to argue that Svidrigailov's experience was only a bad dream, because the manuscript variants prove that Dostoevsky was prepared at one stage to forego the actuality of the sexual outcome between Stavrogin and the child. 'It was just a psychological misunderstanding,' so Stavrogin reassures the bishop in Anna's text:

'Nothing happened. Not a thing.'
'Well, God be praised,' said Tikhon, and crossed himself.[49]

Amidst this confusion, my view of 'At Tikhon's' as a hyperlucid footnote to *Crime and Punishment*, as misconceived crisis and clarity, needs justifying: the very point of Stavrogin's scattering of 'reasons' is that he and his document

---

[47] *Crime and Punishment*, p. 449.   [48] *PSS*, Vol. XII, p. 237.
[49] Ibid., p. 111.

shall not come clear or clinch anything. But, as to clinching things, Stavrogin is not Tikhon, which evokes another of my dicta: Dostoevsky could only satisfy his urge towards crisis and clarity by surrendering it to the enemy. For sure he takes pains to make Tikhon a human puzzle so that he shan't in any obvious way speak God's truth. He looks a bit ill, smiles vaguely, and has a strange rather shy expression. His furniture is a jumble of good and bad; a magnificent Bokhara carpet lies next to straw mats, and engravings of fashionable society and sacred icons confront one another. He appears to enjoy light reading. Perhaps even salacious reading.[50]

But nothing, and certainly not articulating his words 'cheerfully and artlessly', can muffle Tikhon's diagnosis which is that Stavrogin suffers from 'indifference'. At once the two of them fall into a kind of trance. Stavrogin asks the bishop (in cool reason a preposterous question) if he has read the Christian Apocalypse. He then directs him to the message to the angel of the church at Laodicea in the third chapter of Revelation. Tikhon knows the passage by heart and recites it word for word. Its burden is:

I know thy works, that thou art neither hot nor cold: I would that thou wert hot or cold. So then because thou art lukewarm and neither hot nor cold, I will spew thee out of my mouth.[51]

The 'lukewarm' state is of course a biblical and transcendental and authoritative anchoring of 'indifference'. It isolates and ratifies the reason among so many reasons which Stavrogin himself gives: 'the disease of indifference'.[52] Tikhon and Stavrogin have both got it right. But this *it* cannot be said, can only be shown forth as in the suicide letter where Stavrogin writes 'My desires are too weak; they cannot guide me.' We aim straight at the art of *The Possessed* by observing that the follow-up, I'm a lukewarm man, or I'm an indifferent, an apathetic man, is beyond Stavrogin. All self-definition, as Dostoevsky finally shaped and gave Stavrogin to the world, is beyond him. That is why, instead of taking the weakness of his desires to himself, Stavrogin continues in figurative, musing vein, sad and free, very beautiful in context: 'You can

---

[50]   Ibid., Vol. XI, pp. 6–7.   [51]   Ibid., pp. 10–11.   [52]   Ibid., p. 15.

cross a river on a tree-trunk, but not on a chip of wood.' This is the same young man who bit the ear of the governor — and we can only meet and get to know him in the novel itself.

Get to know as opposed to get at. The 'At Tikhon's' chapter, rejected by the editor and finally abandoned by the novelist, gets at, ponders the case of, somebody we never even meet there: the smiling man outside the monastery is Raskolnikov, and the document in his pocket recounts Svidrigailov's deeds. The pondering, the getting at the absent Stavrogin, proves successful; many acute observations buttress the central 'lukewarm' truth about him, and analysis spills over into the notebooks where Tikhon's God's-voice function appears at its clearest. 'Try to hold something sacred, no matter what it be,' he exhorts Stavrogin who replies 'What for?' And then the punch line: 'This isn't done *for something*, it is done *just so*.'[53] At which moment we can sense the warm breath of composition coming off the page, for Dostoevsky first had Tikhon continue 'It carries its own reward' and then crossed these words out in his notebook, no doubt because they are too obvious and touched by the world's wisdom. They aren't worthy of the silent spiritual gesture made by that italicized *'just so'*. Nor is Stavrogin's pert Svidrigailov-like 'What for?' worthy of it, or of himself. And Tikhon's own further move isn't right either: 'If you do not feel a need, and if you love nothing, it follows you are incapable of it.' To this severe driving home of the issue in pursuit of crisis and clarity, Stavrogin might fairly reply that he didn't create himself lukewarm. He would never have had it so. 'I want to want', the underground man's lonely cry, is also his though he doesn't utter it, and biting the governor's ear, like sticking the tongue out, is a one-against-all drumming of the heels of consciousness — but again with a difference which is that the biting extends beyond the notional; it happens and it hurts, though it's a minor foray compared with Raskolnikov's spectacular eruption into actuality with the murder. And at the same time, since Svidrigailov too has been brushed against in this reaching back which is also a

53 Ibid., p. 275.

reaching forward, the incident of the governor's ear can be understood in all its matchless comedy as a desperate man's recourse against boredom.

(iv)

The mere mention of the biting in Anna's manuscript record of 'At Tikhon's' variants is enough to pull the reader back into *The Possessed*, and he can't experience the sudden fierce tug of that novel without realizing simultaneously that the whole 'At Tikhon's' chapter belongs elsewhere, to a different masterpiece. Its footnote status in relation to *Crime and Punishment* constitutes, I admit, a funny sort of belonging, as does the obstructive force of Raskolnikov and Svidrigailov upon Dostoevsky's attempt to give decisively new shape to the Great Sinner of his notebooks and letters and fondest creative hopes. A negative belonging, if you like. But narrative tone is a different and affirmative matter.

A minute later I looked at my watch and noted the time. Evening was drawing in. A fly was buzzing over my head and kept settling on my face. I caught it, held it in my fingers and put it out of the window. A cart drove very loudly into the yard below. Very loudly (and for some time before), a tailor had been singing as he sat at a window in a corner of the yard. He sat at his work and I could see him. It occurred to me that as I had met nobody as I walked through the gate and went upstairs, there was no need to encounter anyone now, going down, and I moved my chair from the window. I picked up a book, but put it down again and began looking at a tiny red spider on the leaf of a geranium, and lost count of time. I remember everything to the very last moment.[54]

This sequence could not occur in *The Possessed* — a dangerous thing to say about a very long and diverse book, but true. Despite the fact that spiders are all over the place in Dostoevsky, not just in Svidrigailov's dirty bathhouse vision of Eternity, and that urban potted plants go back to the beginning in *Poor People*, we are here firmly inside *Crime and Punishment* in its abandoned first-person narrative form ('I am on trial and will tell all'): Petersburg evenings and their hanging summer light, noises from below, happy workmen,

[54] Ibid., p. 19.

blessed 'living life' elsewhere, a lonely man in pain passing through gates, over thresholds, slipping up and down staircases, the buzzing fly of Raskolnikov's dream and his awakening,[55] intense time-consciousness alternating with time-oblivion.

'At Tikhon's' has strayed out of a metropolitan novel into a provincial one which won't accommodate it. To take one's finger off the bounding narrative pulse of *Crime and Punishment* and to open *The Possessed* — to open it anywhere — is to find oneself out in the sticks once again: the 'our town' of the novel and the voice relating its affairs bring back the 'we' of convict life in *The House of the Dead* and the more sketchy collective of that remote Siberian community outside the prison walls. The same dilating and contracting principle informs both novels, a first-person narrator who moves between 'we all thought' and 'it was just my hunch', though the swing is greater in *The Possessed* and its figuration much more complex. If any *House of the Dead* notebooks had survived I would expect them to contain sudden leaps of discovery and creative arrivals like 'Most important — $\boxed{it's\ a\ chronicle}$ ' and

> 'I've had breakfast.
> I'll keep the secret.
> I am a character.'[56]

By drawing a rectangle round '*it's a chronicle*' Dostoevsky suggests a framed narrative for *The Possessed* like the story found by the frame narrator among a deceased ex-convict's effects in *The House of the Dead*; and by declaring 'I am a character' (*kharakter*: a person, not a literary *personazh*) he puts himself inside that frame. The result, therefore, is a framed narrative without a frame narrator — not that he reached the two sides of this conclusion simultaneously. The first came early and firmly, in February of 1870: 'From a provincial chronicle . . . . The system I have adopted is that of a CHRONICLE.'[57] The second was an untidy and protracted business, stretching on through the spring and summer and coinciding with the refusal of *The Pos-*

---

[55] *Crime and Punishment*, pp. 246–7. And 'the awakened flies' that settle on Svidrigailov's untouched food, and which he fails to catch, in the last minutes of his life (p. 450).

[56] *PSS*, Vol. XI, pp. 128, 249.   [57] Ibid., p. 92.

sessed to be contained within the limits of a 'tendentious' sideshow. The novel insisted on reverting to the ampler great-sinner pattern; hence Stavrogin's emergence as 'chief character', 'tragic villain' and so forth during this period, and Peter Verkhovensky's withdrawal to the second rank: Verkhovensky the mere wrecker, the nihilist, the man of the 1860s, the deeper realist's answer to Turgenev.

I look in the same direction to account for the charming note 'Granovsky has got a bit out of hand'.[58] Taken more or less straight from life, Granovsky was to have represented the liberal 1840s in a crisp, neat, polemical generation-gap story. In *The Possessed* he becomes Stepan Trofimovich Verkhovensky (hereafter Stepan), Peter's father and one of the best things Dostoevsky ever did. But in the mean time, whose hand has Granovsky escaped from? This pinpoints the issue of Dostoevsky as author and as 'a character' in the provincial chronicle, the framed narrative. Again we are at the tip of his pen as he draws a box to put himself inside, and as the most private and informative area of the *Possessed* notebooks begins to open up. At first he hadn't even settled on first-person narration; the voice from inside the frame is sometimes 'the chronicler's' or 'the author's', sometimes 'mine'. A double stance develops — inevitably, since the figure inside the frame can't wish away the novelist bent over his notebooks. Thus: 'ABOUT NECHAEV [Peter Verkhovensky]: NECHAEV PLAYS TWO ROLES, THE SECOND OF WHICH I, THE CHRONICLER, DON'T KNOW AT ALL AND AM NOT PRESENTING.'[59] Sometimes we catch the novelist positively shaping and manipulating the narrator: 'The chronicler pretends for his part that he feels the sorrow of a Christian . . . .'[60] And from, or nearly from, the outset there is the hint of a three-cornered relationship in which the future reader of the as yet unwritten *Possessed* joins novelist and narrator in a conspiracy to uphold the truth of the fiction: 'Altogether, when I describe conversations, even *tête-à-tête* conversations between two people — don't worry: either I have hard facts, or perhaps I am *inventing* them myself — but in any case rest assured that everything is true.'[61]

[58] Ibid., p. 94. Or, 'has let his tongue run away with him' (*izboltalsya*).
[59] Ibid., p. 213.   [60] Ibid., p. 119.   [61] Ibid., p. 92.

The man being reassured is the reader. The man reassuring him is, or has the authority of, the omniscient and omnipotent novelist. The 'I' describing conversations he hasn't direct access to, which he wasn't present at, which he may not even have been told about and so may be inventing, is the 'character' Dostoevsky has turned himself into for the purpose of narrating the provincial chronicle. This one sentence from the notebooks goes straight home to the novel which eventually got written. And the novel which got written breathes life into this sentence's very unpromising warrant for the 'truth' of what is being told, namely that there are hard facts or perhaps it is just being made up.

Reassurance is another matter, except at the level where all great art reassures; for a spirit of slippage presides over *The Possessed*. In the opening paragraphs we are introduced to Stepan Verkhovensky:

Nevertheless he was a most intelligent and gifted man, even, so to say, a scholar, though, as far as his scholarship was concerned, well, in a word, his scholarship didn't amount to much, to nothing at all, I think.[62]

A scholar. Not much of a scholar. Really no scholar. Recall Stavrogin's suicide letter. Only negation. Not even negation. Nothing. Doubling in Dostoevsky, which goes back to the very beginning, to Mr Devushkin living and not living in the kitchen, which has its post-Siberian developments in the underground man's now-you-see-me-now-you-don't 'flashing' of his consciousness, in Raskolnikov's and Svidrigailov's different ways of being among but not with us and Porfiry's torture tune of 'There's nothing here, precisely nothing, perhaps absolutely nothing' — doubling takes on a new form in *The Possessed*, closer to the I/We/They/Everybody/Nobody shifts of *The House of the Dead* than anything else before it or to come.

The slippage sentence just quoted concludes with an 'I think'. This 'I' is the first-person narrator inside the frame of

---

[62] p. 2. Verkhovensky is based on an old word *verkhovenstvo* meaning leadership or supremacy, and reflects the novel when it was at the stage of a generation-gap rivalry. Hence 'Granovsky, throughout the novel, is constantly bickering with his son about *verkhovenstvo*,' in an early notebook (*PSS*, Vol. XI, p. 89). This shows the need to be careful over 'interpreting' names in Dostoevsky.

the provincial chronicle, the 'character' Dostoevsky has turned himself into. He is a young friend of Stepan Verkhovensky, and when the notebooks record that Granovsky (Stepan's prototype) has got out of hand they are also heralding the novelist's escape into a fictional mode of enormous suppleness. That Stepan's scholarship amounts to nothing is only what 'I think'. Others may and do think otherwise. A freedom is generated which has its phases of indiscipline, licence, chaos. The book is a stampede, faithful to its title and its Epigraph which is the story of the Gadarene swine possessed by devils and rushing into the lake of Galilee and drowning themselves.

The fury, the energy of *The Possessed* seems quite magically unconvenanted. The slippage principle should make for enervation and a general whittling away. But on the contrary, this world of 'it was rumoured' and 'that may well have been so' followed at once by 'it is more likely that nothing of the sort happened' — again in the opening paragraphs[63] — is as exhilarating as the challenge of life's opacities to a healthy curiosity. Indeed the overall triumph of art in this case is that the novel walks out into our fact rather than ourselves entering its fiction: a very primitive and absolute form of consumer capitulation. Dostoevsky has an impudent way of making his narrator declare 'As a chronicler I confine myself to presenting events exactly as they happened, and it's not my fault if they appear incredible'[64] — like the son of the house writing home about his time on the North-West Frontier of India. The imperial–provincial *idée* is a sovereign one. We read about the governor's bitten ear with the fascination of doting remoteness. Likewise the Audenesque opprobrious act which precedes it.

One of the most respected of our club members, on our committee of management, Pavel Pavlovich Gaganov, an elderly man and highly esteemed, had formed the innocent habit of following anything he had to say with the vehement addition, 'No, sir, you can't lead me by the nose!' Well, there's no harm in that. But one day at the club when he trotted out this phrase during some heated discussion in the midst of a

[63]   p. 3.
[64]   At p. 57, for example. 'I will confine myself to the bare facts' (as at p. 612) is a favourite ploy. Of course it is the last thing 'I' do.

little group of members (all of them persons of some consequence), Nicholas Stavrogin who was standing to one side alone and unnoticed, suddenly went up to Mr Gaganov and, taking him unexpectedly and firmly with two fingers by the nose, managed to drag him two or three steps across the room.[65]

Cantonment goings-on in Peshawar! Goings-on of cruel and rootless hilarity. This is how there is no getting at Stavrogin, and how getting to know him proceeds. And this is what happens to the *podvig* tic which obsesses the notebooks and the 'At Tikhon's' chapter: it becomes deflected and surrealized into eruptive impenetrable little freaks. Or Dostoevsky holds firm to a certain grandness and climactic force, while inverting the *podvig* and rendering it passive, when Stavrogin 'endures' a tremendous punch in the face from Shatov. Stavrogin is a killer — or can be — but he does nothing: 'the light in his eyes seemed to go out.'[66] Though untalkative, he is as inspectable as Hamlet, and no less inscrutable. Quite late in his notebooks Dostoevsky puts the matter thus: Stavrogin 'confides in nobody and is a mystery all round'. Then a few lines further on: Stavrogin 'reveals himself gradually through the action without any explanations'. But the self that gets revealed in the novel's action is a bundle of contradictions, like some people we know well. So there's no inconsistency when Dostoevsky says that what is *'most important'* is the *'special tone of the narrative'* whereby *'everything will be saved'*, and that the tone of the narrative rests in Stavrogin 'not being elucidated'.[67]

Stavrogin's ear-biting and nose-pulling present two small samples of this all-important narrative tone. The first of these revelations which elucidate nothing is introduced as 'completely unthinkable but from another point of view and in one respect all too easy to envisage'.[68] Slippage again: the crumbling, self-thwarting surface of the prose. From what 'point of view' and in which 'respect'? We are never told. Furthermore, unthinkable to whom and envisageable by whom? The chronicler wasn't present at the incident. As with large tracts of *The Possessed* this is in effect third-person narrative, recalling the notebook assurance that whether 'my'

[65] p. 37.　　　　　　　　[66] p. 186.
[67] *PSS*, Vol. XI, pp. 260–1.　　[68] p. 42.

story is based on hard facts or has simply been made up, it is all 'true'.

Nor does the chronicler say whether he was present at the nose-pulling. But nor does it matter; 'our club' will have been seething with talk for days, and 'I' am bound to have heard about Stavrogin's escapade. And the 'they' of more or less the whole town will have heard too. Here *The Possessed* draws close to the I/We/They/Everybody shifts of *The House of the Dead*, and the tone of the narrative, which (Dostoevsky said) is to save everything, demonstrates its airy yet potent, rather Proustian anecdotal scope. 'Our club' presumably overlaps while being smaller than 'the best circles' of this society, whereas the 'they' of 'the whole town' is sometimes, but only sometimes, the 'we' of 'our town'; and 'our group' which springs out of 'my' special relationship with Stepan Verkhovensky and which gathers round Mrs Stavrogin, Nicholas's mother and Stepan's patroness, is different again and again overlapping; and the 'all' buried inside the phrase 'our "old man" — as we all used to call Stepan Trofimovich among ourselves' is probably though not certainly synonymous with this 'group'; while Dostoevsky delights in sly collective evocations like 'civic grief' and in parcellings-out like 'the poorest expectant mothers of the town', and in fouling the whole snobbish provincial nest with such carefully calculated absurdities as 'almost the whole town, that is of course the entire top stratum of our society'.[69]

So there is no difficulty in imagining how the news of the senior citizen's pulled nose got around. In the general excitement — the novel has scarcely begun — it gets borne in upon the reader that Stavrogin's conduct is not the only thing to be puzzled by. Not one of 'us' in the whole town ascribes his action to madness. 'That means we were inclined to expect such behaviour even from a sane Stavrogin.' *That means* — the unsettling authorial logic is neutrally deployed, with no follow-up. Something has bitten 'us'. 'Our' mentality is odd too. The reader must make what he can of it. Everybody in 'our town' feels indignant about the insult to the respected old gentleman, and a proposal gets off the ground

[69]   pp. 7, 21–2, 72, 136, 138.

to give a subscription dinner in his honour; but finally 'we' think better of it, 'perhaps realizing at last that a man had, after all, been pulled by the nose, so there really wasn't any cause for a celebration.'[70]

'Social unsteadiness (*shatost*), as Shatov says.' What has bitten 'us', the transpersonal Gadarene motif of *The Possessed*, manifests itself through the dotty plan for a dinner just as eloquently as through the murder in the park. It's a mistake to have a narrowly political view of the novel, as it is to regard its comedy as somehow decorative. The lightness of its light relief is *shatost* too. 'We', the provincial society, display all the loose-end symptoms of Peter the Great's reforms — though Dostoevsky's overt theorizing about Peter gets left behind in the notebooks. The novel articulates the loose end as boredom, again transpersonalized. 'I find it strange looking at you all,' says Marya Lebyadkin, the crazed visionary cripple, the fool-in-Christ (*yurodivaya*), in a touch-stone meditation; 'I don't understand how it is people are bored.'[71]

Uniting boredom, provinciality, the Gadarene stampede, and paper people, Peter Verkhovensky says: 'I realize that in this godforsaken town you are bored, so you make a rush for any piece of paper with something written on it.'[72] This boredom rotates upon a frivolous–menacing, frenetic–slack, comic–terrible axis which is the book's living principle. In itself the dim complacency of gossip and cards at 'our club' would seem harmless, familiar, merely social; but 'in itself' denatures *The Possessed* where groupings dissolve or collapse into each other, and where the 'merely' social has no place. On his death-bed Stepan Verkhovensky returns to the swine of the gospel story and paraphrases the devils which enter them as a disease afflicting all Russia. In Eternity, like the madman in the story who got rid of his devils when they were driven out of him and into the swine, Russia will sit healed at the feet of Jesus.[73] This dubious eschatology need not worry us because the novel makes no attempt to en-compass it. Jesus and Holy Russia at his feet remain harm-lessly, hypothetically beyond the apocalyptic naturalism

[70] p. 38.   [71] pp. 127–8.   [72] p. 368.   [73] pp. 595–6.

which is everything the book is about: the devils, the disease, the all-pervading unsteadiness.

(v)

Those 'poorest expectant mothers of the town' are the objects of Mrs Stavrogin's competitive philanthropy. She and the new governor's wife, Mrs von Lemke, enter upon a tussle for local ascendancy through their rival charitable undertakings. In the end Mrs Stavrogin and her expectant mothers lose out — if indeed there was ever any winning — while Mrs von Lemke's needy governesses bring that determined woman victory, but then defeat. The fund-raising fête for the governesses is the biggest set-piece *skandal* in all Dostoevsky. Drunks and gatecrashers move in. Grotesque isolated figures — 'a huge pock-marked retired captain'[74] — loom out of the chaos and disappear again. Humble clerks who have gone a bust on clothes for marriageable daughters are outraged but too timid to protest. The book itself seems to go mad. Its flickering epidemic relish at the expense of clerks and governesses and expectant mothers is wilder than irresponsibility and more furious than Saturnalian record. Out of sight, shielded by riot and revelry and now a quarter of a century older, lurks the poet who boasted he had not shown his young mug in *Poor People*: the sober laborious craftsman determined that his tone shall save everything.

An extraordinary number of subscribers and donors had turned up, all the select society of the town; but even the most unselect were admitted, provided they brought the cash.[75]

Trouble ahead! Trouble conveyed in one exactly placed slippage sentence. That is before the fête begins. And at the end, after twelve cancelled variants in one short paragraph, a single sentence, itself the third attempt, tells us 'They would not let the orchestra go, and musicians who attempted to leave were beaten up', which says all we need to know about the unstated 'Keep playing!' whereby the liveliness of the small hours will have been sustained.[76]

[74] p. 423.   [75] p. 288.
[76] p. 465; *PSS*, Vol. XI, p. 413.

On the other hand this skulking novelist told himself in a notebook, as we recall, 'I am a character'; and there is every reason why the narrating 'I' of *The Possessed* should be perfectly visible. Sometimes he is just a secondary figure floating in the novel's bloodstream, as at the fête where he has got roped in with a few other young men to be a marshal and make sure everything goes smoothly. Of course he is incompetent, and as well as being swept along in the muddle and uproar he shares 'our town's' positive transpersonal complicities in what goes on here. All over the place, not only at the fête, a psychic infection rages and erupts in small ugly-comic jests — 'They put a dead cat in my trunk'[77] — but also in affronts to the human self as massive and immemorial as those Homer describes. A very young man has shot himself and 'we' ride off in an inquisitive Gadarene 'cavalcade' ('our ladies had never seen a suicide') to view the corpse; 'everything's so boring' — recall Marya Lebyadkin's words — 'one can't afford to be squeamish about one's amusements so long as they are fun'; and Lyamshin, the man who gets himself asked to parties to mimic women in labour, new-born babies, and peasants in the confessional, steals a bunch of grapes from the room of death.[78]

It's not easy to say what the narrating 'I' is doing at such a scene. Again and again he seems to be in and yet dubiously of the party. In fact the chronicle succeeds in having its cake and eating it, all the way back to the stir caused by Nicholas Stavrogin's arrival in 'our town', when it is recorded among other things that he seemed to know a lot — 'But of course it didn't take much knowledge to astonish us'.[79] Isolated, that looks like straightforward double focus: the first-person narrator inside the chronicle box, unaware of his provincial limitations; and Dostoevsky outside it. One's overall sense of *The Possessed* absolutely refuses to confirm any such duality, and one can pay the novel no simpler or fuller tribute than by saying so.

The slippage principle which should, I remarked, enervate but in truth exhilarates, has a way of positioning the reader

[77] p. 301.   [78] pp. 295–7.
[79] p. 35. 'I was not the only one to be surprised' says the narrator rather touchily.

on the side of the narrative against the narrator. The troubles of the new governor are being described. Cattle plague is rife. Fires keep breaking out. Rumours — that Fama of *The Possessed* which can swell to a raging flood but equally can sink into a hoarse inward whisper — rumours of incendiarism abound. 'Cases of robbery were twice as numerous as usual. But all this, of course, would have been perfectly normal had there not been other more weighty reasons which disturbed the composure of the hitherto cheerful von Lemke.'[80]

How can twice as many robberies as usual be perfectly normal? Of course they can't. Simultaneously the reader responds to the transpersonal unsteadiness, the possessed state of the book, and feels an urge to thrust aside the irresolute self-contradictory narrator and repose upon the story of von Lemke with his cut-out toys and yellow autumn flower. 'However hard it may be to imagine, it was so.' Thus speaks the fool narrator. But this incomparable narrative needs no shoring-up by him. He might as well ask the reader to believe in those supremely credible terrorized musicians scraping and blowing through the small hours.

The intrusive chronicling 'I' can't even make up his mind about numbers. Once the rosetted marshals at the fête are six, and once they are twelve. Very few readers will notice this discrepancy, but all are flicked and jabbed at and irritated — those circling insects[82] — by contradiction, by undetermination followed by overdetermination of reasons, by the narrator's fuss over details which don't matter, his youthful sententiousness about women ('the depths of the female heart'[83]) and other irrelevancies, his moralizing, his way of wantonly bleeding a robust narrative with 'However, that may only have seemed so',[84] his 'I have already described' when he hasn't,[85] his promises to explain later which aren't kept when the reader doesn't want explanation anyhow, he wants the story.[86] Once and once only in six hundred and seventeen pages the narrator gives his readership a disconcerting, impertinent prod by addressing it directly as 'Gentlemen'.[87] These things add up.

[80] p. 311.   [81] pp. 393, 422.   [82] p. 243, above.
[83] p. 11.   [84] p. 304, for example.   [85] p. 153.
[86] As at p. 79.   [87] p. 30 (Constance Garnett's 'my friends').

They add up to a novel of leaking secrets and amputated thoughts, of wildly comic material sometimes dully, almost dutifully deployed, as if the humour had escaped the teller; of people 'missing' each other in dialogue

> 'Perhaps he didn't go out of his mind at all.'
> 'Oh you mean because he started biting people?'[88]

and clashing head-on unforgettably

> 'But I'm your uncle; I carried you about in my arms when you were a baby.'
> 'What do I care what you carried? I didn't ask you to carry me.'[89]

A novel scatty yet dense, as when events are badly related in real life. A novel of little sprouting aphorisms: 'Every man is worth an umbrella'.[90] And enchanted ghost-voice exchanges of extremest purity:

> 'What's that? An allegory?'
> 'N-no — why? Not an allegory, just a leaf, one leaf.'[91]

A novel where actions get unhooked from their (or any) waking rationale:

> The prince too looked at the German, turning his head and collar towards him and putting on his pince-nez, though without the slightest curiosity.[92]

And words as well as actions:

> 'Suppose you had lived on the moon,' Stavrogin interrupted . . . .
> 'I don't know,' replied Kirillov. 'I've not been on the moon,' he added, without any irony, simply as a statement of fact.[93]

And here's another fact:

> 'Nowadays they carry corpses by rail,' said one of the most insignificant young men unexpectedly.[94]

A toneless, disjunctive fact, droll and very uneasy, one of those amputated thoughts I have just mentioned and also a sensation, a crawling sensation of the time being out of joint; there is more *Hamlet* to *The Possessed* than what is personal

---

[88] p. 319. [89] p. 359. [90] p. 245.
[91] p. 214. [92] p. 410. [93] pp. 212–13.
[94] p. 411.

to Stavrogin, 'the Prince' as he first appears, though on the surface of his mind Dostoevsky evidently meant Prince Hal, not the Prince of Denmark.

Nevertheless Stavrogin does contemplate suicide, and the notebook entry 'to be or not to be' bears the date 16 August, so it belongs to the summer when the 'tendentious' political story gets tugged back into great-sinner orbit, growing physically and imaginatively larger and more formidable all the time. Dostoevsky's main troubles were with Stavrogin himself, his new-found 'chief character'. His first and continuing urge was to drive him towards crisis and clarity, which involved, one might almost say which meant, finding a *podvig* that would satisfy his idea of Stavrogin.

And thus suicide comes in. Now the underground man would have extinguished his consciousness if he could, but since the fable of life under the floorboards renders him bodiless and one can't kill consciousness without laying hands on one's body, the matter doesn't arise. Svidrigailov possesses a body, and destroys it. Whether the suicide who teases the murderer about his ability to do something is himself achieving anything deedy by going to his America — that question *Crime and Punishment* never voices, and it is a crucial and inspired omission. And now, writing the same novel all his life, Dostoevsky finds himself doomed to confront suicide as deed, perhaps life's one deed and therefore the *podvig* he is seeking.

During his struggle to get *The Possessed* into shape he came to see that his conception of Stavrogin, as well as obsessed by crisis and clarity, was hopelessly overcrowded. With cornucopian largesse and ramification the notebooks polarize the emerging hero into a man indulging all vileness and in love with the good. In the novel he stays polarized, but without bulk and in a tragic sense without force; he goes through the motions ('the habits of a decent man' and so forth) while his great-sinner infamies are unloaded upon a past which he cannot even renounce. The final letter declares: 'Indignation and shame I can never feel; therefore not despair, either.' His inability to despair makes the soaped rope and spare nail of his suicide at once meticulous and completely open-ended. The doctors rule out insanity, God knows why, just as the club and other circles of 'our town' think a sane Stavrogin capable of ear-biting and nose-pulling.

One recalls the disease of indifference in the abandoned 'At Tikhon's' chapter and observes how odd its symptoms are; or one quotes Stavrogin's notebook rejoinder that simply to live is the hardest thing of all. Anyhow, he kills himself and there is no more to be said. Suicide as *podvig*, on the other hand, must drag a verbalized freight of theory behind it. So the novel frees Stavrogin from 'to be or not to be' and all other trammels of the notebooks, and transfers them to Kirillov. Like Svidrigailov, Kirillov comes to the fore very late and very fast in the process of composition, but unlike *Crime and Punishment*'s self-slaughterer the man in *The Possessed* parades an entire philosophy and theology of suicide. This theorizing is the last thing of all to arrive. Initially, in November, which is three months after Stavrogin was quoting Hamlet, Kirillov's '*ROLE IS A FACTUAL ONE*' — by which Dostoevsky means he 'volunteered to shoot himself for the common cause' and leave a letter claiming responsibility for Shatov's murder, thus diverting the attention of the police from Peter Verkhovensky and the quintet.[95] This framework of suicide and untruthful self-incriminating letter remains. But at the last minute, apparently under the immediate pressure of writing the magazine version of the novel, Dostoevsky realised that '*FACTUAL*' is precisely what Kirillov's role must not, in essence and impact, be.

Kirillov is needed to give *The Possessed* its strand of theoretic absolutism. He is as Gadarene, as possessed, as any one, but at the level of total ideal obsession. While Shatov expounds and disputes ardently, and incidentally takes a lot of good- and God-focused material off the shoulders of the notebook Stavrogin (' "Shatov must be tied up before you can argue with him," Stepan Verkhovensky sometimes joked'), only to Kirillov can it be said and is it said, 'you haven't swallowed an idea, but an idea has swallowed you' — to which he responds delightedly with 'That's good. You've got a bit of sense.'[96]

The idea which has swallowed Kirillov is suicide, not

[95] *PSS*, Vol. XI, p. 241.   [96] pp. 23, 507.

suicide for the common cause of the quintet as Dostoevsky first proposed, but to achieve a metaphysical and religious purpose; and thus he plays a big part in the transformation of a neat political generation-gap story into a larger, more complicated object. He writes the self-incriminating letter because he has promised to. He kills himself, as innumerable commentators have paraphrased and elaborated, in order to kill God. Suicide for this reason — to free mankind of the consoling yet imprisoning fictions of religion — is the highest expression of self-will, a perfectly free action, a divine gesture. The man who kills himself *thus*, becomes god. More exactly, he becomes man-god as opposed to God-man who is the Christ of Christianity. There have been millions of suicides in the history of the world, but none, according to Kirillov, for *this* reason.[97] Therefore mankind, history, eternity, God, all wait upon him and his deed.

While doing rough justice to what Kirillov says, to his brand of mystical atheism, this more or less agreed summary is not convincingly inward with Dostoevsky's creation. In trying to improve on it, perhaps the best plan is to enter where Kirillov does. He is introduced as a 'structural engineer'.[98] I think we should prick our ears at that. Dostoevsky's groping backwards past *Crime and Punishment* towards *Notes from Underground* is not just a matter of arriving at Stavrogin. The seed-bed of Kirillov's structural engineering is the underground man's image of normal human beings as roadbuilders: being somebody, doing something, going somewhere. Of course Kirillov is anything but a normal human being; and that is just the point. His structural engineering never happens. He has arrived from abroad, yet another bird of passage, 'in the hope of getting a job building our railway bridge'. But, so Stepan Verkhovensky tells him, 'They won't let you build our bridge.'[99] Why not? And who are 'they'? A sudden whiff of Kafka. This is the world of the underground man's eruptive and unexplained 'They won't let me — I can't be — good'; which world is itself continuous with that of the pre-Siberian stories, particularly *The Double* where Dostoevsky says he found his underground type. As to

<hr />

[97] p. 103.   [98] p. 79.   [99] pp. 80, 84.

'our bridge' (which is never mentioned again), the reader can if he likes reflect that Kirillov is an odd fish and will no doubt prove himself *persona non grata* in 'our town', or that the local bureaucrats are an officious and/or corrupt lot, or that the central authority thousands of miles away in Petersburg enjoys throwing its weight about. But this would be moving in and making up the message in the style of the 'missing' letters in *Poor People*, the first story of all.

The fact is that *The Possessed*, which can be circumstantial to a calculated fault when it chooses, in this case chooses to say nothing. The novel proposes a man who has been swallowed by a theory of suicide. He lives for us, we can feel him kicking inside the idea's belly, because the bridge-builder who does no bridge-building is vitalized by the nobody to be and nowhere to go of Dostoevsky's inexhaustible inventive fascination. Here, self-exclusion from the feast of life takes a fresh turn. And a new twist is given to the urge to be a Napoleon. In the immediate context of *The Possessed* Kirillov delights even while he is dismaying us by pushing theory — the novel's Paper Person motif, that is — to the very limit, the born gambler's limit. He may be mad. Stavrogin says he is.[100] If so, he is incidentally mad in accord with Kafka's piercing throw-off. He embraces suicide as deed, as the one true act in a false world, as supreme *podvig*, as feat to end feats, God-killing, god-making; and in doing so he exemplifies, as others before and Ivan Karamazov after him, the truth that Dostoevsky can only satisfy his hunger for crisis and clarity by bestowing it on the enemy.

No jokes about America from Kirillov. He has actually been to the actual America — and come back. It was a failure. The novel handles the subject brusquely, whereas a notebook entry about Stavrogin back in the Spring of 1870 suggests a position midway between Svidrigailov and Kirillov: 'Sometimes he complains all of a sudden: "I'm bored!" The S.S. Alabama: "I'll get there!" (dream).'[101] But an unmetaphorical America in *The Possessed* does not mean an unwitty treatment of suicide. What makes the commentators on man-godhood and related themes misleading, why they fail to evoke the real thing, is that they suggest an object which is stable and personal (as opposed to volatile and transpersonal). The obsession has become Kirillov's alone.[102] But the sunrise of impending suicide bathes him and others in fiery metaphysical comedy; 'be as free as you like,' Peter Verkhovensky tells him, 'so long as you don't change your mind' — that is 'so long as your entirely free intention is carried out'.[103] 'Free intention' is the crux. As Kirillov puts it, 'I am killing myself to show my rebelliousness and my new terrible freedom.' He asks rhetorically, apropos the idea which has swallowed him, 'Who will prove it?' and answers 'I'. But Kirillov has himself pointedly ruled out life after death: 'the laws of nature did not spare even *Him*' — Jesus, that is.[104] Then what of this proof and this freedom? Kirillov alive has proved nothing, and Kirillov dead will himself be nothing. Stepan Verkhovensky's naked transcendental 'They won't let you' turns out to be a very suitable preface to a logical joke about time and identity.

Stepan's forward-pointing negative 'won't' is no less important than his collective 'they'. As *The Possessed* is a novel

[102] 'Has become' rather than 'is' because Kirillov caught his idea from Stavrogin. This is one of those psychic infections that ravage *The Possessed*, and it is also one of the ways in which the novel unloads the Stavrogin of the notebooks on other emerging, developing characters. Shatov confronts Stavrogin thus: 'In America I lay three months on straw beside a wretched fellow, and I learnt from him that at the very time you were sowing the seed of God and the fatherland in my heart — at that very time, perhaps during those very days, you were poisoning the heart of that luckless creature, that maniac Kirillov.' This double, simultaneous, contrary infection marks a Gadarene and paper-person apogee of the novel. Infection, obsession, is in the air, rife, transpersonal. Stavrogin himself, of course, was never *obsessed* by anything he said to Shatov or to Kirillov. He won't have had the ontological grounding even to believe it — or disbelieve it. So when he replies to Shatov, 'I wasn't deceiving either of you', that is the toneless truth of the matter (p. 224).

Behind this Stavrogin whom we get to know but can't get at in the novel, lies 'the disease of indifference' in the abandoned 'At Tikhon's' chapter, and behind that again the 'generalhuman' which the *Possessed* notebooks share with Dostoevsky's New Testament annotations and with the text of *Notes from Underground*, and behind yet again the 'I'm all right' ('*Ya sam po sebe*') which had been Mr Golyadkin's empty parrot-cry in *The Double* and now surfaces again in the *Possessed* notebooks: 'yet there remains for him [Stavrogin] the question — what is he himself? The answer for him is "*Nothing*". He is very intelligent and realizes he is not in fact a Russian. He evades the issue with the argument that *he does not find it necessary to be a Russian*, but when shown the absurdity of what he has said he shields himself behind the phrase that he is all right (*sam po sebe*)': *PSS*, Vol. XI, pp. 134, 284.

We begin to see what Dostoevsky meant when he said he had dug very deep into himself to reach Stavrogin.

[103]   pp. 339, 506.   [104]   pp. 563–4.

of groups, circles, sets, quintets, real and imagined, so it is a novel of empty or baffled futurity. Bridge-building is empty because it never happens, God-killing and god-making suicide is baffled because there is only a corpse to point at, there is nobody to attach a fulfilled 'free intention' to. Peter Verkhovensky attacks this bafflement from the other end, from the standpoint of afterwards, as well as that of the not-yet-dead Kirillov who is arguing with him here and now. How is the world going to know it has received a boundless freedom at the hands of an obscure young man lying in some back room in a provincial Russian town? Kirillov replies: 'There is nothing secret that will not be made known. *He* said so.' And with these words he points towards an icon of the Saviour before which he has lighted a lamp — 'to be on the safe side,' Peter suggests. But in response to this Voltairęan jest, the lonely, agonized, perhaps crazed man 'made no answer'.[105] He was no doubt contemplating not futurity but baffled Eternity itself: a universal Revelation outside nature guaranteed by a Christ whom the laws of nature did not spare.

When Stavrogin, who 'poisoned' Kirillov, and who also kills himself, wrote that letter to Dasha Shatov asking her to come and be his nurse, his mind won't have been bent either on or away from suicide; he was neutrally wondering whether she hoped 'to set up some aim for me at last'. He is both rudderless and becalmed, and the futurity conjured by his letter blends the metaphysical frustration of a brilliant unhoused intellectual torpor with human impossibility: you can't cross a river on a chip of wood. This single great emptiness before him has lots of smaller ones inside it. For example, when Dostoevsky abandons the 'At Tikhon's' chapter but retains the brief exchange in which Shatov urges Stavrogin to go to Bishop Tikhon, and Stavrogin replies 'Thank you, I will', let nobody persuade us the novelist has made a mistake.[106]

And the same future tense — 'I will' — has Shatov in its grip. Stavrogin, needling away, elicits from him that he believes in Russia and the Orthodox Church and the body of

Christ. 'But in God? In God?' Stavrogin persists. 'I — I will believe in God,' says Shatov.[107] While Stavrogin never gets to see Tikhon, the immediate future holds murder in store for Shatov. One of his killers is the high-minded Virginsky who 'will never, never abandon these bright hopes' (my italics), and another member of the quintet is Shigalov who pulls out of the affair at the very last moment, not from fear or pity or remorse but because the murder 'is in direct contradiction of my programme' — of Shigalov's own brand of revolutionary ideology. He's not going to warn Shatov or tell the police, he's going to make a statement 'for general edification' — words but no deeds, a turn towards sanity and life that *might have been*, and a horrific–comic *Possessed* moment of subtlest art.[108]

Shigalov does make his statement. The murder goes forward. Thus some things that are said to be going to happen, do happen. 'But they will lose their reason,' says Peter Verkhovensky's lieutenant when Peter has argued that the quintet will hold together after the murder 'unless they've lost their reason'.[109] And sure enough they do panic and run amok, and 'the almost mystical terror which suddenly took hold of our authorities' completes the ruinous and negative side of the Gadarene story.[110]

(vi)

It may be asked what other side *The Possessed* has. For it's no use looking to this novel for even a premonition of a cleansed Russia sitting at the feet of Jesus.

Well now, to hand over crisis and clarity to the enemy is not to revile the hunger, not to mock the passion itself; the handing over resolves an otherwise intractable problem of art; it is not a disavowal; and in any case 'enemy' is only my image. The broader truth is that Dostoevsky cannot foster *any* of his dearest values except obliquely, by stealth, by catching them napping. In *The House of the Dead* he makes us feel that the grim actualities of prison life do this job for

---

[107] pp. 228–9.   [108] p. 547.
[109] p. 570.   [110] p. 554.

him. *The Possessed* works differently. We have already met Lyamshin, the member of the quintet whose party act is to mimic women in labour and new-born babies. Flanking him as it were is the wife of another familiar figure and quintet member, Virginsky. Mrs Virginsky is 'our town's' midwife, a modern woman in Dostoevsky's reshaped generation-gap story, a nihilist and free-thinker.

Our official town doctor Rozanov, himself an accoucheur, declared quite positively that on one occasion when a patient in labour was screaming and calling on the name of the Almighty, a free-thinking sally fired off like a pistol-shot by Mrs Virginsky struck such fear into the patient that delivery was greatly accelerated.[111]

In that sentence humour really is the only thing. Not the next man's humour. A strange wild land out the other side of mockery, even of irresponsibility, indeed beyond all attitude and judgment. No other novelist can reach it.

And as I say, some absolutely precious quarry is being stalked by means of Lyamshin and Mrs Virginsky. Opposite them stands Shatov, and when his wife's and Stavrogin's baby is delivered by Mrs Virginsky, the man who will believe in God declares

'The mystery of the coming of a new creature is a great mystery and incomprehensible, Mrs Virginsky, and what a pity it is that you don't understand it.'

He goes on

'There were two and suddenly there's a third human being, a new spirit, whole, complete, unlike the handiwork of men . . . '.[112]

In this childbirth sequence the prose of an essentially devious and turbid writer clears like a tangled sky. It's not that Shatov is somehow proved right and Mrs Virginsky wrong about new life and (by implication) God, but that the most natural hope begins to stir in the merely legal father's heart;[113] so it would be pompous and artificial to go on

---

[111]   p. 353.

[112]   p. 539. Dostoevsky's humour does not disappear; it lodges in the passionate and muddleheaded thought that it's a pity Mrs Virginsky doesn't understand what is in itself incomprehensible.

[113]   Shatov obliterates the 'merely' of this 'merely legal'. When Mrs Virginsky

talking about futurity, this is *the* future in the mind's eye of one rejoicing man: shared, beautiful, fragile; and the whole novel seems braced to tear itself free of the devils possessing it:

'Marie,' he cried, holding the child in his arms, 'the old nightmare is over — the shame and the death things! Let us work hard and begin a new life, the three of us — yes, yes! Oh yes, and what shall we call him, Marie?'[114]

A new life. The Dostoevsky *voskresenie*, at once regeneration and Resurrection. The knocking off of fetters at the end of *The House of the Dead. Crime and Punishment*'s Epilogue. Shatov's actual words are 'a new road', recalling man the roadbuilder and Kirillov the structural engineer. In a novel where expectations are not so much unfulfilled as positively spited, Shatov's future, his hope, suffers simple tragic extinction with his murder. But he has had his vision of family, home, and work, and that is as real as the thwarting of it.

Note work. In *The Possessed* nobody does any work except Mrs Virginsky.[115] The sky clears in the childbirth sequence because of Shatov's sublime murmurings about the arrival of a new human being, but also because the midwife has her sleeves rolled up, because she is attacking a difficult and strenuous professional job, organizing essentials, masterminding the whole exercise, scolding Marie Shatov who allowed Shatov to get between her and the family in which she was a governess 'with the egotistical object of marrying you',[116] laughing at the distraught husband on his knees

suggests the baby be sent to a foundling home and Shatov refuses, she asks him 'You adopt him as your son?' — to be met with 'He is my son' (p. 539).

[114]   p. 541. The name Marie, so tender and tentative, so surprising and so right in this great sequence, began life in the notebooks as a dry little play in French upon *mari*, the legal husband.

[115]   A woman arrives in our town selling gospels. That is work. But it is work that gets fouled up by Lyamshin and a divinity student who slip obscene photographs into her bundle, so that when she produces the sacred literature to sell it in our shopping arcade, 'the photographs were scattered all over the place' (p. 291). The labourers at the factory outside our town are exploited by the millionaire owners and get cholera (pp. 314–15). That's work too, though we never see them at it, and in any case it's not fit work for human beings.

[116]   p. 535. Like many of Dostoevsky's thrusts against the trendy 1860s, this passes in a narrative flash like something glimpsed from a railway-carriage window.

unable either to bear the sound or block his ears before the birth; and when all is tidied up, 'after some pleasantries about "the happy couple" which were not without a touch of contempt and superciliousness, she went away as well satisfied as before.'[117] She has good reason to be pleased. She has done something, something on a different plane from making a toy church or pipping a social rival at the post or committing a mindless atrocity. Her actions are unquestionably deedy; they bear no theoretical burden, unlike Kirillov's suicide; they run deeper — while she is on the job — than the paper person in her, and they make a rigid, final opposing of the profane midwife and the God-seeking husband academic and quite inadequate to the novel.

Nor does it get us anywhere to learn from Anna Dostoevsky's *Memoirs* that the story of the frantic Shatov, where phrasing seems inevitable and images unsought — it doesn't help to be told by the novelist's widow that these flawless pages lean heavily on his own behaviour while their first child was being born.[118] It's all a question of what a writer can use, what the work in hand will let him use. For example, there's a minor character in *The Possessed*, a quarrelsome eccentric lady, and she believes Lake Geneva gives people toothache. Exactly right — for her. So it produces an odd sensation to learn, again from Anna, that this superstition was in fact Dostoevsky's.[119]

He also goes in for creative self-plundering by way of rhetorical and dialectical self-parody. At the fête Stepan Verkhovensky, the man of the 1840s, makes a speech arguing that Shakespeare matters more than boots, and Raphael more than petroleum; whipping himself up in his peroration to declare that mankind can get on without bread but not without beauty.[120] This is another instance of the novelist promoting his dearest values by stealth. Stepan's aesthetic convictions are Dostoevsky's, and Stepan's speech is an hysterical, summarizing take-off of Dostoevsky's journalism, itself no model of temperateness.[121] The narrative maximizes

---

[117] p. 541.
[118] *Reminiscences*, translated and edited by Beatrice Stillman, pp. 140–4.
[119] p. 56; *PSS*, Vol. XII, p. 290.   [120] pp. 438–41.
[121] The likeness is most obvious in Dostoevsky's polemical piece 'Mr Dobrol-

Stepan's vulnerability, perching him on a platform amid the malcontents and troublemakers and the much larger number of those humble, obscure people who are enduring more or less passively the chaos of the fête. He is holding forth about beauty to an audience which has been short-changed over food and drink and entertainment.

Therefore he is asking for trouble, and he receives it suddenly and in full measure, above the groundswell of heckling, at the hands of a divinity student who reminds him at the top of his voice about Fedka, a dangerous escaped convict now roaming 'our town' and originally a serf of Stepan's whom he sold into military service to pay a gambling debt:

'If you had not lost him at cards, would he have got into prison? Tell me, please. Would he be murdering people now in his struggle for existence? What do you say to that, Mr Aesthete?'[122]

A knock-down blow to the beauty-before-bread man. But far from the end of him. He picks himself up and declares about Fedka, later in the novel, 'I suffered for *ten years* on his account, more than he suffered as a soldier, and — and I'll give him my purse.'[123] Selling was more painful than being sold, a variant of this hurts me more than it hurts you and a comic resourcefulness worthy of Falstaff in his 'let him kill the next Percy himself' vein. But there the likeness ends. Stepan Verkhovensky is prissy, frenchified, very feminine though not at all homosexual. On the one hand, 'My friend, I have discovered something awful: *je suis un* ordinary hanger-on, *et rien de plus! Mais r-r-rien de plus!*'; and on the other, and also out of his own mouth, 'sponging has never been the guiding principle of my actions. It just happened like that.'[124]

It did. Stepan Trofimovich Verkhovensky is the most

yubov and the Question of Art' published in the magazine *Time* in 1861 (*PSS*, Vol. XVIII, p. 70) and translated with some omissions by D. Magarshack, *Dostoevsky's Occasional Writings*, p. 86. Particularly striking, and memorable in its grand anti-utilitarian context, is the argument that art 'responds to man's first need. Beauty is normality, health. Beauty is useful because it is beauty, because a constant need for beauty and its highest ideal resides in mankind . . . . "I am not in need of physical bread, what I need is spiritual bread ." '

[122] p. 441.   [123] p. 576.   [124] pp. 21, 310.

suggestive of all Dostoevsky's accidental men, and it is fitting that the phrase itself should never be used of or by him. He lives and breathes fortuity. Profoundly yet lightly and yet again oh so generously imagined, he turns the novel's trans-personal unsteadiness to joy for us and sheer astonishment, and its cancer-growth of rumour to life's health through art's freedom. The thought of Dostoevsky fostering, however stealthily, his dearest values, through Stepan on beauty, as through Shatov on new life, must be entertained in the context of the journalistic piece on Dobrolyubov:

You must not prescribe aims and preferences for art. Why prescribe anything for it . . . ? It will never get lost or lose its way. It was always true to reality and always walked in line with man's progress and development. The ideal of beauty and normality cannot perish in a healthy society; and for this reason you ought to let art go its own way and be confident that it will not go astray . . . . A single man cannot divine fully the eternal and universal ideal, were he Shakespeare himself, and therefore he cannot prescribe either the ways or the aims for art.[125]

The Possessed looked for a long time like losing its way, and Dostoevsky would surely concede that in so far as the design was, to use his own word, tendentious, this was bound to be so. And yet a novel doesn't write itself, even if some of the very greatest ones appear to; it is written by a man with 'aims and preferences'. But these just happen to be his, he can't 'prescribe' them 'for art'; what he wants to say must come to terms with what the form allows him; art refuses to be imposed upon, to be dictated to, and Dostoevsky's dictum will stand.

(vii)

Perhaps the most remarkable entry in the *Possessed* notebooks is the one which directly opposes Stavrogin and Stepan Ver-khovensky. The narrative tone '*which will save everything*' consists in 'not explaining' Stavrogin but projecting him 'through the action', and equally (and on the contrary) it consists in presenting Stepan '*always with explanations*'.[126]

---

[125] Magarshack, p. 136. See n. 121.   [126] *PSS*, Vol. XI, p. 261.

This belongs to the last days of 1870, more than a year after the murder in the park. It signals the transformation of the large, lucid Great Sinner into the man who is beyond definition and self-definition, beyond calling himself bored, and whose actions — whether he is biting an ear or enduring a punch in the face or hanging by a well-soaped rope — *explain* nothing and nobody. A sort of paring-down: in my analysis a surrender of the crisis-and-clarity urge, and an unloading of all the consecutions of theory upon others, principally Kirillov and Shatov. And conversely, the same notebook entry celebrates the rounding-out of a comic conception miles away from the original, historic Granovsky, scarcely less free than Dostoevsky's ideal of art and lying too deep for tears.

'He, too, saw through me; I mean he clearly perceived that I saw through him . . . .'[127] Stepan and 'I', his young friend, are locked in such mutualities throughout. 'We' are both characters inside the provincial-chronicle box, the framed narrative without a frame narrator, and out of this enclosure liberty proceeds. Stepan reverses the news-from-Peshawar standpoint of the novel by wondering what 'they', those powerful officials in the metropolis, are thinking about 'us' and most especially about himself; the picture of Stepan Trofimovich Verkhovensky as a marked man because of the liberal views he held and very faintly expressed long ago, both frightens him and feeds his self-importance. So that when, in an access of zeal, von Lemke has Stepan's house raided and some old-fashioned radical literature removed, the narrator finds him 'in a surprising condition: upset and in great agitation, but at the same time unquestionably triumphant'. A manuscript draft of this passage survives, and in the draft the narrating 'I' remarks the strange clash of Stepan's emotions. The final text leaves this clash alone, free to speak for itself in a world where the reader believes he understands Stepan better than the narrator does. Still not satisfied with the delicious idea of a soldier taking the doubtful reading matter away in a wheelbarrow, Dostoevsky adds, in Stepan's reportage, 'and covered it with an apron; *oui,*

[127] p. 70.

c'est cela, an apron' — as if in the eyes of Stepan there was something specially affronting or sinister, anyhow notable, about the apron. Relatively weak description of the 'he was very glad of my arrival' sort is cut, and we are left with the histrionic handclasp of Stepan Verkhovensky the actor *manqué* whom no reader of *The Possessed* will ever forget. He imagines he is going to be arrested and whisked off to Siberia. After two fumbled attempts Dostoevsky lands with a leap upon *'Il faut être prêt, voyez-vous'* — he gave me a meaningful look — *'chaque moment* — they may come and take me, and phew! — a man has disappeared!' In the draft he has hidden thirty-five roubles inside a slit in his frock-coat pocket. The final text substitutes waistcoat for frock-coat — 'I don't think they'll get as far as taking my waistcoat off' — even better for the pampered softy with his vein of old-womanish guile. And here the manuscript fragment ends, so we can't tell how much work lies behind such simple touches as Stepan's fear that 'they' will flog him. The narrator objects that he has done nothing. 'All the worse,' replies Stepan. 'They will find out I've done nothing and flog me for it.'[128]

Nor can it be denied that he has done nothing. Nor, unfading in our mind's eye, will this hanger-on and fantasist and self-dramatizer ever do anything, though it's difficult to say so without a chilling, denaturing hint of analytics. Dostoevsky owed a lot to Molière who is to be met in the notebooks but not to be pinned down in the major fiction.[129] While it's true that nobody does any work in *The Possessed* except delivering babies, and true also that Stepan Verkhovensky flowers into a veritable presiding genius of sloth in the guise of footling bustle, nevertheless the reader's heart is not with Mrs Stavrogin, Stepan's patroness, when she hisses at him on his deathbed 'you futile, futile, ignoble, chicken-hearted, always, always futile man'.[130] The reader refuses to let it rest at that. He has been with 'our old friend' too long. It's not the severity that worries him but his inability to

---

[128] pp. 384–91; *PSS*, Vol. XI, pp. 335–9.
[129] The debt to *Tartuffe* in *The Village of Stepanchikovo and its Inhabitants* can't be missed. But *The Village* (Mrs Garnett's *Friend of the Family*) is one of those Dostoevsky failures with fine things in them.
[130] p. 599.

universalize the verdict and therefore take it to himself as he can take 'Vous l'avez voulu, Georges Dandin,' the thing of Molière's Dostoevsky liked to quote.[131] Stepan's own pronouncement, again on his deathbed, strikes more devastatingly deep than Mrs Stavrogin's, and yet the reader inclines his head as to an act of natural justice.

'My friend, all my life I have been lying. Even when I spoke the truth. Never did I speak for the truth's sake but for my own . . . .'[132]

One judges better of others than that, but can only hope better of oneself. And in observing and judging Stepan Verkhovensky one becomes aware that the novelist's self-admonition to present him *'always with explanations'* has been both obeyed and transcended. Details of background, opinions, foibles, are lavished on him as on nobody else. His 'peculiar gloating obsequious humour', his 'sort of capricious self-satisfaction' lurking in the very midst of 'plaintive protestations', are described and pondered. We learn that 'he began to pay great attention to his dreams'.[133] We learn it, though, as a sign of his going to seed — and we wonder. We pause and wonder. We recall that the narrator is a young man. Why going to seed? Leave our friend alone! Don't presume! Why shouldn't he just be getting old?

(vii)

Dostoevsky owed even more to Cervantes than to Molière, and here again, as in his relations with Shakespeare and Pushkin, it's a visitation with no very palpable memorial. An account of how Dostoevsky extrapolated his lifelong leading themes of somebody to be and somewhere to go from Cervantes's huge rhetoric of quest, would be doomed from the start. In fact it is only with Mr Golyadkin very near the beginning of his writing career, and with Stepan Verkhovensky towards the end, that Quixotic features of courtesy and romance become prominent. Mr Golyadkin's response to the elopement letter was a two-in-one attempt to assume a

---

[131] In *The Idiot*, p. 450, it is both quoted and reflected upon.
[132] p. 593.   [133] pp. 47, 53, 69.

chivalric role and reach a lovers' destination. Stepan Verkhovensky has only himself to elope with, and it remains an open
question whether he will go on enduring the indignities of
his hanger-on position, or cut and run, somehow, somewhere.
He remarks to his son that unhappiness is just as necessary to
mankind as happiness — one of those cherished convictions
of Dostoevsky that get slipped in when our attention is elsewhere. But, as Peter immediately tells his father, this is just
the sort of *bon mot* to expect from an idler who is being kept
in the lap of luxury. Such taunts hurt. They are bound to
come to something, Stepan confides to the narrator; 'usually
in our world things come to nothing, but this will end in
something, it's bound to, it's bound to!'[134]

Stepan crystallizes this 'something' in Golyadkin and
Quixote terms when he tells Mrs Stavrogin 'You have always
despised me; but I will end like a knight faithful to my lady,
for your good opinion has always been dearer to me than
anything.'[135] Also, in the same passage, he says he is
going to pack his bag — 'my pauper's bag' — and end up
either dead of starvation in a ditch or earning his keep as a
tutor in some merchant's house. This might seem to be
moving away from Golyadkin, but in point of tone *The
Double* and *The Possessed* draw closest to one another, and
to *Don Quixote*, in the ludicrous materialities of preparation,
and in their juxtaposing of very particular odds and ends
with an airy universality which in lesser hands would be
emptiness. Mr Golyadkin has mustered socks, shirts, shirt-
fronts, flannel vests, uniform, spare trousers, sheets, blankets,
pillows, and a featherbed; but he also tells his servant 'And
now, my friend, I am going away. My dear chap, a different
path lies before each man and no one of us can tell what
road he may chance to follow.'[136] Stepan Verkhovensky kits
himself up with umbrella, travelling-bag, walking stick,
broad-brimmed hat, belted overcoat and top-boots like a
hussar's; and — Quixote overlaid for English readers by
Pickwick, the White Knight, Mr Toad — he talks the language
of 'high adventure' and the open road: 'there's a great idea in
the open road, too!'[137]

[134] p. 194.   [135] p. 310.
[136] *The Eternal Husband*, p. 260.   [137] pp. 488-9, 587.

But he avoids the language of destination. Whereas Mr Golyadkin, incidentally mad, swaddled in a dream of silk ladders and Spanish serenades, aims for Schiller's happy-ever-after hut on the shore, Stepan understands he has nowhere to go: 'to order post-horses one must at least know where one is going. But herein lay his greatest distress at this moment: he was utterly unable to name and fix on a place.'[138] And so he sets off on foot, aiming nowhere. Even to have imagined a destination would have been to raise the question, why this place rather than that? Therefore he keeps walking, 'thinking of nothing so long as he could refrain from thinking'.

Golyadkin country. Our novelist's intellectual humour is asserting itself beneath the narrative. And what narrative! Narrative of Conradian nobility at this suspended moment while Stepan Verkhovensky's road stretches mile upon mile ahead of him 'like a man's life, a man's dream'. There's a quick glance between novelist and reader in that 'dream'. Stepan is falling ill without knowing it; his unspoken, unimagined destination is delirium and death. Chance brings the accidental man up short at a village across a lake from a place called Spasov. The root of that word is 'save'. Chance also throws him together with the itinerant bible-selling woman who was outraged by the hooligans of 'our town' and whom Stepan now, just once, calls his 'saviour' (*spasitelnitsa*).[139] She reads him the story of the Gadarene swine, the novel's Epigraph. Also the Revelation passage on the lukewarm spiritual state. Thus Dostoevsky rescues the disease of indifference from the abandoned 'At Tikhon's' chapter, but also eases its throttling normative grip. In fact there is no grip, it's all drift, in this sequence, as illness brings back Stepan's childhood Church Slavonic, mixed up with Quixotic *politesse* and flagrant falsifying of his own past, and cant about the Russian soul. And as to Spasov and being saved — '*Il me semble que tout le monde va à Spassof*' — there is still some comic devil-life in him as he quotes the Saviour against his bible-selling saviour because she is taking thought for the morrow, and as he turns the gospel on its head with 'Happiness doesn't pay me because I start at once forgiving all my enemies.'[140]

---

[138] p. 574.   [139] p. 592.   [140] pp. 582, 586, 589.

That's no way to set about being saved, so an entirely solemn reader would be bound to think. But, in terms of the tragicomical life of the book, such a reader is himself a fiction, and an empty one. We are all bound for Spasov, and all the fun as well as the sorrow lies in aiming that way. Arrival has no reality in the updated, transposed Quixotic journeying whereby the forward-tilting existential present of *The Double* is rephrased in *The Possessed*. Parajournalist and apocalyptic naturalist through and through, the novelist records anxious speculation in 'our town' as to whether the seventy representatives of the nine hundred workmen at the Spigulin factory are too many to constitute a delegation.[141] We might be reading this morning's dreary inconclusive state of play over secondary picketing. And the sense in which there is no arriving in *The Possessed* is very like that in which there is no reading tomorrow's newspaper. We can only imagine it. When we do we tend to imagine outcomes. For *The Possessed*, outcomes (including Dostoevsky's healed man at the feet of Jesus) are consoling myths. Never trust the artist, trust the tale. And the tale images tomorrow's newspaper as empty or thwarted futurity. I would add open futurity, the future of the open road. After the dying Stepan Verkhovensky has taken the sacrament he says 'however, tomorrow — Tomorrow we shall all set off.'[142] Certainly we are all on the move, if only mentally, and perhaps the open road of Stepan's 'gentle and unresentful heart' will see him to Spasov before *nous les autres*.[143] But in its very nature a possibility is not an outcome.

---

[141] pp. 393–4.   [142] p. 604.   [143] p. 5.

Chapter 8: *The Brothers Karamazov*

(i)

Throughout this final novel the Name Game continues in full swing. *Kara* means black in Turkish. How are Dostoevsky's non-Turkish readers supposed to know that? They aren't. But he gives his Russian readers just one nudge in the course of eight hundred pages. A minor character, a crazed woman with a seeing streak, turns to the youngest brother Alyosha and addresses him with 'a look of extraordinary tenderness' on her face as 'Mr Chernomazov'; and, when corrected, she persists 'Well Karamazov, or whatever it is, but I always say Chernomazov.'[1] Dostoevsky's nudge is the fact that *cherni* means black in Russian.

Kara — Russians would call it a Tartar word — marries up with *mazov* to make a name, and *mazov* beckons us towards the indigenous *mazat*, a verb meaning to daub or smear. Once, again just once, and again a minor character, this time a crafty peasant, says to the eldest brother completely out of the blue 'You're a dyer!' — provoking the instant reply 'For pity's sake I'm Karamazov, Dmitry Karamazov'.[2] So he is. And it is also true that, while falsely accused and convicted of murder, he dyes his hands in the blood of the old servant Grigory.

It may be doubted whether this unhooked 'dyer' moment amounts even to a nudge. The healthy general reader with his appetite to get on, cannot be expected to notice it. But then he is not very likely to take Dostoevsky's 'black' point either. In so far as these are nudges they are first and foremost self-nudges; where the reader experiences nothing at all or a slight fidget in the narrative, the novelist for his part centres himself, reminds himself, as if rapping a tuning fork lightly across his knuckles and holding it to

[1] p. 205.
[2] p. 395. 'Dyer' (*krasilshchik*) rather than 'painter' as in Constance Garnett, or 'house painter' as in Magarshack's Penguin translation.

the shell of his ear. The oddest things can keep an artist on the road, in touch, confident.

The overall tonality of *Karamazov* emerges out of a mass of self-nudges, most obvious and least interesting when they are taken straight from life, as with the christian name and patronymic of the youngest brother which are those of the novelist's recently dead child, and with Chermashnya, the property over which Dmitry and his father quarrel, which is the name of a tiny hamlet, blackened by fire and deep-dyed in poverty and violence, on the Dostoevsky family estate. So even here life and art won't separate neatly; there's more to Chermashnya than a name, and no doubt the same is true of the three-year-old boy in his white coffin.

Then, turning to Schiller and Dostoevsky and *Karamazov*, I see very little point in attempting separation, because Schiller bears equally upon the novelist and his novel. At the age of ten Dostoevsky was taken to a performance of *The Robbers*, and when he was finishing *Karamazov* in the late summer of 1880 he told a correspondent what a 'strong impression' Schiller's play had made on him nearly half a century before, and how it had been 'a very fruitful influence' on his development since.[3] We learn from his widow that he re-read *The Robbers* while writing *Karamazov*, and in the same summer of 1880 he declaimed it to his children.[4] He will of course have been pondering the themes of rivalry between brothers and murder of father by son which are common to play and novel. He also wanted the general direction of his thoughts to be unmistakable. Therefore early in his own story the father points at Ivan his second son and identifies him as 'my most respectful Karl Moor', then at Dmitry 'the most disrespectful Franz Moor, both out of Schiller's *Robbers*, while I — I myself in that case am the *Regierender Graf von Moor*!'[5]

A hefty nudge if ever there was one, but still primarily a self-nudge. I picture Dostoevsky smiling to himself and wondering how many of his readers will remember their Schiller and notice that old Karamazov has got his sons the wrong way round: Ivan will prove the Franz Moor of the

---

[3]   Letter of 18 August.   [4]   *PSS*, Vol. XV, p. 537.   [5]   p. 67.

present piece, hopelessly, messily entangled — a black entanglement — with his brother's fiancée, and smeared (*mazat*) with parricide through his complicity, though that's too definite a word for this web of animal awarenesses, with the actual doer of the deed, the scented epileptic lackey Smerdyakov. Old Karamazov made a mistake. He just got it wrong. In doing so he contributes his mite towards establishing a tonality of chance and mischance cognate with but distinct from that of *The Possessed*. The novelist of accidental men and accidental families turns at the end of his life to an accidental world seen and shaped as the legal conviction of an innocent man. And, because accidental, the result might have been different. Thus on the night of the murder, as Dmitry testifies, the door from his father's room to the garden was shut. The old servant Grigory insists it was open, and cross-examination by the defending lawyer fails to shake him. This clash of evidence is, and both sides repeatedly agree it is, of the first importance. Grigory is sober and truthful and even *akkuratni*,[6] a term which Russians often use to suggest a truly German level of scrupulousness. If Grigory had confirmed Dmitry's account the verdict might very well have gone the other way. But Grigory says the door was open, and about that he is simply wrong. One should know whether a door is open or shut. How did Grigory come to be wrong? Ivan asks Smerdyakov this question and gets the answer 'About that door and Grigory having seen it open, that's just his imagination,' said Smerdyakov with a grin. 'I tell you he's not a man but a stubborn mule: he never saw it, he imagined he saw it — and you won't budge him. It's your luck and mine, him dreaming up this notion, because now it has happened they are sure to convict your brother Dmitry.'[7]

So, as well as sober and truthful and *akkuratni*, old Grigory is stubborn. Once having convinced himself of something he is unlikely to change his mind. But his stubbornness doesn't help us understand why an unfanciful man should suppose a shut door to be open in the first place; we note

---

[6] p. 412. In fact 'most punctilious' (*akkuratneishii*) — so he is described on the night he makes his huge simple blunder.

[7] p. 667.

the stubbornness as a personal trait muddling along with the others, and over that door we have to resign ourselves to the accidental world of *Karamazov* — what Smerdyakov calls luck.

Accident can be turned to the purest fictional gold: recall the proposal of marriage in Tolstoy which is deflected by wood-mushrooms.[8] Or Thomas Hardy's 'haps', often 'neutral-tinted', sometimes inept plot-propellors too sad, too bad to be true. Accident in Dostoevsky is neither golden nor inept. It is obtrusive, unmediated, 'thingy'. A door is a door. Equally a corpse is a corpse: when the famous monastery elder Zossima dies, those who revere him dare to hope his body will be spared corruption as a divine token of his saintliness and a premonition of even greater wonders to come. His enemies want nature to take its course. In the event his corpse begins to stink surprisingly soon, one might say prematurely.

The rising, spreading smell touches off a spiritual crisis in Alyosha Karamazov, Zossima's *protégé*, his dearest disciple, and it drifts round the central chapters of the novel like prowling thunder, a vague transpersonal disquiet. Together with innumerable lesser smells and stains it is the malaise of the book, the miasmic, somewhat Oresteian[9] equivalent of the Gadarene stampede in *The Possessed*.

And as regards accident, the false clue of the door leading onto the garden in the later novel should be paired with the genuine clue of the cap dropped at the scene of the gang murder in the earlier. The *Karamazov* clue is false because the door was shut but Grigory says it was open and the jury believes him. It should not surprise us that commentators do not dwell on this cardinal and perhaps decisive circumstance, for what are they to say? The door is an intractable raw lump such as life throws up. And throws up surprisingly often, one finds oneself adding, which bears both upon Dostoevsky's pre-Siberian, Beckettish thought that freaks are common, and on his Foreword to *Karamazov* where he calls the hero of his novel an odd man out and an exception, but then invites his readers to reflect that the exceptional man

---

[8] *Anna Karenina*, Part 6, Chs. 4 and 5.
[9] I mean what I say, the House of Atreus, not Aeschylus as a whole.

may express the truth about a certain historical period while
the ordinary run of people in the same period 'have for some
reason lost touch with it'.[10]

The corpse that seems in a hurry to stink is also Beckettish,
and also pre-Siberian. As the monks in 'our monastery' sniff
the tainted air, observe each other, feel dismayed or gleeful,
plan ascendancy, seek out allies, a flicker runs back straight
as an arrow, obvious as a fart at school prayers, to the lodging-
house sounds and smells and the domestic pecking order of
Poor People. And over the largest matter of all, that of form,
Dostoevsky's creative end is in his beginning. He started with
an unframed narrative — that is with a novel in letters lacking
authorial introduction, carrying no authorial voice within it,
and finishing in epistolary mid-sentence. His last novel, after
thirty-four years of superficially naive expedients like the
manuscript found in a basket in *The House of the Dead* and
unmistakably subtle ones like the provincial chronicle box
with the narrator inside it in *The Possessed*, returns to the
idea of no frame. It does so by means of the brazen stratagem
of flaunting a frame — I'm thinking of the address 'from the
author' to his readers — which turns into a ghost-frame
before those readers' eyes. The apparently solid and self-
assertive author disappears, or, if you prefer, he collapses into
the novel's first-person narrator. The result is another provincial chronicle, but with a difference pinpointed by that
milestone in the *Possessed* notebooks: 'I'm a character.'
Karamazov's narrator is not a character. He has no age,
friendships, enmities, social standing — none of the things
that shape and fix Stepan Verkhovensky's young friend. He
is unqualitied. We may think we are beginning to 'catch' him
when he doesn't like owning up that the name of 'our town'
is Cattlepen, or says Dmitry made a bad impression on him
at the beginning of the trial proceedings, or speaks of Alyosha's 'untamed and rapturous modesty and chastity'.[11] But
no; most people would dislike living in a place called Cattlepen, Dmitry's manners are impossible and his tact nil, the
words just quoted fumble if not creditably then at least

---

[10] Constance Garnett does not include this short address 'from the author'.
So one must turn to the Penguin translation.

[11] pp. 15, 605, 700.

averagely for Alyosha's elusive spiritual timbre. The author turned narrator has — how could he not? — some generalized attitudes, but he has no stance, no individual flavour, no interest; he's not a man but a crowd in trousers.

While author transforms himself into collective first-person narrating voice, his novel vanishes too. The main burden of *Karamazov's* Foreword is that Dostoevsky wants to write about the doings of his hero Alyosha Karamazov 'in our own day, I mean at this very minute'. To make it intelligible he needs to give an introductory teeing-up account of affairs thirteen years ago; and this *'is not really a novel'* — my italics — 'but just a glimpse of my hero in his first flush of youth'. Of course the main or real novel never gets written, the book in the reader's hands is the elucidatory stuff about the state of play thirteen years back.[12]

No author and no novel — a thoroughgoing way to ensure no frame. Dostoevsky's high-level fooling and his deeper realism go hand in hand here, and they return hand in hand to *Poor People*. If no frame then no form, no art, just life. The boldness of *Poor People*'s life-simulating devices courted and sometimes suffered disaster: the missing and misdated and unfinished (while to all appearances finished) letters were too uncomfortable, it is as simple as that. Not so those narrative gaps, those references without descriptions, glimpsed occasions like the lovers' theatre-going and walks in the park where we move in and, as the Epigraph has it, 'willy nilly get thinking'; for they are the genius, the *life* of Dostoevsky's first book.

And yet what could be more bold and dangerous than the shut door which Grigory testifies is open? *Karamazov's* notebooks are even more emphatic than the novel itself as to the importance of the door: 'CRUCIAL'; 'the door is the overwhelming fact.'[13] We would expect that. The notebooks are the place for clear signposting. Where they cause surprise, initially, is in their complacency about the mistake, the

---

[12] There is evidence that Dostoevsky thought about a second novel (*PSS*, Vol. XV, pp. 485–6), but that of course is irrelevant, as is the letter which points in the opposite direction, towards *Karamazov* as intended to sum up 'all I have pondered, gathered, and set down in the last three years' (*Pisma*, Vol. IV, pp. 198–9).

[13] *PSS*, Vol. XV, pp. 297, 299.

unlikely accident; there's no hint anywhere that the novelist should put in some work on that door. And in fact the work that does get done between notebooks and novel is to build up old Grigory's truthfulness, sobriety, underlying love of Dmitry, *akkuratnost*. Making the accident more sheer and affronting won't have been the sole object of these developments, but it is certainly one result.

Now as to Dostoevsky's habit of nagging himself in his notebooks, we have seen this at its most persistent in the fuss about explaining Raskolnikov's motive for the murder and making Stavrogin cohere in terms of sex, politics and so forth. In the end he gives up; what he has in him to say in *Crime and Punishment* and *The Possessed* proves stronger than his rationalizing anxieties, and Raskolnikov's motive dwindles to the 'I did it because I did it' of his confession to Sonya, while Stavrogin, instead of coming together by virtue of whatever makes him tick, falls apart into 'negation', and then, beyond negation, into 'nothing'.

By contrast the *Karamazov* notebooks know where they are going. They don't dither, there are few false starts and false alarms. Similarly with the later stages of composition. Anna had a complete *Karamazov* manuscript, now lost, and she says it contained 'almost no variants from the printed text'.[14] And later again, as we can see for ourselves, alterations of the magazine version for hardcover publication are insignificant. Everything points to remarkable, indeed unique confidence in follow-through and execution. Also in what I have called overall tonality, dwelling as I have on accident and the unruffled 'thingy' way so much is allowed to depend on a door and a corpse. This trust would be misplaced if *Karamazov*'s life-simulating devices, the equivalents of those mixed successes and failures in *Poor People*, didn't work. But they do, and here are three examples, all like the door connected with Dmitry, to show what I mean.

First. Dmitry writes a letter to one of the two women he is involved with, a wild, drunken letter threatening violence against his father, and this letter is produced at the trial. Reconstructing the scene, the prosecuting lawyer says 'On

[14] *Sobranie Sochinenii* (1958), Vol. X, p. 463.

the evening he wrote that letter, after getting drunk at the pub Metropolis, he was unusually silent, he didn't play billiards, he sat in a corner and talked to nobody. All he did was turn a local shop assistant out of his seat, but that was almost unconscious, a matter of habit because he couldn't go into a pub without picking a quarrel.' Nearly a hundred pages back, when this event was narrated, the only facts vouchsafed were that Dmitry got drunk and asked for pen and paper and wrote the letter.[15]

Second. The same damaging letter mentions a package containing three thousand roubles which old Karamazov keeps 'under his mattress' to entice Grushenka, the other woman Dmitry is involved with. When the lecherous 'old goat' is found murdered and Dmitry is arrested and interrogated — a very long ordeal — he first speaks of the money his father 'kept under his pillow ready for Grushenka'; but later, when the examining magistrate shows him a package ripped open and empty, he exclaims that Smerdyakov must have done the murdering and robbing because only he, Smerdyakov, knew where the money was hidden. The magistrate reminds Dmitry of his earlier statement, provoking the characteristic outburst: 'Nonsense! Absurd! I had no idea it was under the pillow. Anyhow perhaps it wasn't under the pillow at all. I said under the pillow without thinking.' Smerdyakov, confessing both murder and robbery in private to Ivan the second brother, says he told Dmitry the money was under the mattress (thus confirming the drunken letter against the repeated 'pillow' of the interrogation); and then — a thriller-moment uniting *Karamazov* with *Crime and Punishment* — Smerdyakov reveals that the package with the money was never under pillow or mattress. That was the first place any intruder would look. Smerdyakov persuaded the old man to put the package 'in the corner behind the icons, for no one would ever have thought of looking for it there, especially if he was in a hurry'.[16]

Third. My last example is very simple. Remarking Dmitry's impulsive, frantic habit of incriminating himself, of virtually admitting guilt, the prosecuting lawyer clinches his point with

[15]   pp. 654, 746–7.   [16]   pp. 487, 515–16, 663.

'He even shouted to the coachman as they were going along, "Do you know you are driving a murderer?" '[17] Dmitry was afraid he had killed Grigory with the savage blow he dealt him, and some such exclamation as this one to the coachman was evidently in Dostoevsky's mind, for it occurs three times in the notebooks.[18] Nowhere in *Karamazov*, however.

Not talking, not playing billiards, but turning a shop assistant out of his seat. A package under a pillow or a mattress or neither. An alleged question to a peasant coachman. These are mere spoonfuls from the *Karamazov* ocean, but I hope they give some sense and interest to no-frame (*alias* flaunted frame that turns into ghost-frame) and life-simulation in the novel. When readers hear about Dmitry's behaviour in the pub they are unlikely to turn back and check this against the earlier account, they will be too absorbed in learning about Dmitry. Learning from whom though? From the public prosecutor, and from him alone. Author has collapsed into colourless, unqualitied narrator who is neither here nor there when it comes to what really happened. Readers are inside that provincial courtroom, watchful, because they know the prosecutor wants to secure a conviction; and critical, because they understand their Dmitry pretty well by now and won't be fooled. Sitting silent by himself and not playing billiards: that fits his morose *black* humour and his worries of the moment. Turning a shop assistant out of his chair. Alas, that fits too. Dmitry is not at heart a bully but he is uncertain-tempered, especially now, at the end of his tether. And he is peremptory. The army has rubbed off on him a bit — we are never told so, apart from his long military stride, but we can feel it. Perhaps that shop assistant was sitting at a table, and after all Dmitry needed a table, he had a letter to write. Perhaps the assistant once cheated Dmitry, he's a reckless shopper, very cheatable. Perhaps . . . . Willy nilly we get thinking. It's an open prospect, it's life. One thing, though, we will not countenance. While by no means doting on Dmitry — he can be foul, or rather, he does some foul things — we recognize the judgement that he couldn't enter a pub without picking a quarrel for the shallow professional forensic exaggeration it is. Lawyer's stuff. Typical. Tucked away to one side of our riveted attention Dostoevsky is engaged in the largest creative parody he ever tried his hand at.

The package containing the money offers another and different unframed, open prospect; and the question to the coachman is different again. We have no reason to doubt that Smerdyakov told Dmitry the package was under the mattress. Why should Smerdyakov lie to Ivan? In any case this forms part of his larger calculated deception and is confirmed by Dmitry's drunken letter. But equally 'I'd no idea it was under the pillow . . . . I said under the pillow without thinking' carries absolute conviction. It would be impossible to convey the impulsive essence of Dmitry more economically than in the two words *without thinking*. Dostoevsky has the examining magistrate put his finger on the contradiction in Dmitry's evidence but not so the reader shall wonder if he is lying, for he knows Dmitry is not a liar, at least not that sort of liar — it would need a discourse on his highly idiosyncratic sense of honour to say anything more precise. The contradiction is self-enfolded, it is there so it shall not be resolved. In retrospect the reader may guess that Dmitry has Smerdyakov's false tip-off at the back of his mind, as he had when he penned his drunken letter, but now in the heat and weariness of interrogation, and substituting pillow for mattress, he is not conscious of that tip-off, and therefore he tells the whole truth as he knows it when he says he had no idea where the packet was. Further, there is the odd and checking thought that in real life we do say a man has got something in his pocket or up his sleeve or under his pillow or in his bottom drawer, when in fact we haven't the faintest idea where he's keeping it.

And as to that unlucky cry, 'Do you know you are driving a murderer?' the reader never doubts that he understands Dmitry better than the public prosecutor does, and he remains watchful. Like Dostoevsky in his notebooks he apprehends that the words ring true — so true that if he's aware this is the first he has heard of them, his reaction is not that the prosecutor has made them up but that he himself (the reader) was only 'there' for part of the journey and must have missed many things that passed between Dmitry and the coachman, this among them.[19] The reader's childlike surrender to the story, including the gaps in the story, pays tribute to an illusionism comparable to the sense of being inside yet outside Raskolnikov's head — a world both experienced and observed — in *Crime and Punishment*, and the slippage effect of *The Possessed* whereby the novel walks out into our actuality rather than ourselves entering the fiction: comparable to these but closest in principle to *Poor People*'s unframed exchange of letters. While all Dostoevsky's novels draw strength from the fascination of report and rumour, hence transfigured documentary, hence parajournalism, his first and last share a special magic of absence, of not being 'there' in church or theatre with the lovers, not 'there' in the Metropolis with Dmitry when he turned the shop assistant out of his chair. Nothing removes us from the *real* scene of interest more effectively than glimpsing lovers' mutualities or hearing courtroom allegations; and nothing — when Dostoevsky is in charge — stimulates greater, as if no longer borrowed, imaginative appetite. The novelist seems to have dropped dead in his tracks and left us able and anxious to carry through his work.

(ii)

Kara means penalty or punishment in Russian as well as black in Turkish. Dmitry is daubed (*mazat*) with prison and exile for a murder which he didn't commit but in the vague direction of which, so he repeatedly avows, he bent his mind in black smeary passion. We have another murder story, but not a gang murder; and as with *The Double* following *Poor People*, so with *Karamazov* following *Crime and Punishment* there is the question (which I believe Dostoevsky put to himself more consciously and intellectually than the popular idea of art allows) whether vision and technique will invert.

[19] We are 'there' when Dmitry climbs into the cart and drives off (p. 428), and we meet up with him again at 'Meanwhile Dmitry was speeding along the road' (p. 430).

It's of no consequence that *Karamazov* doesn't immediately follow *Crime and Punishment* because the final novel is equidistant, except in time, from all the important works that go before. In it the notion that he was writing the same book all his life comes unhesitatingly home to roost.

Through no-frame and ghost-frame I have stressed the link with *Poor People*. The confessional mode too, at least in name, is pre-Siberian, and in the *Karamazov* notebooks the long extract from Father Zossima's life and teaching is explicitly a confession.[20] The novel itself has a sequence of three 'Confession' chapters. The words 'I admit it, gentlemen' on Dmitry's lips become as identifying as a finger print.

Ivan, the middle brother, squares his shoulders to stand up in court and declare his moral responsibility for the murder. The way in which he is frustrated is as noteworthy as the confessional resolve. Madness stops him, Kafka's incidental madness. Mr Golyadkin was the first and Ivan Karamazov is the last madman in Dostoevsky, and they both serve the same thematic purpose: in other words, there is no separating their going mad from their meeting their doubles. Ivan was sitting in his room 'staring at some object on the sofa against the wall opposite. Somebody appeared to be sitting there . . . .'[21] The question, who is this somebody?, lands us back with a thump inside *The Double*. The all too familiar stranger is and is not Ivan. 'You are me,' Ivan tells him, and 'he is me' he tells Alyosha afterwards — but: 'He told me a great deal that was true, though. I would never have said it to myself.' That catches the one/two equivocation neatly enough, and the follow-up is even more on the spot: ' "You know, Alyosha, you know," Ivan added with terrible earnestness and as though confidentially, "I'd have liked very much that he should really be *himself* and not me." '[22]

That is a naturalizing of Mr Golyadkin's cry 'He's a separate person and I'm separate too' — or rather, it is both a naturalizing and a supernaturalizing; the metaphysical fable is being reworked on the plane of normal and paranormal psychology,

[20] *PSS*, Vol. XV, pp. 232, 242. And so in essence it remains. Therefore the murderer's tale inside Zossima's larger narrative is a confession within a confession (pp. 311–25).

[21] p. 673.   [22] pp. 676, 692.

and of course it has been embedded in a nineteenth-century novel. Even so the unmistakable young-poet flavour hangs over and around this Ivan sequence. 'Could two different people have the same dream?' (that might be a Wittgenstein parody). 'Is it possible to observe oneself going mad?' (so might that). 'Hallucinations in your condition are very likely, but they need to be verified' (the patrician joke disguised as a medical fatuity). And reflection upon 'the extraordinary, though imperceptible benefits' bestowed by Providence would not raise an eyebrow anywhere in Beckett.[23] *The Double's* literal ploy of the Golyadkins Senior and Junior being physically indistinguishable is abandoned in *Karamazov*, so that Ivan tells his familiar he is the same 'only with a different face', but the banality (*poshlost*) which has worried people wanting to establish a Kleist and/or Hoffmann pedigree for *The Double* is retained; the visitor who is Ivan but who tells Ivan things he would never have told himself, is '*poshli*' to both the one of them (two of me can play that lonely doubling game).[24] This obviously Freudian encounter throws up material that might have surprised the master, dying as he did back in 1939. They have gone metric in Hell — 'adopted the metric system, you know' — so the visitor tells Ivan, and he envisages a satellite (*sputnik*) orbiting in space in the form of a surreal axe: 'Astronomers would calculate the rising and setting of the axe . . . . '[25]

Karamazov's vein of twentieth-century humour takes a grim turn when Ivan's visitor extols, ironically, the diagnostic skills of modern doctors: 'You may die but on the other hand you will know perfectly well what disease you died of.'[26] The joke doesn't raise much of a smile, partly because we've heard it live, so to speak, across tables, over drinks, and will hear it again — after all, metricated Hell and axe satellites aren't very funny in the 1980s — and partly because its main thrust is not twentieth-century (pre-Siberian, that is) but in the futurity area of *The Possessed*. It gives another twist to bafflement and emptiness. The medical knowledge forthcoming here is like the advance-notice 'edification' of

[23] pp. 616, 634, 672, 685.   [24] pp. 676, 686.
[25] pp. 678–9, 682.   [26] p. 679.

Shigalov's statement in which he dissociates himself from the murder of Shatov while doing nothing to prevent it. Also, a time-and-identity point is involved, linking the man who expects to die and Kirillov who intends to commit suicide. The sick man won't *know* what he is dying of until he has died of it — and then where is the self to attach this knowledge to?[27] On the other hand if he gets well, which he may, his knowledge is as null as the unrealized 'free intention' of Kirillov who can always change his mind.

Upon this slender and apparently niggling basis Ivan's visitor builds a *Weltanschauung* which is that of Kirillov with suicide removed: 'all that needs to be destroyed is the idea of God in mankind'. Once having disposed of that fabrication the human race will be seized by a new titanic pride and confidence in its power over nature, 'and the man-god will appear'. At one level this is an acceptance of mortality. At another it is the discovery of immortality. The realization that life here is all we've got 'will intensify its fire' unimaginably.[28] We will stand still in that fire in a timeless present, the true eternity.

As I say, this is Kirillov without the lead given by a suicide whose sole purpose is to give the lead. While propounding the man-god argument the visitor asserts, undependably of course, that it is not his but Ivan's. He also teases Ivan about his Grand Inquisitor discourse to Alyosha, provoking an angry and shamefaced response, also undependable since Ivan is going mad. But then some people thought Kirillov was mad, and the very existence of Ivan's visitor, like that of Golyadkin Junior, is dubious. All we have for sure are the words on the page, and three times over these confirm the true Dostoevsky posture of surrender to the enemy. Kirillov the out-and-out theorist, the man swallowed by an idea, seeks to kill God and free mankind by the unique motivation of his suicide. Ivan's visitor, alleging that he merely recalls what Ivan once believed, says men will free themselves and get rid of the God habit as they become more enlightened,

---

[27] Constance Garnett and the Penguin translator both spoil Dostoevsky's little time-and-identity coup by rendering *what you died of* as *what you are dying of*.

[28] p. 688.

a natural process 'analogous with geological phases'.[29] Ivan himself in his big set piece, the Grand Inquisitor, recalls the pessimism of Kirillov; men in the mass are too weak to find and follow their way. But instead of a liberator who shows them the truth he proposes an élite which conceals it. Ivan calls his piece a poem. It is set at the time of the Spanish Inquisition. Men in the mass are the Catholic faithful, and the élite are the church authorities keeping to themselves the fact that Christ lived and died in vain, while they feed the millions a comfortable pappy diet of 'deception'.[30]

Ivan is notably more pessimistic than Kirillov in that his élite does not enjoy the proud and positive ascendancy of man-godhood but is simply strong enough to bear the desolation of the truth. 'We alone shall be unhappy.'[31] And as to the truth, *Karamazov* notebooks and the novel are both clear that the Grand Inquisitor believes there is no God. The notebooks also state that Christ's followers 'will find nothing that has been promised just as he himself found nothing after his cross', and this conclusion is not contradicted in the novel.[32] Division comes where Ivan answers Alyosha's question in the notebooks by saying he sides with the Grand Inquisitor against Christ 'because he loves humanity more', but in the novel he replies 'Why, it's all nonsense, Alyosha, it's only the silly poem of a silly student who has never written two lines of poetry in his life.'[33]

Of the few big shifts that occur between notebooks and novel, this is easily the most important. It distances Ivan from his 'poem', and in so doing it maintains the equidistance (as I termed it) of *Karamazov* from the main trends that go before — an equidistance most apparent in Ivan, the talkative and intellectual brother. His encounter with his visitor reaches back to *The Double* but refuses to be confined there; he has a self-monitoring habit — 'how proficient I am at observing myself' — which fits Mr Golyadkin struggling with the one/two confusions of his fate, and equally the hyperconscious underground man, and equally Raskolnikov

---

[29] Ibid.
[30] p. 260.
[31] p. 267.
[32] *PSS*, Vol. XV, p. 236.
[33] *PSS*, Vol. XV, p. 233; p. 270.

in a spirit of pure naturalism, guilty and pursued, minding his step.[34]

Yet, so mysterious are the workings of local fingertip control in relation to overall tonality, neither of Ivan's brothers could have said he was good at observing himself, and nor could his father. The thought could not have crossed the mind of any other Karamazov — which is a way of remarking that Ivan draws the free-floating mentalism of the book to himself, and in that sense is the only one who thinks at all; the thinking of the others is an inbuilt function of their fighting, fucking, plotting, praying. Thus in a novel riddled with confession only to Ivan does the *abstracted* question of confession occur, the question of confession as *podvig* and false *podvig*. When is a feat not a feat? He tells Alyosha that his visitor taunted him about his resolve to stand up in court and admit his moral responsibility for the murder, saying this is no brave virtuous urge but a manifestation of pride and of the desire to be thought well of.[35] But in the exchange which has just taken place — which Alyosha interrupts — Ivan's visitor said no such thing; it's another example of the reader not being 'there' and of the part played by absence in the novel; we accept, confirm, enhance it as readily as we do Dmitry bawling out 'Do you know you are driving a murderer?' to the peasant coachman. For Ivan is (as well as is not) his visitor, and when he expresses his pain at the thought of confession as false *podvig* Alyosha is (as well as is not) right when he replies 'It's you who are saying this and not he.'

Again Ivan is the only Karamazov who could conceivably say he is 'agonizingly bored'.[36] And this too brings equidistance and especially Svidrigailov to mind. It's no help to

[34] p. 671. Ivan also makes contact with Myshkin over the latter's preoccupation with the mystery of 'double thoughts', simultaneously low and lofty (*The Idiot*, p. 304), and with the entire climactic sequence of *A Raw Youth* (pp. 505–50) whose hero Versilov smashes an icon — or rather not Versilov but his 'double' who is 'chiefly responsible' and who causes Versilov to be 'split in two' and to perpetrate senseless, evil, mad actions — the most extended and least satisfactory rendering of split (*raskol*), doubling, and madness in all Dostoevsky. Much better is 'And what if he is not actually pestering me, but I am pursuing him?' in *The Eternal Husband* where Dostoevsky rehandles the hunter and hunted theme of *The Double* through a woman's husband and lover.
[35] p. 693.　　　　　　　　　　　　[36] p. 686.

somebody worried by the thought that boredom, particularly self-boredom, is not a Karamazov thing, to add that Ivan is bored by his visitor; because whatever else he may be the visitor is Ivan. Likewise when we move from Svidrigailov towards Stavrogin with Ivan's words 'I am a sort of illusion of life and have lost all beginnings and ends and have even got to the state of forgetting what my name is' — a human void apparently destined to negate but in fact 'completely incapable of negation'.³⁷

The very voice of Stavrogin. The end-of-ends spirit of his letter to his 'nurse'. You can't cross a river on a chip of wood. In his Double Act with his visitor Ivan seems to have strayed into the wrong novel, but it's hard to know where he should be sent back to because he has on him clear traces of *The Double*, *Notes from Underground*, *Crime and Punishment*, as well as *The Possessed*. He summarizes an entire tradition of abstractness and life under the floorboards. Most of the time, though, there is no articulated Double Act, no confronting second presence, but something that makes itself felt like an invisible threat, as at the end of the Grand Inquisitor when Ivan suddenly shies away from, diminishes, almost disowns what he has just said by calling it nonsense and a silly student's piece. That stops the reader in his tracks. He is prepared to see the fable of old Spain shrugged off, with its ecclesiastical élite and docile masses, and perhaps even its misguided, defeated Christ. This fable — 'poem' as Ivan calls it — is a construction with a strong smell of paper-person theorizing about it. It is a rationale, a conceptual model. But not so the chapter called 'Rebellion' which prefaces and prompts it; and it is the sense of being thrust back upon this chapter that jolts the reader when Ivan answers Alyosha's direct question as he does.

For 'Rebellion' lays an axe at the base of all theorizing, and in its all-or-nothing absolutism and impulsiveness reveals that Ivan is after all a Karamazov, uttering from within the family and for his own part a great sustained shout of indignation at man's cruelty to man, at a world 'saturated from its crust to its centre with human tears'.³⁸ Philosophies and theologies are väin; they may account for but they cannot justify or undo or make good the suffering of one tortured child. So Ivan's shout is also an argument — an argument against arguing, and thus shot through with irony and pathos; the novel's stray mentalism still clings to him like fluff on an overcoat. His passion is real, savage, prompt — he is a Karamazov — but intellectual, the fruit of study; and we can quote *Love's Labour's Lost* against him: 'How well he's read, to reason against reading', since he has culled his examples largely from books and newspapers. He cites the case of a serf-boy who threw a stone in play and hurt the paw of his owner's favourite hound. The next day, 'a perfect day for hunting', the child was stripped naked and made to run and the whole pack was set on him. He was torn to pieces, says Ivan — a climax of horror in these justly famous pages.[39] In fact, first time round, when the hounds had hunted the serf-boy down they sniffed him and left him alone. Over the whole episode his mother suffered more than she could bear, and she went mad and died.[40]

This morsel of history needed careful parajournalistic handling. Dostoevsky's notebook entry suggests the mother is the centre of the story.[41] In the novel she became incidental and her pitiful end gets no mention at all. The boy comes to the fore (with the doggy sniffing excluded — Dostoevsky and fiasco are never far apart) in relation to what Ivan calls 'solidarity in suffering' and 'solidarity in retribution' among men.[42] It is a Karamazov trait in Ivan, and at first sight surprising, that the idea of us all growing up to sin and to be guilty in relation to each other and to deserve to suffer, does not affront him. 'I understand,' he says, with characteristic conscious address, whereas Dmitry and Alyosha believe this instinctively, and even their old father took it in with his mother's milk — though he won't have drunk much milk since. It's vital for the impact of the novel that solidarity in guilt should loom larger than miscarriage of justice, helping to maintain the equidistance I have been talking about, this time the equidistance of *Karamazov* from *The House of the Dead* where ordinary people call the convicts 'unfortunates'

[39] pp. 248-9.
[40] *PSS*, Vol. XV, p. 554.
[41] Ibid., p. 227.
[42] p. 250.

— sinners like the rest of us, but they happen to be in prison.[43]

So for Dostoevsky acceptance of solidarity in sin and suffering is Russian and not just a Karamazov trait. What distinguishes Ivan from the other members of his family, and what is unRussian about him, is the intellectualism which shaped the Grand Inquisitor myth and troubled itself over the integrity of the urge to confess, and which now turns to the case of the serf-boy reported in the *Russian Herald*. That boy would have grown up into the solidarity of sinful mankind — 'but you see he didn't grow up, he was torn to pieces by dogs at the age of eight'.[44] Solidarity is irrelevant; hence the prominence of the boy at the expense of his mother, and the unflagging stress on children throughout 'Rebellion'.

Ivan's polemic drives Alyosha into a corner, and in so doing exposes the underlying Karamazov rapport between the brothers. What is one to do with the landowner who set his dogs on the serf-boy, asks Ivan: 'Shoot him?'

'Shoot him!' Alyosha said softly, raising his eyes to his brother with a pale, kind of twisted smile.[45]

Of course he retracts, but not before Ivan has exclaimed 'Bravo!', adding 'So that's the kind of little devil squatting in your heart, Alyosha Karamazov!' Now Ivan acquires a devil too — his visitor, his double, the phenomenon inseparable from his going mad. It isn't the same devil as Alyosha's, but akin, brotherly, and called a devil throughout. The momentary accord of the brothers over shooting the landowner strikes us as perfectly natural. And yet, as Ivan points out, vengeance is useless, it doesn't help the serf-boy, indeed it is evil, it just piles pain on pain.[46] Natural, therefore, and devilish. Ivan's 'I must have retribution' is the voice of nature and also of dark powers within and without.

The Russian nature is broad says Dostoevsky in his fiction and elsewhere, and this his final novel asserts the extraordinary breadth of the Karamazov nature.[47] He means that the Karamazovs are very Russian, and he is talking about the

---

[43] *The House of the Dead*, pp. 18, 75; see p. 159 n. 42, above.
[44] p. 250.   [45] p. 249.
[46] p. 251.   [47] pp. 106, 742, 776.

amount of life a nature contains. In his mind's eye there
was — or had been — one nature and one life, the *Life of a
Great Sinner*, the novel which he planned on the scale of *War
and Peace*, at once a spiritual and a sensual odyssey and most
intricately plotted since pilgrimage and profligacy are both
eventful careers.

The author's note to *Karamazov* plays a formal trick with
the fact that the Great Sinner's life never got written. Alyosha
is that sinner, and 'at this very minute' his story is ripe for
telling. However *this minute*, in terms of fictional time, never
comes; he is 'the chief *though future* hero of my story'
(Dostoevsky's italics),[48] and we have to make do with an
eight-hundred page 'glimpse' of him thirteen years ago, a
devout novice commanded by his elder to leave the monastery and go out into the world. Grushenka says she will
pull his cassock off his back.[49] There aren't any facts in
support of her magnificently direct image, but as in *Poor
People* we 'get thinking'. Are there any erotic hints? Well,
Alyosha blushes when Dmitry 'confesses' his womanizing,
'because I am the same as you'; he doesn't think he can help
going the same way.[50] Alyosha loves cherry jam, has loved it
since he was a little boy.[51] Purple stuff. Sugar-sweet like
Grushenka's voice 'and also the somehow inaudible movements of her body'.[52]

Sticky stuff, too. Alyosha also loves 'the sticky little
leaves' of God's springtime. But so does Ivan love the sticky
leaves.[53] What is adoration in Alyosha, at least now (that is a
fictional thirteen years ago), betokens in Ivan a curiously
unpleasant aesthetic fondling, a mental sensualism. Alyosha's
faith is passionate yet beautifully childlike and also, being
human, vulnerable — as a stinking corpse is enough to show:
we await events and turns of mind and changes of heart that
are never realized: all is glimpsing and guessing. Ivan by
contrast has no faith. But despite the agonizing boredom and

---

[48] p. 342.   [49] p. 77.

[50] p. 108. And Dmitry tells Alyosha that 'all of us Karamazovs' have a lust-
storm brewing in the blood (p. 106).

[51] pp. 233-4.

[52] p. 150. '*Leaving Grushenka, he remembers.* SUGARINESS' is a big moment in the notebooks (*PSS*, Vol. XV, p. 264).

[53] pp. 235, 271-2.

the incapacity even for negation revealed in the Double Act with his devil-visitor, the Karamazov appetite holds him. 'I could never commit suicide,' he tells Alyosha after the visitor has gone. 'It's because of my craving for life!'[54] Certainly a broad nature. And what is said by Ivan and guessed about Alyosha relates also to Dmitry and the old father, especially to what they do. They measure, they spreadeagle their broad natures in their doing.

(iii)

In the *Crime and Punishment* notebooks there is a reference to Mrs Svidrigailov's bad breath. Dostoevsky adds that this is to be mentioned 'in passing and *only once*'.[55] The novel relates that 'she always kept a clove or something in her mouth', and that is all.[56] The explicit bad breath has to wait fifteen years, for a different woman, for the right book, for *Karamazov* the novel of evil smells.

The same crazed visionary woman who saw through the Tartar *kara* and substituted the Russian for black, demands 'And why make such a fuss about my breath?' She continues, 'The dead smell even worse', which is visionary in another sense, anticipating the events following the death of the elder Zossima and the chapter 'Odour of Corruption'.[57] She is Mrs Snegirev — a surname Dostoevsky hasn't used since his first novel, *Poor People*, the poem of lodging-house smells: 'in a way it's stuffy, that's not to say there's a bad smell but, if one may so express it, a slightly decaying, a sort of sharpish-sweetish smell.'

Karamazov would never linger over a smell, would never describe; its smells are as unqualitied as its narrator who is its vanished author.[58] Even to call its smells evil, as I did just

---

[54] p. 692.   [55] *PSS*, Vol. VII, p. 162.
[56] *Crime and Punishment*, p. 416.   [57] p. 206.
[58] The author returns very occasionally, as we have just seen, to remind the reader he is a novelist with Alyosha the *future* hero of his unwritten novel. Two reappearances are oddly to one side of this main purpose. Ivan has a love affair 'which profoundly affected the rest of his life: all this could furnish the outline for another story, another novel, which I don't know if I snall ever write' (p. 646). Stranger still, he says of a second-rank character, Perkhotin, that his career 'is remembered to this day with amazement in our little town, and about that we

now, invites the objection that smell is the master metaphor of the novel and that the novel is by no means wholly evil. The prosecuting lawyer unites Karamazov breadth and Karamazov Russianness in terms of smell when he says Dmitry standing there in the dock carries on him 'the very smell' of Russia's past; and that is the truth, and Russia is not evil and nor is Dmitry.[59] He does many bad, smelly things. But he doesn't kill his father. We instantly distinguish the smell of his misdeeds from the psychophysical taint which foreruns the murder and which makes neighbours of *Karamazov* and the *Oresteia*. 'If you ask me, the old man's a sharp one: he smells crime. Your house stinks of it.'[60] Suddenly, the whole novel seems to be tugging at the sleeve of myth.

'Stinks' here is a breath-of-mortal-corruption verb *smerdet*. Throughout the novel it stands in a sensitive relation to the ordinary Russian *vonyat*. The epileptic lackey Smerdyakov who commits the murder is so called after his mother Stinking Lizaveta, a homeless pauper in 'our town'. There's evidence that old Karamazov is Smerdyakov's father. Time and place suggest so, and we know he'd sleep with anybody rather than nobody. As he himself remarks, 'for me ugly women do not exist'.[61] So the lackey is probably a parricide.

And 'lackey' brings to mind the archaic word *smerd* which in a neutral context one might translate 'churl'. I don't recall Dostoevsky using it elsewhere in millions of words of fiction and journalism and letters and notebooks and verse, but it occurs three times in *Karamazov*, and the stink association for eye and ear can scarcely be doubted. Thus the Americans (we know what Dostoevsky, and Dmitry through Dostoevsky, thought of America) are called *smerdi*, where a happy rendering might be 'shits'.[62]

shall perhaps have something to say when we have finished our long tale of the brothers Karamazov' (p. 475). I suppose these two pseudo-aberrations help to foster the life-simulating hugeness and chanciness of the novel.

[59] p. 740.   [60] p. 75.

[61] p. 137. 'You go to Chermashnya, I'll join you there myself and bring you a present. I'll show you one little beauty. I've had my eye on her a long time. Now she's still running about barefoot. Don't fight shy of barefooted little girls, don't despise them — they're pearls.'

[62] p. 808.

Dmitry also calls Rakitin a *smerd*.[63] Rakitin is the only out and out detestable character in the novel, exhausting even Alyosha's charity and patience. 'Dishonourable' is his verdict, and when one of his schoolboy friends talking trendy, obviously second-hand rubbish draws from him the quite uncharacteristically sharp question 'What fool have you got yourself mixed up with?', the fool turns out to be Rakitin.[64] A dangerous, poisonous fool, a shallow-shrewd fool, the kind of worldly novice monk who is likely to end up a millionaire. He degrades everything he touches. He stands alone in the novel because of the way he needles all three Karamazov brothers, trying to mock the faith out of Alyosha, to inflame Ivan's unRussian paper-person tendencies, to exploit Dmitry and his terrible, spectacular troubles with a view to getting his own journalistic career off the ground. He laughs at the idea of the soul and talks physiology, and it's even possible he has been messing about with the unintellectual brother's mind, for Dmitry keeps talking about 'realism' which isn't the sort of abstract word one would expect him to use, and nor is it very clear what he means.[65] But no matter. It doesn't touch his instinctive devoutness, and the voice of the eldest Karamazov brother remains unmistakably his own:

'It's no longer a dream now! It's realism, gentlemen, the realism of actual life! I am the wolf and you are the hunters, and you are hunting the wolf down.'[66]

Though a *smerd*, Rakitin is not Smerdyakov, not the murderer. But then Smerdyakov is only a surrogate murderer.

---

[63]   p. 622.   [64]   pp. 355, 585.

[65]   A positivistic *mélange*, probably. There was a lot of Comte around. The trendy schoolboy also talks 'realism' ('I like to observe realism', p. 555), and why shouldn't this be part of the rubbish he has got from Rakitin?

But popularized Hegel is also possible. The Russians managed to get almost anything out of Hegel. Ivan's devil-visitor jokes about the difference between realism and materialism (p. 674), and the two references to Hegel in the *Karamazov* notebooks (there are none in the notebooks of the other major fiction) occur amid exchanges between Ivan and Satan: *PSS*, Vol. XV, pp. 335–6.

In any event, Dostoevsky's war against the radicals, against Chernishevsky, Dobrolyubov, and Pisarev, continued to the end of his life.

[66]   pp. 387, 393, 402, 497. The first of the two notebook references brackets Hegel and Samsonov, a minor character to whom Dmitry exclaims 'Realism, Kuzma Kuzmich, realism!', p. 387. (Mrs Garnett, perhaps sensing the oddness of this abstract noun in Dmitry's mouth, translates 'realism' as 'a tragedy').

And then again, it is too clearcut to say Smerdyakov is Ivan's deputy and leave it at that. The circumstance of Ivan being out of the way on the fatal night was not a plot, still less was Smerdyakov told to kill the old man. *Karamazov* is a novel of nudges. Fainter, finer than nudges: animal intuition gives the feel and the smell — the book's master metaphor — better than human *bien entendu*. And it would be falsely neat to place the murder solely between the scented lackey and the second brother, his probable half-brother. Dmitry is altogether capable of killing his father, except with cool deliberation. In fact he knocks him down and sets about kicking his face in before Ivan and Alyosha can drag him away; and on the night of the murder, hesitating outside his father's window, brass pestle in hand, overwhelmed with hatred and revulsion — whether an angel kissed him or some stranger wept tears of intercession at that moment or his dead mother offered God a prayer, Dmitry never knew. 'But the devil was vanquished.'

This is one of those wonderful effects built up by accumulation and variation, at the time itself, under interrogation, and during the trial.[67] *Karamazov*'s harvest is breadth, the horrors of holy Russia, a solidarity in sin and retribution which encompasses the murdered evildoer. 'Why does such a man live?' demands Dmitry, and that is the title of the chapter in which he asks the question, and the chapter titles of this novel are uniquely active as to local stress and overall configuration.[68] The old man's complicity in his own murder gets carried by the book's master metaphor. His house stinks. His life stinks. Yet his mystic complicity never quite hardens into the judgment that he deserves to die. His nature is too broad to allow that.

Unlike Rakitin, old Karamazov is not through and through detestable. 'For me ugly women do not exist.' At the heart of his evil ways I find an element of heroic dedication to the senses which I won't call redeeming or even attractive but — broad. He is capable of uttering 'bitter reproaches' over a badly cooked dinner even as he trembles with desire for Grushenka, waiting for her to come to him. When his first wife runs off he decides to go after her, and the fact that he

---

[67] pp. 412, 498, 502, 778-81. [68] p. 70.

has decided to go makes him feel 'fully entitled' to settle down where he is to a terrific drinking bout. One contemptible episode happened long ago so, he says, he isn't ashamed to recount it. He describes himself as 'in the prime of life' and 'a feeble old man' in the same conversation. When Dmitry has beaten him up he chooses a red handkerchief as a bandage and not a white one because he doesn't want to look like a hospital case. He admires his wounds in the mirror with indomitable French bravura — a link with what James called 'the moral enormous' in Victor Hugo, a writer revered and overrated by Dostoevsky.[69]

To Zossima he says 'You know, blessed father, you'd better not encourage me to be my natural self — don't risk it!' We see the point as old Karamazov pictures the monks 'looking at each other and eating cabbage soup' and says Alyosha 'is here being saved' (monastery as salvation shop) and suggests that a soldier who has let himself be flayed alive by Tartars rather than renounce his faith should have his skin sent to some monastery — 'I can imagine the crowds that would flock there and the money the monastery would make' — and complains that God has given us only twenty-four hours in a day which is 'scarcely time to have a good sleep, let alone repent of our sins' and wonders what all the fuss is about death: 'In my opinion a man falls asleep and doesn't wake up, and that's all there is to it.'[70]

And yet when, in this uncontainable comic onslaught, Smerdyakov argues that the soldier-martyr who was flayed alive would not have sinned if he had renounced the name of Christ, and old Karamazov retorts 'You're talking nonsense, my lad, and for that you'll go straight to Hell and be roasted there like mutton', hypocrisy is not the only word for it. The man for whom death is the big sleep says 'I daresay it will be easier going to the next world if you know for certain what it's like there.' Stranger still, the dab hand at blaspheming who raises his arms solemnly over Zossima and pronounces 'Blessed is the womb that bare thee and the paps that gave

[69] pp. 3, 35, 39, 174-6, 290, 410. He thought *Les Misérables* a greater book than *Crime and Punishment*, and as a very young man he had bracketed Victor Hugo and Homer: letter of 1 January 1840.
[70] pp. 31, 37, 85-6, 127, 131, 175.

thee suck — the paps especially!' — stranger still, he does not blaspheme when he makes the sign of the cross over Alyosha and dismisses Ivan with the immemorial Russian 'Christ be with you'. It's a *broader* affair than our sense that humour is the only thing when Mrs Virginsky hastens childbirth by shocking her patients with pistol-shot atheistical sallies. Father and sons gain breadth from each other, without which the Russianness of 'Christ be with you' would be folk-costume, and the solidarity of sin and suffering just a thought. I am saying that the greatest marvel of *Karamazov* is its spatializing the latent temporal energies of the 'Life of a Great Sinner' project, its spreading them in a fierce black smear across the family. The novel presents the classic Dostoevsky no-home; the wreckage of this household is utter. Nevertheless the binding animal awareness we have encountered between Ivan and Smerdyakov affects them all, even Alyosha. Standing in the hall he can tell by the tone of his father's high-pitched laugh in the room beyond that he is 'still far from drunk'. The book swarms with such details. They are great levellers, weakening, even destroying, seniority and juniority and affirming the one broad life, the Karamazov tapestry, the realm of space. When, apropos their womanizing tussle, the father says he was better-looking than the son when he was his age, it feels like an unfair thrust against Dmitry. As if to make amends old Karamazov calls Ivan 'my dear old man' (*otets ti moy rodnoy*, literally 'father mine'), a telltale image. If there must be generations then make them reversible. It's pertinent to the size, haze, and smelly incestuous suggestion of *Karamozov*, that it both is and is not another generation-gap novel.[71]

Likewise it is and is not another crime-and-punishment novel. In the notebooks Dmitry first appears as Ilinsky, and Ilinsky is the real-life name of the convict in *The House of the Dead* who was doing time for a murder — a parricide — which it later transpires he never committed.[72] This 'later' may be the germ of the fictional *Karamazov* 'now' which never arrives, the doings of the great-sinner hero 'at this very

[71]   pp. 20, 38, 122–3, 128, 177, 285, 287. *'Otets ti moy rodnoy'* is Constance Garnett's 'my dear boy' at p. 285.

[72]   p. 134, above.

moment'. Of course it is Alyosha who has been cast as great sinner and Dmitry as the man wrongly convicted of parricide, but that is how the spatializing or spreading of themes across the family actually works. *The House of the Dead's* 'later' is a stop-press device, abrupt and intrusive. *Karamazov*'s 'now' is a crime-and-punishment Epilogue, but an Epilogue magnified and exalted into the real story, and one which Dostoevsky refrains from writing.

It could be argued that the Epilogue of *Crime and Punishment* too is the real story, and that the real story is gestured at, not written. This argument turns on the novel's sovereign concern being acceptance of suffering by the murderer (true confession, that is, as opposed to owning up to the crime), and his reunion with the human family. There's no denying that these things only happen in the Epilogue. But luckily the upshot is that the Epilogue is a mistake which nevertheless does not prevent *Crime and Punishment* being the most powerful statement of alienation through evil-doing in world literature, since *Macbeth*. And when he comes to write *The Possessed* it's as if Dostoevsky had learnt the lesson of that Epilogue, for the 'tomorrow' of Stepan Verkhovensky's 'Tomorrow we shall all set off!' never comes, and this most precious conviction of the novelist is entrusted to the flickering twilight of 'futile' Stepan's dreamlike deathbed chatter: 'Oh, let us forgive, let us forgive, first and last let us forgive all and always. Let us hope that we too shall be forgiven. Yes, because each and every one of us have wronged one another. We are all guilty!'[73]

A case if ever there was one of Dostoevsky creeping up on the blind side of his dearest values. And in *Karamazov* this shared guilt — what Ivan calls solidarity — is entrusted to dream itself. Dmitry is no dreamer, but, exhausted by the party he gives for Grushenka, a *skandal* as intense though not so drawn-out as the *Possessed* fête, 'a revel to end all revels', and then driven further into the ground by interrogation, he falls asleep and dreams a dream, a black dream, a *kara/cherni* dream about 'black cottages' and peasants 'black with black misfortune', and about a starving baby.[74] Later,

[73] *The Possessed* p. 586.   [74] pp. 455, 536–8.

he insists that he is being sent to Siberia 'for that baby'.[75]

But at the time, when he wakes from his dream: 'in a strange voice with a new light as of joy in his face' Dmitry addresses his tormentors 'I have had a good dream, gentlemen'. The most amazing, the strangest 'strange' in all Dostoevsky. Look no further for the gap that separates him from all the others except Tolstoy. What is good about this black dream? It transpires that the new light in Dmitry's face is no false dawn; when he talks about going to Siberia for the starving baby he says 'Alyosha, during these last two months I have become aware of a new man in me — a new man has arisen in me!' *Voskresenie*! Regeneration and Resurrection! He thwarts any inclination we may have to take the baby literally, that is to count it among the helpless little ones of Ivan's 'Rebellion' tirade who do not grow up into our adult solidarity of sin and retribution. 'All of us are "babbies" ' Dmitry says, clinging to the peasant word he heard in his dream; and 'all are responsible for all'.

As to the unrelieved and unexplained suffering of the dream itself, Dmitry finds himself demanding why people are poor and the steppe barren — questions huger even than Russia — and realizing he can neither answer nor help asking them. And, still inside his dream, he wants to do something so there shall be no more pain, no more tears; to do something now, at once, decisively, regardless of all obstacles, 'with all the rash energy of the Karamazovs'. And then he hears Grushenka's voice and wakes up.

And next, an unsurpassable stroke. Dmitry is suddenly struck by the fact that somebody must have put a pillow under his head while he was asleep, because it was not there before.

'Who put that pillow under my head? Who was so kind? he cried with a sort of ecstatic feeling of gratitude and with tears in his voice.

However, 'It was never discovered who that kind man was.' The effect would not be what it is if Dmitry had found himself a bed to rest on. He didn't. He 'lay down on a large chest covered with a rug and fell asleep at once'. The chest

[75] p. 625. 'Rakitin wouldn't understand it' says Dmitry 'in a kind of exaltation', singling out yet again the one *smerd* in the novel.

transfigures the small, very ordinary kindness of the pillow. But it wouldn't do the same for another writer. When I remarked that beds in Dostoevsky are not for repose I wasn't noting a quirk but looking through a peephole upon a world without easy unwatchful relationships, without fresh air and good humour and simple domestic and social routines, a world barred to habit itself unless obsessive. That is why figures like Lieutenant Smekalov sitting at the window with his long pipe are visitants and prodigies. Fresh air! The 'fume-laden hut' where Dmitry nearly gets suffocated is at Chermashnya, the name of the Dostoevsky property, whereas the actual black fire-ravaged place is unmistakably the setting of Dmitry's 'good dream' — the supreme example of a floating hulk of fact swept helplessly into the tiderace of the novelist's invention.

So the hut with the last malfunctioning stove in Dostoevsky borrows the name of the family property, and of course re-emphasises *Karamazov*'s master metaphor of smell; while the historical, terrestrial Chermashnya houses Dmitry's dream. As to the pillow and never finding out who that kind man was, we are face to face with the power of absence and elsewhere and ignorance in relation to the sheer stuff of this 'thingy' novel. A pillow is a pillow. Dmitry waking with his head on it feels intimations of newness, of a new man being born in him as he tells Alyosha afterwards. Hence the 'new light' in his face — which brings us back to the author's foreward to his readers, and the difficulty of presenting these deep-lying Dostoevsky devices as not frivolous. At one level nothing comes of this 'new light', and at another everything. The *Karamazov* 'now' which never arrives has to rub along with out ultimate refusal to doubt that we have the 'real' novel in our hands.

The apocalyptic naturalism stressed by 'regeneration/ resurrection' in the closing words of *The House of the Dead* and *Crime and Punishment*, and by 'salvation' lurking in the place Spasov across the water in *The Possessed*, engrosses *Karamazov* totally. It works backwards as well as forwards in its figuring of timelessness, and interrogation and court proceedings are its perfect vehicle. We learn that the local doctor Herzenstube, a devout, pedantic old bachelor, kept a kindly eye on Dmitry when he was a child, motherless and neglected by his father. He gave him nuts, the simplest of treats, and taught him to name the Trinity in German — Dmitry tended to get stuck over *Gott der Heilige Geist*, but never mind. 'He was taken away', Herzenstube tells the court, 'and I did not see him again.'

'And now twenty-three years later I am sitting one morning in my study, my hair already white, and suddenly a young man looking the picture of health walks in. I would never have recognized him, but he raised his finger and said, laughing, "*Gott der Vater, Gott der Sohn und Gott der Heilige Geist*! I've just arrived and have come to thank you for the pound of nuts, for no one ever bought me a pound of nuts, and you were the only one to do it." And then I remembered the happy time of my youth and the poor boy with no boots in the yard, and my heart turned over, and I said: "You are a grateful young man, for you have remembered all your life the pound of nuts I gave you in your childhood." And I embraced him and blessed him. And I wept. He laughed, but he wept too — for a Russian often laughs when he ought to be weeping. But he wept, and I saw it. And now, alas!'

'And I am weeping now, German, I am weeping now too, you good, good man!' Dmitry shouted suddenly from his seat.[76]

A magical reprise, grateful, sane, 'lawful as eating' Shakespeare might say, amid the tawdriness and hysteria of the courtroom and the nauseating fluency of the lawyers' speeches. And all the more wonderful for Dmitry's bawled interjection from the dock, giving us the whole man — that 'rash energy of the Karamazovs' — in a shout: no posturing but terrific self-projection. This is broad-brush Dostoevsky at his most commanding. But it is close work too, as comparison of notebooks and novel shows. The notebooks have already hit upon the comic and touching idea that old Herzenstube, after decades away from Germany, standing here giving evidence, shall forget the Russian word for nut. He fumbles. The defending lawyer, sensing an advantage, tries to prompt him. Herzenstube still fumbles. 'Yes it grows on a tree' he says in the notebooks.[77] *Karamazov* adds 'and they gather it and give it to everyone', tilting the funny old doctor's discourse, but ever so slightly, towards the visionary strangeness of a world better than ours.

Nuts and the Trinity — a sudden reaching across in a novel which succeeds in being locally immense. And a reaching back. The reader may or may not remember Dmitry mentioning Schiller's *'an die Freude'* to Alyosha six hundred pages ago and saying he doesn't understand German, he just knows the words;[78] and he — the reader — faced with the Trinity now, may or may not ask himself which of us knows more than the words, in German or in any other language, for Father, Son, and Holy Ghost.

And there's another sort of reaching back, from the tempestuous young man charged with murdering his father to the child standing barefoot in Dr Herzenstube's yard. That child was also tended by Grigory the family servant, and when they confront each other now in court and Grigory insists the shut door was open, Dmitry both attempts to refute this devastating and false but honestly given evidence, and thanks the old man for combing lice out of his head long ago.[79] It's already known, in the cumulative manner of *Karamazov*, that Grigory changed the three-year-old boy's clothes and washed him with his own clumsy hands in a tub.[80] We weren't 'there', and apocalyptic naturalism may well be a heavy phrase for what the mind's spatializing eye takes in. But is there a more beautiful and hopeful sight than a child's body? Or better work than helping the helpless? Or a clearer apprehension of 'eternity's sun rise' as William Blake worded it for us?

The child who grew up in his Karamazov breadth — 'broad as our mother Russia'[81] — to have that black but good dream, is at once capable of gratitude and of striking out brutally in the dark outside his father's house at the old man who had been kind to him. It's not clear he recognized Grigory before he struck him or even knew what he was doing, it all happened so fast. Nor is the uncertainty resolved when the scene is rerun during interrogation. Dostoevsky maintains his grip on normal psychology throughout in his handling of this Karamazov impulsiveness. For example, the magistrate asks Dmitry why he grabbed a pestle before running off to his father's place:

[78] p. 104.
[80] pp. 4, 93, 484.
[79] p. 706.
[81] p. 742.

'But what was your object in arming yourself with such a weapon?'
'What object? No object! I just grabbed it and ran off.'
'But why, if you had no object?'[82]

We recognize the seductive logic of an offensive 'weapon' and an 'object' — and which of us has not been in Dmitry's shoes?

But sometimes, though never a cool calculator, Dmitry knows very well what he is doing, and to whom. One of our reasons for finding the lawyer persuasive when he describes the eldest Karamazov brother turning a shop assistant out of his seat in the pub Metropolis, is that we know he has done worse things than that. He once dragged a man into the town square by his beard, to his terrible humiliation and the agony of his young son who ran beside the two men begging Dmitry to forgive his father and let him go. This was Snegirev. No wonder his wife insists on *Cherno*mazov when Alyosha comes to try and make amends, though she never links the name and the incident.

Dmitry, of course, accepts the blackness of both. He also accepts *kara* in its Russian meaning of punishment; it can only be the slenderest extenuation that Snegirev provoked him by his shady financial dealings on behalf of old Karamazov. Dmitry has Snegirev in mind, among many others, when he faces Siberia willingly, affirmatively, for the murder he didn't commit. He is in moral despair at himself. Early on, endearingly blind to the fact that the rest of us are much the same, he confesses that he reads Schiller (in Russian translation) but still doesn't behave any better. His reaction to being falsely accused is that 'men like me need a blow'. He wants to suffer. He's not sure that he is worthy to suffer. He wants to be cleansed by suffering, but can only put the thing interrogatively: 'I will perhaps be cleansed, gentlemen, don't you think?'[84]

In his 'Rebellion' frame of mind Ivan Karamazov would ask the further and wider question, how does this help Snegirev and the others Dmitry has wronged? I doubt if Dostoevsky's readers ask it. They are held to Dmitry himself by his irrepressible life-thrust — the psychic concomitant of

---

[82] pp. 413, 496, 503. [83] p. 207. [84] pp. 105, 538-9, 809.

his raking stride — and by his entirely unintended humour: 'You must take it', he says, meaning his 'confession' of his own 'utter baseness' — 'you must take it at its true value. If not, if you don't take it to heart, then you simply have no respect for me, gentlemen'; and by his way of fusing the bizarre and the overpoweringly evident in an unpursuable dazzling personal essence: 'A human being is not a sheepskin drum, gentlemen.'[85] Readers of *Karamazov* are surely too fascinated and moved by Dmitry to ask what good sending him to Siberia will do for the Snegirev family. But as I say, Ivan would ask this question, and he would answer it along the lines of 'Rebellion' and the Grand Inquisitor myth. To hurt the hurters of the world helps nobody. And even cleansing them cannot work backwards.

Dostoevsky maintains with complete silent confidence and success the fine yet absolute distinction between Dmitry Karamazov's quest for suffering and the narcissistic masochism of several minor, 'lacerated' characters in the novel. As for the vulnerability of Dmitry's quest to Ivan and the Grand Inquisitor, *Karamazov* shows no awareness of it, and the same is true of the notebooks. Dostoevsky's letters tell a different story. Some readers of the magazine serial felt he had given away too much — an extreme case of what I have called the surrender to the enemy of his urge for crisis and clarity. The novelist reassured them. Wait for Book Six, he said. Book Six, 'The Russian Monk', will confound the 'blasphemy' of the 'Rebellion' and Grand Inquisitor sections of Book Five. Be patient and you will find in Book Six 'the novel's culminating stroke', its 'crucial point'.[86]

Thus the *Karamazov* phenomenon of equidistance rears its head again, equidistance from the Christian 'answer' to the underground man and the affirmative Raskolnikov/Sonya exchange and the chapter 'At Tikhon's' — all three censored though the last survives. Dostoevsky believed that *Notes from Underground*, *Crime and Punishment*, and *The Possessed* had all been mutilated by their omission, but, as I argue, he was

---

[85] pp. 484, 524.
[86] Letters of 10 May and 8 July 1879. 'The blasphemy', he writes, 'will be triumphantly refuted' — not 'point by point', but 'as an artistic picture, so to speak'.

wrong and came in due course, and however vaguely, to realize this himself. And now, with *Karamazov*'s 'Russian Monk', he is wrong again — not because the novel would be better without it but because it is no sort of answer to Ivan and the Grand Inquisitor, let alone a refutation. But for the biographical evidence one would never guess it was meant to be. Indeed it is because the clinching urge is resisted, because crisis and clarity really are handed over to the enemy, that Book Six plays the effective part it does.

In 'The Russian Monk' Father Zossima reminisces, meditates, admonishes. He anticipates Dmitry by talking about the suffering that cleanses and about the responsibility of all of us for everybody and everything. He makes contact with Ivan over the true and the false *podvig*. He discusses the sorrows of Russia — factory children and so forth. He extols the monkish life. He describes his own vicious youth and the opening of his eyes to the truth with the limpidity of Tolstoy. Long ago he provoked a man to a duel. Then an internal switch was thrown: 'And I suddenly became aware of the whole truth, in its full light: what was I about to do? I was about to kill a man, a kind, intelligent, admirable man who had done me no wrong . . . '.[87] That might be the later Tolstoy seeing his youthful self as bound for Sevastopol not to do his patriotic duty or even to seek adventure, but simply 'to kill my fellow men who had done me no harm . . . '.[88] However, Dostoevsky's continuation is not Tolstoyan. The young Zossima presents himself for the duel. His opponent shoots and grazes his cheek and ear. Zossima throws away his pistol and apologizes. This breach of decorum enrages the seconds. So Zossima turns and faces them and declares

> 'Gentlemen, is it really so extraordinary in these days to meet a man who will acknowledge his own stupidity and apologise in public for the wrong he has done?'
>
> 'But not in a duel,' shouted my second again.

Zossima has disgraced the regiment. He ought perhaps to be arraigned. But when he announces to his brother officers

---

[87] p. 308.
[88] *Tales of Army Life* (translated by Louise and Aylmer Maude), p. 470.

that he has resigned his commission and intends to enter a monastery, 'they all burst into loud laughter. "You ought to have told us that before. Well, that explains everything. We can't try a monk." '

And so, through the wonderfully funny and brilliant and almost frightening energy of this juxtaposition, Dostoevsky manages to have it both ways — the Tolstoyan way in which Zossima with his 'Gentlemen, is it really so extraordinary ... ?' is the one sane man in a mad world, and the way of that world as to which 'sane' and 'mad' are question-begging, and where 'But not in a duel' catches the incontrovertible facts of life in five words.

Observe too the unflourished riches of 'Well, that explains everything'. On first thought it voices, again with matchless economy and humour, the consummately ludicrous and satisfying address of simple soldiers, practical men, to the mysteries of the spirit. Second time round it dissolves the scene into ironic afterglow — not just the duelling episode but the whole of Book Six: for 'The Russian Monk' explains nothing, clinches nothing, overturns none of the blasphemies Dostoevsky claimed it would. It is beautiful, but removed; I do not mean irrelevant: herein lies its equidistance from the underground man's 'answer' and the others. Even when a fierce beast of the forest is sent meekly on its way with an explicit 'Christ be with you', the moment belongs with Tamino's flute rather than the Cross;[89] or, to put it another way, 'Christ be with you' is strictly for the bears, the bears of Wonderland, it would only make matters worse for Snegirev and his consumptive little boy, clinging to each other, both weeping. They were alone. 'Only God saw us,' says Snegirev afterwards, capping his remark with the bitter barracks-state joke, 'perhaps He will put it on my service record.'[90] Nevertheless they have their dream, father and son, their own avenue of apocalyptic naturalism, a dream of somewhere to go and somebody to be, of another town happier than this one where people won't know about their humiliations and disgraces and they can find their real selves. It's an open-road and an empty-futurity dream, first cousin

[89] p. 304.   [90] p. 212.

to Stepan Verkhovensky's. They need an identified happier town, and a horse and cart and money and health to reach it, and they haven't got these things.

But, in this most *thingy* novel, they have a toy, a 'last year's kite', that sudden stab of the literal, as blunt and native to *Karamazov* as 'A human being is not a sheepskin drum' and 'We can't try a monk', but fringed with hope. The kite is broken so Snegirev proposes to mend it. There also comes to them the possibility of things they haven't got at all, because Alyosha, aware of the family's poverty and Dmitry's affront to Snegirev, tries to persuade him to accept two hundred roubles. As Alyosha and Snegirev confront each other everything I have said about money in Dostoevsky comes home to roost. Snegirev is dazed by the physical stuff, the rainbow colour, the pair of hundred-rouble notes rustling almost like new. Money can buy medicine, a horse and cart. He has just told Ilyusha, his son, 'there are no people on earth stronger than the rich.' It looks as if he is going to take it. 'Do you realize,' he says to Alyosha, 'Ilyusha and I will perhaps really carry out our dream now?' He does take it. Then, with a sudden dizzy swing of the will — staring at the stuff, I said, doing nothing, about to do potentially anything[91] — 'in a kind of frenzy' he crumples up the two notes he has been holding between thumb and forefinger, squeezes them tightly in his right fist, flings them on the ground and grinds them under his heel.[92]

And as for money 'lying about' in Dostoevsky, when the instances are dragged out from *Karamazov*'s vast interstices and turned into a catalogue, the thing begins to read like a joke. We find money or letters of credit inside a French dictionary, in a sock, wrapped in a rag and piece of paper in a hole in an apple tree, behind icons, dropped in a muddy courtyard, sewn in a little bag round the neck, tied up in a parcel, underneath a book called *Sayings of the Holy Father Isaac the Syrian*, even in a cashbox — and allegedly hidden in a pair of boots, under a pillow or mattress, in some crevice or under the floorboards.[93] Money is metaphorically as well as physically thrown away. Dmitry blues it on party treats

[91] p. 6, above.   [92] pp. 212–16.
[93] pp. 67, 113, 126, 487, 515–16, 518, 660–3, 666, 761.

ranging from champagne to toffee — 'toffee, the girls there
love it!' (he is his father's son); and when he thrusts a tip of
fifty roubles upon his peasant coachman, the latter falteringly
but impressively replies that he won't take more than five.[94]
Money is wielded with Karamazov breadth. Thus the old man
devotes one dollop of a thousand roubles to requiem masses
for the soul of his wife, and another of three thousand to
getting Grushenka into bed with him.[95] Non-existent money
fans the flames throughout, from the ghost-inheritance at the
start which deceives Dmitry and encourages his turbulent
way of life, to the ghost-hoard near the end which sets a
greedy innkeeper tearing his very unghostly establishment
apart in search of what was never there.[96]

In this delving, rummaging novel (what an inspiration that
the non-bed on which Dmitry has his black-but-good dream
should be a chest!) money is blandished and hushed up softly
as well as flung away and trampled underfoot. Old Karamazov
seals the envelope containing the thirty hundred-rouble notes
for Grushenka with five seals and ties it across with red
ribbon. On it he writes 'To my angel Grushenka, in case she
decides to come'; and three days later he adds 'And to my
chickabiddy' — that cumulation which both evokes the
restless old lecher and gives us a second look, so to say, at
his parcel. It is an uncomfortable second look, and typical
of *Karamozov*, in that the five seals have become three.[97] We
may reflect that the first description of the parcel is Dmitry's
to Alyosha and the second Smerdyakov's to Ivan, and we
would have to get a 'real' first-hand look at it ourselves to
know which if either of them is right — or has the old man
been fiddling with the seals as well as the inscription? And
indeed to proceed like this is to play Dostoevsky's own game,
to enter into the life-simulating spirit of the thing. Obviously

---

[94] pp. 425, 437.   [95] pp. 18, 120.   [96] pp. 6, 806.
[97] pp. 120, 280–1. In fact we get a third look immediately after the murder
when the envelope has been torn open and left empty on the floor. This confirms
three seals against five, but the red ribbon has become a 'narrow pink' one (p. 480).
And then a fourth glimpse when Dmitry is confronted with it under interrogation!
Again there are three seals, but we learn the new fact that the envelope is 'of the
size used in government offices' (p. 515). Cumulation, life-simulation, playing
Dostoevsky's game: where did old Karamazov get hold of that government-type
envelope?

it's possible that in this case the novelist has made a mistake (though I don't believe so for a moment), and it's likely that more readers will miss the discrepancy than notice it. But in contradicting five with three, and red with pink, if that is a contradiction, *Karamazov* runs true to form and moves close to *The Possessed*; and readers who aren't aware of seals will be aware of other things — pillows and mattresses and so forth. And even if they can name nothing specific they are vexed by a very lifelike undefined annoyance, like somebody trying to concentrate against a door banging somewhere in the house and wondering why his work isn't going well.

Dmitry proves himself his father's son when he spends money on champagne and toffee for the girls, and equally when he stitches together some cloth into a primitive purse and puts fifteen hundred roubles inside it and hangs it round his neck — the younger generation's answer to that sealed and beribboned envelope. A certain fierce and very physical application unites father and son; we glimpse old Karamazov bent on pouring brandy into cold coffee, Dmitry with his handkerchief squeezed into a bloodstained crusty ball.[98] And an inscrutable personal logic, which is another way of approaching Karamazov breadth, unites them too. Dmitry's equivalent of his father's telling the monks to snap out of their dodo ways and observing hallowed ceremonial on one and the same visit to the monastery, is a highly idiosyncratic sense of honour in the service of which he has hung the bag with fifteen hundred roubles inside it round his neck.[99]

It all began when Dmitry's fiancée entrusted him with three thousand roubles to post to relatives in Petersburg. He betrayed her by spending some of it on Grushenka and keeping the rest himself. The bag was a strange idea. The other odd thing was that he made an exact division, spending half and keeping half, which is how the fifteen hundred came to be round his neck. This proves of great importance for the outcome of the trial. It introduces a bad-luck element not

---

[98]   pp. 176, 417. *Karamazov* is a deedy as well as a thingy novel. We are in the world of Mrs Virginsky delivering babies and Fedka the convict sitting down in his sheepskin coat to cold beef and potatoes (p. 507) — the exceptions who prove *The Possessed*'s undeedy rule.

[99]   pp. 31, 87-8.

quite as sheer and as damaging as Grigory's evidence about the door opening onto the garden, but much more complicated.

Why the bag? Dmitry is, as I say, his father's son, and genetics are doing their subtle work throughout the novel — overall tonality again, but tonality for the reader, making the bag right for him, not for those in the courtroom where Dmitry is being tried. Moreover the word Dmitry uses when he tells the examining magistrate about the bag is 'amulet'.[100] Amulet, with its aura of occult charm, hits off (again for the reader) the family blend of religion and superstition and primitiveness exactly: *Karamazov* is a ghostly book like *Crime and Punishment* as well as a diabolic one like *The Possessed*. So the home-made bag/amulet is imaginatively fortunate as well as the truth, but Dmitry cannot produce it, he tore it open and threw it away later when he needed to get at the money, and it is not surprising the jury refuses to believe there ever was a bag.

Why the half-and-half division? This question is teased out during interrogation and at the trial. In fact it has raised its head much earlier, when Dmitry mystifies Alyosha by speaking of his disgrace and smiting his chest with his fist as though this disgrace were actually hanging round his neck, adding that he can still retrieve half of his lost honour.[101] To rationalize Dmitry's attitude: he carries disgrace round his neck because he is keeping his fiancée's money there in order that if Grushenka should decide to run off with him, as she might at the drop of a hat, they shall have the means to elope together; and what could be more contemptible than using one's fiancée's money to improve one's chances with another woman? At the same time, so long as half of the three thousand roubles entrusted to him remains sewn up in the bag, he can return it and thus partially redeem himself. Under interrogation the dividing of the money, in relation to honour and dishonour, hardens into mystic, naive, vulnerable obstinacy; and during the trial itself the exactly equal division gets blown upon by common sense.

---

[100] '*Ladonka*' — Mrs Garnett's 'locket' (p. 518).
[101] p. 159.

Dmitry's obstinacy recalls the unintended humour of his telling his interrogators that if they can't appreciate how shamefully he has behaved, then they simply have no respect for him. He is bracing himself now to meet their formidable argument:

'Surely, the important point is that you appropriated the three thousand and not what you did with them.'[102]

Against this he maintains, simultaneously, that nothing could be lower than keeping some of his fiancée's money on the chance Grushenka will elope with him, and that because he kept some of it and didn't squander it (as he did the rest) in champagne-and-toffee style, he could not *at that time* be called a thief but only a blackguard. Thus he lays himself wide open to two objections, both of which get made: the distinction between blackguard and thief is not very significant, and some of the money had been spent and therefore stolen when the rest, if his story is to be believed, was hanging round his neck in 'the — er — amulet, as you call it'.[103] Dmitry counters with Karamazov passion and the inscrutable personal logic I have just mentioned:

'Yes, I do see it as a vital distinction! Everyone can be a blackguard and I dare say everyone is, but not everyone can be a thief, only an arch-blackguard can be that. Anyhow I'm no good at these subtleties';

and second,

'She would see that since I'd brought back half her money I would also bring back the rest, that is the money I'd squandered, she'd see that I would try to raise it all my life, that I would work to get it and pay it back'.[104]

Again, why *half*? At the trial the prosecuting lawyer makes the ingratiatingly forensic move of inviting the jury to consider whether 'the real Dmitry Karamazov' would have stuck at half.[105] Is there any point in such a division? Even if it was ever made, would the real Dmitry have been restrained by it? Of course not! The dissolute man subjected to, and yielding to, many temptations in recent weeks, and desperate for money — the man with that record would have unstitched

---

[102] pp. 519–20.   [103] p. 525.   [104] p. 520.   [105] pp. 742–3.

his little bag the first time Grushenka said she felt like a treat, and he would have taken out, say, a hundred roubles. After all, he would still be a blackguard but not a thief according to his own absurd reasoning. He could still go back to his fiancée with fourteen hundred roubles and say, look, I'm not a thief. What's the difference between a half and fourteen hundred? Or thirteen hundred? Or one rouble for that matter? No, the real Dmitry would not have stuck at half, he would have dipped into that little bag and dipped again. And Dmitry — our Dmitry, not the lawyer's — has no reply to make; we have only our picture of him in his description of himself to his interrogators, 'craftily, with evil intent' (*ekhidno*) dividing the three thousand roubles into two equal amounts, and spending one half and keeping the other half round his neck for a whole month.[106]

It isn't surprising that our Dmitry fails to come across to the jury as the real one. Likewise to his interrogators, before whom he makes things harder for himself than I have so far suggested. As well as blackguards and thieves, the man who says he is no good at subtleties names and distinguishes those who squander and those who steal. He argues that even if he had spent the whole three thousand but had gone to his fiancée next morning and told her what he had done, then he would have squandered the money but not stolen it.[107] This is his version of Dostoevskian and especially *Possessed* slippage, as is his talk about blackguards and arch-blackguards and thieves and downright thieves. Also, and again not at all surprisingly, he makes a mess of explaining the two-sided nature of the unspent fifteen hundred — the shame in even thinking of using one woman's money to get off with another, the earnest of restitution of the whole — and the more confused and angry he gets, the less credible he appears.

But perhaps the most damaging thing of all is the flat lie Dmitry told at the time he divided the money and blued half. While he spoke to nobody about the two lots of fifteen hundred and the amulet, he positively noised it abroad — 'I told the whole town,' he admits when the interrogators remind him of it[108] — that he had spent three thousand roubles on the party for Grushenka. This lie obviously casts its shadow over everything else he has to say, and it also interlocks with other elements to form the overall bad-luck pattern. Dmitry has always been a great flourisher of money, a conjurer of goodies, a night-of-nights man, and confirmation is forthcoming that he did spend three thousand on that party.[109]

Which begins to bear directly upon old Karamazov's murder. Because a month after the party, on the night when Dmitry comes within an inch of attacking his father and in fact strikes down Grigory and fears he has killed him, and when he is thrown into further turmoil by the arrival of a man — what's more a Pole! — from Grushenka's past and her move to shack up with him: in a frenzy of altruism Dmitry organizes a repeat performance of the party, for Grushenka, for the Pole, for everybody who is around. How does he pay for it? He has been acting penniless these last days and weeks. The amulet is the answer. At last, having kept his hands off it for a month, since the last party, Dmitry tears it open and grabs the remaining fifteen hundred roubles. And that is what he tells his interrogators and the court. But the prosecuting lawyer points in a different direction, at old Karamazov's envelope containing three thousand roubles for Grushenka, which is found torn open and empty at the scene of the murder. An attractive explanation. What is more it has the back-up of witnesses who affirm there was a lot more than fifteen hundred roubles on show that night as there had been (so they wrongly thought) at the earlier party; and Dmitry has again lied about the amount of money he had on him. The night his father was murdered he declared he was carrying three thousand roubles — exactly twice the real amount and so the same lie he told a month before.[110] Arrested and on trial, therefore, Dmitry is telling the truth in the teeth of his father's missing three thousand, and the evidence of others, and his own double lie.

I have paused over these intricacies because of the unexpected life in them, around them, generated by them. They seem to add up to a foregone conclusion. Surely the accused man has no chance. On the contrary, though it is indeed no surprise that our Dmitry fails to come across to the jury as the real one, every reader of *Karamazov* will testify to his excitement as counter-pressures build up and factors like Doctor Herzenstube's evidence exert their force, and the whole affair becomes touch and go. Then there is the blinding simplicity of Alyosha's contribution. Suddenly, in court, he remembers Dmitry smiting his breast — 'I thought at the time: why does he strike himself up there when his heart is lower down?' — smiting his breast and talking about half his disgrace — 'he repeated *half* several times' — and Alyosha now, being cross-examined in the courtroom, realizes Dmitry was striking the amulet and 'half' meant the divided money. The following little exchange between the prosecuting lawyer and Alyosha strikes me as one of the most serene moments in the world's fiction.

'And why are you so absolutely convinced of your brother's innocence?'
'I could not but believe my brother. I know he wouldn't lie to me. I could tell from his face he wasn't lying to me.'
'Only from his face? Is that all the proof you have?'
'I have no other proof.'[111]

Like Dmitry after reading Schiller, we don't behave any better; and as to Dostoevsky's power to melt the hardest, cleanse the foulest heart, it must be remembered that he has put in a lot of work on his readers by this stage of the novel, though it's often difficult to indicate wherein his work consists. Let us return to the bad-luck pattern of things. Dmitry appropriates three thousand roubles, divides them, sews up half in a bag round his neck without telling a soul (though he drops a hint to Alyosha), spends the other half and lies about the amount (which lie is confirmed in all honesty by a number of witnesses), then spends the contents of the bag and again lies about the amount and again the lie is confirmed. On the surface very little effort goes into projecting and sustaining this sequence: there are some vigorous throw-offs like the defending lawyer's 'a hunk of bread always seems larger in another man's hand'; but they are few, and over in a flash.[112]

[111] pp. 717–18. [112] p. 775.

The sustained hard work will not be pinpointed, it is the energy of the accidental novel itself, the narrated mischance of an innocent man's conviction which I introduced by way of a shut door which was pronounced open, a corpse in a hurry to stink, the brothers in Schiller's *Robbers* got the wrong way round. The 'cruel talent' of tsarist Dostoevsky criticism has its wanton and irresponsible aspects, as our regard throughout for fiasco and other emanations of a gleeful creative malice has conceded. But as with madness, so with fiasco, *skandal*, and the rest, it is easy but wrong to represent the incidental as the primary and place the un-doubted cruelty of his genius at the centre of his achievement. With *Karamazov*, to state the issue at its simplest, that would be to imagine a reader who finishes the book gratified that Dmitry has been found guilty — gratified by an indulgence of the evil emotions that are there to be roused in all of us, as opposed to gratified by the justice of great art. It would also be to picture the bad-luck pattern which ruins Dmitry as a superimposed and thumbs-down construction by the novelist and not — what it is — an adventure in the deeper realism.

(iv)

The accused man appropriates his fiancée's money. There's no difficulty in that. It's a blackguard's act as he is the first and loudest to affirm. He takes it because he is a Karamazov, sensual, impulsive, morally unschooled. He proclaims his action's vileness because he is Dmitry Karamazov, extrovert and positive, a man of direct dealing and, though wild in his behaviour, also sensitive and capable of his youngest brother's cloudless blue-sky truthfulness. Thus when he learns his father has been murdered he says he is sorry he hated him so much. 'You feel penitent?' the examining magistrate asks him. 'No,' replies Dmitry, and he gropes for a moment and then comes up with 'I had no right to consider him revolting. That's what I mean. You can write that down if you like.'[113]

He had no right because he is far from a pretty specimen

[113] p. 488.

himself in his own eyes. That makes sense too. And here our
concern is not with straightforward violent uglinesses like
beating up his father and dragging Snegirev through the
streets by his beard while the little son Ilyusha ran alongside
imploring him to stop, but with the bag/amulet and the
money which, once appropriated, was divided and lied about.
To argue over these on behalf of the deeper realism is not to
detract from a supremely ingenious piece of plotting; it's
characteristic of Dostoevsky that the two should go together;
compare the details of Raskolnikov's 'rehearsal' in relation
to the murder itself. In an assiduously 'thingy' novel, ranging
from Ilyusha's toy cannon (contrast the pseudo-toys of the
childless *Possessed*) to Ivan's and Alyosha's sticky leaves,
the amulet is right. By its combining the makeshift thing with
the cutting and stitching deed, a sort of essence of do-it-
yourself, and by its family likeness to old Karamazov's
enticement parcel, the amulet is doubly right, bedrock right.
It is one of the ways in which our Dmitry takes shape over
against the all too plausible figure put across to the jury as
'the real Dmitry Karamazov'.

Then there is the exact half-and-half division. The pros-
ecution makes mock of it, saying it's absurd in itself and
wouldn't have restrained the real Dmitry. But, paying homage
to Dostoevsky's grip on the weirdness of normal psychology,
we all create these arbitrary break points for ourselves like
no drinking before six o'clock, and some of us keep to them.
Of course there's something oddly literalistic and primitive
about *exactly* half and half, but that is the way with instinctively devout young men like Dmitry. He made his break-
point, and it restrained him — for a month.

Alyosha knew his eldest brother wasn't lying when he
denied killing their father; and apropos Dmitry's statement
that he spoke 'without thinking' when he said the old man
kept the enticement parcel under his pillow, I remarked
myself that the words carry absolute conviction, that he is
not that kind of liar. So, what kind of liar is he? When the
magistrate asks him why he lied to the tune of double the
truth about the amount of money he had spent partifying,
Dmitry replies it was perhaps to boast about the amount of
money flooding through his hands, perhaps because he

wanted to forget the half in the amulet — the half in its shameful aspect, we tacitly understand. Then, with a mental shrug, he says: 'Well, I told a lie and that's all there is to it, I told a lie and didn't want to correct it. Why do people tell lies sometimes?'[114]

Why indeed? Overdetermination of reasons dissolving into no reason is a mark of this mercilessly accidental, life-simulating, no-frame novel. At the same time our deeper-realism Dmitry is being further developed against the lawyer's 'real' one. In his infatuation he is a mysterious but very recognizable blend of wastrel and provider, with more than a touch of Mister Big-Talk in him. Shakespeare's 'bounty' and 'dotage' come to mind because, as Raskolnikov is to Hamlet, so in a lesser degree Dmitry is to Antony, while Grushenka tends onward from Cleopatra towards Molly Bloom with her 'I made him promise to believe me and then I told him a lie.'[115]

But Dmitry didn't ask anybody to believe him when on two separate occasions he told all sorts of merrymakers and cadgers and amazed spectators and greedy tradesmen that he had spent a lot more money than was the case; and both times they did believe him. And they weren't the only ones. People who saw him clutching wads of rainbow notes in bloodstained hands or cramming his pockets to overflowing, believed him too; and in this false reckoning, as over the whole bad-luck pattern, Dostoevsky is reaching deep into himself; the notion of equidistance from what has gone before, and of writing the same book all his life, appears at its most pertinent here.

Dmitry wasn't being entirely fair to himself when he suggested a desire to boast as his reason for lying, though he can't know this because he hasn't read his creator's other books. We have, and are able to add that though not centrally a gambler Dmitry comes out of the Dostoevsky all-or-nothing stable, and comes out of it with the addition of an all-*and*-nothing variant. (This brings us back again to Egypt's Queen: the novelist was vastly intrigued by Cleopatra in Pushkin's tale allowing men to sleep with her in return for their lives the next morning.)[116] Gambling and suicide are intertwined throughout Dostoevsky — Cleopatra's takers might be called suicides — and Dmitry sets off for the second party, the repeat performance, intent on blowing his brains out at dawn after this night of nights, among the empty bottles; but events deflect him. Thus while he can talk big, the juster thought would be that all holding back and *half* measures are against his grain; there's something mean-spirited about a party supposedly to end all parties when *half* the wherewithal is hidden under your shirt. And if this doesn't undercut boasting and earmarking half for a possible getaway with Grushenka (which I happen to think it does), then it flows together with those things.

You mustn't expect to find any all-or-nothing or all-and-nothing talk in the novel itself; this is an instance of the reader moving in and making up the message, as I expressed it at the outset; and the objection, why this message rather than any other? can only be met by appealing in the widest way (which needn't be a vague or tentative way) to the Dostoevsky universe, and also to its details. In the present context we are dealing with two parties. At the first Dmitry is carrying three thousand roubles on him, and the all-or-nothing standpoint requires him to proclaim, and incidentally to lie and boast, that he will spend, is spending, has spent, the lot. But at the second he has on him only fifteen hundred, the amulet half, so why should the all-or-nothing standpoint make him say he is devoting three thousand to the party for Grushenka and her Pole and anybody who happens to be around? The answer is it shouldn't and, on closer inspection, it doesn't. The figure of three thousand is in the air because that is the amount originally misappropriated, the amount he must repay, the amount he has been frantically trying to borrow or trade against the property his father has swindled him out of but which he maintains is legally his and reclaim-able, the amount of his lie at the first party, the amount in his father's enticement envelope for Grushenka. Dmitry tells the three-thousand-rouble lie once on the night of the second party, but earlier than the party and unrelated to it. He has

[116] See *The Idiot*, p. 583.

been trying to borrow three thousand from a silly neurotic woman who says she will show him the way to a lot more than that; but it turns out she has been reading his character and believes he is a man with a nose for gold-mines, and her tip is that he sets off at once to find some. Then, with the party and, after that, suicide in mind, and Grigory's blood on his hands and the amulet ripped open and plundered and money apparently everywhere, he goes to an acquaintance to redeem the pistols he has pledged with him.

'Here are your pistols. It's funny, though. You pledged them for ten roubles at six o'clock and now look at you, you've got thousands. Two or three, I'd guess?'

'I'd guess three,' laughed Dmitry, stuffing the money into the side pocket of his trousers.

'You'll lose it like that. You haven't found any gold-mines, have you?'

'Mines? Found gold-mines!' bawled Dmitry at the top of his voice, and roared with laughter. 'Would you like to go chasing gold-mines, Perkhotin? There's a lady here who'll let you have three thousand at once if only you'll go. She let me have it — she's so fond of gold-mines.'[117]

The interview with the silly woman was a magnificently frenetic few minutes of reined-in exasperation and unconscious humour. She had read Dmitry's character by the way he walks — that impatient raking stride yet again; and she tells him 'Oh, believe me, I'm an experienced doctor of the soul.'

'Madam, if you are an experienced doctor, then for my part I'm an experienced patient,' said Dmitry, making an effort to be polite . . . .[118]

But when she springs her gold-mine idea it's too much for him, and he explodes. And now with Perkhotin there's a crowding of hostile elements like small flashing blows. That Perkhotin should use the word gold-mines is the merest grace note in *Karamazov*'s bad-luck pattern, unfortunate but a perfectly natural and dull image with which to salute sudden unexplained wealth. That Dmitry should pounce on the word and twist it his own way and at once pursue that way, is one of those instant revelations of character Dostoevsky achieves

[117] pp. 402-4; 420-1.   [118] p. 402.

so often and, it seems, effortlessly. Dmitry runs off with 'gold-mines' like a dog with a bone. He is a loving man but a poor attender, he is not 'with' Perkhotin, and for this reason among others he is very vulnerable. It so happens Perkhotin means no harm, but he betrays to us an unheedful man, easy to lure and decoy, eminently goadable — the man who has already been sent on a wild goose chase after the three thousand by somebody who does mean harm, to the hut with the stove and charcoal fumes.

Perkhotin is also innocent in overestimating the amount of money in Dmitry's hands, in pushing fifteen hundred up into the thousands, up to 'two or three, I'd guess'. It's bad luck he didn't go on up to four thousand because Dmitry would certainly have followed him and the evil spirit of three thousand would have been exorcized. But he stuck at three, and Dmitry's three-thousand-rouble lie to Perkhotin on the brink of, but unconnected with, the second party is not an all-or-nothing lie like the one on the first occasion, it is an impetuous Karamazov sky's-the-limit lie by an all-or-nothing man.

Again, we are not surprised that Perkhotin did stick at three. He's a sober observant young bureaucrat, thrown by the sight of blood-stained rainbow notes being flourished and dropped on the floor and stuffed into side pockets, but not thrown beyond twice the truth: unlike the frightened old man later on who, 'to the examining magistrate's direct question whether he had noticed how much money Mr Karamazov was holding in his hands . . . replied most categorically: "Twenty thousand, sir." '[119] In terms of Dostoevsky's journey backwards into the nineteenth-century novel this is a naturalizing of Mr Golyadkin's sourceless seven hundred and fifty roubles, and of his scrambling of value and colour, and of his visit to the moneychanger which left him with reduced spending power but a fatter wallet. *Karamazov* retains and enlarges *The Double*'s preoccupation with money as at once the most physical and the most notional stuff in

---

[119] p. 533. Perkhotin's cool caution is reflected in his testimony afterwards, 'that it was difficult to tell at a glance how much money there was, it might have been two thousand, perhaps three, anyhow it was a big bundle, "a fat one" ' (p. 417).

the world. Dmitry made to strip naked (*gol*) so the authorities can search his clothing for money he never had, while he himself ponders the ugliness of the adult human big toe, explores ridiculous and terrible regions closed to Mr Golyadkin by the fiat of the young poet who knew that indubitable big toes and the actualities of money were not for his abstract fable.[120] The very thought voiced by Snegirev to his little boy, that there are none so powerful as the rich, would be enough to break the spell of *The Double*'s subtle, intellectually taxing enchantment.

Dmitry's roubles are sourceless in a different sense from Mr Golyadkin's dubiously existent ones: people see, affirm, testify under oath to — what is certainly not there. They see wrongly but credibly; *The Double*'s metaphysical money has been psychologized, and this is a leading feature of the overall naturalizing process. But as I say, the pre-Siberian physical/notional passion survives. It is indulged at its most bodily by Dmitry's interrogators when they make him turn everything, 'even the small change', out of his pockets, and laboriously reckon a total of eight hundred and thirty-six roubles and forty copecks: so back we go to the 2497½ roubles disgorged by Mr Prokharchin's mattress.[121] As crude as a heap of pebbles. Then at once — hence the sense of coarse or fine weave, depending on how you look at it — they work out in their heads (as the saying is) what Dmitry has spent during the night and add it to the amount in his pockets, and, hopelessly bewildered, ask him as if asking themselves, 'you must have had roughly fifteen hundred at the outset?'[122] A moment tingling with finesse. The question mark, the printer's ink, seems to vaporize. Not roughly fifteen hundred. Exactly fifteen hundred. They have done the sum right. But they refuse to accept it, and thus they are carrying on the underground man's private war against arithmetic.

He could not make two and two add up to five, but he could refuse to submit to four. They can't push their reckoning beyond fifteen hundred. They can, though, refuse to submit to fifteen hundred and, since the Underground has

---

[120] pp. 508–11. [121] p. 112, above. [122] p. 508.

been naturalized, they can suppose that Dmitry has hidden the rest in his clothing and make him strip to let them search for it. Failing there, they can and do assume he has hidden it somewhere in the building, and that is how the matter rests at Dmitry's trial. The money can't be produced. It is one of those counter-pressures that make his case far from lost by the time the jury retires to consider its verdict.

Dmitry's accusers aren't inspired by malice against him. They brush aside their own correct figure of fifteen hundred and press on to a phantom three thousand because they think they are pursuing the truth. Now what actually happens when Dmitry arrives to set the second party rolling is that he says to the innkeeper 'I flung around more than a thousand here last time, Trifon. Remember?' The obsequious Trifon replies he well remembers, adding that he wouldn't be surprised if it was as much as three thousand. 'Well,' says Dmitry, 'I've come to do the same again now — see?' And he pulls out his bundle of notes and holds them in front of the innkeeper's nose.[123] Questioned about this next day, Trifon tells the authorities that as soon as Dmitry got down from the cart he said he had brought three thousand with him. Dmitry protests: 'Come now, Trifon, is that right? Did I really say in so many words I had brought three thousand?' But he doesn't move any closer to denial than that.[124]

Observe how delicately the first exchange is poised, both within itself and in relation to the second, nearly a hundred pages later. Dmitry did spend more than a thousand last time. He asserts this truth, then he emasculates it by responding to Trifon's mention of three thousand with a characteristic brusque 'well' and a perilously equivocal 'same again' which is at once correct (the second fifteen hundred) and a further encouragement to the evil spirit of three thousand that haunts him throughout. He can scarcely contradict Trifon's three thousand in the first exchange since that is what he said himself last time, a month ago. During the second exchange he does attempt something, and affectingly eloquent it is in a fierce-tempered man. He asks 'Come now, Trifon, is that right?' in the face of the statement that he said

[123] p. 437.   [124] p. 529.

three thousand on arriving the night before. We were 'there', and we know he didn't.

This looks like having it both ways, because we were 'there' in the Metropolis when Dmitry wrote that damaging letter to his fiancée, and although we weren't told at the time we are ready (so I argued) to accept afterwards from the prosecuting lawyer that he turned a shop assistant out of his seat.[125] It is indeed the case that Dmitry's arrival for the party has an effect of close-up and blow-by-blow, of not missing a thing, which the pub scene is without. That plays a part. But why be afraid of having it both ways? The claim to have access to our own deeper-realism Dmitry entails that we should. Our Dmitry, overlapping the lawyer's 'real Dmitry Karamazov', is perfectly capable of being rough with a shop assistant, but he would not have arrived for the second party and declared he had three thousand roubles on him. That was the all-or-nothing lie he told when he arrived for the first party a month ago with half the wherewithal hidden under his shirt. Now, the second time round, he is in a sky's-the-limit mood, and the reason this mood has produced one three-thousand rouble lie earlier in the evening is that Perkhotin unluckily guessed three thousand and Dmitry had just tried and failed to borrow that amount from the gold-mines woman.

The distinction between the two sorts of lies is fine but not flimsy, let alone fanciful, though it cannot of course be more than a rationalization made to one side of the novel. It is meant to illuminate the response of the reader, at least of one reader, who sees the familiar wild hyperbolic Dmitry up to his tricks again in the encounter with Perkhotin, but who also feels the breath of sobriety and truth (without 'losing' Dmitry) at 'Come now, Trifon, is that right?' And this reader keeps in touch through the unpromising agency of sums, reckonings, quantification. Three thousand really is an evil family spirit lodging, if you like, in the frou-frou envelope behind the icons in the old man's bedroom, but spreading like a sort of cross-infection (or a stink, if we are to hold to *Karamazov*'s master metaphor) to the money

---

[125] p. 305, above.

entrusted to Dmitry by his fiancée and to his quarrel with his
father over the Chermashnya property which leads to the
self-compromising mess of 'I regarded the envelope with the
three thousand which I knew he kept under his pillow ready
for Grushenka as simply stolen from me. Yes, gentlemen, I
regarded it as belonging to me, as my own property.' No
wonder the public prosecutor 'glanced significantly' at the
examining magistrate when Dmitry said that.[126]

So he doesn't leave the evil spirit behind when he sets off
for the second party. He takes it with him in the way I have
just mentioned, and in others. When his euphoria over
Grushenka's Pole collapses, he offers him and his companion,
a second Pole, three thousand to get out. (In any case the evil
spirit was waiting for him when he arrived in the shape of the
innkeeper who pushed his truthful 'more than a thousand'
up to three.) Dmitry does not pretend to the Poles, any more
than he did to Trifon, that he has three thousand on him.
He says he has three thousand hidden at home.[127] Here and
now he offers them five hundred 'by way of advance', and
when they hesitate he raises his offer to seven, which is still
one hundred and thirty-six roubles and a few copecks inside
what the authorities find when they make him turn his
pockets out.[128] That highly idiosyncratic sense of honour
works in odd but convincing ways; it makes Dmitry a calculator while never meanly or even shrewdly calculating; it
produces absurd, touching mental rigidities and stiff rhetorical gestures, all of which are liable to be swamped at any
moment by a comic and liberating intellectual chaos —
'Everybody can be a blackguard and I dare say everybody is'

[126] p. 487.
[127] We understand him to mean the enticement envelope; he doesn't yet
know his father has been murdered and the money taken. Later (p. 532) he says
he had in mind transferring to Grushenka's Pole his claim to the Chermashnya
property; but by now, towards the end of the interrogation, he is exhausted and
confused and has forgotten — there is no question of lying — and has to be
reminded what, in a mood of high excitement, he promised the Poles. It comes
naturally, we note, to speak of the enticement envelope as 'hidden', but not an
unexecuted legal document. And it is straining ordinary usage to speak of such
a document as money. (Of course we can't rule out the possibility, though it's not
my feel of Dmitry, that he was telling the Poles a deliberate half-lie in the first
place.)
[128] p. 451.

— and betrayed, not lived up to, by that Karamazov breadth which Dmitry calls baseness as it rampages through, in creative friction with, a plot of extreme temporal and spatial and numerical tightness and control. So while Dmitry does not say he has three thousand when he arrives for the second party, he is not the man to say he has only fifteen hundred either. He suggests, even asserts, he has more, 'much more'.[129] The sky's the limit. We are back with the kinds of lies Dmitry tells and doesn't tell, and under what conditions; and we are back with the ponderable human stuff informing the difference between three thousand and much more than fifteen hundred.

Not that the deeper realism makes all judgment certain, it would be quite unrealistic if it did. Trifon the innkeeper accuses Dmitry: 'And in the big room, when you were treating the chorus, you shouted straight out that you were leaving your sixth thousand here — that is with what you spent before, that's how to understand it.'[130] Trifon calls on various people to confirm this, and they all do except the one educated man among them who agrees he was standing near and heard mention of a sixth thousand, but doesn't say he heard it from Dmitry's lips. What are we to believe? We weren't 'there' with Dmitry and his rustled-up chorus of peasant girls; we glimpsed them now and then through the wild night; it's not like his arrival for the party. The evil spirit of three thousand begets six thousand — three then and three now, as Trifon says, and we can imagine Dmitry being goaded upwards, skywards, along the lines of his encounter with Perkhotin. On the other hand Trifon misjudged the money flourished in front of his nose as 'far more than fifteen hundred', and he and the peasants are anxious to tell the local big-wigs what they want to hear. And so on. The fact is, we don't know. We register a difference, in terms of our Dmitry, between saying on arrival one has three thousand and shouting out something about a sixth thousand at the height of the fun and games; but we still don't know.

[129] p. 508.　　　　　[130] p. 530.

At this point the narrative opens up a second front in the private war against arithmetic.

The evidence as to the sixth thousand made an extraordinary impression on the interrogators. They liked this new form of reckoning: three and three made six, which meant three thousand then and three thousand now — and here they had the six thousand, a straightforward sum.

When the figures added up to fifteen hundred the interrogators didn't like the result. They couldn't deny their own arithmetic, so they circumvented it. Now they do like the result and they embrace it and impose it upon what the underground man called living life. The fifteen hundred was real — was living — in so far as it had been translated into Strasburg pies and champagne and toffee. The part that would only translate into the coloured paper and metal in Dmitry's pockets had the twilight reality of money's imputed value throughout Dostoevsky: a grey and nugatory twilight because money, unlike toffee, is nothing other than it is willed and deemed; but at the same time, the human will being what it is, a jungle twilight of almost boundless rapacity and fear and dozing, stirring power.

And the present six thousand? It has been compounded of two three thousands which never existed and is therefore a product of mental arithmetic in Dostoevsky's meaning of that phrase. It won't translate into toffee or money or anything else. It is unattached, a sort of sky-writing, a morsel of quantification in the air. But it does its work effectively enough, there's something in it to wage war against; and so we conclude not that it is unreal but that *Karamazov* houses realities other than the underground man's living life. More sudden and less pervasive than the novel's three thousand, this six thousand is equally an evil spirit, a ghost at the lucid extreme of *Karamazov*'s psychic spectrum.

Because that spectrum is continuous, the clear and simple sum engages with the obscurest urges towards order, certainty, assurance, arrival, in the hearts of human beings: Dmitry's interrogators are not, I repeat, malicious men. Conversely, his own declaration (which of course does him no good) that misappropriating his fiancée's money is a baser act than 'the murder and robbing of my father, supposing I had murdered and robbed him', marries the grotesque confusions of his sense of honour to the palpable deed which sets the impalpable but mentally obvious three-thousand-rouble ghost straying across the open spaces of the novel.[131]

The opaque ghosts, as befits a black and smeary book, and the dark and sticky cherry jam over which Ivan and Alyosha 'get to know each other', far outnumber the pellucid ones. Old Karamazov concedes cheerfully that he may be harbouring an evil spirit. If so it must be as inscrutable a mix as his own brandy-laced cold coffee. In any case, he adds, it could not amount to much; 'a more important evil spirit would have chosen some other lodging'.[132] Disarmingly outrageous. This is the man who can't look solemn without looking vicious, the man we have seen punishing the bottle with black mourning crepe round his hat.[133] Among other things he's a great tease. Other people haven't really got more important evil spirits, apart from Ivan and his Devil Double. In fact people in *Karamazov* are visited rather than possessed: Ivan precisely by his visitor; old Karamazov 'by spiritual terror, when drunk, and moral perturbation which almost produced, so to say, a physical impact'; and Dmitry has a recurring dream of pursuit at night, of hiding himself in utter panic and humiliation behind a door or cupboard from someone who knows perfectly well where he is 'but pretends as if on purpose not to know'.[134]

And Smerdyakov, apropos his epileptic fits, also talks about pretending on purpose.[135] It's both colloquial Russian and one of those apparently otiose Dostoevsky phrases. What would pretending *not* on purpose be like? Yet it has a sinister rightness for *Karamazov*, this threat of poltergeists shaking up language in the night, and thought and action both flowing at two or more levels while we struggle with the self-tightening knot of our futile readerly pursuit after the reason people do things. Smerdyakov has the look of a castrate, a member of the religious sect of *skoptsi*.[136] He doesn't beget the murder, he

[131] p. 507.　　　　　[132] p. 36.　　　　　[133] pp. 65, 96–7.
[134] pp. 91, 497.　　　[135] p. 644.
[136] p. 125 (Mrs Garnett's 'strangely emasculate').

has it fathered on him by virtue of his resentment, vanity, shallow Westernism, vicarious deededness (but not always vicarious: 'As a boy he was very fond of hanging cats and then burying them with ceremony'), and so on. But however long and accurate the list, it will never constitute a generative reason or complex of reasons. Smerdyakov wants to make Ivan the natural father of the deed and himself a sort of eunuch-procurer. That won't do either because, as we have seen, the death of the old man does not lie neatly or solely between the two of them. The really important evil spirits of *Karamazov* are interpersonal.

Smerdyakov seeks or pretends — pretends on purpose? — to rationalize this murky scene by separating the murder and the killing. He accuses Ivan of the first ('you alone are the real murderer') and takes the second on himself which in some fashion he must since he is bent on his own style of confession; and then he describes in detail how he did it. He needed to gain access to the bedroom leading onto the garden. Deeply suspicious and frightened of Dmitry, old Karamazov had locked himself in there at night, making Smerdyakov keep watch on the house and grounds. Between them they had arranged a code of taps on the window frame by which Smerdyakov would keep the old man informed of what was going on, particularly as regards Grushenka. On the fateful night — the word fateful is everywhere in this novel — Dmitry had been and had run off again, striking down Grigory when he tried to intercept him. Smerdyakov now saw his chance. Dmitry and Grigory were safely out of the way. He crept up to the open window and found old Karamazov striding round inside in high agitation, his dominant mood of fear and lust. Smerdyakov told him Grushenka had come:

'She's here,' I says, 'She's come, Miss Svetlov has, she wants to be let in.' And you know he shook all over like an infant. 'Where is she? Where?' That's how he gasped, but he didn't believe me. 'There she is,' I says, 'she's standing there. Open the door.' He looked at me out of the window and was in two minds whether to believe me, but he was afraid to open the door. He's frightened of me, I thinks to myself. And a very funny thing. I suddenly took it into my head to tap out on the window frame before his eyes those taps we'd agreed on as a signal

Grushenka had come. He didn't believe my words, but when I tapped out the signal he ran at once to open the door. So he opens it.'[137]

Yes it is 'a very funny thing'. What gave Smerdyakov the idea of tapping? Why did the old man believe the taps but not the words? Such details fall within the all-embracing funniness of *Karamazov* which is both very linguistic — pretending on purpose and so forth — and liable as here to sweep language aside in its 'deedy' and 'thingy' thrust towards tapping on a window frame. The funniness of accident yields a novel *par excellence* of the sneeze and the nosebleed.[138] And, in various senses, ejaculation. 'I've oiled plenty of locks in my time' — so the old man reports Father Zossima, falsely of course but shedding true light on himself and on Smerdyakov, the outcome of brisk copulation in back-alleys, Stinking Lizaveta's child, a monster, as it were an unaborted abortion, a walking and talking reminder of life's biggest single accident, getting conceived.[139] I harp on accident both at the level of a nosebleed and of the book's overall bad-luck pattern which interpersonal forces like the three-thousand-rouble ghost affirm and sustain. Fateful accident: the phrase jostles uncomfortably within itself, like pretending on purpose, but casts a calm and royal eye outward upon the bedroom-window encounter between Smerdyakov and the old man his probable father. The almost unbearable vividness of that encounter proceeds equally from a tenterhooks disquiet where anything might happen and a subliminal trancelike doom, a narrative sleepwalk, in which nothing else could.

(vi)

The conjuring of human beings as animals is even more powerful in *Karamazov* than in *Crime and Punishment* and *The Possessed*. Also of human beings as spiritual animals.

---

[137] pp. 664-5.   [138] pp. 231, 317.

[139] p. 136. Mrs Garnett's 'I've plenty of tricks in my time' is not very meaningful, but we must each make what we can of Karamazov's neologism *'naaphonil'* which he has blasphemously constructed out of Athos (*Aphon*), the Holy Mountain, the greatest of eastern sanctuaries. I have tilted it the way I have because he has just said of Zossima 'he's such a sensualist that I'd be afraid for my daughter or wife if she went to confess to him.'

The novel has an Epigraph taken from St John which focuses on the original fateful accident of conception, fertility, new life, in relation to death:

Verily, verily, I say unto you, except a corn of wheat fall into the ground and die, it abideth alone: but if it die, it bringeth forth much fruit.

And this invites comparison with *The Possessed*'s Epigraph, again from the New Testament, where the mad Gadarene stampede and self-destruction are what the novel achieves, and where the healed man at Christ's feet is what it doesn't: but no matter, because it doesn't attempt to; the coat of the parable gets cut according to the cloth of Dostoevsky's available creative energies.

Karamazov's relation to its Epigraph is different, but with the family likeness that runs through all the major works. According to St John it has been wrong of me to speak of the novel's pattern as a bad-luck one, and with no more than an eye to the Epigraph we must allow that it has been pre-judging the issue to do so. Men like me need a sudden blow, says Dmitry.[140] He is less concerned about its human injustice than the mystic legalism (or divine justice) of going to Siberia for the starving baby in his black-but-good dream, which means becoming worthy to suffer, which means the death of the old self and the birth of the new. Which means, or rather is poised to mean, bringing forth much fruit — the end to which the Epigraph directs us.

Dostoevsky does not suggest what the hero, a man made new, did after the end of *The House of the Dead*, when his fetters were knocked off. Or what the new life held in store for Raskolnikov, penitent at last and accepting suffering in *Crime and Punishment*'s Epilogue. And we have no idea whether the dead Stepan Verkhovensky got to Spasov. And now, and finally, there is no afterwards in which Dmitry Karamazov demonstrates ('By their fruits ye shall know them') that it was no bad-luck pattern which brought him to judgement, but fateful accident theologized: we sneeze as the fit takes us, and every sneeze is numbered.

---

[140] p. 538.

In *The Possessed*, when Shatov envisages a new start for the new baby and for himself and his wife, one gets no premonition of a miraculously healed man (Dostoevsky's Russia); rather, of three thwarted human futures, sane futures in a mad world; but the sanity is of and within nature: 'let us work hard,' says Shatov, displaying the novelist's uncanny touch. But when in *Karamazov* 'some kind man' places a pillow under Dmitry's head while he lies asleep on a chest, the fruit of the spirit, thing and deed, is inescapably present and evident. The kind man disappears and is never found, never identified. Dmitry awakes and weeps inwardly to see the pillow: 'his whole soul was shaken with tears.' The fruit of the spirit is watered by the spiritual animal's tears of gratitude.

'To recognize our friends is a god,' Euripides says.[141] Dmitry greets his unknown benefactor; and the entire relationship between *Karamazov* and its Epigraph is one of mutual awareness, and therefore of simultaneity, and of co-presence which may or may not be physical, may be a pillow or compassion. This is not a roundabout way of saying the Epigraph gets realized in the novel. I am arguing that outcome and hereafter, so insistent in the healed man of the *Possessed* parable, have disappeared, and that the spatializing of a pointedly temporal theme, already remarked by me of this novel *qua* generation-gap story, extends beyond the Karamazovs, father and sons and two dead mothers, to crime, investigation, trial, conviction, sentence, where what seems intractably sequential is reprocessed and re-reprocessed through interrogation, the evidence of witnesses, the lawyers' reconstructive speeches — all agents of space and then-and-now simultaneity. The cumulation which distinguishes *Karamazov* throughout is, in imaginative substance, a widening of vision not a passing of days, a learning of what is there and not what happens next. Excitements, very genuine and sequential excitements, like Smerdyakov's account of how he did it, are held in the amber of retrospect. And it is no contradiction to speak of mounting tension at the trial, because a book takes time to read. This temporal mounting

[141] *Helen*, l. 560.

accompanies the temporal experience of turning the pages. Inside those pages there is the lateral spread from claustrophobic courtroom to the naked little boy in a bath-tub and the young man returning to recite the Trinity in German to Doctor Herzenstube and the not quite so young man restrained perhaps by his dead mother's prayers from killing his father. Dmitry's wrongful conviction is not a climax but an irony smeared across the whole enormous episode at its close by a voice from the dispersing crowd which pronounces 'our dear old peasants' (the jury) 'have stood up for themselves'.[142] *Karamazov* is a book without climaxes. Nothing could be less like the unrelenting drive of *Crime and Punishment* towards murder and then towards the climb up the spiral staircase to admit to murder.

But, like *Crime and Punishment*, Dostoevsky's last novel has an Epilogue — as well as an Epigraph like *The Possessed*. It may be asked what there is left to say, to consign to an Epilogue, if *Karamazov* is truly a story without climaxes and if outcome and aftermath have disappeared. Certainly no regeneration/resurrection (*voskresenie*). We have seen what there is to see of the death of the old Dmitry and the birth of the new. He first mentioned this change in the immediate aftermath of his black-but-good dream, long before he was tried and convicted; but the reader feels it from the start, as does Father Zossima who prostrates himself before a man instinct with great and creative suffering.[143] Thus, though Dmitry was not to know, it's misleading to talk about a change since what we have here is the abiding mutual awareness of Dostoevsky's novel and Jesus' hard gospel saying reported by John. One supposes Dmitry will go on behaving badly, perhaps worse than badly sometimes. But he, the old Dmitry, dies daily, and it hurts. 'God knows my heart. He sees my despair. He sees it all.'[144] He talks a lot about God, and never profanely. And the same is true of Grushenka who matches Dmitry's heavy direct passion with a feather-brained, let's call it trigger-happy, pious flair. She crosses

---

[142] p. 799. This standing up for themselves is planted firmly in the chapter-title, like gold-mines, and Ivan and Alyosha getting to know each other, and many other threads which the novelist wants to pull apart before he knits them together.

[143] p. 71.   [144] p. 121.

herself 'devoutly' when she hears the news of Father Zossima's death, then remembers she is sitting on Alyosha's knee and jumps off.[145] Next things next. There's birth around as well as death, and birth hurts too, though Grushenka, unlike Dmitry, does not go in for simple shouts of pain. She's a very different spiritual animal.

(vii)

The disappearance of outcome and aftermath is the 'now' which never arrives, the 'real' novel which never gets written, as experienced from inside *Karamazov*. Dmitry must be called the hero of our book. Alyosha is the hero of the 'real' one: the author tells his readers so.[146] This means — again of course from inside *Karamazov* — that death and birth in the spirit are themes articulated through Dmitry, and the blow which sends a man sprawling, the blow 'men like me need', is explicitly his portion; while the mutualities of novel and corn-of-wheat Epigraph appear at their most tender and tentative in Alyosha. And as to Aloysha, no reader feels cheated unless he is determined to. Tentativeness, imaged by Grushenka perching herself on the novice monk's knee, is sufficiency of knowledge within *Karamazov*; whether she ever got the cassock off his back or seriously tried belongs to the 'now' whose positive and gratifying role is never to come.

In the central chapters of the novel Zossima dies, the master metaphor of smell is literalized, and Alyosha's young life is assailed by nature in the everyday form of mortal corruption. Dmitry wouldn't have batted an eyelid. 'God knows my heart'; his immediate striding access to the Maker of that heart strikes me as the most wonderful and elusive achievement in all Dostoevsky. Alyosha's faith, though ardent, is not sure like that, and despite his loving gentle open ways and sweet sleep and innocent dreams and gift with children and live habit of prayer — stupendous feats too — he is to be feared for. This is tentativeness apprehended as

---

[145] p. 366. Contrast the true profanity of the fashionable doctor called in to treat the consumptive Ilyusha Snegirev: ' "What can I do, I'm not God" replied the doctor in an off-hand voice but with his usual impressiveness' (p. 590).

[146] p. 302, above.

danger. A smell infects him with Ivan's 'rebellion' and reduces him to wanting to believe.[147] Eros awaits. (Perhaps Eros *should* await: there is no 'real' novel and this is not a real question in the one we have.) Also he is the pretty boy around the place, inside and outside the monastery, and some will think they catch a hint, the merest head-toss, of sulky flirting.

With the impression of Grushenka clear and warm upon him, though unaroused by her, he returns to the monastery and finds a window open and a monk reading the New Testament over Zossima's coffin. 'So the smell must have become stronger,' he thinks. He kneels to pray and, exhausted, falls into a doze.

Dmitry goes to sleep on a chest and dreams of starving peasants. 'Why are people poor?' is his dream-question. And, 'Why don't they embrace and kiss one another? Why don't they sing joyful songs?' He longs to put all of it right. Life should be something else.

As Alyosha dozes on his knees, life becomes something else — somewhere else. The monk is reading of Jesus' first miracle when he turned water into wine for the wedding guests at Cana. Half asleep, Alyosha thinks how poor they must have been, those people there, not to have enough wine even for a wedding.[148]

So, yet again, the image of the party. In *The Possessed*, and exquisitely comic it is in the telling, we have a political meeting disguised as a birthday party.[149] At the centre of *Karamazov* is a wedding party portrayed as a party but transfigured by a miracle. Both novels have Epigraphs in search of true community, one from the starting-point of false community (the Gadarene 'herd') and the other of no community ('it abideth alone'). False community and no community go back to the beginning in Dostoevsky — to office and lodging-house and seamstress's lonely room. True community gets its first festive apocalyptic twist in the

---

[147] p. 354. ' "I did believe, I do believe, and I want to believe, and I will believe, what more do you want!" cried Alyosha irritably.' More troubled still, 'I don't think I even believe in God,' at the prospect of losing Father Zossima through death (p. 257).

[148] pp. 374–9.   [149] pp. 352–74.

house with the lights and music outside which Mr Golyadkin stands in the rain trying to look at all its windows at once.

The warm dry house is the somewhere else where life is something else. But of course *The Double*'s party is no less dubious than 'our hero's' invitation to it. *Karamazov* doesn't ask whether the wine really flowed from outside nature at Cana, or whether, beyond the iconic wedding feast, Christianity is true and the God-man invites us all to the party of eternal life. One knows what Dostoevsky believed, but that is irrelevant. One also knows that the greatness of his novel permits none but a hooligan to receive the somewhere and something else of Alyosha's dozing apprehension at the level of the land of nod and drinks on the house.

The dubiousness in and around Mr Golyadkin has evolved into the huge spiritual tentativeness of Alyosha's destiny. Like Dmitry, and with all the passion of a Karamazov, he grasps his apocalyptic visitation as the opposite of tentative, as decisive. He senses a new world unfold before him, and the reader remembers Stepan Verkhovensky taking to the open road and hears again something very like the voice of Joseph Conrad:

The vault of heaven stretched boundlessly wide above him, full of soft, shining stars. From the zenith to the horizon the Milky Way ran in two pale streams. The fresh, motionless, serene night enfolded the earth . . . . The silence of the earth seemed to merge with the silence of the heavens, the mystery of the earth came into contact with the mystery of the stars.[150]

Nobody could be remoter from Alyosha in personal timbre and circumstances than Stepan Verkhovensky. And yet the same man made them both, imagining one as parasite, the other as monk — monks *are* parasites according to old Karamazov — one launched upon quintessentially comic and inconclusive journeying, 'futile' by Mrs Stavrogin's cruel verdict, and the other contemplating the words of Father Zossima 'who had bidden him "sojourn in the world" '.[151]

The Cana chapter reads free, shy, very rare. No novelist's thumb in the balance. And when Alyosha believes 'something firm and unshakable as that vault of heaven had entered his

[150] p. 378.   [151] p. 379.

soul', whereas the overall feel of Alyosha in *Karamazov* is tentative, the conclusion should be that the novel is bigger than he is, not that his experience in the cell with the corpse and gospel reading and open window was false or shallow. He can only speak for himself, and his destiny is not only for himself, it does not cleave to him as if it were the clothes he stands up in. The fulfilment of Alyosha's destiny is spread in the broad and spatial way of *Karamazov* across the 'now' which never arrives; and the 'tomorrow we shall all set off' of Stepan's death across the lake from Spasov, which was an ever-receding horizon in *The Possessed*, a novel of movement, becomes in *Karamazov*, that novel of sojourn (for Zossima chose his word carefully), the envelope which surrounds but has no part in the action, and within which the actors position themselves, perforce temporarily, and therefore perch, singly like the young man at prayer and the girl on the same young man's knee; or collectively like the blood-relations in the smelly tottering house of wrath and lust, and like the wider community of Cattlepen, a place of rotten wood and broken roads and jerry-building and miserable dank back-alleys, including 'moral ones'.[152] Taking the two novels at a single glance, life as shanty town in *Karamazov* complements life as gold rush in *The Possessed*.

Sojourner at the start, Alyosha is equipped with pillow and mattress which his father (what a father!) exhorts him to bring home (and what a home!) from the monastery.[153] At the end, in the novel's Epilogue, he is still travelling light and going nowhere except in the context of his spiritual destiny and Zossima's admonition. Ilyusha Snegirev has died, and good with children as always Alyosha attends the funeral and burial with Ilyusha's school friends.

There will be a funeral feast afterwards. Kolya Krasotkin, a precocious child, remarks the incongruity of eating pancakes while you mourn. Kolya has been infected by Rakitin, the novel's one *smerd* and turner of life's wine into water.

---

[152] p. 107. Dmitry is talking about another provincial town, but there are plenty of moral back-alleys in Cattlepen too.
[153] pp. 88, 123.

'Don't let it worry you that we shall be eating pancakes. It's an old, age-old custom and there's something nice about that,' Alyosha laughed.[154]

Life goes on. Alyosha lays pancakes alongside death very much as Doctor Herzenstube laid nuts alongside the Trinity at Dmitry's trial. Both of them do justice to the breadth of *Karamazov*. Alyosha has just been assuring Kolya and his friends of the truth of the Resurrection, the theological *voskresenie*, so he is no less doctrinally embroiled than was the good doctor. But Herzenstube's Trinity, inside *Karamazov*, is a business of knowing the German words — which in no way detracts from the sublime encounter of healer and little boy who becomes the young man newly returned, the picture of health, who becomes the accused person roaring to everybody in court that he is weeping now. And the Epilogue's Resurrection is the language of ardent youth, again sublime and in no way a snug orthodoxy.

However, youth also throws a brick at a flock of sparrows, there being no boy to throw stones at, because he is dead.[155] And others are not young, and neither are they ardent on the one hand or, on the other, nature's stone-throwers.

'Yes, yes, let's go back to Mummy,' Snegirev suddenly recollected again. 'They'll make up his little bed, they'll make up his bed!' he added as though afraid they would really make up the bed, and he jumped up and ran home again.[156]

The Snegirev hovel is the last no-home in Dostoevsky, and the grieving half-crazed father's fear for his child's bed, following Dmitry's chest with a rug on it and Alyosha's portable mattress and pillow, is the final dislocation of the idea of repose.

[154] pp. 818–21.
[155] pp. 180, 816–7.
[156] Constance Garnett translates 'make up' in its primary sense of 'take away', but *ubirat postel* does mean to make a bed, and I prefer the more surprising thought.

Index

OXFORD

MORE OXFORD PAPERBACKS

Details of a selection of other books follow. A complete list of Oxford Paperbacks, including The World's Classics, Twentieth-Century Classics, OPUS, Past Masters, Oxford Authors, Oxford Shakespeare, and Oxford Paperback Reference, is available in the UK from the General Publicity Department, Oxford University Press, Walton Street, Oxford, OX2 6DP.

In the USA, complete lists are available from the Paperbacks Marketing Manager, Oxford University Press, 200 Madison Avenue, New York, NY 10016.

CRIME AND PUNISHMENT
Fedor Dostoevsky

Crime and Punishment is the story of a murder committed on principle, of a killer who wishes by his action to set himself outside and above society. A novel of fearful tension, it is set against the backdrop of St. Petersburg, sinisterly evoked by Dostoevsky, and constitutes a battle between the pressures of the law and the killer's own conscience.

This remarkable work of fiction was marked by Dostoevsky's own harrowing experiences of interrogation, trial, and death penalty—a sentence commuted to penal servitude.

The World's Classics

MEMOIRS FROM THE HOUSE OF THE DEAD

Fedor Dostoevsky

'I know no better book in all modern literature' was Tolstoy's verdict on *Memoirs from the House of the Dead*. In this almost documentary account of his own experience of penal servitude in Siberia, Dostoevsky describes in relentless detail the physical and mental suffering of the convicts, the squalor and the degradation, parts of which were compared by Turgenev to passages from Dante's *Inferno*.

The World's Classics

CHILDHOOD, YOUTH AND EXILE

Alexander Herzen

Childhood, Youth and Exile comprises the first two parts of Herzen's autobiography, *My Past and Thoughts*, one of the greatest monuments of Russian literature, comparable to the major works of Tolstoy, Dostoevsky and Turgenev.

Ends and Beginnings is the sequel to *Childhood, Youth and Exile* which comprises an autobiographical selection from the later parts of *My Past and Thoughts*.

The World's Classics

FIVE PLAYS

Anton Chekhov

'Where does one get to with your heroes? From the sofa to the privy and from the privy back to the sofa' was Tolstoy's baffled—and inaccurate—comment on Russia's greatest dramatist; and the five plays (*Ivanov, The Seagull, Uncle Vanya, Three Sisters,* and *The Cherry Orchard*), on which Chekhov's worldwide reputation rests, still defy attempts to determine what they are about. Chekhov induces our involvement with the emotional experiences of his individual characters as they seek for a pattern and meaning in their lives.

The World's Classics

THE RUSSIAN MASTER AND
OTHER STORIES

Anton Chekhov

The loss of ideals and the poverty of actual experience are Chekhov's themes in the stories collected here. Chekhov's Russians, at the close of the nineteenth century, are trapped in a prison of frustration; he never depicted with greater laconic power their spiritual desperation and search for ways of escape.

The World's Classics